Restoring History

Western Cultural and Political Conservatism

Frederick J. Hutchison

Edited by Julie F. Klusty

JFK
INK

Columbus, Ohio

Greg — Thanks for your patriot heart! Some things are worth fighting for — FREEDOM!

Julie Klusty

Restoring History – Western Cultural and Political Conservatism

Property of Julie F. Klusty and JFK Ink, an imprint of JFK Administrative Services, ltd, an Ohio company.

Requests for information: jfklusty@gmail.com

All images included in this publication were obtained from public use records, unless otherwise noted.

Scripture quotations are taken from:
The Holy Bible, New International Version (NIV). Copyright 1973, 1978, 1984 by the International Bible Society. Used by permission of Zondervan Publishing House. All rights reserved.
The Message (MSG). Copyright 2002 by Eugene H. Peterson. Navpress Publishing Group. All rights reserved.
The Holy Bible, King James Version (KJV). Set Forth in 1611. Distributed by the American Bible Society, New York.

ISBN: 978-0-615-56496-8

Library of Congress Control Number: 2011944962

First Edition: January 2012

Cover designed by Heidi Adams, www.heidiadamsdesign.com. Cover art entitled *Gravity of Thought: How Great Minds Shaped the Fabric of History* – includes the images of (front cover) Saint Thomas Aquinas, William F. Buckley, Jr., Thomas Paine, Jesus the Christ, (back cover) Saint Anselm, Vladimir Lenin, William Blackstone and Georg Hegel.

Dedicated to Fred
(1949-2010)

Many have undertaken to draw up an account of the things that have been fulfilled among us, just as they were handed down to us by those who from the first were eyewitnesses and servants of the word. Therefore, since I myself have carefully investigated everything from the beginning, it seemed good also to me to write an orderly account for you, most excellent Theophilus, so that you may know the certainty of the things you have been taught. Luke 1:1-4 (NIV)

"Reconciliation and philosophical interaction between conservatism's five historical forms can restore an intellectually vigorous, culturally fruitful, morally coherent and politically potent society." ~ Frederick J. Hutchison, 2009.

Put the question to our ancestors, study what they learned from their ancestors. For we're newcomers at this, with a lot to learn, and not too long to learn it. So why not let the ancients teach you, tell you what's what, instruct you in what they knew from experience? Job 8:8-10 (MSG)

As Fred's sister, I perhaps knew him better than anyone else. We were very close all our lives, having been raised as Air Force children and moving from airbase to airbase: from Oklahoma City to Arizona, to Florida, to Cleveland, to France and back to Cleveland Heights where we both went to Cleveland Heights High School and Cuyahoga Community College. We did many things together and had many friends in common.

During Fred's two years at Miami University in Oxford, Ohio, he invited me down for a weekend to meet his college friends and experience some time with the university fellowship he was attending. He was passionate about sharing the salvation message, as he was a new convert himself. After putting him off for several years, I finally did find what he was talking about in a new relationship with Jesus Christ. By that time, he had graduated and was employed in downtown Cleveland at Union Commerce Bank.

Fred had majored in finance and was seeking a different career ladder. He was attending Cleveland State University to get his Master's degree in business. He remained in the Cleveland area several years more. Three years after I made the decision to follow Christ, I returned to Columbus to attend a graduate program at Ohio State University and became involved in a campus ministry, having been referred by Fred to a person he knew there. It was such a wonderful group and I was learning so much that I invited him to come down and live in Columbus to be a part of the group. He made some visits and eventually did come down to stay four years after I moved. He did some temporary work until he connected with the Auditor of State of Ohio's office and was hired as an auditor. He spent the next 19 years there, auditing mostly state agencies but spending one year in Cincinnati as a line manager before returning to state agency auditing in Columbus. He also did some work on quality assurance and conducted some training sessions.

Fred was planning to go back to school and change careers again and he moved in with our parents in order to save some money toward this purpose. Shortly thereafter, a brain tumor was discovered in the winter of 1997. He had surgery at OSU Hospitals and recovered at Dodd Hall. In spite of his undiminished mental prowess, the Auditor's office did not take him back after his rehabilitation but instead granted him a disability pension and freed him to do the things he was passionate about. At the time, he could walk and move his left arm and hand but had lost finger dexterity in the left hand. He wound up writing his documents on the computer with only his right hand, and was avidly researching areas of interest. This was the beginning to a twelve year period of authorship of a book entitled *The Stages of Sanctification*[1] and many articles and essays published by RenewAmerica.com and some letters to the Columbus Dispatch. He started with an email group that he sent essays and writings to, and developed his following from there. I loved the poems he wrote in addition to the many different topics he addressed.

Fred was a man of many interests and had a passion for intellectual exchange, the arts, culture, history, politics, and spiritual studies. He was a brilliant seeker of truth. He was an author, mentor, speaker, counselor (to close friends) and witness to everyone who knew him. Fred was passionate about restoration of Christian values in the United States and was a frequent contributor to the RenewAmerica blog.[2] His essays on the history of conservatism came out of a desire to see real, meaningful cultural and spiritual awakening in this country.

---

[1] (F. J. Hutchison 2000)
[2] (F. Hutchison, RenewAmerica - Fred Hutchison column 2009)

I am sure that as I write this, Fred is cheering the rest of us on from heaven. Those who knew him and loved him were fortunate to have a passionate advocate on their side, who would do anything he could to encourage, support, and befriend them at dark times in their lives.

The last two years of his life, Fred's brain tumor recurred and he had surgery and chemotherapy resulting in sickness and weakness. By this time, Mom had died and Fred was still living with Dad with in home caregivers for both of them. Dad was at the end of his life as well. Eventually, when Fred died at age 60 on August 10, 2010, he told me he was ready to go. During that time, the SALT fellowship group he had been part of for many years at Upper Arlington Lutheran Church, became Christ to him. They came to see him, brought specially prepared foods, prayed with and for him, hugged him, helped him with personal care, took the Bible study to him and generally speaking did everything they could do to care for him. I will never stop thanking God for this group of sincere believers and friends who made Fred's last days so blessed and wonderful with the outpouring of their love. Dad died a few months after Fred.

It was Fred's wish that this collection of essays, originally titled *A Brief History of Conservatism*, be published in book form, and so we decided to do it. Julie Klusty, one of the SALT group members, has edited these essays on the history of conservatism. Many thanks to the caregivers that helped Fred realize his dreams of publishing, and to the friends that made his life brighter, happier and filled with Christ's love – and thank you to everyone who participated in some way with the publication of this book.

Leila L. Leidtke, Fred's big sister

ABOUT THE EDITOR

Julie F. Klusty attended The Ohio State University, Max M. Fisher College of Business, where she received a BS in Business Administration/Marketing. She is an experienced administrative manager and provided years of support, insight and problem solving contributions for residential management, manufacturing and civil engineering firms. In 2010, she started her own business, JFK Administrative Services, ltd (JFK), which offers professional administrative management to diverse clients. Julie's heritage as a direct descendant of prominent, founding American citizens inspired her to become active in several local, state and national patriot groups. She is a 30 year resident of Columbus, Ohio, where she lives with her loving husband and two dogs.

"Watch out for people who try to dazzle you with big words and intellectual double-talk. They want to drag you off into endless arguments that never amount to anything. They spread their ideas through the empty traditions of human beings and the empty superstitions of spirit beings. But that's not the way of Christ. Everything of God gets expressed in him, so you can see and hear him clearly. You don't need a telescope, a microscope, or a horoscope to realize the fullness of Christ, and the emptiness of the universe without him. When you come to him, that fullness comes together for you, too. His power extends over everything." Colossians 2:8-10 (MSG)

I met Fred in the spring of 1997, as I walked through the double doors of our church narthex and almost ran into the tall, gaunt man hobbling towards the parking lot on a cane too short for his height. We both stopped abruptly and considered each other in silence for a moment before speaking. I was taken by the frailty of the giant man as I pulled my eyes from his trembling hands and bent my neck upward to survey the massive scar freshly carved around his skull and the wisps of badly unkempt hair that spoke of recent chemotherapy. ─This guy is obviously about to die," I thought to myself.

Then my eyes locked onto a pair of piercing baby blues that demanded recognition with steely resolve from behind smudged bifocals. He weakly pulled himself to his full height, tucked his cane beneath his bad arm, and chuckled in a deep baritone voice, ─Why, I think I have met a hobbit!" A beautiful smile completely enveloped his face and all vestiges of illness were swept away as I stepped into the shade of his friendship. Several years later, the ***Lord of the Rings*** books and movies would introduce me to the wonder of J.R.R. Tolkien's epic fantasy and the resident hobbits Fred was so fond of, and I would come to understand that this initial meeting reflected the joyful abandon of Gandalf as Frodo Baggins jumped into his greeting arms. I was blessed to enjoy the opening of these movies with Fred, who was still very much alive.

Before we parted that day, Fred jotted down my email address on the back of a folded piece of paper he kept in his shirt pocket beside his two pens, promising to add me to his contact list. Over the next twelve years, I came to cherish his writings, sometimes proofing an article for him without really understanding the significance of his brilliance. Yet, the real blessing he gave me was the depth of friendship he shared – he was always available to listen, counsel and enjoy his friends. His quirky sense of humor and stubborn opinion on every subject created a continuous stream of appreciation and hostility from friends and acquaintances – he was never afraid to speak his mind.

During the next several years, a group of my single gal friends took Fred under our feminine wings and challenged his intelligence, wit, emotional maturity and obtuse opinions. His insight into culture and history was a fantastic addition to the many jaunts we took to area plays, musicals, movies and parties. He could debate endlessly over beer and brats, and as we pushed into the arguments, all of us came away with greatly expanded and inspired minds. He was a special blessing in our lives and a reminder that God's love for us was an ever present challenge to go deeper, higher, broader and wider. When my husband showed up in my life, Fred instantly enveloped him as a dearly loved brother with the same mantle of friendship.

As Fred's health began to wane, he anxiously reached out to friends to calm his fears and reassure him of God's love. It was a pleasure that none of us would have missed. He exhorted each of us individually as to our future responsibilities, giving charges as a dying general would to his officers. He specifically urged me to see that the book he had been working on got published – hence this work. His last days were hard on him, but the joy of communion with his brethren never left him until his last breath – he continued to seek the true, the beautiful, and the good until he could no longer speak. He worshiped and honored his Lord and Savior until he was embraced by the One his heart desired above all else.

Working on his manuscripts was a challenge, because I wanted to stay true to his work, but found myself still arguing about his subjective opinions. I could not write them out of the book – so I researched deeper into historical sources and added information I thought necessary to clarify or explain his position. In the process, my own intelligence was challenged, and I recognized perhaps for the first time just how brilliant he was. This work is not only timely and deep; it holds the seeds that could turn our floundering country back to cultural health as spoken in Scripture:

> *"If my people, which are called by my name, shall humble themselves, and pray, and seek my face, and turn from their wicked ways; then will I hear from heaven, and will forgive their sin, and will heal their land." 2 Chronicles 7:14 (KJV)*

I have confidence that Americans can be used by God to rebuild the Republic – we have a great treasure house of past wisdom, splendid history, truth principles and values, and sterling examples with which to build. We can win the battle against deeply entrenched postmodernism if we humble ourselves enough to stand with confidence on the giant shoulders of those who have gone before us. May we receive God's special anointing of deep joy in the uniting of like-minded patriots, as we roll up our sleeves to begin the hard work.

Structure Notes

- Fred Hutchison's personal comments, opinions and stories are footnoted and/or text boxed as a " Fred Critique."
- Early chapters build the foundation for later chapters. As such, the first several chapters are thick with history and philosophy, and are a laundry list of ancient knowledge. Press through them!
- The chapters were originally articles posted on RenewAmerica.com and encompass over 2,800 years in less than 200 pages – many details were not included. Some sections of the initial essays have been moved so that chronology, context and topic could be more seamless.
- Non-chronological text that remains in the original essay locations because of specific points Fred was making is denoted by gray text shading.
- As you read, you will notice that some material is revisited from different perspectives. Approach the text as though combing through long hair from the top of the head to the bottom of the hair, smoothing the strands after each sequential stroke.

Special Thanks

I want to thank Leila and Byron Leidtke for giving me the opportunity to make Fred's publishing dreams come true. Thanks also go to David and Kelly Kullberg for encouraging me to take up the challenge and for sharing their book publishing experience. I extend my sincere appreciation to those friends who volunteered to proof the working draft: Norma Bruce, Phil Donner and Eve Tomassini. Thank you to Stephen Stone, President of RenewAmerica, who offered to promote the publication on RA's website. I especially thank my loving and supportive husband, Bob, for the countless dinners and chores he picked up while I sat in front of the computer. Grateful thanks goes to God the Father, Son and Holy Ghost, who cleared my life schedule and motivated my mind and heart to complete the project. Finally, thank you, Fred, for letting me stand on your giant shoulders – I look forward to our long embrace in the presence of our King!

I close with my favorite e-prayer, Fred's *#99 The Pursuit of Happiness*, which mystically healed the shards of my own broken mind and heart in an instant. ~ Julie F. Klusty

From my youth I sought happiness.
I thought that is what we are here to do.
Have not our fathers said,
"Life, Liberty, and the Pursuit of Happiness?"
Is not that what they came here for?
And are we not their heirs?
But what is happiness,
And how do we pursue?

At tender age happiness is sunny play,
But in the course of years the play goes stale,
And the tedious vexation of ennui
Drives all my pleasures away.
All the pleasures of the adult senses,
Do likewise decay and yield a harvest
Of futility, vexation, and irritated temper.
O deliver me from this misery!

Perhaps high ambition shows the way.
Win the palm, gather your trophies,
Bear your blushing honors in the limelight
Before the cheering crowds.
Inflate your image in the eyes of men
And gratify your hungry pride.
Then sated by the admiring eyes of men
Happiness will burst forth
From the breast of swollen pride.

But that is not worshipful admiration I see.
Their eyes are filled with bitter envy.
I feel more hatred than love.
And those very few who really love me
Are led astray because I have become an idol to them.
Thus, my achievement has bred
Only hatred, strife, and idolatry
And has filled my little world with misery.

The shining moment in the sun
Withheld the joy I sought.
Someone has deceived me
But my own heart was eager to be fooled.
I remember only from those sweaty and fretted days
A dizzy whirl of frenzied toil
And heavy burdens to carry home at night
And a prison of care awaiting me in the morn.
I thought to console myself
In the thought that power and influence, wisely used
Can bring a little good upon earth.
But no sooner were my little sandcastles built
But they were washed out to sea,
Soon forgotten and all the good
Carried off by the hastening tide and
Dissolved in the boundless sea.

And then I remembered
The long struggle to fend off the hungry wolves
Who lusted for my place in the manic pack
And who thought I possessed what they craved
And did not know that
I had nothing good in my hands.
The thrill of pride in power and promotion
Lasts but a moment
And soon leaves a sickened emptiness in the heart.
The legion of the mediocrities,
The surly and mangy pack,
Ringed round me snarling and snapping.
They Hated me with hearty energy
And greatly celebrated in my fall.
They have found their dark and slimy happiness
In the ruin of my pride.

The deepest wounds were made by
The jaws of envious friends.
My fleeting day of a little measure of glory
Was too much for them to endure.
Tormented by the agonies of jealousy
They sharpened the daggers of revenge,
And greedily planned their treachery.
The bitter wounds of betrayed love
Are poisoned by an adders venom
And often repeat their stings
In the many weary years of memory's review.

Perhaps the consolations of work
Will carry me through the weary trek.
Maybe happiness is hidden in work.
Let us look to the journey
And not to the destination.
Ah, this is better.
There is a satisfaction
In a day of wholesome labor.
Whatever the outcome.
It was a good day engrossed in the task;
Free from care, with happy moments
And flashes of merriment and convivial sentiments.
But still my heart hungers in its core.
It says "feed me or I perish."
What food do you seek, O my heart?
My soul, why are you still downcast?

Perhaps, I need a quest of higher worth;
An adventure in the great cosmic battle
Of good at war with evil.
Ah, the thrill of battle!
Defying evil and despising danger.
I tell you there is a joy in it.
But the hero's lot is not a happy one.
He multiplies enemies
In a battle with no respite.

And while he is facing down his foes
He faces a darker battle within
As his inner demons lay siege
Upon the bulwarks of his proud righteousness.
There is no rest or surcease
In the watches of the night.
The inner battle rages on
In dreams of horror
Or in sleepless nights of dread.
At length his proud resolve cracks
And he fades into acedia and lassitude.
And finally comes despair
As his high blown pride is humbled once again.

Perhaps the pursuit of Truth
Will be a higher and better way.
Ah yes, this is better indeed!
Ah, the depths and the glories of knowledge and truth
Which delight the nobler precincts of the heart
And exalt the mind to loftier planes.
I tell you there is joy in it!
Yet the joy comes unexpectedly,
Lingers briefly, and flies.
And when it is gone,
The mind sinks into an exhaustion
Heavier than any workman knows
And the heart turns to lead.
I shall rest and try again tomorrow.
But tomorrow the joy and the inspiration are gone,
The knowledge is stale,
And the dark poison of pride
Seeps up from the roots
And contaminates the work
Transforming a thing of beauty into ugliness.

Oh God! Where now shall I turn?
Who can redeem this ruined and blighted life?
At the end of my strength
I give this mangled life to you.
Can you salvage it?
Even happiness I forsake.
Oh illusion, there is hidden in your pursuit
A deadly snare to our feet.
From henceforth I forsake the world
And pursue God and Him alone.

And there He is waiting to meet me:
His long suffering patience looking to the day
That I forsook the dismal chase
Of this lost world's desperate strife
And turn my face to Him.
And in His presence
A glory overwhelms me
That uplifts my mind
As it tears my heart in shreds.
A joy so great that it wounds.
A wound which bleeds tears
Of purest bliss.
An awakened life so intense
That is like a death.
And all the world
Awakens to new lights, colors, fragrances
And the dismal earth
Takes on the sweet aspect of heaven.

I try to ask Him, is this happiness?
But cannot say the words.
Instead there comes forth
A flood of tears mixed with laughter.
"Enough, enough" I cry.
"Take this flood of angelic happiness away.
I am only a weak mortal man
And I can endure it no more."

Fred Hutchison, 1999

"Of all the dispositions and habits which lead to political prosperity, **religion** and **morality** are indispensable supports. In vain would that man claim the tribute of patriotism who should labor to subvert these great pillars of **human happiness**, these firmest props of the duties of men and citizens." George Washington, Farewell Address, 1796

Restoring History
Western Cultural and Political Conservatism

TABLE OF CONTENTS

TABLE OF FIGURES

Restoring History

Western Cultural and Political Conservatism

Figure 1.   Chapters 1-3 Timeline (800 BC-1800 AD)

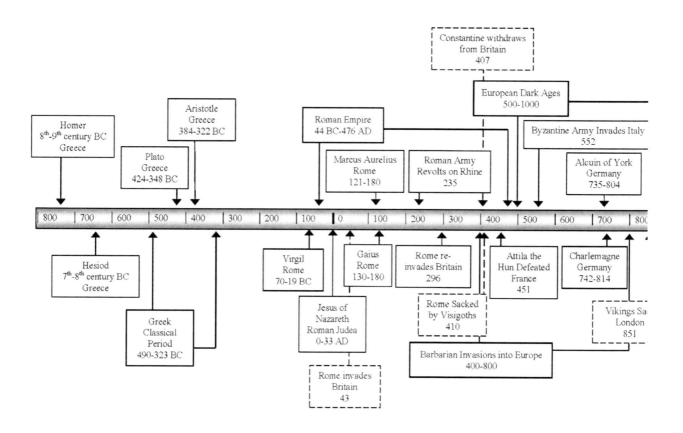

The differing box and line dashes are meant to
help with visual tracking in congested time spaces.

Not every person mentioned in the text is shown.

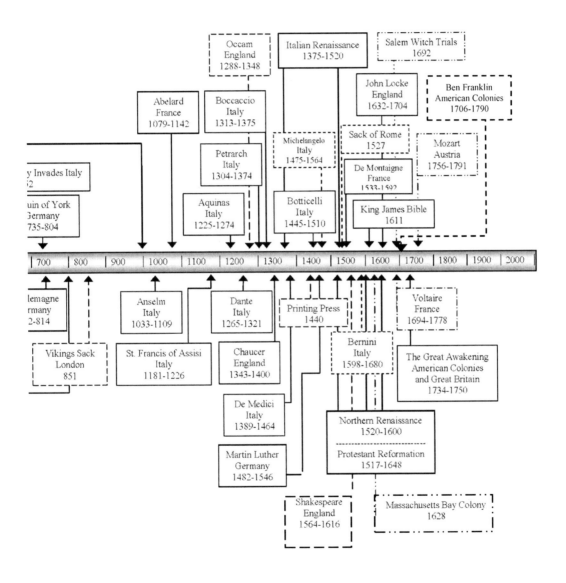

Occam
England
1288-1348

Italian Renaissance
1375-1520

Salem Witch Trials
1692

Abelard
France
1079-1142

Boccaccio
Italy
1313-1375

John Locke
England
1632-1704

Ben Franklin
American Colonies
1706-1790

Petrarch
Italy
1304-1374

Michelangelo
Italy
1475-1564

Sack of Rome
1527

Mozart
Austria
1756-1791

y Invades Italy
2

De Montaigne
France
1533-1592

uin of York
Germany
735-804

Aquinas
Italy
1225-1274

Botticelli
Italy
1445-1510

King James Bible
1611

700 | 800 | 900 | 1000 | 1100 | 1200 | 1300 | 1400 | 1500 | 1600 | 1700 | 1800 | 1900 | 2000

lemagne
rmany
2-814

Anselm
Italy
1033-1109

Dante
Italy
1265-1321

Printing Press
1440

Voltaire
France
1694-1778

Vikings Sack
London
851

St. Francis of Assisi
Italy
1181-1226

Chaucer
England
1343-1400

Bernini
Italy
1598-1680

The Great Awakening
American Colonies
and Great Britain
1734-1750

De Medici
Italy
1389-1464

Northern Renaissance
1520-1600

Protestant Reformation
1517-1648

Martin Luther
Germany
1482-1546

Shakespeare
England
1564-1616

Massachusetts Bay Colony
1628

Sam: It's like in the great stories Mr. Frodo, the ones that really mattered. Full of darkness and danger they were, and sometimes you didn't want to know the end because how could the end be happy? How could the world go back to the way it was when so much bad had happened? But in the end it's only a passing thing this shadow, even darkness must pass. A new day will come, and when the sun shines it'll shine out the clearer. Those were the stories that stayed with you, that meant something even if you were too small to understand why. But I think Mr. Frodo, I do understand, I know now folk in those stories had lots of chances of turning back, only they didn't. They kept going because they were holding on to something.

Frodo: What are we holding onto, Sam?

Sam: That there's some good in the world, Mr. Frodo, and it's worth fighting for.

*Samwise Gamgee, **The Lord of the Rings: The Two Towers**, J.R.R. Tolkien, 1954*

Parthenon from Ancient Greece

Current political and cultural arenas provide a good backdrop to consider the vital role of conservatism in Western history. Conservative ideals provided a crucial function in the Western civilization's rise to become the world premiere in literature, philosophy, art, music, architecture, economics, commerce, exploration, science, technology, war and politics. Western culture is often equated with European civilization and broadly refers to a heritage of social norms, ethics, traditions, religious beliefs, political systems, and specific artifacts and technologies. Conservative principles and values have consistently produced beneficial effects on culture.

In contrast, liberalism has often been destructive to Western culture, propagating false views about the nature of man, society, government and the cosmos – and only produces a mixed blessing. There is an illusion in the land that liberalism is an old tradition, and that conservatism arose in the late 1940's as a reactionary force. In fact, four of the five types of conservatism were very old when liberalism first appeared during the 18th century, *after* the West had already established dominance.

This chapter introduces each of the five major schools of conservatism in the order of historical appearance: 1) Literary Traditionalism, 2) Christian Conservatism, 3) Natural Law Conservatism, 4) Neoconservatism, and briefly mentions 5) Libertarianism.

LITERARY TRADITIONALISM

LOOKING BACK IS THE WAY FORWARD

The decisive ideal of Western Traditionalism in the ancient world was the belief in a golden age of the mythical past. Societies with glorious visions of their cultural past sought to recover and preserve as much of it as possible. Tradition was valued as a means of embracing the wisdom and blessings of the past, and preserving the culture from decay. In working to "*conserve*" precious cultural treasures, they became known as "*conservatives.*"

After gaining historical and cultural traction, Western traditionalists stopped looking back to a largely mythical, distant golden age, and started looking back to the great thinkers and the literary masters who went before them. The process began when the oral poetry of Homer (9th and 8th century BC) and Hesiod (8th and 7th century BC) were committed to writing. As each new great thinker and writer appeared, he was added to literary canon and became indispensable to the culture. Literary Traditionalism was essential to the Greek cultural renaissance in Athens (5th and 4th century BC), the Roman cultural renewal (2nd century AD), the cultural flourishing of the High Middle Ages (12th and 13th century), and the Italian Renaissance (14th and 15th century). Chapter 2 will take an extended look at Literary Traditionalism.

> *Fred Critique*
>
> *To inspire the cultural improvement of a society, hindsight is often the way forward.*

Some have argued that looking to the past blocks progress. History indicates that where culture is concerned, almost the opposite is true. Every cultural renaissance mentioned in Chapter 1 was inspired by backward-looking conservative ideals. To inspire the cultural improvement of a society, hindsight is often the way forward.

THE GOLDEN AGE

We remember the Mycenaean Greek Bronze Age because of the Trojan War (12th or 11th centuries BC), which is among the most important events in Greek mythology and was narrated in many works of Greek literature. Mycenaean civilization collapsed during the invasion of the Dorian barbarians, two generations after the Trojan War, and a long Greek Dark Age followed.

During those dismal times, the hearing of epic tales such as Homer's (8th century BC) *The Iliad*[3] and *The Odyssey*,[4] kept the people from despair. The memory of heroes and the myths of a golden age were preserved by tribal poets and

Hesiod

storytellers, such as Hesiod (between 750-650 BC), who memorized a huge corpus of literature and poetry, often set to song and accompanied by the harp. These long enchanted songs produced a kind of proto-Traditionalism among the Greek tribes.

Hesiod's poem, *Works and Days*,[5] sang of the golden first age of man when people enjoyed peace, harmony, abundance, and freedom from physical affliction. These happy people lived in idyllic innocence, in a pastoral paradise of delight, and were vivacious, playful and carefree — always frolicking, feasting and making merry. A charming quality of lighthearted playfulness can be traced from the time of Hesiod through the historic age of classical Greek culture (4th and

5th centuries BC). The image of seven Muses singing and dancing atop Mount Parnassus is an archetypal image of the sweetness and vivacity that was Greece. Our modern day Olympic Games are a remnant of Greek sport and playfulness.

The Greek Orphic mystery religion[6] (6th century BC) adopted the cult of the golden age. The philosopher Empedocles (5th century BC) emphasized the mythical golden age of Greece at the very time Athens was experiencing a *real* golden age. Apparently, enchantment with an imagined golden age was partly responsible for the Greek cultural renaissance in the 5th and 4th centuries BC.

THE BIRTH OF WESTERN CULTURE

Apollo of the
Belvedere

Greeks of the classical period (490-323 BC) retained a polytheist religion, but looked to golden age mythology to provide spiritual ideals. The traditional highly individualistic gods retained historical names, but were converted into spiritual archetypes. As idealism animated cultural and creative energies, statues of gods began to share the same stylized face. The *Apollo of the Belvedere*[7] by sculptor Leochares (4th century BC), bears the unrecognizable romanticized image of the perfect man, who Greeks imagined must have lived in the golden age. When the Greek confederation defeated the Persian Empire in two wars, they believed they were invincible and ready to enjoy another golden age. As their innovative vigor was unleashed, Western culture was born in Athens' enlightened, intellectual ferment.

---

[3] The Iliad (1194-1184 BC) tells of the story of the Trojan War, a ten-year siege of the city of Troy (Ilium) by an alliance of Greek states, and features the quarrel between King Agamemnon and Achilles the warrior.
[4] The Odyssey is a sequel to the Iliad that focuses on the Greek hero Odysseus (Ulysses in Roman myth) and his journey home after the fall of Troy.
[5] (Hesiod 1st Printed Edition 1493)
[6] Orphism is an ancient Greek and the Hellenistic religion associated with literature ascribed to the mythical poet Orpheus, who descended into Hades and returned. Classical sources, such as Plato, refer to mysterious Orphic initiation rites, which promised advantages in the afterlife.
[7] The Apollo Belvedere is a white marble sculpture from Classical Antiquity rediscovered in central Italy in the late 15th century, during the Renaissance. Neoclassicists consider it the greatest ancient sculpture. It epitomizes the aesthetically perfect ideals of Western Europeans.

CHRISTIAN CONSERVATISM AND THE GOLDEN AGE

The Judeo-Christian belief in Adam's expulsion from the Garden of Eden and mankind's subsequent longing for utopia was quite compatible with Hesiod's vision of returning to the virtuous golden age of living close to nature, uncorrupted by civilization. Idyllic **Arcadian** paradise[8] was recaptured poetically with all the unspoiled wilderness, bountiful natural splendor and blissful harmony. Since the majority of early Christians spoke Greek as a first language and lived in culturally Greek cities, the linkage of Christianity to Greek Traditionalism came easily.

ARISTOTELIAN NATURAL LAW CONSERVATISM

Aristotle (4th century BC) defined virtue and the good life in terms of human nature, laying essential conceptual foundations for **Natural Law**[9] philosophy. Further traces of natural law ideas are discovered among the **Roman Stoics**,[10] who were uncomfortable with the Arcadian concept of playful song. Saint Thomas Aquinas (13th century AD) would later borrow concepts from Aristotle and write the first comprehensive natural law philosophy, which deeply influenced Western culture. This chapter will revisit the subject of Natural Law in Rome and Europe.

ROMAN AMBIVALENCE ABOUT ARCADIA

Plato and Aristotle

The Romans established innumerable deity cults to worship the gods of ancestors, founders, kings, conquered nations and allies, which influenced every aspect of both the natural world and human affairs – religious negligence could provoke divine wrath against the State. Rome's temples and statues displayed a tendency towards sternness, and were lacking in the Greek quality of playful sweetness.

Roman poets wrote golden age epics, most notably Virgil (1st century BC), who implied in *Georgics* (29 BC) that man's loss of paradise was worth the journey in spite of immense toil, hardship, conflict and sorrow. He encouraged the benefits of waking men from the sweet slumber of Arcadia to a world of harsh challenges, so they could develop wits, virtues, intellectual powers, and force of will – in order to build cities, participate in a civilized community, and enjoy a sophisticated culture. At the price of immense labors, suffering and warfare, man had developed and matured through Roman civilization, if only for a fleeting moment of glory. Virgil wrote that Saturn's golden age of a tranquil Arcadia was superseded by Jupiter's iron age of work and striving. Likewise, Greek rustic grace and charm must concede to Roman cosmopolitan glory.

THE ROMAN BATTLE OF LIFE

In contrast to Greek optimism and infatuation with nature, Virgil regarded farming as war between man and nature. Romans recognized that just as man must combat the tangled natural world, he must also struggle against the internal conflict between good and evil. Virgil's poetry and the philosophy of Stoicism were intended to triumph over the inner

---

[8] Arcadia refers to pastoral harmony with nature and is a poetic term for unspoiled wilderness. The term is derived from the mountainous topography and sparse population of the ancient Greek province of Arcadia.

[9] Natural law, or the law of nature, is any system of law determined by nature, and is thus universal. Classically, natural law refers to the use of reason to analyze human nature and deduce binding rules of moral behavior.

[10] Stoicism is a Hellenistic philosophy founded in Athens by Zeno of Citium in the early 3rd century BC. Stoics believed that destructive emotions resulted from errors in judgment, and that people of *"moral and intellectual perfection,"* would not suffer such emotions.

battle, an elemental contradiction in man that became an essential insight and enduring trait of Western Conservatism. Christian doctrine of the Fall reinforced the pessimistic Roman view.[11]

Virgil believed that a civilized Roman political regime must wage war against chaos to create social and political order. This battle involved fighting against disordered men, political rebels, barbarians and hostile nations. Victory was the key to history, according to Virgil, because Rome's glorious destiny was to bring law, order and civilization to the world. He celebrated the legendary origin of Rome in *The Aeneid*[12] several years before the birth of Christ. This masterpiece was written at the request of Caesar Augustus (63 BC-14 AD), who credited himself with bringing peace and order to the world after a century of sundry insurrections, and foreign and civil wars.

A ROMAN PROTO-NEOCONSERVATIVE

Although Virgil constantly quoted or made allusions to literary masters from both Greece and Rome, he was a forerunner and perfect example of the literary branch of the modern neoconservative movement as it relates to U.S. foreign policy, i.e., national interests include the defense of other nations with similar principles for geopolitical purposes. The difference between Greek Literary Traditionalism and Virgil's formative neoconservative sentiments

Virgil

was the Roman social, political and military agenda to bring order and civilization to the world. While Athens had a regional maritime empire in the Aegean Sea, no Greek prior to or after Alexander had an international agenda. The focus of every Greek was Athens, just as the focus of every Frenchman is Paris. Neoconservatism is *Roman* in quality, just as Americans tend to use economic and military power to bring democracy and capitalism to other countries.

Virgil hinted at neoconservative sentiments in *Georgics* and *The Aeneid*. He believed that in order for human nature to flourish, there must be literature, poetry, art and architecture, along with sophisticated conversation and a cultured community. None of these graces can be cultivated without virtuous men, victory in war, suppression of the disordered barbarians, social order, and a government of rational law. Once order is achieved, men can turn to the classics and cultivate philosophic minds, poetic discernment, and aesthetic taste. Augustus was able to sponsor men of letters like Virgil, after he established order. Virgil's influence on Dante (14th century) to Milton (17th century) will be reviewed in Chapter 2.

ROMAN RENAISSANCE OF THE SECOND CENTURY AD

Christianity emerged in Judea (30-33 AD) as a Jewish religious sect and spread throughout the Roman Empire and beyond, attracting people from diverse ethnicities and cultures.[13] Christian virtue stood out in vivid contrast to Roman depravity in the 1st century. For example, infanticide was a common and government endorsed practice – unwanted babies (mainly those born female or abnormal) were often killed, sacrificed to a pagan god, or left out in the elements to die. To Christians, all babies (whether male, female, perfect or imperfect) were created in the image of God and therefore had value. Society was fundamentally altered when the early church began to rescue and raise discarded babies as Christians.

Young Roman men soon faced a lack of eligible young women for brides, while the church had a surplus of virgin maidens of good character. The church allowed them to marry their virgins on the condition that the men convert to

---

[11] Source of insight (Thornton Spring 2007)
[12] The Aeneid (29-19 BC) is Virgil's epic poem about the adventures of Aeneas the Trojan and ancestor of the Romans, in Italy.
[13] (Luke 60-64 AD)

Christianity and promise to raise their children as Christians. Thus, Christian virtue and charity led to the rapid growth of the church – and increasingly shamed the Romans for their vice.

The loss of integrity weighed heavily on 2nd century conservatives. Rome enjoyed a century of prosperity and cultural renaissance under what English historian Edward Gibbons (1737-1794) called the *"five good emperors"* – Nerva (8-98), Trajan (53-117), Hadrian (76-138), Antoninus Pius (86-161) and Marcus Aurelius (121-180). This revival involved a renewed interest in the classics of literature and philosophy, and a rediscovery of ancient Roman virtue.

The quest to recover timeless values and principles that lead to the marriages of virile Roman men to sweet Christian virgins became a cultural prototype in the West. Centuries later, courtly 12th and 13th century romances sometimes featured a manly knight of military renown giving court to a pure lady of the castle who exemplified culture and spirituality. Extensive love poetry, written entirely by men known today as troubadours, was developed to celebrate the beauty, purity, and exquisite qualities of unattainable ladies of noble birth.

ROMAN UNIVERSAL LAW

Second century Romans rose to the challenge of Christian virtue by seeking ethics through **Stoicism**[14] (the belief that moral and intellectual perfection is attainable by rejecting emotions, which are the result of destructive errors in judgment) and **Manichaeism**[15] (the belief in the struggle between a good, spiritual world of light, and an evil, material world of darkness). Epictetus (55-135), Greek by birth and a slave in Rome, and Marcus Aurelius, an emperor noted for military exploits, were the greatest Roman Stoic philosophers. Stoicism became a popular religion/philosophy of the aristocracy.

Roman Stoics connected natural law to human ethics, but did not consider it a higher law. As **Pantheists** (which teaches that nature and God are identical), they believed that natural law was a manifest essence in both nature and man. They were interested in following a rational and purposeful natural order to find virtue. Stoics spread the idea of a *"universal moral law."* The Apostle Paul must have anticipated this when he wrote:

> *"Indeed, when Gentiles, who do not have the law, do by nature things required by the law, they are a law for themselves, even though they do not have the law, since they show that the requirements of the law are written on their hearts, their consciences also bearing witness, and their thoughts now accusing, now even defending them." Romans 2:14-15 (NIV)*

Paul linked law written in the heart with nature when he said the gentiles *"do by nature ... the law."* During his Roman education, Paul would have read Marcus Tullius Cicero (106 BC-43 AD), so he would not have been surprised that Romans had discovered the principle. Cicero first studied Epicurean philosophy, then Platonism, and finally the moderate cosmopolitan Roman Stoicism of his era – he exposed political and philosophical errors with his view that good laws, sound government and happy human relations rest soundly in natural law.

Gaius (130-180), the greatest Roman jurist of the 2nd century, wrote ***The Institutes*** (161 AD) in which he distinguished between *"Civil Law"* as a law peculiar to a people, and *"The Law of all Nations"* that is revealed by natural reason. Surprisingly, Gaius did not acquire the idea of a universal law for all nations from the mature Stoic philosophers of his day, but from Cicero.

---

[14] (Wikipedia 2011) (Huffman 2012)
[15] (Wikipedia 2011) (R. W. Smith 2012)

THE CHURCH'S CULTURAL PRESERVATION PROGRAM

During the invasions of Vandals, Goths and other migrating barbarian tribes (400-800), Christian monks fled to remote locations to sing the liturgy and hand copy old manuscripts of the Scriptures in relative safety, thereby saving the Bible for future generations. These scholars also reproduced the classics of Greece and Rome, to nourish the minds of students and prepare for civilization's revival. Mankind came exceedingly close to losing these precious manuscripts, and with them the Western cultural heritage. Art Historian Kenneth Clark (1903-1983) said, *"We came through by the skin of our teeth."* We have the Traditionalist Conservatism of Christian monks to thank for saving Western culture from barbarism.

THE SWEET SONG OF CHRISTIAN CULTURE VERSUS THE WRETCHED CRIES OF BARBARISM

Beowulf fighting the dragon

During the Dark Ages (500-1000), articulate and musical students were educated at the monasteries and Cathedral schools of the Catholic Church. Alcuin of York (735-804), Headmaster of Charlemagne's Palace school, decreed that every Cathedral school should teach the Seven Liberal Arts (grammar, logic, rhetoric, arithmetic, astronomy, geometry and music). The first three all developed articulate speech; the seventh was music. A barbarian bereft of speech and music was thought to be a creature devoid of blessing, little better than a beast.

Beowulf (unknown date, 8th-11th century) is the epic Anglo-Saxon Dark Age poem concerning the exploits of Beowulf, a warrior champion, which displays a strange blend of Christian and pagan cultural elements. The hero's opponent was a monster named Grendel, or *"a won saeli wer"* – meaning *"a being bereft of blessedness"* – who roared beastly cries and could not understand or speak human language. Grendel attacked Hrothgar's Hall where people were singing a *"sweet song."*[16] The unknown writer of ***Beowulf*** envisioned blessed Christian students speaking articulately and singing sweetly, as the inarticulate barbarian (typified by Grendel), stood outside the hall, empty of blessings and howling in pain. American scholar Fred Hutchison (1949-2010) believed that barbarism has returned, and we hear Grendel once more in the screams of rock stars – inarticulate creatures incapable of singing beautiful songs can only shriek to ventilate their rage and pain.

> *Fred Critique*
>
> *We hear Grendel once more in the screams of rock stars – inarticulate creatures incapable of singing beautiful songs can only shriek to ventilate their rage and pain.*

THE MEDIEVAL RENAISSANCE OF RATIONAL PHILOSOPHY

During the decades following 1100, the University of Paris was founded by disciples of the Italian noble, Saint Anselm of Canterbury (1033-1109). Europe was rapidly recovering from the Dark Ages because powerful nobles provided regional protection – this security facilitated agricultural inventions that fed the growing population and new urban centers, attracted immigrants, allowed for safe trade routes, and spread Christian influence. Castles, cathedrals and walled cities sprang up. Students in Paris were debating philosophy with an enthusiasm reminiscent of the philosophic debates in Athens fifteen hundred years before. The awakening of philosophical debate and scholasticism was built upon *four foundations:*

1. Sponsorship of education by the Catholic Church (all debaters were learned church men seeking truth).

---

[16] (Lerer 2007)

2. Teaching of grammar, logic and rhetoric by the cathedral schools.

3. Saint Anselm's teaching about beginning with faith, embracing a first principle or authoritative presupposition, and reasoning deductively to a conclusion. Anselm's theory in his article ***De Veritate*** affirms the existence of absolute truth in which all other truth participates. This absolute truth is God, who is the ultimate principle of things and thought – it is necessary to first make God clear to reason and demonstrate His real existence. He wrote, *"Nor do I seek to understand that I may believe, but I believe that I may understand. For this, too, I believe, that, unless I first believe, I shall not understand."*

4. Aristotle's logic, particularly the **syllogism**.[17] The recovery of Aristotle's work was a major breakthrough in philosophy, since some of his views discounted a personal God, immortal souls and creation.[18] Various Catholic Church leaders censored his views for decades.[19]

Scholastic philosophers of the 12th and 13th centuries possessed a process of reasoning more free from logical fallacies than any philosophy before or since. Some 21st century thinkers believe that appreciation for reason has fallen to historically low ebbs. When modern theorists scoff at scholastic philosophy, it could be a symptom of a cultural epidemic of tolerance for logical fallacies.

CITY AIR MAKES ONE FREE

A number of medieval cities became communes or semiautonomous republics, where a popular slogan describing a principle of law was *"City Air Makes One Free"* or *"Stadtluft macht frei."* Although leaders of these city-states had more enthusiasm for regulation than Americans might appreciate, these urban republics were pioneers in the European quest for freedom within community. The development of individualism is a product of these societies, whose emphasis on individual liberties and freedom emerged in opposition to the authoritarian oppression of the feudal system.

Some city-states in Italy became rich and powerful, setting the stage for the Renaissance. Many factors facilitated the urban movement including: a boom in commerce and enterprise; a cultural flowering centered in the cities; rationality and articulate communication promoted by cathedral schools and university-trained scholars; the emergence of brilliant church-trained leaders; and the concept of natural law that emerged in stages during the 12th and 13th centuries.

AQUINAS AND NATURAL LAW

Saint Thomas Aquinas (1225-1274), a **Dominican**[20] priest and great scholastic philosopher, developed the ideals of Natural Law. He dissented from the Stoics, who had no concept of a law transcendent to nature, and followed Gratian (12th century), the founder of canon law, in equating natural law with divine law. Aquinas believed *"that for the knowledge of any truth whatsoever man needs divine help, that the intellect may be moved by God to its act."*

---

[17] Syllogism is a form of deductive reasoning consisting of a major premise, a minor premise and a conclusion.
[18] Latin texts of Aristotle were brought to Paris from Cordova by Muslim and Jewish scholars during the 12th-13th centuries.
[19] Thomas Aquinas reconciled Aristotle's viewpoints and Christianity in his work ***Summa Theologica*** (1265-1274).
[20] Dominicans are a Catholic religious order founded by Saint Dominic (1216) in France that has produced many famous theologians and philosophers, and are known for having strong intellectual life and sound theology.

St. Thomas Aquinas

Aristotle (4th century BC) made a distinction between laws of nature, and human laws and conventions in his *Nicomachean Ethics*.[21] Aquinas connected the concepts of natural justice and natural right, which share some characteristics, and he conflated the two into a single identity in a way Aristotle may not have intended, as the differences appear to become lost. Thus, Aquinas is generally credited with introducing the proposition that human rights exist and are based upon laws of nature.

Aquinas decreed that human laws are to be measured by natural law to determine justice, and held that an unjust law is no law at all. As feudal peasants gained awareness of upper class privileges compared to the slavish misery they suffered under, popular revolts arose against unjust barons and/or bishops who ruled medieval towns, and little republics where justice prevailed formed. The words of Aquinas also proclaim a fore-gleam of the American Revolution – a revolt against arbitrary and unjust law.

Aquinas taught his students to employ the faculty of reason to discover what natural law requires, and what is incongruent with human nature. Since God designed both man and nature, natural law has divine sanction. Mankind is not to consider what is normal for a brute – but what is natural according to God's design. However, Aquinas was careful to distinguish between **divine law**, which is a concern of the church and the believer, and **natural law**, which is a concern of government, commerce and public life. It was great men like Aquinas, a lowly Dominican friar, who taught us how to differentiate between church and state without erecting artificial barriers, and without separating the state from God.

SELF-EVIDENT TRUTHS, FOUR GOOD THINGS, AND SEVEN VIRTUES

Aquinas believed that natural law is imprinted upon the conscience of every man and its principles are self-evident. This is the origin of the phrase *"We hold these truths to be self-evident,"* which Jefferson wrote in the Declaration of independence. The first tenet of Aquinas' natural law is that every man is obliged to do good and eschew evil – the four codes of good are: 1) procreation, 2) education of children, 3) living in society, and 4) worshiping God. Subsidiary rules help citizens accomplish the good, while drunkenness, theft, etc., are evil because of the injury they cause to the good.

Aristotle's list of seven virtues enable individuals to make moral choices – lacking any one of them impairs wisdom. The first four are called **Cardinal Virtues**, can be ascertained by applying common sense reasoning to nature, and include prudence, justice, fortitude and temperance. The three **Theological Virtues** are hope, charity and faith.

TENSION BETWEEN NATURAL LAW AND TRADITIONALISM

Traditionalism is ambivalent about Aquinas' unabashed confidence in reason, arguing that when reason stands alone spinning theories, it tends to be abstract, simplistic and naive about the realities of life, so is not by itself adequate to discover natural law. However indispensable to human life, no man can navigate successfully through life on reason

---

[21] The Nicomachean Ethics is Aristotle's best known work on ethics, and plays a pre-eminent role in defining Aristotelian ethics. It originally consisted of ten separate scrolls, and is based on notes from his lectures at the Lyceum, which were edited by Aristotle's son, Nicomachus.

alone. God has endowed man with other faculties that must also be exercised in order to gain wisdom. Among these is the ability to accumulate lessons about life based upon experience.

Justice Antonin Scalia

An admirable modern attempt to reconcile Natural Law Conservatism and Traditionalist Conservatism is Justice Antonin Scalia's (1936-) doctrine of text and tradition, which purports that while the jurist should rationally determine the meaning of the text, he should also consider legal precedent and the wisdom of cumulative social experience. The understanding of long tradition ought to be respected by the courts, argued Scalia, and not summarily breached by jurists who arrogantly assume that their abstract logic and personal preferences are wiser than the time-tested and wholesome traditions of a successful and happy society. Judges are not authorized by the U.S. Constitution to be tribunes of the people or reformers of society, which is why Scalia dissented from the court's decision that a private, traditional, military boy's school must admit girls.

IDEAS HAVE CONSEQUENCES

The culture war has deep philosophical roots. Plato stated that universals have independent existence, while particulars are shadowy and inferior versions of universals. Aristotle taught that universals subsist in particulars, but have no independent existence apart from them. Ancient Greeks were amazingly intelligent and talented, but were unable to solve this contradiction, since they lacked an essential central foundation that Christian Europe would later enjoy. The unresolved riddle of universals and particulars may be why Athens' classical period was so brief – glorious cultural ferment lasted only about 50 years.

Statue of Plato

According to cultural historian Richard Weaver (1910-1963), *"Ideas have consequences."*[22] Two interlocking concepts played significant roles in the rise of the West: 1) **universals and particulars**; and 2) **the one and the many**. Western culture provided satisfying solutions to these intellectual dilemmas in the 12th and 13th centuries – and is still the only civilization to do so. The Christian doctrine of the Trinity provided the solution for these foundational paradoxes.

UNIVERSALS AND PARTICULARS

Universals are truths, laws, archetypes, paradigms and systems that are everlasting, unchanging, ubiquitous and essential – they are the same necessary realities every time, every place and in all cases (i.e., universal moral law, strength, humanity.) **Particulars** are individual specifics unique to time and place such as people, animals, geography and weather – detailed, irreducible concepts are also particulars.

---

[22] (Weaver 1948)

THE BRILLIANCE AND RESILIENCE OF EUROPE

The vigorous European culture advanced from 1050-1800 AD with four successive Renaissance eras. The brilliance and resilience of Western civilization emanated from the foundational truths and faith that was embraced by strong, wise and talented men. The first generation of scholastic philosophers continued the Greek debate, arguing that universals have independent existence. Disciples of the Benedictine monk, Saint Anselm (1033-1109), called this **Realism** – claiming that reality exists apart from observation. The Realist debate with non-Realist philosophers and unbalanced extremes went through turbulent wrestling to sift bad ideas from the good ones. The intellectual dynamo of these heroic challenges established foundational truth, and is opposite to the lassitude of postmodern universities where scholars no longer believe one idea could be intrinsically superior to another.

INTELLECTUAL IMPERIALISM

Peter Abelard

Realists promptly faced a proud and tough opponent who practiced intellectual imperialism, medieval French scholastic philosopher Peter Abélard (1079-1142), a champion debater and popular celebrity. Abélard was a **Conceptualist**, meaning he believed that universals only exist as concepts. This speculation was within the realm of his intellectual mastery – he could not tolerate an independent existence for universals, because that would place them beyond his understanding and control. He was the prototype of culturally destructive academia that exalts the mind beyond its proper jurisdiction within the whole of life.

Civilization can be threatened from many directions. Modern science follows Abélard's pattern of **epistemology**, meaning what we can know and how we can know it. Epistemological imperialism is summarized by sweeping claims such as: *"We are the initiated elite. We alone have the key to knowledge. No other kind of knowledge is valid. Our special knowledge enables us to eventually acquire all knowledge about all things. Nothing exists that we cannot eventually learn about and master. If it is outside the competence of our kind of knowledge, it doesn't exist."*[23]

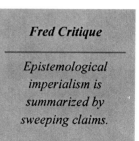

Fred Critique

Epistemological imperialism is summarized by sweeping claims.

Science becomes destructive to the human soul and Western culture according to the extent of the establishment's belief and promotion of these utopian myths. Two contemporary examples include: 1) the refusal to listen to criticism from outside the scientific fraternity or to dissenting mavericks inside; and 2) recent neuroscientific investigations claiming that reason, consciousness and free will are illusions, and if controlled methods cannot find something, it must not exist.[24]

A LOGOCENTRIC WORLD

"The heavens declare the glory of God, and the firmament shows His handiwork. Day unto day utters speech, and night unto night shows knowledge. There is no speech nor language where their voice is not heard." Psalms 19:1-3 (KJV)

---

[23] (F. Hutchison, Brief History of Conservatism 2009)
[24] (Neuroscience of Free Will 2010) (Trevena and Miller 2010)

William of Occam

Nominalism has two main versions – one denies the reality of universals, and the other refutes the existence of abstract objects that do not exist in space and time. Abélard's teacher, French philosopher Roscelin of Compiègne (1050-1125), was a Nominalist who claimed that universals exist only as names. William of Occam (1288-1348) denied the authenticity of metaphysical universals and argued that only individuals exist – he held that universals are products of abstraction by individual human minds and have no extra-mental existence. Postmodern scholars insist that words are arbitrary signs void of meaning – this nominalism often leads to poisoned skepticism and subsequent cynicism, nihilism and despair.[25]

In contrast, Realists are **Logocentric** (*Logo* = word, *centric* = centered; or reason centered), a term coined by postmodern German philosopher Ludwig Klages (1872-1956) referring to traditional Western science and philosophy belief in a *"metaphysical presence"* or a *"transcendence signified."* This model situates the logos (*the word* or the *act of speech*) as epistemologically superior in a metaphysical system, assuming an original, irreducible object to which the logos represents. The French deconstructionist philosopher, Jacques Derrida (1930-2004), used the term to explain what he wanted to destroy about Western culture.

Logocentric Realists disagree with the Nominalist position that words are merely arbitrary signs, believing that words carry meaning and have an independent existence – just as universals do. Words are not merely names of things, they are things. Anglo-American writer W.H. Auden (1907-1973) sometimes asked aspiring rhymesters why they wanted to be poets. If they viewed poetry as the means to get out a message, Auden saw no hope for their goal. However, if the young writer loved to linger among words and listen to what they said to each other, he recognized a promising poet.[26]

True poetry is possible in a Logocentric world, but impossible in a Nominalist world. If words are real things, poets are oracles of what words are saying as part of creation – they bear messages from the Creator and the universe. If words are mere arbitrary signs, the cosmos grows silent and man, a creature of words, finds himself exiled in a silent, alien world. Scripture speaks of a world filled with declarative voices coming from heaven and nature: *"The heavens declare the glory of God; the skies proclaim the work of his hands. Day after day they pour forth speech; night after night they reveal knowledge." Psalms 19:1-2 (NIV)*

A friend of Fred Hutchison who owned a gigantic personal library once said that books have souls.[27] Such beliefs are life nourishing and in stark contrast to the life-destroying nihilism of nominalism. Realist monks who copied and stored manuscripts during the Dark Ages prevented the extinction of Western civilization by saving great documents; one of them was the Bible, a spirit-breathed tome with a soul. Books can revive our crumbling culture because they have souls.

> *Fred Critique*
>
> ---
>
> *Books can revive our crumbling culture because they have souls.*

FOUNDATIONS OF WESTERN CULTURE

Realists who adhered to St. Anselm's views came close to solving the problem of universals and particulars. Italian Dominican priest and scholar, St. Thomas Aquinas (1225-1274), crafted the finishing touches for a definitive solution that vindicated and enhanced both. He corrected extreme Realism's platonic tendency to cut universals off from

---

[25] (F. Hutchison, Brief History of Conservatism 2009)

[26] This paragraph was inspired by a Mars Hill Audio interview with Scott Cairns, author of **Compass of Affection**. (Cairns 2004)

[27] (F. Hutchison, Brief History of Conservatism 2009)

particulars, and diminish or define particulars entirely in terms of universals. Aquinas determined that universals have independent existence, but also subsist in particulars – thereby giving particulars essence, meaning and unique detail more relevant than a condensed expression of universals.[28] Always before, philosophers either emphasized universals at the expense of particulars, or vice versa – this formulation enabled a mutually furnished world.

St. Thomas Aquinas

With the age-old riddle clearly and definitively solved, the foundation of Western culture was securely laid and construction began. A wondrous Logocentric society was now possible, since words could share in the essence of universals without forfeiting their integrity as particulars. Tongues and pens were loosened from long muteness.

Aquinas' explanation was believable and satisfying to most Christians – since the Creator is transcendent to creation, it stands to reason that universals are transcendent to particulars. If Creator and creation both truly exist, then universals and particulars have collective ontological existence, i.e., they are really *"out there."* If God's nature and glory are manifested in the universe, and the cosmos is deeply embroidered with a plenitude of particulars, then logic demands that universals subsist in particulars. If three particular personalities exist in the one Trinity Godhead, then a universal God honors the distinct individuals and particulars of nature.

Aquinas' influence on Western culture is extensive. Much of modern philosophy was formulated in reaction against, or agreement with his ideas, particularly in ethics, natural law and political theory. His ground rules facilitated the flowering of literature when four eminent writers equipped with powerful Logocentric words appeared – Dante, Chaucer, Petrarch and Boccaccio. These voices speak as clearly today as they did to their own generation. As discussed in Chapter 2, Petrarch and Boccaccio laid literary foundations for the Italian Renaissance and trained first generation leaders for the Republic of Letters in Florence.

CIVILIZED PEASANTS

An upsurge of interest in universals and particulars during the 1050-1100 period corresponded with a simultaneous rise of attention towards the mystery of Christ's presence in Holy Communion.[29] Everyone who understood Aquinas' explanation of how the body and blood of Christ are offered universally for all people, yet subsist particularly in the sacramental bread and wine, had a grasp of the reconciliation between universals and particulars. Peasants were not isolated from the general culture – medieval tradition maintained an organic view of society that included rural workers as a living part of the organism as powerful, civilizing ideas filtered down to them through the church. Uneducated peasants were instructed by parish priests, and now possessed elemental conceptions that eluded Greek philosophers. This era is remembered by the benchmark Romanesque architecture of the great abbey churches.

Frodo the Hobbit from the
"Lord of the Rings" movies

This acculturation of peasants may account for the charming, civilized countryside in various places, most notably Northern Italy, Southern France, the Rhineland and the Western Midlands of England. These blissful Elysian fields stand in stark contrast to the hellish wilderness that comprised most of Northern Europe in the 10th century. The English West Midland counties of Worcestershire, Shropshire, Warwickshire and

---

[28] (Aquinas 2008)
[29] See Chapter 15 for a detailed account of this spiritual awakening.

Staffordshire were idealized and affectionately satirized by Tolkien as *"The Shire."* The resident Hobbits were caricatures of merry, eccentric English peasants living in their beloved countryside. The Shire was described as a small but beautiful and fruitful land with an extensive agricultural system, and pocketed with forests similar to the English landscape.[30] Just as Tolkien recuperated from trench fever in Staffordshire, Frodo recovered from the Nazgul stab wound to his shoulder in Rivendell. Just as Tolkien could not return to dwell in Worcestershire after surviving the Battle of the Somme in World War I, Frodo could not remain in the Shire after visiting Mount Doom.[31]

THE GENIUS OF A TRINITARIAN SOCIETY

Saint Anselm of Canterbury

Only a **Trinitarian**[32] society is likely to settle upon the balanced philosophical realism proposed by Anselm and Aquinas. It is highly improbable that non-Trinitarian civilizations come to that conclusion – polytheistic Greeks could not solve the problem of universals and particulars. Monotheistic Muslims rejected the Trinity but loved Aristotle; yet they could not solve the problem of universals/particulars and refused the Christian solution. As a partial result, the Muslim Ottoman Empire, Europe's chief rival, began to lose momentum after 1700, while the West accelerated in development as a great civilization.

> *Fred Critique*
>
> *A Trinitarian society is uniquely compatible with Republics, and only a Republic can fully implement the political connotations of the Trinity.*

Trinitarian Realism and Logocentricity are the basis for the characteristic rationality of the West. It is no accident that the scientific method arose first in Christian Europe. A Trinitarian society is uniquely compatible with Republics, and only a Republic can fully implement the political connotations of the Trinity. This follows the American Founding Fathers' natural law presuppositions that only a Republic is in accord with human nature.

HERESY AND CONFUSION ABOUT UNIVERSALS

Abélard's clever and hugely popular academic debates and inquiries concerning rational philosophy were taken as sheer revolt by the French abbot, Saint Bernard of Clairvaux (1090-1153), who personified passionate and unwavering faith. The unwavering Bernard worked to crush the rising evil in the person of the boldest offender, and had Abélard tried for the heresy of Sabellianism under the church's authority. The curious fact that the greatest commissioned

advisor to kings and popes would personally deal with an upstart teacher is a clue into the vital import of the issue.

Sabellianism is the non-Trinitarian notion that the three divine persons of the Trinity (Heavenly Father, Resurrected Son and Holy Spirit) are merely three modes or aspects of one God, rather than three distinct persons in God – the formulation denies the members' particularity and personhood. God is universal because he is the creator, redeemer and object of worship for all mankind – his three entities makes him personal and particular. The incarnation of the complete man, Jesus of Nazareth, bridges the gap between transcendent universal and indwelling particular. Trinitarians understand that observable particulars in nature do not contradict implicit universals, because a

---

[30] (Tolkien, The Hobbit 1937) (Jackson 2001-2003)
[31] (Tolkien, The Lord of the Rings 1954) (Jackson 2001-2003)
[32] Believing or professing belief in the Christian Trinity or the doctrine of the Trinity.

triple deity concept does not disprove Godhead oneness (three in one = trinity). According to Saint Anselm, Sabellianism is a true heresy because if Christ is not a real person, his death and resurrection would have no effect in securing the believer's eternal salvation.

Abélard's confusion about the Trinity is directly related to his unbelief in the reality of universals and particulars. Trinitarians recognize both in philosophy and nature because they accept a Triune God – a unified Godhead of three persons is the archetype of universals and particulars that is implicit in creation and the rational human mind, which is incomplete without these concepts. This comprehension is a foundational reason for Western renown in so many stellar achievements of intellect and imagination.

Abélard stumbled on the mystery of the Trinity, therefore denying the independent reality of universals – just like postmodern multiculturalists. The contemporary **Emerging Church**[33] movement of renegade Evangelicals slid into Sabellianism because of intellectual laziness towards carefully teaching the Trinity. When congregations lose interest in universal truth, they engross themselves in depraved, contemporary culture fads. As they embrace Abélard's heresy, they deny Anselm's and Luther's doctrine of atonement. This may be happening right now at a mega-church near you!

LAYING FOUNDATIONS

Charlemagne

After the fall of Rome and the barbarian invasions, Northern and Western Europe slowly converted from paganism to Christianity as heroic missionary monks completed the work of evangelism and established monasteries throughout the wilderness. The fruits of Christian spirituality required six centuries to slowly work into the pagan darkness, as leaven is worked through lumps of dough. By forcibly Christianizing the Saxons and banning Germanic paganism on penalty of death, Charlemagne (aka) Charles the Great (742-814) integrated them into his realm. The conversion of the Franks paved the way for a Christian empire – Pope Leo III (750-816) crowned Charlemagne the *"Holy Roman Emperor"* on December 25, 800. King Charles is regarded as the founding father of the French and German monarchies, the Ottonian dynasty, and Europe – his empire united most of Western and Central Europe and encouraged the formation of a common identity.

This empire collapsed and gave way to the local rule of land owners, most of whom were baptized Christians. These barons were gradually able to make headway in fighting off pagan raiding parties, brigands, freebooters and war lords. From 900 AD forward, the elaborate codes and rites of feudalism steadily evolved towards a semi-civilized, semi-Christian society of landed aristocracy complete with a code of honor and Christian knight ideals. By 1050, these standards of chivalry were taken seriously by many of the warrior class. Legends of knight-errant champions are partly mythological, but have a solid factual basis – after 1100, courtly romances and troubadour stories about heroic knights on quest were extremely popular throughout Europe.

During the same period, the office of bishop grew in importance and began to rival the barons in power and prestige. Ordinary people were more likely to know the name of their bishopric and parish than their barony, duchy or kingdom. The church and priesthood became a powerful new establishment, which in due time would transform the culture.

---

[33] The emerging church is a late 20th-early 21st century Christian movement that crosses political, theological and denominational boundaries. Advocates call it a *"conversation"* to emphasize a commitment to dialogue that is aimed at developing a decentralized structure while including the extensive points of view in *"postmodern"* society. Participants agree on disillusionment with the organized and institutional church, and the need to deconstruct the nature of modern Christian worship, evangelism and community.

Europe was not yet a true civilization because it lacked permanent free-standing metropolitan cities and urban culture. The peripheral settlements in the shadow of fortresses, monasteries or trading posts lacked permanence and were dependent for survival on military, religious or mercantile sponsors.[34]

WHITE MANTLE OF CHURCHES

By 1000, Europe had an impressive network of monasteries. Monastic chronicler Raoul (or Rodulfus) Glaber (985-1047) wrote, "...it was as though the very world had shaken herself and cast off her old age and were clothing herself in the white mantle of churches,"[35] referring to the monasteries that covered Europe. After Glaber died at the Monastery of Cluny, the region began erecting the most fabulous church of the day (Cluny III, or the third church of Cluny). The

Raoul Glaber

great cathedral was laid out in a cruciform pattern with six towers, one for each of the wounds of Christ: two signifying the wounded feet of Christ at the west portal; two indicative of nail pierced hands at the transepts; one for the crown of thorns at the choir; and one at the east end of the nave for Christ's wounded side. The great church had dozens of side altars and chapels located in semicircular chambers built into the walls. The multiplication of these satellite prayer chapels indicates that throngs of people were seeking a sanctified and sheltered place to pray. It was the largest church in Christendom prior to the erection of Saint Peter's Basilica in Rome.

Deep spirituality preceded and conditioned the spiritual hurricane that led to the construction of Cluny III. Cluniac monasteries provided the foundation for a series of reform popes who emerged as spiritual and cultural leaders after the renewal began. Four factors made it possible for men who were spiritually shaped and educated by Cluny to ascend the papal throne:

1. Cluny reported directly to Rome, so the Abbot always had personal contact with the pope;

2. Cluny controlled hundreds of daughter churches, making it one of the most powerful and influential institutions in Europe;

3. Cluny supplied men who were spiritually minded, well educated, and had administrative experience – the exact type needed to staff Vatican bureaucracy; and

4. The spiritual revival made it possible for men of lowly birth to rise to great heights – especially in the church.[36]

EARLY HARBINGERS OF CIVILIZATION

There were hundreds of Benedictine monasteries (daughter houses of Cluny) that had impressive literary and artistic culture prior to 1050. Society was also blossoming in the courts of great lords – as in Charlemagne's retinue and the great ducal assemblies. The inspiring awakening was an early harbinger of Europe and contributed greatly to development, but it was only the promise of future social order, not true civilization. Proper civilization requires cities. Civilized culture came slowly to monasteries and courts, but arrived quickly in new cities that began to appear.

Fred Critique

Proper civilization requires cities.

---

[34] (Dawson 1959)
[35] (Glaber 1027)
[36] (Dawson 1959)

RISING ABOVE THE CLASS SYSTEM

Peasants' Crusade

No new civilization is possible if society is weighed down with the heavy apparatus of a class system. In the case of Europe, breaking away involved temporarily suspending class system divisions during transcendent moments of general spiritual awakening – these were periods of remarkable unity and cheerful sacrifice. The spiritual awakening of 1050-1100 did not disannul the social class system, but lifted the weight and transcended many limitations, especially in new cities.

The prevailing assumption that only aristocrats and knights had *"honor"* was shattered, if the definition means noble personal sacrifice for a higher cause. The Peasants' Crusade"[37] (1096-1099) demonstrated that devotion to high ideals and impossible causes permeated every social class. The premise that proud Lords and Ladies would never work beside those from the servant class was also refuted. In those days, spiritual unity trumped social class.

THE SUDDEN APPEARANCE OF EUROPEAN CIVILIZATION

"But seek ye first the kingdom of God, and his righteousness; and all these things shall be added unto you." Matthew 6:6 (KJV)

As the city of God is pursued in a single-minded way, civilizations come into being – they seem to emerge as a by-product of a united spiritual quest. Europe rose quickly and unexpectedly as people sought to build God's kingdom. Considering Dark Age conditions, this was one of the least likely places for a stable society. After six centuries of darkness, European civilization amazingly appeared over a fifty-year period (1050-1100). The explosive growth was driven by winds of almost unprecedented power – a spiritual hurricane that did not come out of nowhere. The ground was prepared prior to the cyclone, as religious and spiritual foundations were slowly laid over the previous centuries.

SEPERATION OF CHURCH AND STATE

Heinrich (Henry) IV (1050-1106) was installed as Holy Roman Emperor at the age of six when Heinrich III (1017-1056) died. The Pope used this weakness to break free of Holy Roman Empire control, insisting that priests and bishops serve only the Church and refusing appointments by the Emperor. Heinrich IV later attempted to select his own bishops to help him regain ruling power of the empire, but was excommunicated for his insolence. He was reinstated into the Church only after forced penance, literally kneeling in snow to the Pope at Canossa in northern Italy (1077).[38]

This brief break in the power structure (1050-1100) enabled a spiritual awakening and the free flourishing of mankind to blossom. The flowering of thought during this short fifty-year period can be attributed to the rebellion against a state sanctioned church and the desire to return to biblical principles. The Church was never meant to brandish the sword,

---

[37] The Peasants' or People's Crusade lasted from April to October 1096, and was destroyed by Turk forces. It was part of the First Crusade (1096-1099) military expedition by Western Christianity under Pope Urban II to regain the Holy Lands taken by Muslim's, ultimately resulting in the recapture of Jerusalem and the freeing of Eastern Christians from Islamic rule.
[38] (Knight 2009) (Carr 2011)

nor was the state meant to institute worship.[39] The Early Renaissance is subsequentially dated 1050-1300 by many reliable sources – citing improving religious, social, military and economic factors.[40]

SPIRITUAL HURRICANE

The word *"revival"* is inadequate to describe the religious upheaval in late 11th century Europe – the word *"hurricane"* is more appropriate, because landscape is altered after they pass. Before the spiritual hurricane, Northern and Western Europe was a wilderness full of deep forests, bogs, thorn thickets, wild animals and human marauders –villages and modest towns were scattered here and there. After 1100, many forests were cleared, marshes were drained, the land was cultivated, and proud new cities sprang up.

These cities were impressively surrounded by castle-like stone walls brandishing battlements and citadels, with many church spires visible above the walls. Elegant stone palaces on hilltops replaced the old earthen and timber fortresses. The new metropolis areas had bustling marketplaces supported by commercial networks. A revolution in windmills, water mills and mechanical devices was used in construction. New universities were founded by scholars with great zeal for seeking truth, and debating theology and philosophy.[41]

THE FIRST BREATH OF FREEDOM

Some cities became communes, meaning they were Christian republics with some common features of later bourgeois democracies. The communities had craft guilds, Christian **confraternities**,[42] and urban monastery orders – each institution included civic and philanthropic functions and many had festive specialties. For example, commune authorities sometimes granted particular guilds a monopoly to perform Christmas plays.

Serfs in the feudal countryside were not slaves; they did have a few hereditary rights and entitlements. But they were not free; they were bound to the land and loaded with heavy duties. Runaway serfs could flee to the sanctuary of a church to find refuge from being arrested, and then skip from church to church until entering city walls to find final release from bondage. Charitable confraternities sponsored escapees until they found servant or laborer jobs, or trade/craft apprenticeships.[43]

Although the communes had more municipal regulations and offered less privacy than modern Americans would tolerate, they offered a real measure of freedom. *"City air makes one free"* was a popular proverb. These miniature republics offered the first tantalizing breath of freedom to European man. Without civilization and cities, there can be no individual freedom. Freedom came first to urban republics that were intensely Christian, and which enjoyed the energies, vitality and culture of high civilization. The quest to save civilization and the mission to preserve freedom go hand and hand.

> **Fred Critique**
>
> *Without civilization and cities, there can be no individual freedom.*

---

[39] (Barton, Wallbuilders: The Separation of Church and State 2001)
[40] (Earle 1996)
[41] (Dawson 1959)
[42] Confraternities are lay brotherhoods devoted to some purpose, especially religious or charitable service.
[43] (Dawson 1959)

ENTHUSIASTIC SACRIFICE

The new Romanesque cathedrals were formidable constructions for any era – great mountains of stone were originally surrounded by clusters of thatched cottages, offering an idea of community priorities. The exertions, expenses and sacrifices made by people of every social class to build immense palaces of heaven were enormous. This was not a case of pharaoh cruelly driving slaves. Chroniclers occasionally describe workers cheerfully and joyfully contributing their share of labor to build city walls and cathedrals. Citizens were enraptured about building the Kingdom of God on earth. Sometimes profound silence would fall as they worked, class distinctions melted, many forgave enemies, and the spirit of brotherhood prevailed.[44]

People living in the cottages may well have said, *"It matters not that the roof leaks and we sleep a half dozen people to a room. We live near the great Cathedral where God dwells, which is decorated with gold and jewels and fine tapestries. We provided supplies for the workers who built it. We helped build Christ's kingdom on earth. That is all that matters."*

The phrase *"Christ's kingdom"* was shortened to *"Christendom"* in common parlance, and became synonymous with Christian Europe. According to art historian Kenneth Clark, civilization rose within the span of a single human lifetime – perhaps the span of a resident of the early cottages.[45] Inhabitants could have been born in tiny village huts at the forest edges during the Dark Age's last days, and died in impressive walled cities with great cathedrals. The forest fears of childhood must have seemed far away to old timers standing in the gilded splendor of cathedrals – it must have seemed like life's journey began in hell on earth, and ended in heaven.

> *Fred Critique*
> _____
> *It must have seemed like life's journey began in hell on earth, and ended in heaven.*

THE SPIRITUALITY OF THE CROSS

The dominant form of religion for common folk was the spirituality of the cross – every church congregation knelt before the crucifix, identifying with Christ in his sacrificial death. Houses of worship were designed with an ambulatory, a circular walk around the altar, and people slowly walked around it to gaze with wonder upon the consecrated host, i.e., the crucified Christ indwelling the bread and wine of communion. Every confessional had lines of contrite people waiting to confess sins.

Country roads all maintained shrines consisting of a crucifix under a shelter. The roads to pilgrimage churches were clogged with penitents walking barefoot and wearing sack cloth. Millions traveled in all weather, trying to reconcile with God – horrible storms were regarded as penance. People who survived sojourns to sacred distant lands and returned home were hailed as folk heroes. Those returning from the Holy Land would wear palm fronds, and were admiringly dubbed *"palmers."*[46]

BREATHTAKING PROMOTIONS

> *"Almost every boss in America claims to promote on the basis of merit, but in this day of mediocrity they are the exception rather than the rule."* Fred Hutchison, 2009

---

[44] (Dawson 1959)
[45] (Clark, A Guide to Civilisation: The Kenneth Clark Films on the Cultural Life of Western Man 1970)
[46] (Dawson 1959)

Only in a rapidly rising civilization like Early Renaissance Europe, or societies with a flourishing culture like Renaissance Italy, are authentic merit promotions commonplace. Mediocrities in Renaissance Florence were not only winnowed out, but were subject to public humiliation – even coming in second in public artistic competitions could ruin a promising artist's career. The pursuit of excellence was ruthless for artists and hard-nosed businessmen alike.

Bernard of Clairvaux

Breathtaking promotions are possible during spiritual hurricanes – when people are passionate about building the kingdom of heaven on earth, they focus on doing an excellent job and getting it finished for God's glory. Sculptors who created gargoyles positioned at cathedral pinnacles where no human eye could see them strived for excellence *"because God sees them."* In this environment, the most able are used in strategic roles, and issues of rank and family entitlement often fall aside. Many extraordinary leaders emerged after breathtaking promotions in the late 11th and 12th centuries, including:

- Pope Innocent III (1160-1216) who is commemorated as one of the world's great lawmakers.

- Saint Dominic of Osma (1170-1221) who founded the Dominican Order and is the patron saint of astronomers.

- Saint Francis of Assisi (1181-1226), the founder of the Franciscan Order and known as the patron saint of animals and the environment.

- Pope Gregory VII (1015-1085), the heroic reformer of humble Cluny origins who challenged the authority of European monarchies to appoint church officials.

- Lanfranc (1005-1089) and Anselm (1033-1109), two successive Italian scholars who were appointed Archbishop of Canterbury and were lauded by the English – the reward for monastic scholarship was a bishop's throne.

- Abbot Bernard of Clairvaux (1090-1153) became the most powerful and influential man in Europe – kings, emperors, bishops and popes trembled at his rebuke.

- Abbott Suger (1081-1151), inventor of Gothic architecture, became the Regent of France.[47]

DYNAMIC MOVEMENT

When God intends to create a new civilization, his breath is like divine wind sweeping across the land, putting people in motion. Instead of the listless Dark Age stagnation, there was dynamic movement – people on pilgrimage, merchants with loads, and traveling scholars. There was vibrant development in cities as the kingdom of God on earth was pursued. Great armies eager to battle heathens, heretics or wicked princes marched to distant lands. Many intrepid knights were lost, charging headlong into the ranks of death in pursuit of glory – in some cases pursuing earthly fame and in others, heavenly.[48]

King Richard I

King Richard I of England (Cœur de Lion, or Richard the Lionheart) (1157-1199) was an extraordinary warrior so fierce in battle that his mere appearance at the head of his troops could turn the battle tide. Salāh ad-Dīn Yūsuf ibn Ayyūb (1138-1193), better known as Saladin, was the first Sultan of Egypt and Syria and founded the Ayyubid dynasty. He led

---

[47] (Dawson 1959)
[48] (Dawson 1959)

Muslim and Arab opposition to the Franks and other Europeans – his forces defeated the Crusaders at the Battle of Hattin, near Tiberias in present day Israel, leading the way to his re-capture of Palestine. His chivalrous behavior was noted by Christian chroniclers, and despite being their nemesis, he won the respect of many Crusaders, including Richard the Lionheart. Saladin's generally victorious army once fled from the field rather than face the formidable rage of Richard, even though greatly outnumbering the English forces. Arab parents threatened naughty children with the admonition *"King Richard will get you"* well into the late nineteenth century[49] – he became the ultimate bogeyman in tribute to his daring exploits, which made him larger than life.

LARGER THAN LIFE

Kenneth Clark characterized the period 1050-1200 (the fifty years of divine hurricane plus the following century of momentum) as the *"great thaw"* in his book *Civilization* – a time of extraordinary energy. *"...in every branch of life – action, philosophy, organization, technology – there was an extraordinary outpouring of energy, an intensification of existence. Popes, emperors, kings, saints, scholars, philosophers were all larger than life, and the incidents of history – Henry II at Canossa, Pope Urban announcing the First Crusade, Heloise and Abelard, the martyrdom of Saint Thomas a Becket – are great historical dramas, or symbolic acts, that still stir our hearts."*[50]

This describes a dam-burst of human energy more than a thaw. The events could also be interpreted as being caused by a divine wind. There is no question that the maelstrom of action and drama involving larger-than-life men occurred during a great spiritual awakening – perhaps the greatest vivid personalities since the apostles.

> *Fred Critique*
>
> *There is no question that the maelstrom of action and drama involving larger-than-life men occurred during a great spiritual awakening – perhaps the greatest vivid personalities since the apostles.*

MIDWAY IN THE JOURNEY

Chapter 1 has journeyed 2,100 years through Western cultural history. Many elements of the conservative movement existed by 1300. The next chapter will follow the trail of Petrarch, Boccaccio and Salutati to Bruni (central figures of the early Renaissance); explore how the Italian Renaissance (15th century) brought Literary Conservatism to its logical conclusion in a Republic of Letters; and investigate Renaissance men from Machiavelli to Montaigne to Shakespeare.

The Reformation (16th century) brought the Bible, faith, morality and education to ordinary people on an individual basis. Natural law ideas developed further in the 17th and 18th centuries. The popularity of Virgil and his conservative Roman ideas, and the great inspiration of two titans of literature, Dante and Milton, continued unabated until the 18th century.

Liberalism and the Romantic Movement were born during the 18th century. In response, Traditionalist Conservatives developed new concepts to stand in opposition. A revival of Classicism would furnish the West with cultural critics who shunned Romanticism. Classical liberalism would leave a seedbed of ideas, some of which would sprout as Libertarian Conservatism. By 1800, most of the essential ideas of the modern debate between conservatives and liberals had come into play.

---

[49] (Fletcher 2003)
[50] (Clark, A Guide to Civilisation: The Kenneth Clark Films on the Cultural Life of Western Man 1970)

Chapter 1 detailed how four streams of early Conservatism contributed to Western culture: 1) Literary Traditionalism, 2) Christian Conservatism, 3) Natural Law Conservatism and 4) Neoconservatism. This chapter picks up the story at Dante (1300 AD) with a journey through the proto-Renaissance of literature (1300-1375), followed by a quick tour of the Italian Renaissance (1375-1520), and finishing with Shakespeare during the Northern Renaissance (1520-1600). Chapter 2 explores how Literary Traditionalism led to the Renaissance, how the great works of Dante and Chaucer were triggered by their personal reckoning with God, how Christian civilization produced fruitful life, and how the very education of learned men carried the seeds of fallacy and disillusionment. Historical lessons will be identified and itemized at the end of this chapter.

POETRY, AN EARLY HARBINGER OF RENAISSANCE

Cultural Renaissance develops along a timeline: magnificent poetry and literature generally emerge first; brilliant fine artists and architects appear second; and illustrious philosophers and composers arrive late in the game. The appearance of superlative 14th century poets, like Dante and Petrarch, was an early harbinger of the Italian Renaissance. Two Centuries later Michelangelo painted the Sistine Chapel and perfected the design of Saint Peter's Cathedral during the High Renaissance. Baroque music developed because of Renaissance innovations in tonality and harmony, but was not perfected until after 1700, when Bach, Handel, Vivaldi and Telemann appeared. Trends in philosophy that began during the late Renaissance found their synthesis and finale in Immanuel Kant during the late 18th century.

To explain this pattern, consider poets to be the prophets of cultural ideals that will prevail during the subsequent intellectual renewal. Four immortal writers emerged during the 14th century: Dante, Petrarch, Boccaccio and Chaucer. Great artists and architects reveal the fashions of current society, according to art historians John Ruskin (1819-1900) and Kenneth Clark (1903-1983). Philosophers and composers slowly digest cultural ideals over time, and develop elaborate and technically complex means of giving mature expression to them.

> *Fred Critique*
>
> *Poets are the prophets of cultural ideals... Philosophers and composers digest cultural ideals and develop elaborate and technically complex means of mature expression.*

MIDWAY IN THE JOURNEY

Dante

"Midway in the journey of life I found myself in a dark wood, for the straight way was lost." Divine Comedy, Dante Alighieri

Dante Alighieri (1265-1321) wrote these lines in 1312, as he harkened back to a spiritual event he experienced in the jubilee year of 1300 at the age of 35, when he was *"midway in his journey of life."* On Good Friday of that year, Dante was convicted of heavy sin, hence his words, *"...I found myself in a dark wood, for the straight way was lost."* His inner pilgrimage to find the —straight way" was expressed in the **Divine Comedy**, his literary classic of a metaphorical journey through Inferno, Purgatorio and Paradiso (hell, purgatory and heaven).[51]

---

[51] (Alighieri 1315)

Dante's spiritual crisis is an excellent example of how Christian passion can stimulate culture. As a man of conviction who possessed superb literary gifts, his magnum opus could not be composed until a spiritual catharsis had reawakened faith and restored him to the straight and narrow path. His renewed spiritual journey was the basis for his epic poetry.

THE CLASSICISM OF DANTE AND PETRARCH

Dante and Petrarch are perfect examples of *Literary Traditionalism*, which is recognized as one of the oldest streams of cultural conservatism. According to a tabulation of ***Great Books of the Western World***,[52] Dante cited more ancient authors than any Western author who had gone before except Epictetus (Stoic philosopher, 2nd century AD). Dante was profoundly influenced by Virgil, who was the greatest of the literary traditionalism masters.

Francesco Petrarch (1304-1374) cited more traditionalist authors than Dante, and was the first European classicist who seriously attempted to understand historic writers on their own terms, instead of from a **Gothic**[53] perspective. Renaissance men following him would build upon Petrarch's insights until they excelled in understanding the classical mind, thereby expanding Western mankind's world view with renewed versatility and creativity. Architecture and literacy were revived, which was seen as finite evidence of a new golden age of learning and refinement.

THE PROUD POET LAUREATE

Dante was proud of his literary talents, but humbly conceded to the superiority of Virgil. In contrast, Petrarch was egotistical about his intellect and resented living under the literary shadow of Dante. Petrarch could not accept being the second best poet of the century, and his attempts to parody Dante were too subtle to have the desired effect.

Francesco Petrarch

In some ways, Petrarch was the first modern man: he was the first European man to climb a mountain purely for individual adventure; he traveled more than most men of his era; he was cosmopolitan in outlook and was a sociable man of great personal charm, adept at forming friendships; and he was free of parochial interests. As an international celebrity poet, Petrarch was equally famous in Rome, Paris and Avignon. When Paris and Rome simultaneously offered him the laurel crown award of poetry, it gave Petrarch the added tribute of choice when he received the honor of **poet laureate**[54] in Rome.

Petrarch was imitated by so many Renaissance authors that his own fame was gradually eclipsed. Literary historians have failed to give Petrarch his due while lionizing Dante and Chaucer, yet Petrarch arguably had a greater effect on the Renaissance than any other writer.[55] Writers freely raided the immense corpus of Petrarch's work as though it was a public treasury – Shakespeare borrowed heavily from Petrarch, without giving him credit. Art historian Kenneth Clark conceded that Petrarch was the first European to read the classical authors with real insight, but slyly called Petrarch *"the false dawn of the Renaissance."* However, Petrarch was the true father of the Renaissance, for without him the stimulation for launching the revival

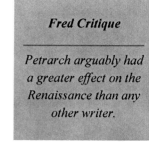

Fred Critique

Petrarch arguably had a greater effect on the Renaissance than any other writer.

---

[52] (M. J. Adler 1952)

[53] Gothic, a term first used in 1611, refers to the melding of two major influences in European cultural development, the Roman Empire and the Germanic tribe of Goths that invaded it. The word is used to mean Germanic, medieval, not classical, barbarous, and is also an architectural and art style.

[54] A poet laureate was officially appointed by a government and was often expected to compose poems for state occasions and events.

[55] (F. Hutchison, Brief History of Conservatism 2009)

would not have existed. To a significant degree, the class of men and leaders during the early Renaissance were launched by the vision of Petrarch.

CHAUCER AND SOCIABILITY

Like Dante, English poet and statesman Geoffrey Chaucer (1343-1400) took a spiritual pilgrimage, but in Chaucer's case it was a physical journey. Although he could afford a carriage, Chaucer walked to Canterbury Cathedral as an act of penance. His objective was to venerate the bones of Saint Thomas of Becket, whom Chaucer called *"the holy bliss-ful martyr."* His ***Canterbury Tales***[56] is the saga of the pilgrims who traveled with him. The genial and kind Chaucer has retained his appeal in the modern age, perhaps because contemporary literature and performance art emphasizes character and personality stories.

GOTHIC ARCADIA VERSES MEDIEVAL CALAMITY

Toward the end of the 13th century, the Little Ice Age brought harsher winters with reduced harvests, followed by the Famine of 1315, the outbreak of the Hundred Years' War (1337), and the rapid spread of Bubonic Plague (1346-1350). Food shortages, inflation, black markets and pirates, malnutrition and disease, wars and labor shortages, and religious upheavals contributed to a cycle of mass destruction and death.[57] Although the 14th century suffered under biblical scale calamities, a paradox of high spirits, playfulness, exquisite manners, congenial banter and cultivated taste reigned in the hearts of mankind. The Duke of Berry held court in a rich and sophisticated version of Greek Arcadia. The Arcadian season in Florence, Italy gave verse to its home town son, Boccaccio.

LA DOUCEUR DE VIVRE

The joyous play of Gothic life was a celebration of what the French call *"la douceur de vivre"* (the sweetness of life). This unique amusement was not the cruel and lewd games of barbarians, nor the obsessive entertainment of modern sportsmen. Gothic citizens loved the troubadour stories of romance and adventure that reduced courtship to an elaborate game. Kenneth Clark described the Gothic world as:

> *"A world of chivalry, courtesy, and romance; a world in which serious things were done with a sense*
> *of play – where even war and theology could become a sort of game; and when architecture reached*
> *a point of extravagance unequaled in history."*

Giovanni Boccaccio

A remarkable illustration of this sweet playfulness was exhibited by the twelve disciples of Saint Francis of Assisi (1181-1226) when they were called before Pope Innocent III. While this mighty pontiff could elicit trembling in the kings of Europe, who were either his feudal vassals or under political dominion, the humble *"friars minor"* (little brothers) gazed upon the great Bishop of Rome in all his glory, and began to sing and dance around the great papal throne – the perfect example of unwashed ragamuffin *"la douceur de vivre"* in spiritual form.

The serious dignity of the Renaissance drove playful vivacity out of the Gothic era. Sweet, sunny, dreamy days of the young culture gave way to the adult solemnity of Renaissance maturity. However, two great authors – Boccaccio and his inspired admirer, Baldassare

---

[56] (Chaucer late 14th century)
[57] (Wikipedia 2011) (Allmand 2012)

Castiglione (1478-1529) – preserved the finest Gothic courtly delights for transmission to future generations, configuring a gentleman code of honor. Sophisticated and gentle playfulness is an enduring charm of Western gentry. Giovanni Boccaccio (1313-1375) was a protégé and colleague of Petrarch, serving as a virtual link between the aging Petrarch and the Italian Renaissance. Boccaccio's contribution to Western culture was crucial.

FROLICKING DURING THE PLAGUE

When the Black Death plague came to Florence, Italy in 1348, seven ladies and three gentlemen fled to a beautiful Tuscan hills villa and spent a fortnight celebrating the sweetness of life. The shadow of death hovered over the valley, but these genial youth chose to enjoy each other's company with an extended picnic that included songs, dances, games and practical jokes. Their lively conversation is recorded in Boccaccio's **The Decameron**,[58] a distinctive work that describes in detail the physical, psychological and social effects of the Bubonic Plague.

The young Florentines devoted the ten day retreat to playful festivities, taking turns presiding as king or queen for a day, and electing their successors. To pass the time, each member told one story every night, according to the royally chosen theme of the day. Daily themes included misfortunes that bring a person to a state of unexpected happiness; people who have achieved an object they greatly desired, or recovered a thing previously lost; love stories that ended unhappily; love that survived disaster; those who have avoided danger; tricks women have played on their husbands; tricks both men and women play on each other; and those who have given very generously whether for love or another endeavor. They spoke of nature as a pleasant garden and an eternal spring for the enjoyment of youth – similar to Greek Arcadia. Nature was the sublime inspiration for beauty, order, symmetry and natural luxury, as well as natural morality and balanced intelligence – showing a hint of Natural Law philosophy, one of the cultural streams of conservatism.

Interestingly, the zestful Boccaccio and the congenial Chaucer were the first men of European civilization to publish the words of women speaking in their own voice and on their own terms. During the shared experience of *"la douceur de vivre,"* the feminine voice was verbalized, and men were interested enough to publish the transcripts.

PLANNING THE RENAISSANCE

Petrarch, Boccaccio and a circle of young scholars in Florence often mused over the future of education and cultured society. Petrarch predicted that gentlemen would supplant clerics in civic leadership – a visionary insight considering that Castiglione's **The Courtier** would not be written for more than a century. Young Christian gentleman would need strong political, cultural and educational foundations to prepare for imminent leadership. Since wise, learned and virtuous leaders are required to raise intellectual tones, these associates became the nucleus of the early Renaissance.

THE HOUSE OF JOY

The Italian Renaissance did not spontaneously erupt, but was the fruit of well planned cultural and educational reform. Great schools inspired by Petrarch, Salutati, Bruni and their associates produced "enlightened men" who became famous for their sophisticated culture and versatile talents. Renaissance Humanism engaged scholars, writers and civic leaders, today known as humanists, and prepared students to be doctors, lawyers or professional theologians.

---

[58] (Boccaccio 1353)

The greatest schoolmaster of the Renaissance, and one of the first modern educators, was Vittorino da Feltre Ramboldini (1378-1446), who was invited by the marquis of Mantua to educate his children. In 1423, Vittorino founded the first elite secular boarding school, *La Giancosa* (The House of Joy), where he taught the children of prominent families alongside many poor children, treating them all as equals. Influenced by the Greek education

Vittorino da Feltre

model that involved training mind and body, *La Giancosa* was furnished with sports fields, while Vittorino taught the humanities and emphasized religious, moral and physical instruction. His unique education methods included: adapting the teaching process to the ability and needs of each child; well lit and well constructed buildings; curriculum that included field trips; attention to student health; and elevating the status of teachers.

Vittorino admired Eusebius of Caesarea (263-339), the Roman Christian historian and church father who believed that education can be a means to moral character development. As a devout Christian, Vittorino believed the pagan classics of Greece and Rome could be reconciled with a Christian education, an idea many Catholic educators adhered to for centuries. Students were required to master grammar and become fluent in Latin and Greek, before turning to history, morality, poetry and rhetoric. Classical history focused on the memorable deeds of great men and their example of virtue. The moral illumination included spiritual exercises meant to nurture young Christians in the faith, and encouraged personal relationships between master and student.

La Giancosa glowed in the imagination of all who hoped to acquire an agreeable classical education. Humanists sought to produce citizens (including women) able to speak and write with eloquence and clarity, so they would be capable of engaging in civic life and persuading others to virtuous and wise actions. The arduous process of education was sweetened with splendid settings, as the school grounds included a palace with beautiful gardens for the student's enjoyment and aesthetic refinement. To the Renaissance educators, learning and maturing were part of the pursuit of happiness, and a good life required the full development and subsequent use of the human faculties. Therefore, formal education was viewed as the glory of civilization and an illustrious season in a life well lived. Vittorino's greatest student was Federigo da Montefeltra (1422-1482), the future Duke of Urbino, who transformed the palace of Urbino into the High Renaissance court where Castiglione would listen to elegant conversations and become inspired to compose **The Courtier**.

REPUBLIC OF LETTERS

The Republic of Florence, a city-state located in modern Tuscany, Italy, was founded in 1115. The Republic was ruled by a council of nine members (*signoria*), which was chosen by the ruler of the city (*gonfaloniere*), who was elected every two months by Florentine guild members. Though not an official member of the Republic's elected political government, the Chancellor of Florence held the most important bureaucratic position, wielding considerable political influence. The Chancellors, serving as civil service leaders, included some of the most famous scholars, political thinkers and humanists of the Renaissance.

Coluccio Salutati (1331-1406) was Petrarch's most gifted disciple, and the first of three Great Chancellors of Florence. Leonardo Bruni (1369-1444) was Salutati's greatest student and the most famous of the three Chancellors. Poggio Bracciolini (1380 -1459), the third notable Chancellor, was a young protégé of the elderly Salutati. This chain of literary masters – Virgil, Dante, Petrarch, Salutati, Bruni and Bracciolini – led to an extremely rare historical entity referred to as a **Republic of Letters**, a self-proclaimed community of scholars and literary figures that stretched across time and national boundaries, but respected differences in language and culture.

Early Renaissance leaders were devout churchmen with highly versatile talents. Each of the three Chancellors made original contributions to literature and were pioneers in literary research, having been drafted under Papal authority for special assignments and scholarly projects. From the Dark Ages until the 18th century, the church was a great sponsor of culture, particularly during the 11th and 12th centuries in France, and the 15th century Italian Renaissance.

Salutati was appointed Chancellor of Florence in 1375, marking the beginning of the Early Renaissance. Art historian Kenneth Clark said:

> "For thirty years the fortunes of the Republic (of Florence) ... were directed by a group of the most intelligent individuals who have ever been elected to power by a democratic government. From Salutati onwards, the Florentine chancellors were scholars, believers in the studia humanitas, in which learning could be used to achieve a happy life, believers in the application of free intelligence to public affairs, and believers, above all, in Florence."

The circulation of handwritten letters was necessary for a Republic of Letters to function because it enabled intellectuals to correspond with each other from great distances. Educated citizens exchanged published papers and pamphlets, and considered it their duty to bring others into the Republic through the expansion of correspondence.

Bracciolini was appointed Chancellor in 1453, and served until his death in 1459. Cosimo de' Medici gained control of the Republic in 1454. The ascendency of the House of Medici in Florence diminished the political power of the scholar-chancellors, but they retained considerable cultural influence. The Medici family proved to be generous civil servants in their patronage of the arts and letters, and maintained power until 1494.

The great Republic of Letters thus ran from 1375-1459, which also dates the Early Renaissance. The High Renaissance can subsequently be dated 1459-1527, during which time Rome supplanted Florence as the Renaissance center. The republican government was disestablished in 1532, when Pope Clement VII appointed Alessandro de' Medici *"Duke of the Florentine Republic,"* thereafter making the Republic a hereditary monarchy.

A MANUAL FOR GENTLEMEN

Baldassare Castiglione

Under the patronage of Eleonora Gonzaga, Duchess of Urbino (1493-1570), a circle of Renaissance men discussed the qualities a perfect aristocrat should possess. Castiglione was inspired by the conversation to write ***The Book of the Courtier (Italian: Il Cortegiano)***,[59] which he hoped would compare favorably with Boccaccio's ***Decameron***. The Courtier esteemed conservative ideals to create a gentleman archetype, highlighting the best traits of virtuous men from the classical past, the Gothic era, and Christianity.

While the Urbino dialogue preserved *"la douceur de vivre,"* the ribald humor and cruel tricks were tamed, and replaced with chivalry, honor, romance, courtesy, elegant conversation, wit and manly demeanor. Sports, swordsmanship, horsemanship and the arts of war were regarded as essential to the making of a gentleman, as was the ability to embrace philosophical, literary and artistic discernment. Christian cardinal and theological virtues, as delineated by Saint Aquinas, and the courtly virtues of tact, magnanimity, gallantry and social finesse were indispensable character qualities. Infamous Renaissance versatility was perfectly portrayed in ***The Courtier***, which became the indispensable gentleman's handbook for almost four centuries, and was instrumental in developing European high culture.

---

[59] (Castiglione 1528)

Cosimo de Medici

Cosimo de' Medici (1389-1464) reestablished Plato's Academy in Florence, appointing Marsilio Ficino (1433-1499) as headmaster. Ficino, who was the first translator of Plato's classic writings from Greek to Latin, was one of the most influential humanist philosophers of the early Italian Renaissance. He was a noted astrologer, who was in touch with every major academic thinker and writer of his day – and he attempted to revive ancient Greek astrology and Platonism by synthesizing it with Christianity, without neglecting his own faith. The Florentine Academy had enormous influence on the direction and tenor of the Italian Renaissance and the development of European philosophy.

High Renaissance grandiosity was partly caused by intoxication from the stimulating mixture of Christianity and Neoplatonism, or *"platonic inflation."* Michelangelo Simoni's (1475-1564) titanic figures on the ceiling of the Sistine Chapel are a perfect example of platonic inflation. As an apprentice artist in the house of Medici, the sponsor of the Platonic Academy, Michelangelo came by his grandiosity honestly – he absorbed platonic inflation along with his daily sculpture and painting lessons.

PLATONIC INFLATION AND LIBERAL HUMANISM

Platonic inflation became the source of new ideas referred to as *"liberal humanism"* that were contrary to ancient conservative principles. Such ideas included: man is the measure of all things; human nature is malleable; the potential of man is unlimited; and utopia is a possibility. Such notions flowed from the pens of Renaissance men such as Leonardo Bruni (1389-1444), Leon Alberti (1404-1472), Pico Mirandola (1463-1494) and Sir Thomas More (1478-1535).

The four conservative traditions detailed in Chapter 1 (Literary Traditionalism, Christian Conservatism, Natural Law Conservatism and Neoconservatism) were contrary to these ideas. Conservatives held that one cannot find *"the measure of all things"* in man, but must look to transcendent sources and ancient wisdom. They agreed that man has an established nature within limits, but to mold man contrary to his true nature is damaging. Traditionalists believed that man has developmental potential according to his design, but cannot break free to soar beyond inherent limits. Finally, utopia is not possible – the dark side of human nature and the inner contradictions all people wrestle with prevent the existence of an ideal community that possesses a perfect socio-politico-legal system. The conservative culture of Europe could not digest the ideas of liberal humanism, and society suffered a century of disillusionment with the Renaissance, culminating with Shakespeare's furious disappointment with man.

THE DAWN OF MODERN TASTE

Sandro Botticelli (1445-1510) painted pagan goddesses and Madonnas, all of whom resembled the blond daughters of Northern Italian gentlemen. These were the first women depicted in European art that are beautiful according to modern tastes – their beauty is instantly accessible to the modern eye. The first music that sounds beautiful to the modern untrained ear was composed during the late Renaissance – a trained ear can find beauty in medieval music, but to most moderns the aesthetics of Gothic sounds are illusive. A modern man might glory in a Gothic Cathedral, but his spirit finds repose and comfort under the arches and arbors of Renaissance settings. For good or ill, the Renaissance shaped enduring artistic sensibilities.

THE BONFIRE OF VANITIES, DAMNATION OF FAUST AND SACK OF ROME

The Medici family's grip on power weakened as the French-Italian wars began (1494). The expensive Renaissance art and culture paid for by wealthy Italian families was a mockery to the growing misery in Italy, creating a backlash of resentment among common people. Girolamo Savonarola (1452-1498), an Italian Dominican friar and influential political contributor, preached hellfire sermons on the streets of Florence against moral corruption committed by many of the citizens and clergy. His main opponent was Rodrigo Borgia, who was also Pope Alexander VI from 1492-1498. The chastened populace brought their proudest possessions (mirrors, cosmetics, lewd pictures, pagan books, immoral sculptures and art, gaming tables, chess pieces, lutes and other musical instruments, fine dresses, women's hats, and the works of immoral and ancient poets) – items Savonarola associated with moral laxity – to the public square and burned them all in the *"Bonfire of the Vanities"* (1497). Many fine Florentine Renaissance artworks were lost in these notorious bonfires.

Martin Luther (1483-1546), the German priest and professor of theology who initiated the Protestant Reformation, and other church leaders denounced the platonic inflation and immorality of the High Renaissance. Luther also condemned Dr. Johann Georg Faust (1480-1540), a charlatan whose name became legend. German storytellers portrayed Faust as a man demented by platonic inflation, and like Renaissance men, he mastered every field of study. Still dissatisfied and rankling against mortal limits, he sold his soul to the Devil (*Mephistopheles*) for limitless new powers. The terrifying damnation of Faust resonated in the northern lands of the Reformation, where many were disgusted with Renaissance megalomania – the delusional fantasies of wealth, power and omnipotence.

From Michelangelo's *"Last Judgment"*

The **Sack of Rome** (1527) was a military event carried out by the mutinous German troops of Charles V, Holy Roman Emperor (1500-1558). The massacre effectively ended the Italian Renaissance, and brought great disillusionment to enlightened men and their obsession with extravagance. Michelangelo, who had painted the titanic figures on the Sistine Chapel ceiling (1512) before the Sack of Rome, went on to paint the terrifying ***Last Judgment*** (1541) above the altar of the same chapel. The pleasant bubble burst, and terror of damnation replaced the hubris of platonic inflation.

THE DISILLUSIONED NORTHERN RENAISSANCE MAN

The Renaissance shifted north, but disillusionment hung on for a century. Desiderius Erasmus Roterodamus (1466-

Michel de Montaigne

1536) was a Dutch Renaissance humanist, Catholic priest and theologian. Sir Thomas More (1478-1535) was an English lawyer, social philosopher, author, statesman and noted Renaissance humanist who served Henry VIII of England and was an opponent of the Protestant Reformation. Both these northern Renaissance men were shaken in their faith in man, but stood strong in their faith in God.

Michel de Montaigne (1533-1592) was one of the most influential French Renaissance writers, known as the father of Modern Skepticism. He became famous for his effortless ability to merge serious intellectual speculation with casual anecdotes and autobiography, and was intensely skeptical about religious faith. Montaigne had direct influence on

William Shakespeare (1564-1616), the English poet and playwright who is widely regarded as the greatest writer in the English language and the world's pre-eminent dramatist. Shakespeare was ambivalent about religious faith, but suffered a crisis of severe disillusionment with man and grief about the futility of life. He wrote:

> *"Tomorrow and tomorrow and tomorrow, creeps in this petty pace from day to day, to the last sylla-ble of recorded time; and all our yesterdays have lighted fools the way to dusty death. Out! Out brief candle! Life's but a walking shadow, a poor player who struts and frets his hour upon the stage and then is heard no more. It is a tale told by an idiot, full of sound and fury, signifying nothing."*
> **Macbeth, Act V, 1607**

After these furious words about man's titanic despair, optimism could make no recovery and the Northern Renaissance ended with Shakespeare. Paradoxically, Literary Traditionalism increased in intensity during the Northern Renaissance, perhaps because of the invention of the printing press by Johannes Gutenberg around 1440.

THE IVORY TOWER

Michel de Montaigne's library was located at the top of a round citadel and contained thousands of books. The walls of his *"ivory tower"* library were covered with the maxims of classical authors written in Latin and Greek. Montaigne's massive volume ***Essais***[60] (translated literally as "Attempts") was filled with the ideas of Petrarch and the classic authors, which stimulated deep personal contemplation and musings concerning the condition of mankind. His writing penetrated into places within the realm of self-reflection that no Western author had explored before. As a young man, Shakespeare avidly read the works the older Montaigne and soon surpassed him in the intensity and depth of his introspective explorations.

HISTORICAL LESSONS

The lessons gleaned from history identified in this chapter can be itemized by comparing conservative wisdom with liberal folly.

1. The Literary Traditionalism that led to the Renaissance contrasts significantly with progressivism, historicism and multiculturalism.

   a. Progressivism looks upon the cultural past with contempt, lionizes the mediocrities of present day, and idealizes an unknown future.

   b. Historicism values only the present culture and finds cultural history and traditional morality irrelevant to the needs and values of the present moment.

   c. Multiculturalism in liberal academia demeans the works of "dead white European males," and exalts contemporary works with no regard for innate merit, but valued solely on whether the works are authentic expressions of favored cultures.

2. The great works of Dante and Chaucer were triggered by their conviction of sin, repentance and the process they chose to get right with God. This brief history will point to several occasions when a reckoning with God was the turning point of culture.

---

[60] (Montaigne 1580)

Modern liberalism is hostile to doctrinally orthodox Christianity, and is fighting to remove Christ from the culture. As a result, Western culture is losing its resilience and its historical ability to be healed and rejuvenated through spiritual renewal.

3. One of the fruits of high culture development was *la douceur de vivre* (the sweetness of life). Contrary to the lies told about the Middle Ages during the French Enlightenment, Christian civilization produced a sweetness and joy of life. Even now, there is a striking contrast between the life-embracing gusto of conservatives with the frowning bitterness of liberals.

4. The masterpiece of education that produced the versatile Renaissance man and the elegant and learned gentlemen contrasts substantively with contemporary academia, which is producing narrow specialists who are cultural barbarians.

5. The delusions of the Renaissance included the belief that man is the measure of all things, the unlimited potential of man, and the possibility of utopia. These fallacies stimulated culture in the short run, but led to tremendous disillusionment. However, Western civilization was resilient, and worked these false ideas out of its system by 1600. Modern liberalism revived all these errors.

6. This chapter cited three instances of small group discussions by intelligent people that brought about great cultural changes.

    a. Petrarch, Boccaccio and their disciples,

    b. The ten young Florentines recounted in ***The Decameron***, and

    c. Renaissance men at Urbino retold in ***The Courtier***.

    Every great cultural renewal in European history was preceded with intense discussions by intelligent people. If intelligent conservatives wish to see a change in the culture, they must be prepared to have extensive conversations with other intelligent conservatives.

> ***Fred Critique***
>
> *If intelligent conservatives wish to see a change in the culture, they must be prepared to have extensive conversations with other intelligent conservatives.*

STAY TUNED

Chapter 3 will begin by tracing the continued rise of Western culture (1600-1750), and will then examine the conservative reaction to French Enlightenment (1750-1800) and the Romantic Movement, which will furnish clues about modern conservatives.

King James Bible

Historically, Europe enjoyed three periods of rapid cultural advancement: 1050-1250; 1375-1520; and 1600-1750. During this seven-century developmental period, Western culture was vigorously advancing two-thirds of the time, and the culture was consolidating and preparing for the next progress one-third of the time. This third chapter tracks the third spike of European cultural development, commonly called the Baroque era, beginning in 1611 with the *King James Bible* and ending in 1750 with the world of Samuel Johnson, Voltaire and Benjamin Franklin.

1600 ITALY

Giovnanni Bernini (1598-1680) was the century's greatest Western sculptor and the supreme architect of Baroque era art, architecture and stage craft. Claudio Monteverdi (1567-1643) was an extraordinarily influential composer who developed dramatic opera into an enduring art form, and transformed Renaissance music into early Baroque music. Monteverdi set the direction Western music composers would follow for one hundred and fifty years.

MELODRAMA AND TECHNICAL PERFECTION

Giovnanni Bernini

Giovanni Bernini called the church of Saint Andrea al Quirinale (Saint Andrew of the Quirinal Hill) his *"only perfect work"* of architecture. Built for a Jesuit seminary in Rome, Bernini spent hours sitting inside, appreciating his achievement of Baroque grandeur, dramatic impressions and technical virtuosity. The combination of theatrical melodrama and technical perfection is the defining mark of Baroque culture – the spectacular interior of Saint Andrea would impress even Hollywood special effects wizards with the painted dome, lighting and design, heroic scale, and genius sculptures and decorations. Painting, sculpture and architecture are blended in this spiritual theater to visually inspire a vision of the exaltation of St Andrew to divine level.

Bernini was arguably the most skillful sculptor who ever lived. His sculpture was very close to perfection in its form, detail and texture – he could so wonderfully imitate human flesh with cold marble that it seemed warm and soft. His statues depict beautiful women, biblical heroes, or haggard old men with such brilliance that they seemed ready to step off their pedestals on to stage, as actors with their melodramatic expressions and postures.

A THEATRICAL CULTURE

Art historians often criticize Bernini for the theatrical quality of his art – indeed, as the greatest theater and opera set designer in Europe, he often staged lavishly dramatic scenery pieces and planted practical jokes. One of his sculpted figures on the *Piazza Navona Fountain* in Rome has his arm raised in alarm as though trying to block out a revolting sight of horror and disgust; the scene he looks upon is a building designed by one of Bernini's rivals. His carving of the Coronado family, famous art patrons, sits in a theater box gazing at *The Ecstasy of Saint Theresa*, which is his master-piece of theatrical fantasy – the real Saint Theresa was homely, sensible and stoically resisted exhibitionism, quite unlike the sculptured angelic young beauty swooning in blissful agony like an opera prima donna on stage. The stern

Spanish saint and no-nonsense Mother Superior, who rebuked novices for falling into majestic swoons or visions, would have been outraged with Bernini's dramatic portrayal.

IS BAROQUE MELODRAMA TRUE ART?

It has been argued that the sheer intelligence, talent and humane sensitivity of Baroque art, architecture and music redeem the unrestrained theatrical elements from predictable or disappointing pomp. These elaborate, ornate arts do not diminish the serious dignity and depth of Renaissance brilliance, but are authentic and represent a genuine advance in culture.

While Bernini's sculptures lack the power, intensity and heroism of Michelangelo's work, his marvelous technique humanized statues by adding drama and human feeling, using sweeter and more perfect forms, and putting a brilliantly textured finish on the marble. The enchantment of Bernini figures gently awakens and instructs aesthetic sensibilities – demonstrating depth of soul while entertaining emotions.

Michelangelo's figures seem almost crude and inhuman in comparison to Bernini's living marble-fleshed people. The platonic inflation and blatant distortion of Michelangelo's sculpted human forms are glorious mutants that shock and frighten – the work of a half-mad genius whose images of dread terrified popes, cardinals and courtiers.

1600 PROTESTANT EUROPE

William Shakespeare

Shakespeare wrote *Hamlet* in 1600, as Queen Elizabeth I (1533-1603) sat on the British throne after having led England to prominence since 1558. The elderly monarch was the daughter of King Henry VIII and the vanquished and imprisoned Anne Boleyn, who had predicted to King Henry that she would yet triumph through her daughter, Elizabeth. The following year, a proposal to translate the Bible was submitted to King James IV of Scotland, the son of the conquered and caged Mary Queen of Scotts, who had prophesied to Elizabeth I that she would gain victory through her son, James. At the death of the childless Elizabeth, James IV of Scotland became James I of England.

Protestant England was ready for an official English Bible sponsored by King James, who was raised to be a scholarly Protestant while his Catholic mother was in jail, and so *The Authorized King James Bible* was published in 1611. Most Protestant spiritual revivals and renewals for the next three hundred years were centered upon teaching and preaching from this Bible version.

SHAKESPEARE'S MELODRAMA AND VIRTUOSITY

In spite of William Shakespeare's weakness for the sublime-grotesque, a trait he shared with Michelangelo, many of his plays have a proto-Baroque balance. For example, Shakespeare's most wildly unrestrained lines are typically framed by intelligent soliloquy, or balanced by moments of levity. His plays are as melodramatic and uninhibited as an Italian opera – the emotions expressed are deeply felt, elegantly expressed, and lavish. Haunting and reverberating words explored the new territory of human psyche.

Shakespeare shared the virtuosity of Bernini and Monteverdi to an extent. His manuscripts resemble corrected rough drafts and at times the cursory edits seem chaotic, as though making it up as he went along. Indeed, some plays were still being edited the day they opened – gaining greatness through the on stage improvisation and subsequent improved script. The playwright made no money from his plays, and opposed all suggestions to publish them lest a rival theater use them. He earned a modest fortune as a successful actor, and a larger fortune as a theater company partner and new theater investor.

Shakespeare regarded his true genius to be as an actor, director and impresario. Considering the wise advice given to a troop of actors in the play **Hamlet**,[61] he must have been a superlative director and mentor. Typically writing two plays a year while concurrently running a business, promoting plays, directing actors and appearing on stage, he wrote plays to parade his acting talents and to flaunt protégés he trained and directed – coveting the public's opinion that his actors were better than those of rival theater companies. Though he wanted to sell tickets for his spellbinding stage creations, he also cared deeply for the art and craftsmanship of acting. He possessed a great performer gift in his perfect pitch for the music of words – engrossed in emotional intimacy with the audience, he could sculpt words and make pithy phrases echo in minds long after the curtain fell.

THE BARD WENT TOO FAR

"King Lear and the Fool in the Storm"

Perpetually experimenting with storms of emotion on stage, Shakespeare could not resist pushing the envelope of human passions to the limit – and then step beyond the boundary into the inhuman grotesque. The bard went too far with **King Lear**,[62] making the king into a madman who, in his titanic fury, was transformed into a cosmic demon. This Faustian element in Shakespeare also haunted Michelangelo in their descriptions of ambition surrendering moral integrity to achieve power and success; or making *"deals with the devil."* However, the temptation to break free from human limits did not always open doors of the monstrous. Baroque art also soared upwards towards the heavens with the domed ceilings of churches, palaces and opera houses, which are adorned with images of heavenly harmony.

Fred Critique

This Faustian element in Shakespeare also haunted Michelangelo in their descriptions of ambition surrendering moral integrity to achieve power and success; or making "deals with the devil."

WORDS OF FIRE

The English language was transformed and improved under the influence of the King James Bible, and the writings of William Shakespeare and John Milton.

> *"But his word was in mine heart like a burning fire shut up in my bones, and I was weary with refraining and I could not stay [i.e., I could not hold it in.]" Jeremiah 20:18 (KJV)*

---

[61] (Shakespeare, Hamlet 1600)
[62] (Shakespeare, King Lear 1608)

Satin in *Paradise Lost*

"Oh for a muse of fire, that would ascend the highest heaven of invention!"
King Henry V, *Shakespeare, 1599*

"Him (Satan) the Almighty Power hurld headlong flaming from th'Etherial Skies with hideous ruine and combustion down to bottomless perdition, there to dwell in Adamantine chains and penal fire." **Paradise Lost**, *Milton, 1667*

Puritan preachers used the vigorous and forceful Geneva Bible (1560), which influenced the translators of the King James Bible, and explains the extraordinary zeal of the Puritan movement at its zenith. A Puritan-like passion is sometimes seen in the mission field, when newly literate people of the third world read the Bible for the first time in their own language. Enthusiastic readers often ascribe Scripture with absolute authority, acting upon the heart burning words as though they are personally addressed to them by God, Himself.

"Did not our hearts burn within us while He talked with us along the way and opened to us the scriptures?" Luke 24:32 (KJV)

SPIRITUAL WILDFIRES

The printing press, invented in Germany during the Renaissance by Johannes Gutenberg, launched an era of mass communication that permanently altered the structure of society. During the Protestant Reformation (1517-1648), unrestricted circulation of information and (revolutionary) ideas crossed borders, informing the masses and threatening the power of political and religious authorities. A sharp increase in literacy broke the education and learning monopoly of the elite ruling nobility, bolstered the emerging middle class, and laid the foundation for modern economy.

The presses ran day and night to feed the insatiable appetite of the newly literate general public for affordable reading material. Books by bestselling authors like Luther and Erasmus were sold by the hundreds of thousands. Luther's German translation of the Bible, along with his sermons and a blizzard of fiery religious tracts and hostile anti-papal pieces, sparked a wildfire of spiritual zeal in Germany.

The explosive quality of the early Reformation could not be contained, and the movement flew to extremes and shattered Europe into pieces. Northern Europe, with the exception of Ireland and pockets of Britain, turned Protestant, and southern Europe remained Catholic, while fierce battles and warfare took place in the center. Luther's main task became teaching and correcting extremists, in order to harmonize and balance doctrinal principles. *The Augsburg Confession* (Lutheran Church, 1530) and *The Westminster Confession* (Reformed Church, 1646) helped confute the extremists and established sound doctrines, which remain a bulwark of orthodoxy and a defense against heresy to this day.

CULTURAL BLOSSOMING AFTER CATACLYSM

The Thirty Years War (1618-1648) and the English Civil War (1642-1651) were driven by politics and a religious fervor spurred on by Biblical knowledge that drove soldiers to fight with exceptional ferocity. Although these wars were particularly destructive, they were not entirely a disaster for culture. In the case of the English Civil War, the victory of Oliver Cromwell's army was a major step towards the supremacy of Parliament over the Monarchy.

During the next two centuries, the strong English Parliament attracted extraordinary men who had a positive influence on literature and the sciences. Of special note was Christopher Wren, a distinguished scientist and architect, and a founder of the **Royal Society of London for Improving Natural Knowledge** (1660), known simply as the Royal Society, which is possibly the oldest learned scientific institution in existence. After the great fire of London (1666), Wren was commissioned by Parliament and the Crown to lay architectural plans for the rebuilding of the city. His beautiful architectural creations are some of the most cherished landmarks of modern London.

HEAVENLY HARMONY

From harmony, from heavenly harmony
This universal frame began.
When Nature underneath a heap
Of jarring atoms lay
A tuneful voice was heard from high:
"Arise ye more than dead."
Then cold, and hot, and moist, and dry,

In order to their stations leap,
And Music's power obey.
From harmony, from heavenly harmony
The universal frame began:
From harmony to harmony
Through all the compass of the notes it ran,
The diapason closing full on man.

This is the first stanza of *A Song for St. Cecelia's Day* (1687) by English poet John Dryden (1631-1700), who lived during the era of Baroque music (1600-1750). Dryden described a primal state of chaotic nature, followed by a tuneful voice from heaven that commanded the atoms. According to Dryden, God used the power of music to frame the primal elements into ordered creation, infusing nature with strains of heavenly harmony. A **diapason** is an octave, a harmonious musical interval, or the harmonious resolution of a musical passage. Dryden used the expression *"the diapason closing full on man"* to say that the harmony of creation found complete resolution in the creation of man. If God's acts of creation were a symphony, the final chords of the grand finale represent man, the symphonic conclusion and fulfillment of creation.

Dryden's concept of music as the ordering and harmonizing cosmic power perfectly describes the inspirational ideal of Baroque composers and musicians. They believed musical compositions and performances participated in the harmonies of heaven and nature, therefore the phenomena of music was the most important of the arts. *"The idea that the universe is bound together by harmony or concord is fundamental in Elizabethan cosmology. The music of the spheres orders the heavens, and music alike orders human passions and social forces."*[63]

1600 NEW WORLD

THE SIREN SONG OF UTOPIA

The temptation to separatist utopianism came early to the American shores and was rejected by wise and seasoned Puritan leaders. The siren song of **utopia**, an ideal community or society possessing a perfect socio-politico-legal system, has sounded many times. A recurring task of the American conservative movement has been to expose and confute utopianism in all its fictional guises.

> **Fred Critique**
>
> *American conservatives must expose and confute utopianism in all its fictional guises.*

---

[63] *The Norton Anthology of English Literature, Volume 1*, page 1049. (Greenblatt, et al. 2006)

SPIRITUAL WILDFIRES IN MASSACHUSETTS

The worn-out pages of Puritan Bibles and the threadbare knees of Puritan breeches offer a glimpse into the intense personal spirituality in Massachusetts Bay Colony (founded in 1628). Fiery zeal was so great that the populace could scarcely restrain their own hearts, and the leaders struggled to maintain influence. Indians and starvation were not the greatest dangers to early Massachusetts settlements – the biggest threat was hyper-holiness wildfire breaking out, causing the community to disintegrate like ash. An inundation of burning-heart saints strained the fledgling society to the breaking point.

God-intoxicated men, who were prone to fiery prophesy, spiritual extremism and perfectionism, organized small circles of hyper-saints to counter a community they felt was less than perfect in its holiness or doctrines. They sometimes withdrew into exclusive circles and refused to share the Lord's Table with less than perfect neighbors. Their zeal for the Lord was accompanied by the desire to *"withdraw from the dung-hill of this world,"* in Roger Williams' salty phrase. Serious court cases were brought

Puritans in Massachusetts

against leaders of divisive hyper-holy factions, as the small wilderness settlement could not survive perfectionist fragments. Grievances were decided in favor of an imperfect but united community with a chance to survive, against dozens of separatist utopias that would perish on their own.

Puritans disapproved of the Pilgrim settlement eighty miles south at Plymouth, because they were radical separatists who had renounced the Church of England. Leaders insisted they were neither separatists nor nonconformists, but sought to purify the Church. However, these reformers contended with the reality of their own perfectionists who yearned for holy separation.

THE WITCHCRAFT FIASCO

The Salem witch trials (1692) occurred more than sixty years after the founding of Massachusetts. The Puritan movement was no longer spiritually robust, having lapsed into deadening legalism. Many were haunted by guilt for falling away from the faith of their forefathers, and by fears of divine judgment for this abandonment. These worries spurred the public hysteria; however, the witchcraft fiasco was a brief anomaly.

Occult activity actually did exist in Salem, beginning when a slave woman who practiced Voodoo passed along a few secret practices to a clique of impressionable teenage girls. There were also reports of poltergeists – mischievous spirits who tease and annoy – allegedly annoying folks through *"things that go bump in the night."* Petty nighttime vexation did not warrant mass panic, but the deadly legalism and strain of disappointed perfectionism created a fit of collective paranoia in the descendants of God-intoxicated men.

Very few witches per capita were executed in Massachusetts Bay Colony – far more were slaughtered during that era in the European nations – yet only the Western hemisphere punishes itself over the ancestral abuse. Due to a lingering strain of disappointed utopianism, America cannot quite get over the fact of not being, and never having been, perfect. Thanks to the animosity of modern educators towards America's Christian roots, all many students know about Puritans is the witchcraft controversy. The episode has been used in political rhetoric and popular literature as a caution against the dangers of isolated religious extremism, false charges, lapses in legal rights, and governmental intrusion on individual liberties.

Educators, scholars and cultural historians have taught that the Reformation was bad for culture, pointing to such events as when German Protestants stormed Catholic churches to smash statues (1524), while simultaneously failing to mention Luther's rebuke of said statue-smashers. We are often reminded of when Oliver Cromwell closed the theaters (1655); however, critics fail to consider how profane, lewd and perverse the theaters had become. After the Reformation fires had died down, an enduring moral fiber was left behind among the common people. Having regained a consensus about right vs. wrong and good vs. evil that had been absent since the Middle Ages, normal morality emphasized sexual fidelity in marriage and principled rearing of children. It is impossible to underestimate what strong, moral families contributed to Western culture.

> *Fred Critique*
>
> *It is impossible to underestimate what strong, moral families contributed to Western culture.*

Family and community vitality fostered a healthy balance between freedom and order in Great Britain and the American colonies. While Catholic Europe moved in the opposite direction, towards the supreme power of great monarchies, the benefits of a Catholic Counter-reformation (1545-1648) set the stage for an extraordinary flourishing of **high culture**.[64] Although freedom is essential to the full flourishing of human nature, a brilliant culture is equally vital.

THE ANGLO-SAXON AWAKENING

Millions of ordinary people had not been participating in the high culture of the day, since the Renaissance only reached a tiny, elite segment of the population. Thanks to Protestant schools,[65] the Reformation opened the hearts and minds of the butcher, the baker, and the candlestick maker, who could now read and had Bibles tucked away in their back rooms. The effects of this advancement lasted longest in **Anglo-Saxon**[66] lands because of recurring spiritual revivals. The **Great Awakening** (1734-1750) had its highest impact in New England, and enjoyed widespread influence throughout the American colonies and many parts of Great Britain. Many who were wakened from commonplace slumber by the Reformation and later revivals became interested in community and cultural affairs, reading newspapers and arguing politics. Puritans and their Yankee descendants are famous for debates in town halls and incessant agitation for public improvements.

ONE ROOM SCHOOLHOUSES

Yankees replaced their Puritan forefathers' zeal for God with zeal for education. Young men who had been educated in New England traveled to every region of America to become schoolmasters and educate a nation. Textbook pioneer, Noah Webster (1758-1843), authored a speller, a grammar, and a dictionary – he insisted that every schoolmaster require grammatically correct, Americanized speech from students. Webster's goal was to provide a uniquely American approach to training children. Every child who feared the hickory stick was obliged to clearly pronounce

---

[64] High culture refers to cultural products, mainly in the arts, held in high esteem – the elite culture of the aristocracy or intelligentsia, a repository of broad cultural knowledge, and a way of transcending the class system. It is contrasted with the low or popular culture of the less well-educated, barbarians, or the masses. (Wikipedia 2011) (Donnelly 2012)

[65] Lutherans, Quakers, Presbyterians, Moravians, Mennonites, German and Dutch Reformed, Baptists, Methodists and Anglicans established elementary schools and academies. (Protestant School Systems - Colonial and Nineteenth-Century Protestant Schooling, Early Twentieth-Century Protestant Schooling 2011)

[66] Anglo-Saxon is the historical term for Germanic tribes who invaded and settled Great Britain beginning in the 5th century.

every syllable, every consonant, and every vowel read aloud in class. Americans in log cabins and Western towns often spoke clearer, more articulate English than was heard on the streets of London.

Children in little school houses learned Shakespeare, Milton and the King James Bible. The New England Primer began with the famous verse, *"In Adam's fall we sinned all."* McGuffey Readers for older children included **The Fall of Cardinal Wolsey**, by Shakespeare. This vigorous education, centered on articulate speech, helped secure the success of democratic politics and constitutional government.

NATURAL LAW AND THE WISDOM OF GOD

John Locke (1632-1704), an English philosopher and physician, agreed with St. Thomas Aquinas that God ordained natural law, weaving it into the fabric of creation. According to this philosophy, one of God's intentions for bestowing human reason in the design of the universe was to encourage man's participation in divine wisdom. This intimate involvement in the big picture would push wise composers to seek the heavenly harmonies woven through creation, and drive rational philosophers to discover natural laws that govern human nature and society.

LOCKE AND BACH

Johann Sebastian Bach

Contemporaries during the era of Baroque music, John Locke and Johann Sebastian Bach (1685-1750) held similar world views. Locke sought philosophical wisdom in the decrees of God woven through the strands of His creation, thinking the design of natural law was beautiful and harmonious. As a composer, Bach sought heavenly harmonies that were expressions of order and a reflection of law and science. In Bach's **Well-Tempered Clavier** series[67] (1722 and 1742), a collection of solo keyboard music composed *"for the profit and use of musical youth desirous of learning, and especially for the pastime of those already skilled in this study,"* he revised and improved tonal scale so that compositions could be written in a greater number of keys, and the harmonies would be more perfect according to mathematical intervals of tone. Bach was the creator of musical form – he established a standard of metered music and established mathematical composition rules. The **Well-Tempered Clavier** is generally regarded as one of the most influential works in the history of Western classical music. Reading John Locke while Bach is playing in the background can create an ambiance of intellectual depth, technical command and artistic beauty.

> *Fred Critique*
>
> *Reading John Locke while Bach is playing in the background can create an ambiance of intellectual depth, technical command and artistic beauty.*

IS MAN A POLITICAL ANIMAL?

"Government is not a solution to our problem, government is the problem." Ronald Reagan, 1981

St. Thomas Aquinas followed Aristotle's teaching that man is a political animal, and human government is natural and necessary to complete human flourishing because it helps care for the common good. John Locke argued that man is not a political animal, and that government is not natural or necessary to prosper mankind. Furthermore, Locke insisted that people do not require instruction or supervision about caring for the common good.

---

[67] (Bach 1722-1742)

According to Locke, government is an artificial contrivance brought into being by *"social contract,"* for the purpose of defending certain unalienable rights based upon the laws of nature. Governmental authorities do a better job of protecting the life, liberty and property of citizens using the laws, police and courts than any lone individual can do in protecting himself. Defending the intrinsic dignity of citizens, which is essential to human flourishing, is the only justification for the existence of government.

LOCKE AND CONSERVATISM

Since Locke's social contract is formed to protect human rights based on natural law, the role of government is limited to that agreement. A contracted administration is not *"natural,"* but is a mere artifact of human device – therefore it holds no authority to produce utopia or seek social engineering. Likewise, the laws of nature demand certain protections: property rights declare it unjust for an agency to redistribute income or seize property for arbitrary reasons; children in the womb must be granted the right to life and justly protected by prohibiting abortion; criminal punishment is necessary to uphold and vindicate universal moral law; and parental rights to teach their children universal moral law concerning sexual promiscuity and homosexuality conflict with compulsory, tax supported, values-neutral sex education, which has no permission to exist.

LOCKE, CLASSICAL LIBERALISM AND LIBERTARIANISM

John Locke

Locke believed that when a citizen surrenders the personal defense of his rights to the police and courts through the social contract, he is not relieved of moral responsibility – rights and freedoms are accompanied by moral and social obligations. The universal moral law compels people to respect neighbors' rights and treat them respectfully. The government must inter-vene when these rights are violated, but it has no jurisdiction over how individual freedom is used to support and encourage neighbors according to conscience. Conscientious people often serve their communities beyond requirements, by dutifully volunteering time and skill with civic organizations, ministries or political office.

Classical liberalism is based on the political theories of John Locke and the economic theories of Adam Smith (1723-1790) and David Ricardo (1772-1823). In the 19th century, classical liberals in government were focused on property rights, free enterprise and the personal freedom of citizens under a limited government. Many 21st century Libertarians endorse all these ideas, imagining themselves to be classical liberals.

Fred Critique

No orderly cosmos can exist that contains beings that have rights, but no obligations. Such a world would be chaos.

Some modern Libertarians believe moral obligations are limited to not violating someone else's rights. Beyond that, they consider themselves to possess the right of absolute freedom, and deny that the liability for collective good applies to them. To believe this, one must embrace a metaphysically incoherent philosophy – if there is no universal moral law, there can be no rights based on natural law. Without such rights, the claim to freedom is arbitrary. Furthermore, no orderly cosmos can exist that contains beings that have rights, but no obligations. Such a world would be chaos.

THE MERIDIAN SPLENDOR OF A GREAT CIVILIZATION

At the peak of great cultures, distinguished sages appear. François-Marie Arouet (1694-1778), better known as Voltaire, was a French Enlightenment satirical writer, historian and philosopher famous for invincible wit and the advocacy of civil liberties, including freedom of religion and free trade. Voltaire was an outspoken supporter of social reform in the Paris salons where brilliant discussions were held, despite strict censorship laws and harsh penalties for those who broke them.

London intellectuals flocked to coffee houses to witness various attempts to defeat the famous Samuel Johnson (1709-1784) in debate. Often referred to as Dr Johnson, this devout and eloquent author made lasting contributions to English literature as a poet, essayist, moralist, literary critic, biographer and editor.

The polymath, Benjamin Franklin (1706-1790) of Philadelphia, demonstrated the ability to make original contributions in many fields of expertise. One of the United States of America Founding Fathers, Franklin was a leading author and printer, political theorist, politician, postmaster, scientist, inventor, satirist, civic activist, statesman and diplomat. He was foundational in defining American culture based on the values of thrift, hard work, education, community spirit, self-governing institutions, and opposition to both political and religious authoritarianism, coupled with the scientific and tolerant values of the Enlightenment. As historian Henry Steele Commager (1902-1998) stated, Franklin *"merged the virtues of Puritanism without its defects, (and) the illumination of the Enlightenment without its heat."*

By 1750, Europe was the premiere civilization of the world. The triumph of Christianity, natural law and conservative principles produced a brilliantly ordered civilization in which esteemed Baroque musicians – Bach, Handel, Vivaldi and Telemann – lived and composed. In commerce, industry, science, technology and the military arts, Europe outdistanced its most dangerous rival, the Ottoman Turks, who were leaders of the Muslim world.

> **Fred Critique**
>
> *The triumph of Christianity, natural law and conservative principles produced a brilliantly ordered civilization.*

WHAT WENT WRONG?

In the midst of all this glory, something began to go terribly wrong. By the end of the 18th century, France had suffered a ruinous revolution, and the great powers of Europe were fighting a war of unprecedented violence. Chapter 4 will explore what went wrong during two long and colorful centuries (1600-1800) of fitful cultural decline.

Figure 2.   Chapters 4-10 Timeline (1550-2005 AD)

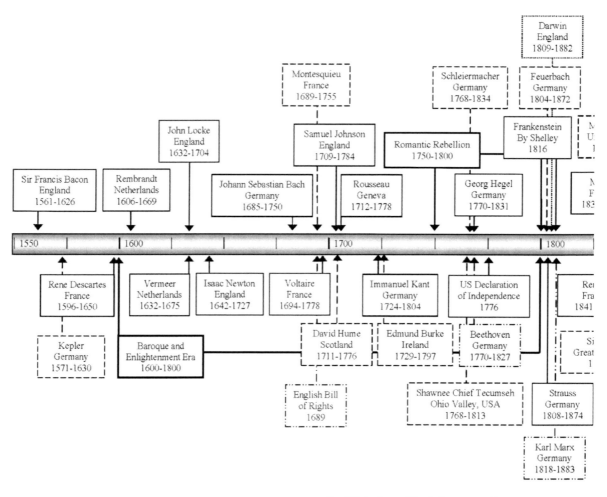

The differing box and line dashes are meant to
help with visual tracking in congested time spaces.

Not every person mentioned in the text is shown.

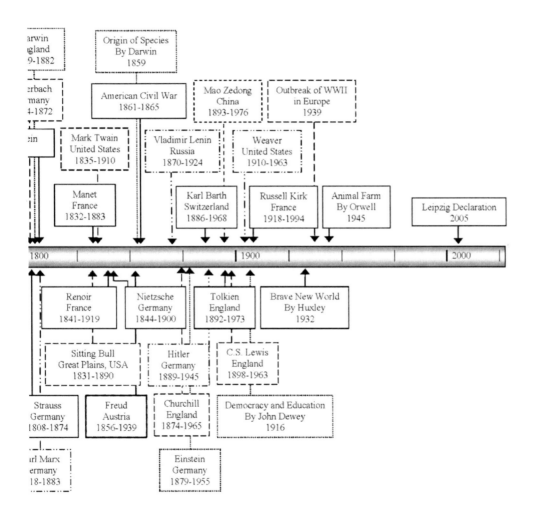

Conservative traditionalism instructs that a large part of our wisdom comes to us from the past. Christian conservatism teaches that man is a fallen creature, and all human works contain the seeds of their own destruction. Therefore, our challenge is to weed out falsehoods and follies sown in prior generations, while embracing the brilliant Western cultural heritage as a whole.

The first three chapters have traced the development of Western culture from 800 BC-1750 AD and reviewed the role played by conservative principles. Chapter 4 will identify some bad seeds planted during the Baroque and Enlightenment Eras (1600-1800) that set the stage for long-term cultural decline.

A BIFURCATING CULTURE

Although Western culture developed rapidly during the Baroque and Enlightenment Eras, some streams of society flowed toward the metaphysical, while others branched away from metaphysics. This **bifurcation**, or two branch division, gradually became a **dichotomy**[68] in tension, which has developed into the schism known today as the *"culture war."*

Metaphysics (roughly meaning *"beyond the physical world"*) pertains to the essence of things or the nature of reality that is higher and deeper than palpable daily experience. Philosopher Immanuel Kant (1724-1804) called the superficial material world observed with the eyes *"phenomena,"* and the true nature of things concealed beneath phenomena *"noumena."* Unseen reality, or **noumina**, exists in the metaphysical realm. A spiritual realm that transcends the material world is also part of the metaphysical. First principles, final ends, ultimate truth, universal moral law, natural law, and the nature of being and knowing also pertain to metaphysics. When poets and philosophers speak of *"the true, the beautiful, and the good,"* they are communicating metaphysics.

CONSERVATIVES, LIBERALS AND METAPHYSICS

Most branches of metaphysics find a home somewhere within the various streams of Western conservatism. When a conservative says *"man has a nature,"* he is making a metaphysical declaration. If man has a nature, human customs should only include things beneficial to mankind and should exclude the harmful, since an inner being would possess intrinsic value. Human beings with innate meaning and designed purpose are capable of rich culture because of the great depths for creative individuals to explore.

In contrast, the whole of liberalism is anti-metaphysical. When liberals insist that mankind has no nature other than how society has shaped them or how they have molded themselves, it reveals an implicit skepticism towards metaphysics. If man is pliable clay to be molded by culture or self, anything can be included and anything goes – nothing should be considered fallacious, tawdry, mediocre, pornographic, malevolent, or evil – and nothing holy or honorable must be respected. Human beings who are mere

---

[68] A dichotomy is any splitting of a whole into two non-overlapping parts.

modeling clay, however molded, will be superficial in construct and have no value beyond instrumental or utilitarian calculations. Anti-metaphysical culture must give way to nihilism, anarchy and the upsurge of unchecked evil.

The difference in the cultural impact of these two points of view is tremendous. The culture war is essentially a struggle to determine the victor between metaphysical versus anti-metaphysical culture. Thus, long-term prospects for the survival of Western Civilization will be determined by the outcome of the culture war.

> **Fred Critique**
>
> ---
>
> *Long-term survival of Western Civilization will be determined by the culture war.*

METAPHYSICS, FAITH AND REASON

There is a connection between metaphysics, faith and reason. Faith and reason help us connect with the metaphysical realm. Metaphysics enriches and stabilizes both faith and reason. For example, metaphysical theology and ethics provide boundaries in which faith and reason must operate.

Western metaphysics produced a culture that was uniquely rational and welcoming to religious faith. Prior to the bifurcation of Western culture, faith and reason were strongly allied. After the division, faith and reason were in opposition. Today, faith and reason are hostile to one another in some quarters, which is historically abnormal and culturally unhealthy.

METAPHYSICAL MUSIC, ANTI-METAPHYSICAL PHILOSOPHY

"God listens to Bach while the angels listen to Mozart." Karl Barth (1886-1968)

During the Baroque era, music took the lead in metaphysical expression and reached a summit in the compositions of Johann Sebastian Bach (1685-1750). Baroque music drew the arts and architecture towards high metaphysics, as discussed in Chapter 3. Meanwhile, philosophy steered the sciences and practical affairs away from metaphysics. While historians call it *"The Age of Reason,"* the Baroque Era was a time when metaphysics was challenged by persuasive opponents, and reason began to be gradually eclipsed by experience and feelings.

Western rationalism was developed by Greek, Roman and European philosophers who used reasoning powers to explore metaphysical questions. The foundations for reason were undercut when metaphysics came under siege from rogue philosophers. The tide decisively turned against metaphysics among the intelligentsia during 1750-1800, when the Romantic rebellion against reason was unleashed. This started reason's long toboggan ride down to the depths of 20th century **existentialism** (emphasizing the uniqueness and isolation of individual experience in a hostile or indifferent universe; regarding human existence as unexplainable; and stressing freedom of choice and responsibility for the consequences of one's acts), **postmodernism** (belief that many, if not all, apparent realities are only social constructs, as they are subject to change according to time and place), and **narcissistic nihilism** (self-absorbed rejection of all distinctions in moral or religious values and a willingness to repudiate all previous theories of morality or religious belief.)[69]

---

[69] (Various 1961)

METAPHYSICS AND CULTURE

Besides shoring up faith and reason, metaphysics contributes at least the following to culture:

1. Metaphysics connects us to the cultural past in ways that are more stable, rational and enriching than memory and nostalgia. An example of this is the appreciation of classical art and literature.

2. Metaphysics connects us to the noumina of the present world, which is why some artists, writers, poets and composers are drawn to the spiritually charged *"numinous"* qualities of nature, human life and civilization.

3. Metaphysics gives hope and purpose by persuading us of our influence upon a future world, and assuring us that the future matters.

4. Metaphysics encourages individuals by revealing their inherent nature, identity, design, destiny and value as a person.

5. Metaphysics furnishes culture with core ideals and archetypal principles from which to fashion a numinous society that is scented with those ethical standards.

THE BIRTH OF A CIVILIZATION

Intellectual historian Richard Weaver (1910-1963) said that every civilization must have a *"metaphysical dream,"* or set of unifying ideals. Every new culture comes into existence by a united striving of inspired people to build the kingdom of their gods on earth, or by trying to realize their shared ideals and spiritual aspirations in their communities. New civilizations must have a powerful faith, a shared vision, and vigorous resources of reason – a shared metaphysical dream makes this possible. European society rose rapidly from barbarism because of robust faith, strong vision, and resources of reason and metaphysics that were deep.[70] They longed to build the Kingdom of Christ on earth, which they called *"Christendom."*

FRANCIS BACON STARTS ANEW

Francis Bacon

Sir Francis Bacon (1561-1626) was an English philosopher, statesman, scientist, lawyer, jurist, author and father of the scientific method. His work laid the indispensable empirical foundation for inductive methodologies, enabling science to become the glory of European culture. He also introduced a handful of logical fallacies in which many scientists still believe. As the father of Western skepticism, Bacon's implicit hostility towards metaphysics greatly damaged culture by providing philosophical grounds for brushing aside the cultural and intellectual heritage of the West.

Bacon had a brilliant mind, and was a great writer and political genius – but he was also proud, greedy and inordinately ambitious. He made a fortune as a lawyer, and subsequently had a great career in government from 1613-1620. He rose to be Chancellor of England, ruling the nation while King James I was out of the country; however the king removed Bacon from power after he was convicted on charges of corruption. After starting life anew as a private citizen, Bacon proposed that everyone should follow his lead and turn to science and philosophy – deciding that if he could not rule a kingdom, he would rule the realm of human intellect.

---

[70] (F. Hutchison, Brief History of Conservatism 2009)

BACON'S EXPURGATION OF THE PAST

Bacon proposed that society should cancel all knowledge of the past and start from scratch, using a scientific method for acquiring understanding that he developed. He claimed that all learning brought forward from the past is tainted with preconceptions, prejudices, assumptions, theories and obsolete knowledge – which he referred to as *"Idols (false images) of the mind"* – and should be purged. Unfortunately, Bacon's most important intellectual contributions were laced with fallacies – the man who would cure civilization of ancient erroneous beliefs was himself a great sower of new fallacies and myths. Francis Bacon's assertions should have made him public enemy number one among all conservatives from that day forward, but his contribution to the empirical foundation of modern science was so great that he has generally escaped the censure of all future generations.

Western culture after 1800 declined in direct proportion to the extent that Western man cut himself off from the cultural past. Those individuals most persuaded by Bacon and his philosophical heirs went the furthest in cutting themselves off from their heritage. Great thinkers such as Descartes, Locke, Rousseau, Diderot and Hume were among Bacon's successors, and gave weight and momentum to the program of cutting humanity off from the past and building a new world on the ashes. They agreed that new foundations must be constructed, but held different opinions about the details of those constraints.[71]

> ***Fred Critique***
>
> *Western culture after 1800 declined in direct proportion to the extent that Western man cut himself off from the cultural past.*

BACON'S POISONED SKEPTICISM

> *"[W]hat is now done in science is only a whirling about, a perpetual agitation, ending where it begins..."*
>
> *"Human knowledge as we have it is a mere medley and ill digested mass, made up of credulity and mere accident, and also of childish notions that are first imbibed." Sir Francis Bacon*

Skepticism is a double-edged sword, because it can produce good or bad results. Certain vocations including scientific research, law, medicine, detective work, auditing and journalism require *"professional skepticism."* The specialized experts in these fields cannot jump to premature conclusions, but must prove every hypothesis with factual evidence. This is good skepticism.

In contrast, Bacon's radical skepticism was foolish and **misanthropic**[72] in its generalized distrust, disgust and contempt of humanity. According to Bacon, not only science but all human knowledge has been tainted. His blanket skepticism was malicious and poisonous, and his egoistic presumption and condescension were egregious. However, because he was a very persuasive writer, many people were taken in by him on their first reading.

BACON'S IMPLICIT HOSTILITY TO METAPHYSICS

When Bacon swept aside the entire cultural and intellectual heritage of the West, he rejected a rich metaphysical tradition. His methodology for gaining knowledge started with an implicit defiance of metaphysics, claiming that all true

---

[71] This is the same dilemma that brought the campus rebellion of the late 1960s, detailed in Chapter 14, to a hopeless impasse –
"Let us destroy the established system and build anew on the ashes... but what then shall we build?" (F. Hutchison, Brief History of Conservatism 2009)
[72] Misanthropic means marked by a hatred, distrust or contempt for humankind.

understanding begins with examining the material details of phenomena while ignoring noumina. The hostile skepticism he advocated would be used by Voltaire to laugh at metaphysical ideas.

If all knowledge comes from careful examination of material evidence, as Bacon claimed, then the world must be no more than an empty material shell. Thus, Bacon threw away the succulent fruit of metaphysics and left the dry surface crust for future philosophy pupils to feed upon. This factor is why many students complain that philosophy is dry and abstract – and why reason fell out of favor.

BACON'S EPISTEMOLOGICAL IMPERIALISM

Bacon claimed that his method of empirically-based inductive reasoning was the only way mankind could obtain true and unlimited knowledge – he asserted that no other method could yield reliable information. Modern scientists who are heirs to Bacon's empiricism often make the same declaration, routinely claiming the only comprehension worth possessing. This epistemological imperialism has narrowed the minds of many scientists, who make bold statements that everything not known will eventually be learned.

These exaggerated echoes of their father fall contrary to the very method that has sharply limited what science can learn. While promising all knowledge to his protégés, Bacon has taken away some of the keys of knowledge. His reduction of man to one narrow method of obtaining knowledge contracts and distorts human nature. If man is designed to know things in several ways and he is only permitted to learn and know in one way, he suffers an unhealthy deprivation. When students are given a dry rind and told it is the only true knowledge, they suffer from short term psychological indigestion and long term intellectual malnutrition.

BACON'S SCIENTIFIC MYTHS

The principal myths in Sir Francis Bacon's empirical philosophy are these:

1. The First Myth of Neutrality – Starting With the Facts.

    Bacon proposed that scientific study should start by observing the facts and then following wherever the data leads – no researcher has ever achieved this, because it is impossible to accomplish. Scientists always form a **hypothesis** (educated guess or theory) first, which guides them in planning research, selecting observation objects, and defining what they seek during the examination of discovered evidence. Without a starting point premise, no systematic research can be performed, and no intelligent selection, observation and interpretation of proof can be made concerning the discovery of truth. Investigations cannot start with proof; they must start with a hypothesis.

    Since a hypothesis is grounded in theory and analysis, it automatically introduces a personal preconception – neutral and unbiased agendas do not exist. Discovered facts can refute a project theory, of course, but the manner of selection, examination, and the interpretation method of data are based on strategy developed to support the hypothesis. Thus, bias is unavoidable.

    Nevertheless, scientists persistently maintain the prevailing mythical claim that research starts with facts, which then escort them toward the detection of reality. The assertion is justified by arguing that research will be neutral and free from bias with this starting point. They employ tactics that attempt to falsify a premise – to the extent that this is actually completed, the analyses can be redeemed. However, no one puts forward a hypothesis and designs research hoping the theory will fail. The belated attempt to falsify a hypothesis is like closing the barn door after the horses have already escaped.

2.   The Second Myth of Neutrality – Facts Speak.

In the last chapter, we briefly considered John Locke's concept that the human mind is a blank slate or *"tabula rasa."* He borrowed this idea from Bacon and developed it to demonstrate that sense perceptions make impressions on the mind, which are the building blocks of knowledge. The absurdity of this claim surfaces with a glimpse at intangible objects that are passive and cannot actively intrude upon a passive mind. The mind is active and oversees what is written upon it from passive sensory data. German philosopher Immanuel Kant (1724-1804) believed that sensory perceptions are stage-managed by the mind, which then interprets these perceptions on its own terms and using its own methods. Therefore, there can be no such thing as a neutral perception, or a neutral interpretation of a perception.

3.   The Third Myth of Neutrality – Inductive Reasoning.

Bacon proposed that we examine facts and use **inductive reasoning** (interpretation from specifics to generalities) to draw conclusions. However, any number of inductive calculations can be based upon a factor and the way it is interpreted. The specifics themselves cannot guide the research framework toward the inductive analysis. Since the researcher can frame interpretations and inductive reasoning to advance his agenda, all inductive reasoning contains an element of bias.

4.   The Fourth Myth of Neutrality – The Staircase of Induction.

Bacon proposed an ascending staircase of induction in which the conclusion of each step up is the foundation for the next step of reasoning. This model commences with facts at the bottom of the staircase, and after a series of inductive reasoning steps, concludes with general principles at the top of the staircase. Unfortunately, a neutral ascending stairway of induction leading straight from specifics to a general concept does not exist. This is another myth of science. An unguided chain of inductive reasoning will follow a random course, as any computer programmer knows – actually, it might travel in circles like a processor caught in a loop.

The only way an alleged sequence of induction can lead straight from specific facts to general principles is purposeful rigging by the researcher. Top-down reasoning must be employed in order to construct the series, starting with the desired general principle of proof and carefully calculating down to the details. While working downward, careful attention must be given to the facts needed to support the predetermined conclusion. This is obviously not an **ascending chain of induction**, but a **descending shackle of deduction** rigged to resemble an ascending staircase. This practice is a routine fraud of the scientific method!

Bacon mistakenly thought that if researchers ascended the staircase of induction in a slow, careful, methodical way, they could avoid skipping steps and flying into sweeping generalities. This cautious technique sought to avoid bias. However, since it is necessary for the researcher to rig the staircase, presumption is built into every step.

René Descartes (1596-1650) became disillusioned with scholasticism and metaphysics, but had great confidence in mathematics. He invented the **Cartesian coordinate system of geometry**[73] after he noticed that mathematical axioms were developed from *"self-evident truths."* Such truths cannot be proven, but cannot be doubted. By an *"intuition of pure reason,"* one understands a self-evident truth of mathematics. By starting with truths that cannot be proven, mathematicians can prove other concepts that are not self-evident.

Descartes set out to reject the presuppositions of scholasticism, and find a replacement for them in self-evident truths through a program of doubt. He intended to distrust everything until he could find a proposition he could not doubt. This program required skepticism more thorough and systematic than Bacon's, and laid the foundation for Hume's nihilistic disbelief a century later.

"I THINK, THEREFORE I AM"

"Cogito ergo sum." ("I think, therefore I am.") René Descartes

Ontology is the philosophical study of the nature of being, existence or reality as such, as well as the basic categories of being and their relations. Traditionally listed as a part of the major branch of philosophy known as metaphysics, ontology deals with questions concerning what entities exist or can be said to exist, and how such entities can be grouped, related within a hierarchy, and subdivided according to similarities and differences.[74]

Rene Descartes

"I think, therefore I am" is an ontological statement by Descartes that pertains to being. But it is not good metaphysics – quite the contrary, it is horrific logic. As Descartes systematically tried to doubt everything, he found that he could not doubt that he was thinking. If he indubitably thinks, he must exist. Correct? No again – this is more scrambled logic. Who is doing the thinking? Who is aware of the thinking? Who is *"I"* in *"I think therefore, I am"*? Descartes seemed to believe that his mind was both thinking and observing the thinking – that he and his mind were the same entity – the *"I am."*

All these assumption are highly dubious. The mind observing itself is like a cog in a clock trying to observe the system of gears. It would be absurd for a cog to proclaim it had realized a self-evident truth about the gear system. A cog is so close to the system, it can know nothing of the system as a whole. Only an observer detached from the gear system can view the system as a whole.

In like manner, only a human faculty separate from the mind can observe the mind as it thinks and be aware of that observation. The observing faculty can say *"I observe thinking,"* but it cannot say *"I think."* By definition, what I observe another entity doing is not what I am doing. Therefore, the *"self-evident truth"* that Descartes was not able to doubt is an absurdity. A better ontological statement would be *"I am a spirit being, I have a mind, and I dwell in a body."* If I am a spirit being with consciousness, I can

> *Fred Critique*
> ───────────
> *"I am a spirit being, I have a mind, and I dwell in a body."*

---

[73] The Cartesian coordinate system specifies points in a plane by pairs of numerical coordinates, which are the distances from the point to reference lines commonly labeled the X and Y axis – three dimensional systems utilize an additional Z axis. Geometric shapes are described by Cartesian equations.

[74] (Singer 2012) (Various 2012) (http://en.wikipedia.org/wiki/Ontology)

observe my mind as it thinks and be aware of the observation. This must be true if I am morally responsible for my thoughts.[75]

AN IMPOSSIBLE DUALISM

Descartes built an impossible dualism because he started with a false foundation. He claimed that the mind is a spiritual entity while the body is a material entity. However a duality of kinds of being is nonexistent in nature – a unitary creature cannot be radically divided. Descartes never established a convincing explanation for how the spiritual, incorporeal mind communicates and commands the physical, corporeal body to take action. His purely mechanistic views of the body have generally prevailed in modern science and medicine, resulting in impersonal and dehumanizing views of the body. As metaphysics has faded, Western civilization has become more detached and amoral about the human body.

IMPOSSIBLE ALTERNATIVES

Determinism is the name of a broad philosophical view, which conjectures that every type of event, including human cognition (behavior, decision and action) is causally determined by previous events. In philosophical arguments, the concept of determinism in the domain of human action is often contrasted with free will.[76]

Thanks to Descartes, most modern people think the only ontological alternatives available are either a purely material mind, or dualism of mind and body. Both alternatives are impossible, and the philosophical stakes are high. A purely material mind would be deterministic and therefore would eliminate the possibility of reason, free will, conscience and consciousness – which is absurd. To a purely physical being, metaphysics is nonsense and human beings are reduced to existing as automatons, or dead men drifting upon a dead sea.

The idea of a purely spiritual mind floating in the ether and unable to communicate with a purely material body is equally absurd. If the spiritual is cut off from the material, the metaphysics that the mind can enjoy is irrelevant to the body – physical life on earth is cut off from the realm of purpose and meaning. As dying bodies float through a dead sea cut off from meaning, they become detached from physical and cultural predicaments and have only the stark consolation of philosophy to cling to. An existence reduced to living in abstract thoughts, as Descartes did, results in a civilization that considers the body and the problems of society irrelevant.

THE DECLINE OF METAPHYSICS AND CULTURAL CONSEQUENCES

Rembrandt self-portrait

The decline of metaphysics leads to cultural shallowness and chaos because it is difficult to sustain the pursuit of excellence and the search for truth, beauty and the good in an environment with no ethics. A shallow society holds no exemplary ideals to inspire literature, the arts, architecture and philosophy. As metaphysics retreated in the early 19th century, the first great disillusionment of Romanticism filled the vacuum with inherently unstable images of suffering and disillusionment. Modern artistic chaos indicates a superficial civilization with no shared principles, artistic values, or numinous impressions.

Famous examples of numinous impressions include the works of Dutch painters Rembrandt Harmenszoon van Rijn (1606-1669) and Johan Vermeer (1632-1675), and

---

[75] (F. Hutchison, Brief History of Conservatism 2009)
[76] (http://en.wikipedia.org/wiki/Determinism) (Various 2012) (Jesseph 2012)

French impressionists Pierre-Auguste Renoir (1841-1919) and Édouard Manet (1832-1883). These artists managed to impart a numinous glow into their paintings: Rembrandt's portraits display a radiance of spiritual and psychological depth; Vermeer's quiet scenes of almost photographic realism are bathed in peace; Renoir's bright vistas of happy young people overflow with the sweetness of life; Manet's works escort us into the pleasant ambience of place and time.

In contrast, modern art often seems to lack a numinous quality, leaving many scenes depressingly empty no matter how much material content the canvas displays. Subjects in recent paintings frequently resemble manikins more than living persons with essence. In a world swept clean of metaphysics, artists and poets somehow manage to soullessly drain the life out of images, so every scene implicitly portrays dead men in a dead world. The determining vision after the Romantic Movement disillusionment was the triumph of death.

DEAD MEN ON A DEAD SEA

"Water, water everywhere,
And all the boards did shrink;
Water, water everywhere,
Nor any drop to drink.

The very deep did rot, O Christ!
That ever this should be!
Yea, slimy things did walk with legs
Upon the slimy sea.

Alone, alone, all, all alone
Alone on a wide, wide sea!
And never a saint took pity on
My soul in agony.

The many men so beautiful!
And they all dead did lie:
And a thousand thousand slimy things
Lived on and so did I."

The Rime of the Ancient Mariner, 1798

Samuel Taylor Coleridge (1772-1834) wrote **The Rime of the Ancient Mariner**, which described a crew of dead men on a ghost ship drifting on a desolate sea. Although the love of nature eventually redeemed the protagonist, the conclusion of the poem reveals the ship's master to be Death, exposing the real message of the hopeless dead on a sea of mortality.

THE FALLACIES OF HOPE

"Aloft all hands, strike the top-masts and belay; Yon angry setting sun and fierce-edged clouds Declare the Typhon's coming. Before it sweeps your decks, throw overboard The dead and dying - ne'er heed their chains. Hope, Hope, fallacious Hope! Where is thy market now?" **The Fallacies of Hope, 1840**

The Raft of the Medusa

Joseph Turner (1775-1851), the most versatile and controversial landscape painter of 19th century England, followed Coleridge's motif of inhumanity and horror at sea with his poem **The Fallacies of Hope**, an indictment of the slave trade's calculated evil. In order to further illuminate his meaning, Turner painted a picture of a slave ship casting chained slaves into shark infested waters as sailors prepared for a typhoon.

Another example of the disillusioned Romantic obsession with hideous disasters at sea is **The Raft of the Medusa**, a painting by Théodore Géricault (1791-1824). This picture depicts the aftermath of the 1816 shipwreck of the French naval frigate Méduse, which ran aground off the North African coast of Mauritania. Nearly 150 people on board hurriedly constructed a raft, but only fifteen of them survived after enduring thirteen days of starvation, dehydration, cannibalism and madness. The event became an international scandal when Géricault consciously selected the well-known incident to generate great public interest with his gruesome depiction of dying victims wretchedly clinging to a small raft at sea.

FALLACIES ABOUT HUMAN NATURE

In the absence of metaphysical ideas about the nature of man, speculative thinkers could redefine human nature at will. Jean Jacques Rousseau (1712-1778), a Romantic political philosopher, writer, and composer, asserted that man is naturally good and all human evil and corruption are caused by society. Western liberalism was born from this false idea about mankind that was built solely on the strength of Rousseau's personal mystical experience.

Reason built on metaphysical foundations can easily see through Rousseau's illusions, which is precisely why his deceptions and liberal delusions did not become prevalent in the West until metaphysics was in serious decline. Although his ideas are contrary to the accumulated wisdom of Western culture and common sense, they have become extremely popular. Liberal utopian fantasies are only possible for a shallow flatland society.[77]

THE REVOLT OF THE SKEPTICS

François-Marie Arouet (1694-1778), better known by the pen name Voltaire, ridiculed metaphysics in his popular novel *Candide*,[78] a sharp witted and insightful portrayal of the human condition. It was clear to sophisticated readers that the targets were Lutheran rationalist philosophers Gottfried Liebnitz (1648-1716) and Christian Wolff (1679-1754). The great popular success of *Candide* demonstrated the growing hostility of the intelligentsia towards metaphysics, and enjoyed both great success and great scandal. The book was widely banned for the religious blasphemy, political

sedition and intellectual hostility hidden under a thin veil of naïveté. Although Voltaire was not an atheist, he was a shallow Deist and a bitter opponent of the French Catholic clergy who preached faith and taught the meaty metaphysics of St. Thomas Aquinas, on which superficial men choke.

Philosopher David Hume (1711-1776) was even more skeptical than Voltaire. He agreed with John Locke that sensory impressions are imprinted on the blank slate of the mind, but denied that intellectual concepts cobbled together from those impressions have any validity. His extreme pessimism about what can be known bordered on **epistemological nihilism** (denial of the existence of knowledge). Hume, who was admired by Voltaire, was influential in convincing the intelligentsia of the West to scuttle metaphysics.

Immanuel Kant (1704-1824) corrected Hume's fallacies about the reasoning mind, but reinforced his rejection of metaphysics. Kant reaffirmed that noumina existed, but denied that humans could ever have knowledge of it – therefore, metaphysical reasoning cannot lead to the truth.[79] Kant's arbitrary restrictions on how the mind can know things forced him into an impasse that has continued. For the last two hundred years, radical skepticism has slowly eaten away at the vitals of Western culture. The children of this philosophy are with us today, ventilating radical skepticism

---

[77] (F. Hutchison, Brief History of Conservatism 2009)
[78] (Voltaire 1759)
[79] If humans cannot have knowledge of noumina, how did Kant know it existed?

in all its malice and stupidity. Attempts at intelligent discussion on college campuses are often quickly dissolved in the acid bath of know-nothing skepticism.

UTOPIAS AND GILDED AGES

The disillusionment of artists with Romanticism was agonizing because the movement was quasi-utopian – the first of many false utopias to vex the modern era. The collapse of metaphysics and the accompanying decline of reason and faith left people without hope. Utopian hucksters filled this vacuum by offering false expectations to the hollowed out and declining culture, which swallowed the fictitious dreams of bliss to fill the emptiness. Death of the false paradise inflicted deep spiritual wounds on true believers, inevitably resulting in bitter disillusionment.[80]

Mark Twain (1835-1910) and Charles Dudley Warner (1829-1900) coined the term *"Gilded Age"* in their co-authored novel ***The Gilded Age: A Tale of Today***,[81] a satire of greed and political corruption during the rapid economic and population growth in post-Civil War and post-Reconstruction America. The expression referred to the process of trimming an object with a superficial gilded layer of gold, and intended to ridicule the grandiose display of wealth with a word play on the phrase *"golden age."*

Utopian reformers railed at greedy materialists because of the superficial nature of wealth. Interestingly, the lures of utopia and the seductions of a gilded age flourish in the same shallow environment. As people are blinded to numinous realities, they are drawn to apparent glamour. The bright illusions take the form of either the artificial ideals of a heavenly fantasy, or the glittery surfaces of wealth that deceived Jay Gatsby,

F. Scott Fitzgerald's archetypically dubious, self-made American businessman from ***The Great Gatsby***.[82] The cultural deceptions of utopia and greed are spiritually similar – the human spirit, crying out for numinous reality, is fed with cheap substitutes.

Cultural fads such as Romanticism, the worship of nature, Transcendentalism, and the New Age movement promise a more intense experience of life as a substitute for the loss of meaning in a shallow culture. —Consciousness-raising" guru Joseph Campbell (1904-1987) made the bald assertion in a posthumous 1988 television broadcast with American journalist and public commentator Bill Moyers that people do not care about the meaning of life, but only about the *"experience of being alive."* Such a fallacious assertion could only go unchallenged in a culture so shallow that the innate human desire for meaning has been eliminated.[83]

> ### *Fred Critique*
>
> *Fallacious assertions only go unchallenged in cultures so shallow that the innate human desire for meaning has been eliminated.*

---

[80] (F. Hutchison, Brief History of Conservatism 2009)
[81] (Twain and Warner 1873)
[82] (Fitzgerald 1925)
[83] (F. Hutchison, Brief History of Conservatism 2009)

"I am a spirit, I have a mind, and I live in a body." Fred Hutchison, 2007

As a spirit, we have consciousness and a conscience. Unlike the body, the spirit is imperishable and can know God. Contrary to the beliefs of Bacon and Kant, the spirit can know things beyond what the mind can know. The spirit can intuitively sense the numinous realm, which can inspire cultural expressions such as poetry, literature and painting.

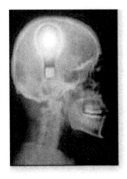

The spirit and the body have different natures – the human psyche is a hybrid being of spirit and body that continuously intermediates between the two. The body is not cast adrift on the *"raft of the Medusa"* in alien seas, but remains on the mother ship with its spirit. The spirit requires relationship with the body in order to discover noumina within the phenomenon, as did Rembrandt, Vermeer, Renoir and Manet. This world is lush with numinous life for the enjoyment of living people.

The mind appears to be a hybrid being of spirit and brain. We can observe what our minds are thinking because we are a spirit. We are responsible for what we think because we are aware of it, and have a conscience and a free will. The mind is not cut off from the body, but can rise to the realm of metaphysics because it is partly spirit and is connected to the intangible human soul. Therefore, the mind is not limited to the dry rind of knowledge – it has access to the luscious, juicy fruit inside.

Finally, Christians who believe in the incarnation of Christ know that spirit and body can be united – for Christ is both God the spirit being, and man the physical being at the same time. Therefore, Christians should dismiss outrageous assertions that man is, of necessity, entirely material in composition, or that he is an irreconcilable duality.

> **Fred Critique**
>
> *Christians should dismiss outrageous assertions that man is, of necessity, entirely material in composition, or that he is an irreconcilable duality.*

NEXT TIME

Stay tuned for Chapter 5, which will consider the new conservatism of modernity, whose fathers include John Locke, Samuel Johnson, Montesquieu, Edmund Burke, Johann Wolfgang von Goethe and James Madison.

Prior to 1600, most Western people took many of the ideas now regarded as conservative for granted. Although a few counter-cultural views emerged during the late Medieval and Renaissance eras, they had no long-term historical traction. Chapter 4 considered how leading Western philosophers from 1600-1800 undercut rational metaphysics and faith to promote destructive skepticism – thereby setting the stage for a rising liberal tide and a long-term cultural decline after 1800. During the same period, a series of great men laid the foundations of modern conservatism.

Although Western conservative principles and ideals are ancient, as outlined in Chapters 1-3, reinforced foundations were needed to ensure a tough and resilient conservatism that could weather the intellectual, moral and spiritual storms of modernity, and which could be a robust competitor of liberalism. Chapter 5 reviews a few founders of modern conservatism who lived from 1600-1800.

STANDING ATHWART HISTORY

"The purpose of my newly-founded magazine is to stand athwart history yelling „STOP.' "
William F. Buckley, Jr., **National Review,** *1955*

Buckley's phrase belongs to modern conservatism, which defies the dark, incoming tide of liberalism. Interestingly, only one conservative hero mentioned in this chapter, Edmund Burke (1729-1797), had the self-conscious idea that he was standing against the tides of history, which is why he is viewed as the first truly modern conservative.

Edmund Burke was an Anglo-Irish statesman, author, orator, political theorist and philosopher who served for many years in the House of Commons of Great Britain as a member of the Whig party. Burke used his influence as a member of parliament to promote conciliation with the American colonies. He supported the American Revolutionaries and was sympathetic towards the American Founding Fathers, who fought to preserve the rights of Englishmen.

Burke later opposed the French Revolution as he came to realize that the surge was flowing in the wrong direction. Before the uprising, France had a brilliant culture and provided trusted leadership to the West. The rebellion inflicted such profound damage to the culture and social fabric of the country that it never entirely recovered its former glory and brilliance. For those who cared about civilization and refined society, the French Revolution was a catastrophe, and Burke pronounced bitter condemnation on those who destroyed a culture in the name of abstract theory.

THE REACTIONARY INSIGHT

Conservatism has always had more substance than merely defending history and yelling stop. A few traditionalists might relate to Canute the Great (995-1035), the king of Denmark, England, Norway and parts of Sweden who stemmed the Viking tide on England's shores, but could not stop the sea when he sat on the shore and futilely commanded the tide. Unlike Canute, principled conservatives have slowed the incoming liberal tide and sometimes pushed the waters back.[84]

> *Fred Critique*
>
> *Principled conservatives have slowed the incoming liberal tide.*

---

[84] (F. Hutchison, Brief History of Conservatism 2009)

German philosopher Karl Marx (1818-1883) called modern conservatism *"reactionary,"* and he was not entirely wrong, as many people have become conservatives in reaction to liberalism. However, its metaphysical base is founded on principles that are deeper, sounder and more exalted than mere opposition to liberalism. In the 19th century, conservatism won its share of victories, and liberalism suffered its share of setbacks. Prior to World War I, it was not clear whether conservatism or liberalism would win the cultural and political struggle of the West.

EARLY MODERN AND MODERN CONSERVATIVE EXAMPLES

"Any man who is under thirty, and is not a liberal, has no heart; and any man who is over thirty, and is not a conservative, has no brains." Winston Churchill

Liberalism is the cultural counterpart of the Romantic Movement, as both sprang from Rousseau's tormented imagination. Remarkably, three of the conservative founders made important contributions to the anti-metaphysical world of emerging liberalism/romanticism as relatively young men, but switched sides as their wise old heads and advancing maturity moved them to the right in the cosmic struggle. Most of the early architects made significant contributions to conservatism's foundation in their middle or mature years.

Samuel Johnson

In contrast to the bold stands Burke and Buckley took against the tides of history, literary intellectual Samuel Johnson (1709-1784) had no concept of the liberal deluge. Johnson occasionally ridiculed and criticized the Romantic Movement, but assumed the idealistic notions would be dismissed as nonsense and regarded them unworthy of serious attention from grown, sensible men. A contemporary of Burke, Johnson was one of the early modern conservatives at heart.

Modern conservative and political doctrine pundit William F. Buckley, Jr. (1925-2008) devoted a major portion of his life to criticizing and dismissing the controversial nonsense of liberal opinion. Buckley's youthful awakening to the importance of resisting liberal deluge is demonstrated by his first book, ***God and Man at Yale***,[85] published when he was only twenty-six. He held superlative influence in the United States as a modern intellectual, and was responsible for blending traditional American political conservatism with broadminded economics and anti-communism.

JOHN LOCKE, THE FATHER OF LIBERALISM AND CONSERVATISM

John Locke (1634-1704) was as an indispensable founding father of political philosophy. Locke laid the foundation for liberal **epistemology** (how we know and what we can know), and conservative **ontology** (what entities exist or can be said to exist). He never noticed the contradiction between these two positions, because he was still arguing about human nature and natural law during his later years. The challenge is painfully apparent in the present culture war, as we find Locke's liberal heirs fighting his conservative heirs.

John Locke

JOHN LOCKE AND THE FOUNDATIONS OF LIBERALISM

Locke worked with several leading English scientists in his early career, which was devoted to medicine and science. His immersion in the empirical process that emphasized observation and experiment, and his familiarity with the applied philosophies of Francis Bacon and Pierre Gassendi, led to him author ***An Essay Concerning Human***

---

[85] (Buckley 1951)

Understanding,[86] in which he articulated how the mind learns and knows. As mentioned in Chapter 4, Locke believed that the mind is a *"tabula rasa,"* or blank slate. He postulated that sensory impressions engrave themselves upon the passive mind, and all human knowledge is built upon these monographs of the senses.

FALLACIES OF LOCKE'S EPISTEMOLOGY

The following points – essential to liberals, but outrageous to conservatives – are implicit in Locke's theory that the mind is a blank slate:

1. If the mind is a blank slate, humans are modeling clay, and by implication, entirely the construct of environmental molding. This concept made it possible for Rousseau to claim that all wickedness is caused by civilization.

2. If humans are modeling clay, man has no innate nature and can be shaped into anything. Therefore, the metaphysically-based principles that life has meaning and purpose can be dismissed. If man is a programmed automaton in an empty world, faith and reason based upon metaphysics are unwarranted. Western cultural heritage can be cast overboard as excess baggage holding man in the past.

3. If man has a pliable nature, unlimited progress and a future utopia are possible. Therefore, start from scratch using education and governmental social engineering programs to create a new man and a new world.

   Comment: If man is meaningless mud, what is the point of a better world – and who determines that one existence is better than another? This tension has always existed in liberal thought, but the mandate to build a better society has prevailed. Furthermore, stubborn denial that one culture can be superior to another has triumphed during the present postmodern darkness. Postmodernism slants towards anti-science and prefers group participation (i.e., we find our identity in group participation) over and against individualism and self-reliance as a basis for human existence.

4. When metaphysics collapses, the retreat of faith and reason is near at hand. A clay creature should only have faith in the potter – namely, in educators and social program designers. The monster must trust the creator Dr. Frankenstein, just as good citizens ought to believe in the ruling elite – our new molders and creators.

   Comment: If those who intend to mold us have themselves been molded, why should we trust them? This is essentially the question campus rebels asked in the late sixties and why they revolted against the establishment. In the same way, postmodern liberals revolt when ruling liberals are not sufficiently anti-establishment – i.e., Cindy Sheehan's campaign against Nancy Pelosi.

   Point of theology: Man can trust an uncreated Creator, but not a created creator. Therefore, the subversive question "Where did God come from?" is only asked by those with no faith.

5. Without a metaphysical foundation, independent reason and logic is not viable. Education and government sculptors will indoctrinate people via politically-correct speech codes so they know what to think.

   Comment: Without metaphysics, wisdom has no foundation and no voice of authority. Therefore, assertions of independent logic seem arrogant and arbitrary. Why should a postmodernist believe one package of mental programming is better than another? Why bother to protest against indoctrination? On the other hand, if reason is really an illusion, those who claim the right to command are not rational beings. Therefore, why submit to their brainwashing?

---

[86] (Locke, An Essay Concerning Human Understanding 1690)

LOCKE VERSUS LOCKE

As a Christian, Locke held reason, faith and metaphysics in high esteem, and did not believe in the implied fallacies of his blank slate theory. He almost certainly would have considered these notions outrageous — but the ideas would not have been possible without his epistemology. Universal rules have no application for pottery creatures.

Jean-Jacques Rousseau

A difficulty in logic emerged during the postmodern shipwreck – if individuals construct reality from experiential sensory fragments, then each person's inner space is unique and incompatible with everyone else's – all knowledge is unique. In such a world, no universal knowledge or authentic communication is possible; anarchy is man's natural state, and civilizing order is oppressive (according to Rousseau.) If everyone is a unique, random construct of independent self-creation, the very idea of universal principles, morality and natural law is absurd.

Natural law and a universal moral law are only applicable in a world where all men have a nature according to a creator's design. In order for Locke's conservative principles to apply and resonate, the mind must possess a nature that employs innate faculties of reason, intuition, conscience and will. Humans must be able to discover the internal imprint of natural law to be persuaded and convicted by such principles. Furthermore, innate knowledge must be available at birth to harvest further knowledge (as argued by Aquinas and Kant). Reason makes use of inborn comprehension to find meaning in sensory phenomena. Sensory imprints on the mind are experiences, not knowledge – even a sea slug has sensory imprints on its microscopic brain.

LOCKE DEFENDS THE ENGLISH BILL OF RIGHTS

John Locke was an articulate supporter of *The Glorious Revolution of 1688* when King James II of England (James VII of Scotland) was deposed, and William and Mary of Orange were installed on the throne. He provided a philosophical defense of the *Declaration of Rights*, also called the *Bill of Rights (1689)*, which established the civil liberties of Englishmen, and defined the king's acts that required the consent of parliament, a measure that limited the abuses of arbitrary power. The Bill clarified that the king was subject to the law, and had no authority to establish his own courts or preside as judge. These rights included:

1. The right to petition the government for redress of grievances;

2. The right to bear arms;

3. Freedom from a standing army during peace time without the consent of parliament;

4. Freedom from taxation without representation;

5. Freedom to elect members of parliament;

6. Freedom of speech in parliament;

7. Freedom from royal interference with the law;

8. Freedom from cruel and unusual punishments and excessive bail; and

9. Freedom from fines and forfeitures without trial in a legal civil court.

Some of these rights were included in the American Bill of Rights by the Founding Fathers, who sought to recover English rights that colonists had enjoyed before being dismissed by the actions of King George III, Lord North and Parliament. Therefore, the American Revolution was essentially a conservative event – a fight to protect treasured ancient rights and privileges.

Thanks to John Locke's philosophical defense of the ***English Bill of Rights***, Englishmen came to understand that enumerated rights were supported by natural law, and thereby belonged to them according to the laws of nature. Ordinary citizens began enjoying these rights, and the subsequent flourishing of human nature produced remarkable vitality and energy that enabled Great Britain to become the world premier economic and political power by 1850. The tiny nation pioneered the industrial revolution and came to rule one-third of the globe through this exceptional human vigor, strength and self-discipline.

American colonists from Great Britain assumed these rights crossed the Atlantic with them, since they remained the rough equivalent of Englishmen. The question quickly arose concerning whether the French, Spanish and Germans in America were entitled to the rights of Englishmen. Locke's premise obviously meant all inclusive human nature when he was developing these ideas before the Glorious Revolution, even though he dedicated the published work in defense of the ***English Bill of Rights***.

Americans gradually came to understand that rights derived from natural law are metaphysical and universal – not merely traditional privileges or legal entitlements for Englishmen and their colonial descendants. The Creator endowed these rights upon all mankind including the Scots, Irish, Germans, French, Spanish, indentured servants and black slaves. The Civil War tested the proposition that a black slave is a man, and therefore has rights endowed by God and nature that cannot justly be withheld by owners.

Interestingly, the debate about universal rights has not yet played out in American foreign policy. Some conservatives argue that the federal government's only constitutional and natural law mandate is to defend human rights for citizens on national soil. Other conservatives contend that since human rights derived from natural law are universal, America should express vigorous concern for the deprivation of civil liberties abroad by tyranny.[87]

> *Fred Critique*
> _____
>
> *The debate about universal rights has not yet played out in American foreign policy.*

LOCKE VERSUS THE FEDERALIST PAPERS

Locke's famous work of political philosophy, ***Two Treatises of Government***,[88] was to the Glorious Revolution and English Bill of Rights what the Federalist Papers were to the American Constitution – except that the Federalist Papers were more practical and less metaphysical. Originally published anonymously, the First Treatise attacks patriarchalism and the Second Treatise outlines political and civil society based on innate rights and contract system. Every well-educated citizen during the American Revolution had read Locke, so the metaphysics of Natural Law was widely understood.

The failure to adequately recapitulate these principles in the Federalist Papers might have been a mistake, since Locke's theory was grounded in his Christian world view and natural law. Some Americans also followed **Deism**, which is a philosophy claiming that organized religion is not necessary since reason and observation can determine that a supreme being created the natural universe, but this deity does not intervene in human affairs with supernatural powers. This thin metaphysical gruel opened the door to serious misunderstandings.

---

[87] (F. Hutchison, Brief History of Conservatism 2009)
[88] (Locke, Two Treatises of Government 1689) http://www.gutenberg.org/files/7370/7370-h/7370-h.htm

JEFFERSON'S CORRUPTION OF NATURAL LAW

Locke's *Two Treatises of Government* contains the following concepts:

- Property acquired by mixing one's labor with the gifts of nature is properly one's own;

- No one can rightly feel himself ill-used or unjustly deprived solely because his neighbor possesses property;

- One can dispose of his property as he wills provided he does so within the boundaries of the moral law;

- No one should be deprived of life, liberty or property without due process of law; and

- The arbitrary appropriation of one's property deprives a man of his rightful freedom in essential ways.

God gave humans an intrinsic nature that includes reason and free will, so they could acquire property to meet their material needs and function as free men. Without legal protection for private property, freedom withers away. Every

Thomas Jefferson

conservative understands this in the marrow of his bones. Locke's work clearly established the words *"Life, Liberty and Property."* Many modern American conservatives have reservations when they hear the original *"property"* instead of *"pursuit of happiness,"* as Thomas Jefferson wrote into the Declaration of Independence.

"The Pursuit of Happiness" was the motto of the Romantic Movement, which was based upon subjective experience, had no metaphysical foundations, and was incompatible with natural law that assumes man has an innate nature. Romantics were in rebellion against the boundaries of nature. The result of living in a metaphysical vacuum is that people stumble over the concept that man has a right to property. Liberals love the pursuit of happiness, but have no metaphysical foundation for claiming it as a right.

The right to privacy idea is not founded upon natural law either, but flows from the romantic notion of the pursuit of happiness. The concept of privacy, as understood in North America, is not universal to all civilizations and was virtually unheard of in some cultures until recently. Liberals assume that anything done privately under the personal agenda of the pursuit of happiness must be valid, even actions that are contrary to nature and moral law. The attempt to mingle rational law concepts with misty romantic aspirations generates bewilderment, which is why contemporary jurisprudence about an imagined right to privacy is so deeply confused and conflicted.

MONTESQUIEU: THE ARISTOCRAT BECOMES A LIBERAL

Charles-Louis de Secondat, Baron of Brede and Baron of Montesquieu (1689-1755), was a young man of high social rank and great political powers. During his twenties, he was an ultraconservative of the old order and celebrated the aristocracy and the feudal system. He was an intellectual at heart and extensively studied law, history and science.

At age 32, Montesquieu surprised everyone by suddenly veering towards skepticism and liberalism, as expressed in his *Persian Letters*,[89] a satirical work recounting the experiences of two Persian noblemen traveling through France. He became the new Michel de Montaigne (1533-1592), the French Renaissance father of Modern Skepticism who was legendary for his ability to fuse formal intellectual theory with relaxed anecdotes and autobiography. Separated by two centuries, both Montesquieu and Montaigne were intellectual French noblemen who lived near Bordeaux, were

---

[89] (Montesquieu, Persian Letters 1721) (French: *Lettres persanes*)

celebrated in Paris for their witty and devastating critique of every aspect of French social order, and were prominent in the provincial government.

During his thirties and forties, Montesquieu slowly gravitated towards the English intellectual world, partly through his affiliation with Henry St John, 1st Viscount Bolingbroke (1678-1751) and Philip Dormer Stanhope, 4th Earl of Chesterfield (1694-1773), and partly due to his election as a Fellow of the Royal Society, a high honor among the community of scientists. As an intimate friend of English dukes, he attended parliamentary debates and was welcomed at court by the Prince of Wales. He read English political journals and anonymously published an essay on the English Constitution (1748), which was incorporated into his classic political treatise *The Spirit of the Laws*.[90] He was no longer a liberal.

MONTESQUIEU CONSIDERS THE FALL OF ROME

The English delighted in comparing themselves with the Romans. English historian, Edward Gibbon, published the six volumes of *The History of the Decline and Fall of the Roman Empire*,[91] which impart liberal views for

Montesquieu

Rome's deterioration. Montesquieu published *Reflection on the Causes of the Grandeur and Declension of Romans*,[92] a major work about ancient Rome's decline that became a major milestone in his journey towards a conservative perspective. Montesquieu had a special flair for political science and regretted the loss of the Roman Republic, which was the first government to separate executive, legislative and judicial powers while placing a premium on civic virtue. The empire excelled in governing foreign dependencies, but destroyed the liberty and character of citizens throughout the provinces by concentrating power in a few hands in Rome.

Montesquieu's litany of significant causes for the fall of Rome echo like a 21st century American conservative lamenting the United States. They include: moral decay; cultural decline; excessive immigration of aliens who were unformed by Roman culture and traditions; high taxes; inflation; corruption of office holders; the sapping of military virility and discipline by new anti-war religious cults; the softening of character by wealth and luxurious living; the abandonment of Roman farms; and the servility, indolence and fickleness of the multicultural rabble in Rome.

THE SPIRIT OF THE LAWS

> *"The tyranny of a prince in an oligarchy is not so dangerous to the public welfare as the apathy of a citizen in a democracy."* Charles de Montesquieu

After twenty years of scholarly toil, Montesquieu published his magnum opus, *The Spirit of the Laws*, one of the greatest works of political theory and legal history ever written. The publication encouraged constitutionalism, separation of powers, preservation of civil liberties, rule of law, abolition of slavery, and the concept that political and legal institutions should reflect a community's cultural and geographical character. At the age of 61, he had become an international sage.

---

[90] (Montesquieu, The Spirit of the Laws 1750) (French: *De l'esprit des lois*)
[91] (Gibbon 1776-1788)
[92] (Montesquieu, Reflection on the Causes of the Grandeur and Declension of Romans 1734) (French: *Considérations sur les causes de la grandeur des Romains et de leur décadence*)

One famous doctrine declared that *the animating principle of republics is virtue, the animating principle of monarchies is honor, and the animating principle of despotisms is fear."* According to Montesquieu, a republic that protects a broad set of citizens' rights is a *"democratic republic."* If citizen rights are narrowly defined in a republic, it is an *"aristocratic republic."* The **English Bill of Rights** was a political philosophy movement away from an aristocratic republic and towards a democratic republic.

Henry St. John Viscount
Bolingbroke

The Tory political philosophy was a traditionalist and conservative ideology whose ethics were summed up with the phrase *"God, King and Country."* Tories opposed the radical liberalism of the Whig faction, whose foundation rested on constitutional monarchism and resistance to absolute rule. Montesquieu formulated his vision as a protégé of philosopher and Tory leader, Henry St John Bolingbroke (1678-1751), who had composed hostile arguments expressing Tory opposition to Whig leader, Robert Walpole, 1st Earl of Orford, (1676-1745).

As a student of John Locke's natural law ideas, Bolingbroke proposed formulating decrees by legislative power, which inspired Montesquieu. Using the English Constitution as a model, Montesquieu wrote that a republic should place executive, legislative and judicial powers in different hands, providing balanced authority to prevent tyranny. Book XI, Chapter VII in *The Spirit of the Laws* expressed these principles, and subsequently inspired Thomas Paine (1737-1809) to pen *The Rights of Man*,[93] and James Madison (1751-1836) to contribute to *The Constitution of the United States*.[94]

ROMANTICISM VERSUS CLASSICISM

During this era, the cultural counterpart of conservatism was classicism, and the cultural counterpart of liberalism was romanticism. However, human nature is complex and paradoxical, and there have been plenty of conservative romantics and liberal classicists. Classicism in the arts emphasized and cherished beauty, harmony, universal and timeless qualities of human nature, reason, order, and traditional continuity with the ancient past. Artistic romanticism accentuated individual emotional experience, and encouraged a rebellious breaking free from the confining boundaries of mundane reason, order, tradition and existence to soar into sublime insights.

OUTGROWING ROMANTICISM

> *"Bliss it was in that dawn to be alive but to be young was very heaven."* **The Prelude**, *William Wordsworth, 1850*

Thirty-three years before he wrote the essay identifying him as the father of traditionalist conservatism, Edmund Burke developed a concept that became essential to the Romantic Movement. As a young man, Johann Wolfgang von Goethe (1749-1832) was a leading poetry, drama and literature contributor to the German Romantic Movement – at age 37, he went to Italy, observed classical art and architecture, and converted to classicism. Apparently, Burke and Goethe both outgrew romanticism.

Does man gradually burn out on romantic experience and seek meaning in the harmony and beauty of classicism? Not necessarily, but it is certainly true of some cases. Several French painters became disenchanted – Renoir returned to classicism after he tired of impressionism. The young English poet, William Wordsworth (1770-1850), visited

[93] (Paine 1791)
[94] (Convention 1787)

Revolutionary France where he fell in love with a French girl and the sheer romanticism of the Revolution. Wordsworth mainly gazed at nature to inspire minstrel raptures of romanticism – he wrote, *"Nature never did betray the heart who loved her."* However, nature did betray him with chronic illness, and his works began to decline around the mid-1810s, which paralleled a change of lifestyle that demonstrated his exhaustion with romanticism.

BEAUTY VERSUS THE SUBLIME

Edmund Burke

Burke wrote *A Philosophical Inquiry into the Sublime and the Beautiful*,[95] which was immediately hailed a classic, and is still required reading for students of aesthetics and art history. Although a central theme of Western art for 2,300 years, Burke narrowed the concept of beauty to sharply contrast it with the sublime. While most people assumed that attractiveness and inspiration overlap, Burke insisted that a gulf exists between the two. He narrowed and embellished the concept of beauty to include the pretty, cute, petite, round and babyish, in order to exaggerate the difference between prettiness and magnificence.

Some Victorian artists followed Burke's idea of cute sugar-coated sweetness to personify beauty – the more sentimental and nostalgic, the gushier and effeminate creations became. Classical purists who emphasized harmony, archetypal themes, universal ideas and tradition laughed at the sugary art, while romantic artists were revolted by the syrupy concept and declared war upon beauty.

A present day artist who painted abstract expressionist works of the Jackson Pollock genre had mastered every form of art in college, proving it by painting beautiful murals on Fred Hutchison's walls, but he could not sell his paint smears on canvas. When Hutchison suggested that he paint pictures of cute puppies in order to pay the bills, he angrily retorted, *"That would be selling out."*[96]

Modern artists are not entirely wrong in their objection to the art of prettiness and cuteness. As every good-looking high school girl knows, attractiveness can be used to manipulate and exploit. Tragically, the overreaction of modern artists against manipulative saccharine led to a renunciation of beauty that devastated 20th century art and reduced aesthetics to the level of barbarism. The revolt against beauty and the philosophical appreciation of beauty has been extreme.[97]

> *Fred Critique*
>
> *The revolt against beauty and the philosophical appreciation of beauty has been extreme.*

THE HIDEOUS SUBLIME

Some artists, like Renoir, veered away from colossal eruptions of romantic feeling and defected to the art of prettiness – after all, romanticism set the feelings free, and sentimental art is all about feelings. Mainstream romantics regarded this as a betrayal because of the way had Burke defined the sublime. By way of an explanation, Romantic orthodoxy insisted that art should reflect magnificence in the radical way Burke had defined it, who correctly recognized that every culture's concept differed. Burke's sublime was to be gigantic, monstrous, terrifying, hideous, dark and beyond the grasp of intellect and imagination – the exact opposite of his caricature for beauty as small, round, cute and sweet. Because of this, romantic painters ceased to think of a majestic mountaintop as sublime and began to consider nocturnal forest fears of fevered imagination.

---

[95] (Burke, A Philosophical Inquiry into the Sublime and the Beautiful 1757)
[96] (F. Hutchison, Brief History of Conservatism 2009)
[97] (F. Hutchison, Brief History of Conservatism 2009)

Frankenstein's monster

The hideous sublime flourished in western art and literature during the 19th century, taking on dark overtones of the occult. Obvious examples include Samuel Taylor Coleridge's *The Rhyme of the Ancient Mariner* (1797), Mary Shelley's *Frankenstein* (1816), Edgar Allen Poe's *The Raven* (1845), Robert Louis Stevenson's *Dr. Jeckle and Mr. Hyde* (1886), Bram Stoker's *Dracula* (1897), Oscar Wilde's *The Picture of Dorian Grey* (1890), and Gaston Leroux's *The Phantom of the Opera* (1909). Such fare continues to be popular because of the Romantic Movement's artistic triumph.

TOLKIEN'S REVENGE

J.R.R. Tolkien (1892-1973), a 20th century Christian writer, authored *The Hobbit*,[98] *The Lord of the Rings*,[99] and *The Silmarillion*,[100] high fantasies featuring sublime monsters that terrify cute Hobbits. The stories involved a cosmic battle between the forces of good and evil – his dark, sublime beasts were entirely tools on the side of evil and were hideous brutes in appearance and ferocity. The creatures were so despicable that readers have no sympathy for them, as some readers do for Frankenstein's monster, Mr. Hyde, the Phantom, Dracula and Dorian Grey. The war raged against the allied forces of good that included admirable human heroes. By ensuring hatred for the legion of great wickedness and love for the good champions, Tolkien equipped his sublime tales to be compatible with Christianity. He established the small and cuddly inhabitants of the Shire in the grand scheme without displacing the classical nature of the true, the beautiful and the good.

BURKE, THE ROMANTIC CONSERVATIVE

Edmund Burke did not renounce romanticism, but superseded it with conservative values that moved away from dark sublime elements. Like Tolkien, Burke was a romantic conservative. To explain how individuals can embrace these two juxtaposed ideas, recall that a portion of the Romantic Movement abandoned the cult of the sublime and became nostalgically sentimental. Traditionalist conservatives became romantically nostalgic, as demonstrated in Tolkien's wistful, heroic tales about ancient Anglo-Saxons – epic sagas following the legendary tradition of *The Iliad* and *Odyssey*. Burke maintained romantic nostalgia for high European culture – he was horrified by the destruction of France's brilliant culture, and considered the rabble that set fire to magnificent art and artifacts as abhorrent as Tolkien regarded the horde of orcs and goblins that rampaged Middle Earth.

THE FATHER OF MODERN CONSERVATISM

Burke's *Reflections on the Revolutions in France*[101] won the sympathy of many Englishmen because they were shaken by the French Revolution. Burke cleverly used the essay against his liberal-progressive opponents in parliament who were infatuated by social-engineering and reform projects. He argued that the social fabric of a blessed culture slowly accumulates the deep and subtle wisdom of centuries, reflecting profound truths about human nature, the treasures of high culture, a distillation of divine

Fred Critique

Edmund Burke, the father of modern traditionalist conservatism, taught us to defend the social fabric, to cherish the high culture that is our heritage, and to resist the liberal tide.

---

[98] (Tolkien, The Hobbit 1937)
[99] (Tolkien, The Lord of the Rings 1954)
[100] (Tolkien, The Silmarillion 1977)
[101] (Burke, Reflections on the Revolutions in France 1790)

reality, and a providential outworking of God's economy. In contrast, the vague general principles of the reformers are destructive when applied to real people in an organic society – the blunt hammer of the utopian destroys the delicate web of civil structure.

Edmund Burke was undeniably the father of modern traditionalist conservatism. He taught us to defend the social fabric, to cherish the high culture that is our heritage, and to resist the liberal tide. He stood athwart history yelling, *"STOP."*

NEXT CHAPTER — MODERNITY!

The next chapter shall venture into the modern world of the 19th century. Stay tuned!

CHAPTER 6
THE CATACLYSM OF STATES: 1861-1865

Conservatism passed through a series of fiery trials during the 19th century. Chapter 6 shall view conservatism and Christianity in the crucible of the American Civil War. Chapter 7 shall consider seven dark ideological waves that swept over land during the 19th century: 1) German *"higher criticism"* of the Bible; 2) Hegel's Historicism; 3) Marx; 4) Darwin; 5) Freud; 6) James' Pragmatism; and 7) Dewey's Instrumentalism. Each of these philosophies is hostile to conservatism, Christianity and Western culture.

Civil War scene

The American Civil War (1861-1865) illustrates several important epic conflicts of the century. In order to distill these elements, two campaigns from the Civil War hostilities shall be addressed: 1) the war to preserve the union versus the secession movement; and 2) the war to free the slaves versus the alleged rights of slave owners.

The cataclysm of states drama encompasses a number of historical movements including evangelical revivalism, abolitionism, states' rights, blood and soil romantic movement, transcendentalism, conservative traditionalism, natural law conservatism, and the struggle to define the nation state. Some conflicts between these movements were decisively resolved by the Civil War, others endured through the century, and some are still undecided.

RALLY ROUND THE FLAG, BOYS

Union troops sang *Let Us Rally Round the Flag, Boys*, meaning unite under the stars and stripes, the emblem of the federal union. Confederate troops sang *Hurrah for the Bonny Blue Flag Which Bears a Single Star*, meaning cheer for the flag of secession. Born in Ohio, Ulysses S. Grant (1822-1885) regarded the United States as his country, but respected states rights. Robert E. Lee (1807-1870) regarded Virginia as his country, but regretted to see the federal union dissolved.

Although Lee was a distinguished American Army general with proven Mexican War battle-field experience, he rejected the offer to be supreme commander of the Union Army when the Civil War began, and resigned his commission. The weight of loyalty for his beloved Virginia was heavier than his devotion to the Union he had served all his adult life. Like many American citizens of the day who were struggling to define the nation-state concept and determine personal duty due to the Republic, Lee had difficulty weighing the conflicting allegiance.

Robert E. Lee

In our own day, conservatives remain loyal to the federal republic, while many progressive liberals now prefer transnational associations to national interests. For example, liberals are often offended when America behaves as a sovereign nation-state in matters of war, diplomacy and enforcing the law concerning border security and illegal aliens. We must return to the Civil War to understand the origins of this fateful split in loyalties.

DEFINING A NATION

*"...To assume among the nations of the earth, the separate and equal station to which the laws of nature and nature's God entitle them." **Declaration of Independence**, 1776*

As the era of kings passed, European nations were no longer united by loyalty to a royal house – citizens of republics with powerless or dethroned kings had to form new fidelities. America, Germany and Italy faced great difficulties in sorting out provincial duty from allegiance to the nation state. Napoleon settled the issue for his countrymen – loyalty to France would forever be supreme. However, the string of 19th century revolutions left the definition of French faithfulness an open question, because both sides in each upheaval claimed true devotion and accused the opponents of treason. The English were steadfastly loyal to king and country, but failed to clarify if the dedication encompassed England, Great Britain, or the entire British Empire. Thomas Jefferson rejected the British Empire and believed every people group had a right to its own country, but while he did not consider Virginia a nation, he did regard the thirteen colony union a nation in embryonic form.

NATIONHOOD, VIRTUE AND CULTURE

Roman Coliseum

According to Montesquieu, virtue is the most essential value for a successful republic. The separation of legislative, executive and judicial powers under the Roman Republic protected liberties and encouraged virtue among citizens. When it became an empire, great power concentrated in too few hands, causing the eventual loss of public freedom and character. Although Augustus continued the outward organizational form, he gradually condensed all real power as his own.

Natural law conservatives have sometimes wondered if God created man to live in tribes, empires, commonwealths or nations. Combining Locke's natural law principles with Montesquieu's vision of a Republic, many conservatives came to believe God (or nature) designed man to excel in nations, but not in empires or tribes. Empires like the Roman or British realms can stimulate culture for a season, but as freedom and virtue wane, men decay and culture languishes. Tribal life does not protect individual rights or encourage independent thought; nor do tribes produce civilizations or high cultures that allow the full flowering of human nature. Only nations or city-states that assume high quality values and principles can provide a stable foundation for a healthy society.

BLOOD AND SOIL

The German Romantic Movement developed the theory of *"Blood and Soil"* (German: *"Blut und Boden"*) wherein the culture of a people close to the land they occupy and cultivate mystically emerges from the soil and blood of kindred souls – the nation is an organic entity that emerges from grassroots. The philosophy focuses on descent and homeland ethnicity, and places high value on rural living. Robert E. Lee considered Virginia his country – not the Federal Union or the Southern Confederacy. His natural law perception of the Virginian people-group determined their entitlement to nationhood.

Blood and soil can certainly produce a narrow tribal culture, but probably cannot generate an authentic nation and a worthy national culture. While this ideology has merit, and cherishing folk lore can be beneficial, the belief that culture rises bottom up instead of descending top down did significant damage to Western culture during the modern era. As we painfully learned in the 20th century, the continuous feeding of fads and moods in popular music and art eventually leads to a primitivism lower than the culture of barbarian tribes. Without hierarchy, there can be no high civilization – taste and cultural aspiration must trickle down to mass society from the assumed national elite that is imbued with the best of their cultural heritage.

500 TRIBES

Tecumseh

The two great attempts to confederate Indian tribes in opposition to white settlement failed because both allied forces shattered after suffering military defeats. Ohio born Shawnee Chief Tecumseh (1768-1813), who led an attempt to unite northwestern American Indians to defend the Ohio Valley against white expansion, was killed while aligned with the British Army against American forces during the Battle of the Thames near Moraviantown, Ontario – the tribes in his confederacy surrendered to William Henry Harrison shortly after the battle. The Dakota Territory Sioux holy man, Sitting Bull (1831-1890), who inspired the Battle of Little Bighorn that ultimately annihilated most of George Armstrong Custer's (1839-1876) 7th Cavalry Regiment of the U.S. Army, was made *"Supreme Chief of the whole Sioux Nation"* during the years of the Great Plains Native American resistance; but the superior American military weaponry forced the Indians to surrender, and he was eventually killed during an attempt to arrest him. In spite of legendary courage from individual warriors while fighting for their people, tribes were easily spooked by *"bad medicine"* after the defeat of alliances – the Sioux became wary of the Apache.

These confederated tribes could be formidable in united victories, as Custer discovered, but shattered into fragments when defeated. The 500 Indian Nations concept is a myth – these were 500 *tribes*, each with a unique culture drawing upon the memories, traditions and habitations of the tribe, as filtered through the trances of their medicine men. The only recorded melding of American Indian tribes occurred long before white colonists appeared, when a visionary Huron elder united the five Hodenosaunee, or Iroquois tribes – Mohawks, Oneidas, Onondagas, Cayugas and Senecas – with a powerful message of peace and unity comprised of thirteen laws similar to the Ten Commandments and the U.S. Constitution combined.[102]

HURRAH FOR THE BONNY BLUE FLAG

The romantic notion of blood and soil took root in the American South. The 1861 confederate marching song, ***The Bonny Blue Flag***,[103] starts with the words, *"We are a band of brothers and native to the soil, fighting for our Liberty, with treasure, blood and toil..."* Blood and soil made them brothers, and therefore a people-group entitled to their own country – this is precisely why many Southerners argued for secession and fought so bitterly against invading Union troops. Numinous blood ties enabled the band of southern brothers to operate like a tribe. The link of soil connected the feudal caste society of landed aristocracy to the agrarian community of small farmers. Nevertheless, simple explanations for the complex enigma of the South do not exist.

Northern Yankees, however similar in language, race and religion, had no comparable concept of blood and soil brotherhood, and therefore had no part in the southern fraternity. While the rebels did not think Yankees prayed to

---

[102] (Josephy 1994) DVD/book documentary on the Native Americans of North and Central America from pre-Columbian to the end of the 19th century. (http://500nations.com) Information website for Native American casinos, powwows, places to visit, and tribes in every state and province in the United States and Canada.
[103] (McCarthy 1861)

different gods, they did consider them money grubbers without honor, grace, manners or common decency – ignorance of the Southern code made them outsiders to the clique, bound to a negative perception. This position was similar to the Sioux's suspicious opinion of menacing Apache habits.

THE SOCIAL FABRIC

Traditionalist conservatives noticed that the social fabric was more tightly woven in the South – this cultural unity was a considerable advantage during the early part of the war. The North was more urban, mercantile and entrepreneurial, but had three advantages to offset community limitations – Christianity, idealism and transcendentalism. Northerners were generally more religious and idealistic, and their optimism for the Union proved remarkably durable. Prior to the Civil War, the Bible Belt was in the North – faith filled Union troops often displayed remarkable coolness in the face of death. However, there was considerable contradiction between Biblical Christianity and a cult called transcendentalism.

TRANSCENDENTALISM

The Romantic Movement in the North was not the German format of blood and soil, but the New England system of **transcendentalism**, a literature and philosophy protest movement against the condition of society that developed during the 1830s and 1840s. Core group beliefs included mystical, pantheistic and universalistic qualities that *"transcend"* the physical and empirical — ideal spirituality was realized through individual intuition rather than religious doctrine.

Major figures were Ralph Waldo Emerson (1803-1882), Henry David Thoreau (1817-1862), Walt Whitman (1819-1892), Emily Dickinson (1830-1886) and Margaret Fuller (1810-1850), who all wrote literary classics in the decade prior to the Civil War. Transcendentalism worked in the opposite direction of blood and soil ideas, making Northerners of different states more willing to cast aside parochial interests and join hands to fight secessionism. Transcendentalists loved the Union and hated secession – sometimes their wrath was comparable to that of the abolitionists against slavery.

A forerunner of the astrological Age of Aquarius, transcendental poetry was almost as cloudy and murky as **New Age Movement**[104] verse. Unfortunately, later generations of transcendentalists and their heirs wanted to transcend more than spiritual and artistic advancement, they sought to surpass the federal union and embrace trans-national confederations. This is why some contemporary liberals are enthusiastic about internationalism, but cool towards nationalism, particularly American patriotism.

Multiculturalism is a social response towards multiple cultures at the administrative level (i.e., schools, communities, businesses, cities or countries) intended to create respect for ethnic diversity. It attempts to broaden the political environment by promoting positive support for distinct cultural and religious groups, without endorsing specific values. The contemporary cult of multiculturalism is a distant heir of

> *Fred Critique*
>
> *Some contemporary liberals are enthusiastic about internationalism, but cool towards nationalism, particularly American patriotism.*

---

[104] The New Age spiritual movement's central precepts "draw on both Eastern and Western spiritual and metaphysical traditions and then infuse them with influences from self-help and motivational psychology, holistic health, parapsychology, consciousness research and quantum physics." It aims to create "a spirituality without borders or confining dogmas" that is inclusive and pluralistic. Another primary trait is holding to "a holistic worldview," emphasizing that Mind, Body and Spirit are interrelated and that there is a form of Monism and unity in the universe. (Kyle 2012)

transcendentalism – liberals have touted it to promise protection for all types of minority communities, to fight racism, and to reverse rules preventing full access to the equal opportunity and freedom that is the legacy of Western civilization. However, at the phenomena's core is contempt for Western culture and America, although this is bitterly denied. Devout multiculturalists habitually blame capitalism, Western heritage and/or America for everything wrong in the world, or insist they are the moral equivalent of evil enemies. The historical hostility of transcendentalists towards secessionists and states' rights advocates is similar to the present antagonism of environmentalists and multi-culturalists toward American nationalism and patriotism.

THE GOSPEL VERSUS BLOOD AND SOIL

For two hundred years, Quakers had condemned slavery; it was not until the spiritual revivals of the 18th and 19th centuries that evangelicals began to join them in denouncing bound servitude. According to Biblical Scripture, Christ called believers to preach the good news of freedom to every nation, tribe and person, which would include both the tribes in remotest Africa and the slaves in Virginia. If a black slave could walk the streets of gold in heaven, hand in hand with the Southern planter, why must he wear chains in Virginia?

Black slaves had no foothold in Southern society on the basis of blood and soil, since there was no blood relationship with the white man – or none that society acknowledged or accepted. Southern whites romanticized an exaggerated idea of blood kinship, because they celebrated superiority over the downtrodden Negroes in their midst. Even poor whites gloried in their superior bloodlines and brotherhood with other Southern whites. This white race solidarity increased until the Civil War.

NATIVIST CONTRADICTIONS

Nativism favors the interests of certain established inhabitants of an area or nation as compared to claims of newcomers or immigrants. It may also include the re-establishment or perpetuation of such individuals or their culture. Nativism typically means opposition to immigration or efforts to lower the political or legal status of specific ethnic or cultural groups because the groups are considered hostile or alien to the natural culture, and it is assumed that they cannot be assimilated.[105]

Southern white men believed that they alone had a vested interest in the soil. Although black slaves might be close to and work the land, only those who owned the land were *"native to the soil."* While landless whites were potential owners and therefore honorary natives, slaves were deemed unworthy of consideration according to blood and soil principles. The black slaves, who were at the very bottom of the hierarchy, were closer to the soil than any other group. This self-contradictory reasoning indicates that Southern bottom-up *"blood and soil"* nativism had been subsumed by a top-down caste system. In contrast, race and land ownership had no bearing upon United States citizenship, therefore black volunteers were eagerly recruited to fight for the Union Army.

---

[105] http://en.wikipedia.org/wiki/Nativism_(politics) (Various 2012)

THE FIERY GOSPEL

I have seen Him in the watch-fires of a hundred circling camps.
They have builded Him an altar in the evening dews and damps.
I can read His righteous sentence by the dim and flaring lamps,
His day is marching on.

I have read a fiery gospel writ in burnished rows of steel,
'As ye deal with my condemners so with you my grace shall deal.'
Let the hero born of woman crush the serpent with his heel,
Since God is marching on.

Battle Hymn of the Republic, *2nd and 3rd verses, Julia Ward Howe, 1861*

It is necessary to look through the fiery lens of gospel revival to appreciate the intense words in the ***Battle Hymn of the Republic***. Historians seldom understand how fiercely religious the Civil War was – it was fought in the middle of the longest and most broadly experienced revival in world history (the Second and Third Great Awakening, 1800-1900). No other spiritual renewal has come close to the depth and lasting change it brought to American national character, politics and religious orientations. Many Christian chroniclers are drawn to charismatic preachers, and over-rate revivals that enjoyed spectacular evangelists. The mid-19th century awakening had no human leader or preacher who stood out, yet no rebirth permeated American consciousness throughout the land like this one.

A REVIVAL OF PRAYER

On September 21, 1857, a Christian layman named Jeremiah Lanphier (1809-?) started a noon prayer meeting for fellow New York businessmen – six men attended. By March 1858, big-city newspapers devoted front-page coverage to the *Layman's Prayer Revival*, reporting that over 6,000 people were attending assorted prayer meetings in both New York and Pittsburgh. Large cities and small towns across the country recorded a multitude of praying citizens: Chicago, 2,000; Philadelphia, 4,000; Charlestown, South Carolina, 2,000; and Louisville, Kentucky, 1,000. By late spring, many assemblies had sprung up with attendance of 10,000 people – Washington, D.C. offered prayer groups five times a day to accommodate the crowds. One man's obedience to prayer blossomed into a revival that transformed America.

LET US DIE TO SET MEN FREE

"I have seen him in the watch-fires of a hundred circling camps... ...As he died to make men holy, let us die to make men free." ***Battle Hymn of the Republic***

The Civil War broke out in 1861, and first big battle was fought at Bull Run on July 1861. Fervent prayer continued in the cities, but the revival focus shifted to the camps of both Union and Confederate soldiers. Most congregations in the camps were small circles of troops gathered around a lay minister who had joined the army. These impromptu gospel encounters were everywhere amidst the *"hundred circling camps."*

At first, transcendental sentiments to crush secessionists prevailed among the troops, but the philosophic gruel of this watery pabulum was unsatisfying to men facing death in battle. The soldiers hungered for the red meat substance of God's judgment, death and hell, and Christ's bloody ordeal on the cross that opens the door of heaven. They began to view themselves as holy crusaders entrusted to free the slaves and crush the bondman. Since Jesus died to rescue them from sin, condemnation and hell, many soldiers responded by offering their lives in battle to free the slaves.

THE SOUTHERN BIBLE BELT

After the Civil War, substantial parts of the South were a smoldering ruin. In their agony and despair, many Southerners cried out to God for mercy and succor, and revival shifted southward. Ever since the great days of the Southern revival preachers, most American evangelists of national stature have come from the South. After 1970, a disproportionate number of conservative leaders have appeared in the Southern states, which are now classified as *"red states"* during presidential elections, meaning that they usually vote for Republican candidates.

FRUITS OF VICTORY

Civil War Victory was a vindication for the Union, the gospel and the natural law rights of individuals. Transcendental romanticism was encouraged, while blood and soil romanticism was discouraged. America's destiny as a continental, industrial, mercantile and entrepreneurial power was confirmed. Hereafter, Americans in both the North and South would be patriotic about the nation, not their state of residence.

Every great resolution of history has a downside, and Civil War baggage still weighs heavily upon our national shoulders. Having been set free from blood and soil ties, Americans gradually became hyper-individualistic at the expense of community. With these roles in the formation of culture now dismissed, the doors to mass immigration were opened wide. The concept of nationhood and citizenship became cloudier and more abstract as transcendental sentiments encouraged utopian notions of internationalism and the rejection of national patriotism. Although liberals angrily deny it, disparagement of American loyalty almost always comes from the left, and almost never from the right. Sometimes liberals attribute patriotism to nativism, forgetting that the rise of American patriotism involved a renunciation of Southern nativism.

A BULWARK FOR THE NATIONS

The continued tone of American devotion is one that rises above parochial interests to celebrate the common participation and fortuitous history of the national entity that is blessed by God. The ultimate significance of the Civil War is that America emerged as a strong and essentially Christian nation in ideals – it retained the character of a republic, and was capable of extraordinary unity in times of peril. The Republic preserves the three branch separation of government, as called for by Locke and Montesquieu. However, the President wields exceptional executive powers in times of war, as Lincoln demonstrated. The astonishing combination of strength and freedom is unusual in history, enabling the American spirit to soar when trouble comes and citizens rise up to help. The United States of America is a gift of providence to the world – a bulwark of freedom during a time when extraordinary evil is rising in the Muslim east.

DEPREDATIONS OF MODERNISM

Chapter 7 will continue with a consideration of the immoral and degenerate modernism that passed over the land during the 19th century, including German *"higher criticism"* of the Bible, Hegel, Marx and the cult of modernism.

Conservatism passed through a series of fiery trials during the 19th century. Chapter 6 reviewed conservatism and Christianity in the crucible of war – the next two chapters are devoted to eight dark waves of depraved modernism that passed over during the 19th century. Chapter 7 will consider: 1) German *"higher criticism"* of the Bible; 2) Hegel; 3) Marx; and 4) the cult of modernism. Chapter 8 will tackle: 5) Darwin; 6) Freud; 7) William James; and 8) John Dewey. Each of these ideologies is hostile towards conservatism, Christianity and Western culture.

GERMAN HIGHER CRITICISM

During the 19th century, liberal theologians and philosophers influenced by romanticism and German idealism were skeptical about Christian faith, and began to attack the authority of Scripture. They published fancy expositions that seemed scholarly on the surface, but were deeply illogical in content. These *"higher critics"* loaded circular reasoning and intellectual assumptions into their arguments to predetermine the conclusions – a famous logical fallacy. *"I do not believe the Bible, therefore A, therefore B, therefore C, therefore I do not believe the Bible."* These skeptics reasoned in a circle specifically designed to reach a predetermined conclusion.[106]

SCHLEIERMACHER

Western Christian **High Scholasticism** is a comprehensive handling of theology that supplements revelation with deductions of reason. Martin Luther began Lutheranism with a forceful protest against scholasticism, as he sought assurances about life and faith. Luther believed reason could be utilized to question men and institutions, but not God – humans could only understand God through the divine revelation of Scripture. The **Pietist** movement blended Lutheranism with the Calvinist emphasis on individual piety and enthusiastic works of faith, reacting against theological rationalism they dubbed *"Lutheran scholasticism."*

German Lutheran pietist, Friedrich Schleiermacher (1768-1834), was one of the first of the *"higher critics."* As a pietist, Schleiermacher stressed that the feeling of dependence upon God was the core of religion. His opinion was not entirely wrong, since surrender, trust and reliance on God are indispensable attributes of belief. However faith is not a feeling, although it is often accompanied by emotion. Schleiermacher insisted that feeling alone is responsible for dogmatic theology, and he rejected the role of scripture and rational theology as a source of doctrine.

Friedrich Schleiermacher

While most pietists did not reject the authority of scripture, Schleiermacher was intellectually influenced by German Idealists Johann Gottlieb Fichte (1762-1814) and Friedrich Wilhelm Joseph Schelling (1775-1854). The philosophy of **German idealism** emerged in the late 18th and early 19th centuries, stemming from Immanuel Kant's work and closely linked to both romanticism and the revolutionary politics of the Enlightenment. Schleiermacher may have been emotionally influenced by German Romantic culture, since he wrote praises for the movement – the revolt against reason might account for part of the higher critics' irrationality.

---

[106] (F. Hutchison, Brief History of Conservatism 2009)

German Idealists emphasized the will and the subjective faculties of the mind. German Romantic poets emphasized feelings and rejected reason. Both rejected transcendent truth and authorities for truth like the Bible, the Augsburg Confession, and Lutheran Church teaching. They felt that truth can only be found subjectively within man, which is exactly what Schleiermacher claimed.

AN IMPOSSIBLE COSMOS

Postmodern liberals still believe Schleiermacher's dictum – situational ethics, moral relativism and the cultural relativism of truth claims are based on the idea that truth must be discovered subjectively. **Relativism** is the philosophical theory that all points of view are equally valid and do not contain absolute truth or validity, having only relative, subjective value according to differences in individual perception and consideration. This presumption enabled idealist philosopher Georg Wilhelm Friedrich Hegel (1770-1831) to invent his own cosmos, arguing that truth changes over time in accordance with his theory of historicism.

> *Fred Critique*
>
> *Situational ethics, moral relativism and the cultural relativism of truth claims are based on the idea that truth must be discovered subjectively.*

Hegel's historicist position proposes that every human society and activity (i.e., science, art, philosophy, etc.) is defined by its history, so its fundamental nature can only be acquired through understanding. The history of any human venture simultaneously builds upon and reacts against what has gone before. His historicist and idealist explanation for reality revolutionized European philosophy and became a vital forerunner to Marxism.

However, historicism is logically impossible – no cosmos can exist in which every individual invents his own truth claims. Historicists believe that each generation must subjectively discover its own truth; but contemporaries seeking truth individually could never agree on group truth claims, because the personal search requires each person to create his own reality. Hegel could not invent a private cosmos without implicitly inviting everyone to concoct their own universe. Any society that invites people to engage in this process will shatter into fragments and collapse.

Interestingly, postmodern liberal leaders insist that everyone should invent their own truth, while concurrently demanding conformance to a political correctness code. This contradiction is not lost on young liberals who feel their own discovery of individual truth entitles them to rebel against the authority of older liberals – just as the higher critics rebelled against the Bible's authority.[107]

HEGEL, STRAUSS AND NIETZSCHE

David Strauss

Georg Hegel claimed that history is governed by impersonal spiritual forces. This assumption explicitly rules out divine revelation and the miraculous intervention of an infinite and personal God. Following the trail of Hegel and Schleiermacher, David Friedrich Strauss (1808-1874) adopted an anti-supernatural position. Strauss believed that since dogmatic theology is based purely upon subjective human feelings and not the Bible, then the Bible must be a collection of myths, and he proceeded to *"demythologize"* it.[108]

Using circular reasoning, Strauss reduced biblical miracles to folklore or events with rational explanations, essentially saying, *"I don't believe in biblical miracles because I don't believe in*

---

[107] (F. Hutchison, Brief History of Conservatism 2009)
[108] (Strauss, On Christian Doctrine 1840) (German: *Christliche Glaubenslehre)*

miracles of any kind." Strauss claimed that the life of Christ was fabricated by early Christians based upon their messianic expectations. This claim was not based upon scholarly examination of documents or historical evidence; he simply applied his prior assumptions based on current fads in German philosophy to the Bible, again reverting to circular reasoning. *"The life of Christ in the Bible is a concocted story because I believe the Bible is a collection of myths."* [109]

Friedrich Wilhelm Nietzsche (1844-1900) was a German philosopher, poet and classical historian who wrote crucial texts on religion, morality, culture, philosophy and science. He developed a radical questioning method for determining the value and objectivity of truth, resulting in a profusion of interpretation and analysis – his influence remains significant in modern philosophy, nihilism, existentialism and postmodernism. Nietzsche's major ideas included the will to power and the death of God.

AN UPSIDE DOWN WORLD

"That which may be known of God is manifest in them; for God has shown it to them. For the invisible things of him from the creation of the world are clearly seen, being understood by things that are made, even his power and Godhead, so they are without excuse." Romans 1:19-20 (KJV)

During the Middle Ages, religious metaphors about nature were popular in medieval literature. Holly thorns represented Christ's crown of thorns, while the berries were red to imply the blood of Christ. Birds were images for angels. The griffin (half lion, half eagle) suggested the God/man Christ. The pelican signified the sacrifice of Christ because people thought the chicks were fed with their own blood. The phoenix rose from the ashes as a resurrection prototype. Notice how the imaginative descriptions ascended from nature to the transcendent spiritual realm – just as the interior columns of gothic churches soar upwards with inspiring magnificence. This symbolizes a right-side-up world.

God stocked nature with metaphors and archetypes of a higher spiritual world. Writers C.S. Lewis (1898-1963) and Dallas Willard (1935-) wrote with special fascination about how the created world sometimes operates like a portal to a transcendent spiritual world, which briefly opens to give glimpses of heaven. During those rare moments when nature takes on a sacramental sheen, mediation between material nature and the spiritual realm can occur.

When Strauss wrote that the Bible was fable,[110] the great ship of Western culture listed to the left and began to roll. By reducing Christ's life to myth and metaphor, Strauss overturned Western spiritual imagination. His insistence ruled out a higher spiritual world, and divine abstractions collapsed. Instead of projecting beyond nature to God, Western philosophy began to envision downwards to earth, looking for mythical origins in man. Dallas Willard wrote, *"We are living in an upside-down world."*

THE MAGICAL THINKING OF NARCISSISTS

German philosophical idealism was a great engine of pride, which explains the breathtaking arrogance of Strauss' assertions. Idealists held to the ridiculous proverb that if a tree falls in the forest and no one hears it, it makes no noise – for that matter, the tree does not exist if nobody sees and accepts its reality. If the mere lack of human acknowledgment can disestablish elements of creation, the presumption to dissolve scripture revelation into myths by mere denials is not

---

[109] (Strauss, The Life of Jesus, Critically Examined - English Translation 1860) (German: *Das Leben Jesu, kritisch bearbeitet*)
[110] (Strauss, On Christian Doctrine 1840)

surprising. This magical thinking inflated Strauss' opinions to the point where he could blithely wave away miracles and historicity with no grounds other than personal disregard.

Nietzsche apparently lost his faith while reading Strauss' *The Life of Jesus*,[111] in spite of the raw assertions – the God complex he suffered from made him vulnerable to mysterious philosophy. Every step of the downward journey was led by narcissists, who could not tolerate considering the possibility of a heavenly being greater than themselves. It left Nietzsche's supreme vanity to declare, *"God is dead,"* prior to succumbing to madness. Insanity is the egotist's last refuge – they flee to imaginary sand castle worlds to safely focus on their sick, self inflated fantasies while presuming their own godhood.

FEUERBACH AND HEGEL

Ludwig Feuerbach

Ludwig Feuerbach (1804-1872) belonged to a politically liberal, left-wing Hegelian faction in college. After studying Baruch de Spinoza (1632-1677) and Hegel, he bitterly rejected the possibility of revelation from a transcendent God and embraced **pantheism**, the view that the universe (nature) and God are identical. As an atheist and materialist, he rejected the Bible and Christian theology to pursue nature – claiming that after death, we are absorbed back into nature – as the romantic pantheists of the day asserted. Many of his philosophical writings presented a critical analysis of Christianity. Feuerbach adopted Hegel's historicism, asserting that the fixed idea of Christianity blocks the way of progress for a constantly changing civilization. The existence of fixed or absolute truth contradicts the changing truth design of Hegel's historicism fantasy, which is the basis for the myth of progress that has reigned supreme in the West for the last two centuries, and is the core idea of the cult of modernism.

THE MYTH OF PROGRESS

The **myth of progress** is based on the assumption that human nature is constantly changing because impersonal forces of history alter man, therefore truth is changing – or at least the truth that applies to man. If God created man and designed human nature, the appeal for *"progress"* and a changing human nature is preposterous. However, someone who actually believes in a constantly fluxing, pantheistic world of detached powers that push toward an irresistible march of progress can find meaning in such claims.

It is high time for the restoration of common sense through public questioning and debate – for those individuals with intelligence to be doubtful about the preposterous cosmos that skeptics have dreamed up. How can impersonal forces be creative and have a plan? How can impersonal forces know or care if man makes progress? How can impersonal forces change a personal world? Is "p*rogress"* the evolution of man and society towards a mythical utopia? Is utopia the final pantheistic oneness that lies in the future? Such harmony is presumably the ultimate good; however, pantheists insist everything already exists in great union. If so, do we not already live in utopia? Keep in mind that we must have our consciousness elevated to recognize the oneness before we can have utopia, because German idealists maintain nothing exists until man recognizes it. No sane answers seem to be forthcoming.[112]

> *Fred Critique*
>
> *It is high time for the restoration of common sense through public questioning and debate.*

---

[111] (Strauss, Das Leben Jesu 1835)
[112] (F. Hutchison, Brief History of Conservatism 2009)

Oddly, people believe these strange fables today – they try to collectively raise their consciousness through a haze of sex and drugs to embrace the *"oneness,"* in order to usher in spiritual utopia. Magical idealism and postmodern murkiness are the slender threads on which 19th and 20th century men based their faith in the inevitability of progress. Such belief validates irrational minds that grasp at preposterous ideas in order to find a substitute for Christianity – the Apostle Paul called it a *"reprobate mind."*[113] English musician and singer-songwriter, John Lennon (1940-1980), envisioned a psychedelic utopia world with no nations, no religion, and a never-ending sex orgy among all people. If only we would all imagine this, so it would magically come true. Such a utopia would be a good thing only because Mr. Lennon was able to dream.[114]

> *"You may say that I'm a dreamer, but I'm not the only one. I hope someday you'll join us, and the world will be as one."* John Lennon, 1971

HEGEL'S RIGHT AND LEFT GROUPIES

Georg Hegel

Ludwig Feuerbach was hailed by left-wing Hegelian radicals as a hero of the **German Revolution of 1848**,[115] which stemmed from a popular longing for increased political freedom, liberal state policies, democracy and nationalism. In contrast, right-wing Hegelians backed the established authorities, believing that the great leader of the state (German: *"der fuhrer"*) was the vanguard of historic forces. Historians obsess over the left-wing actions during the troubles and routinely ignore the right-wing, but it is safe to assume that they were politically aligned against each other in 1848.

In the 20th century, the left-wing was absorbed into the Communist parties of the West, and the right-wing was swallowed into the Nazi and fascist movements. German opposition to the red communist menace fueled Hitler's rise. When Hitler invaded the Soviet Union in 1942, he was carrying the 1848 implications to a logical conclusion – as heirs of Hegel's right-wing groupies, Nazis were at war with Communists, heirs of the left.

The majority of men fighting and dying in Europe during World War II fought on the Eastern front, where Nazis fought Communists. The European Western front was a side show until the Normandy invasion on June 6, 1944 — five years after the September 1, 1939 outbreak of war, and ten months before the April 7, 1945 conclusion. It can be reasonably argued that World War II was essentially a bloody quarrel between Hegel's right-wing madmen (Nazis) versus his left-wing maniacs (Communists); more blood was shed in that colossal conflict between the two poles of modernism than all other World War II casualties. Modernism is fiercely self-destructive and schizophrenic in nearly destroying what traditional Western culture has built.

HEGELIANISM VERSUS CONSERVATISM

Some modern liberals cannot differentiate between conservatives and Nazis because the Hegelian ideology spectrum distorts their perception. Liberals are the ideological first cousins of Hegel's left-wing Communists, which is the basis for historical liberal sympathy for communism – Communists have never returned the favor, thinking of liberals as

---

[113] Romans 1:28 (KJV)

[114] (F. Hutchison, Brief History of Conservatism 2009)

[115] The German Revolution of 1848 was a series of protests and rebellions in the German Confederation states and the Austrian Empire that sought to unify all European German-speaking populations into a single nation-state. Middle class insurgents fought for liberal principles while the working class rebels sought working and living condition improvements. This rift caused the Revolution to split, and the conservative aristocracy defeated it, forcing many into exile.

"useful idiots."[116] Progressive liberals and Nazis are also philosophical cousins, both rising from Hegelian right-wing doctrine – the furious conflict between them is a family quarrel. Communists, Nazis and progressive liberals all share the Hegelian belief in inevitable progress towards utopia.

Anti-communism played an important role in conservative progress after World War II, as those who championed traditional Western culture and rejected Hegel's fantasies reacted to the propositions of Karl Marx (1818-1883). Conservatives are opposed to all branches of Hegelian tenets, and reject utopian thinking and myths of progress. If conservatives fully realized their intellectual and spiritual independence from the Communist/Nazi/liberal continuum of Hegel's world, they would recognize that all departments of the modernist agenda are hostile to their values. Joining ranks in diametric opposition to these delusions would further the conservative agenda, and rescue Western civilization and culture from destruction by suicidal modernism. Such deliverance requires the intervention of a savior, namely Jesus Christ.

MARX AND HEGEL

Dialectical method is the exchange of ideas between individuals who hold different viewpoints about a subject, but attempt to establish the truth of the matter with logical dialogue and debate. Immanuel Kant invented a dialectical process for metaphysics that included thesis, antithesis and synthesis – the synthesis of two contrary ideas produces a higher metaphysical idea. Hegel applied this method to historical spiritual forces instead of metaphysical ideas. The synthesis of opposing spiritual forces purportedly brings about a higher state of being for man, and a more advanced civilization. According to Hegel, this *"dialectic"* is how human progress occurs.

Karl Marx

Karl Marx (1818-1883) borrowed the same process and applied it to history using economic forces. Marx was a strict atheist and materialist, and he rejected Hegel's spiritual forces stating that, *"Nothing exists but matter in motion."* In order to contrast his system with Hegel's, he called his model *"dialectical materialism."* Both men agreed that the dialectic gradually perfects human nature and leads to utopia. However, Hegel claimed that man was perfected by impersonal spiritual forces, and Marx pronounced that ultimate man is created through economic influence.

Hegel and Marx were both progressive determinists – they claimed that the forces of history are irresistible, progress is inevitable, human nature will be perfected, and utopia will come. Hegel's determinism and utopianism is the source of widespread belief in the inevitability of progress. A moderate version of Marx's economic determinism was popular among 20th century liberals.

ECONOMIC DETERMINISM

Economic determinism is a radical reduction and crude caricature of highly complex human nature. Even worse, it often denies that man has a nature, implicitly reducing humans to the status of modeling clay that requires shaping by economic forces to become whatever the determining pressure decrees. If economic determinism is true, mankind is nothing but programmed automatons – the invisible hands of economic class would have created all social structures. Of course, this is a magical thinking myth.

---

[116] The term *"useful idiot"* is political jargon used to describe Soviet sympathizers in Western countries – it implies that the people in question naïvely think themselves an ally of communism, when they are actually held in contempt and are being cynically used for a cause they do not understand. The earliest known Western media usage was a 1948 article in the social-democratic Italian paper ***L'Umanita***.

Liberals have been obsessed with Marx's idea of economic determinism for more than a century. Any time a social problem is mentioned, liberals invariably speak of *"root causes,"* meaning economic origins. For example, while many liberals claim that poverty is the cause of terrorism, careful studies have revealed that most terrorists are comparatively affluent and well-educated.

SOCIAL JUSTICE

Leaping forward in time, former vice-presidential candidate John Edwards' (1953-) presented a 2004 campaign speech concerning *"Two Americas,"* which is an expression of three Marxist concepts: economic root causes, social justice and class warfare. The lecture referred to social stratification in American society, referring to haves and have-nots. Edwards suggested that affluent America is composed of a different variety of people than working class America, because economics determines what we become.[117] If Edwards actually believes this mummery, he is deluded about human nature.

John Edwards

According to social justice presumptions, the divide between affluent and poor is presumably unjust because the rich are molded better than the working class and poor. Therefore, the underprivileged class suffer unjust privations and have the *"right"* to a *"better life"* — i.e., the right to have more money. Social justice ideas are absurd unless one first subscribes to the Marxist scheme of economic determinism – they purposely instigate antagonism between social classes. Marx actually encouraged class warfare because he thought it was the engine of progress (thesis, antithesis, synthesis, etc.)

CLASS WARFARE

The Democratic Party's great failing for the last eighty years has been using the Marxist program of class warfare to win elections. Marx believed that feudalism in medieval Europe created warfare between the landholding aristocracy and laboring peasants, purportedly leading to a new synthesis that produced capitalism. Capitalism then wrought conflict involving the *bourgeoisie* (French: *city dweller*) who possessed the means of production, i.e., steel factories, etc., and the *proletariat* (French: *iron worker*) who provided their labor for a wage. The clash allegedly led to a synthesis called **socialism**, where the means of production are publicly or commonly owned and controlled by government.

The kind of socialism Marx called for was *"the dictatorship of the proletariat,"* in which a deliberately harsh regime was required to perfect human nature by exterminating evil bourgeoisie characteristics. Russian revolutionary, Vladimir Lenin (1870-1924), and Chinese mastermind, Mao Tse-tung (1893-1976), gave top priority to the duty of eliminating the bourgeoisie – thus tens of millions of people were murdered based on economic class.

After the Soviet Union's seventy-year run, it was clear that the dictatorship had not perfected human nature. One cause of the U.S.S.R. collapse was the loss of faith that totalitarian socialism could improve individual character – corruption was everywhere, alcoholism and suicide were common, and the Russian family and society was in ruins. Russian despair was summed up by the statement, *"They did more than take our youth away. They took away the men we were going to be."*[118]

---

[117] (Edwards 2004)
[118] (Amis 2007)

Wisdom formulated on the teachings of American Christian theologian and philosopher, Francis Schaefer (1912-1984), states that, *"Any false idea about human nature inflicts injury on people to the extent that it is believed and acted upon."* Damage is further multiplied if the false idea is forced upon people by a dictatorial government. False Marxist dogma has generated more human despair and led more people to ruin than any other ideological notion ever propagated on earth.

RUSSELL KIRK RESPONDS

Russell Kirk with Ronald Reagan

Throughout the generations, conservatives fighting a rear guard battle have responded to the lies of higher criticism, modernism, Hegel and Marx – debunkers of Communism have been particularly conspicuous. The incomparably quotable Englishman, G.K. Chesterton (1874-1936), was a piecemeal debunker of modernism who is memorable for his wit and paradox. A less witty but more comprehensive opponent, Russell Kirk (1918-1994),[119] was more than a modern Edwin Burke keeping traditionalist conservatism alive; he was more than a systematic version of Chesterton, who arrived to thoroughly refute the fallacies of modernism; he was more than an advocate of Western literary classics. Kirk was a great American synthesizer for age-old strands of conservatism who appeared in history just when he was needed the most – when the cause of conservatism was on the ropes.[120] Kirk's masterpiece ***The Conservative Mind: From Burke to Eliot***[121] launched the modern American conservative movement by establishing that the Founding Fathers were deeply influenced by intellectual traditions and history. Kirk was guided by eight general principles,[122] all of which contradict the ideas of modernism considered in this chapter, as quoted from "Conservative Fundamentals,"[123] a book review article by Gillis Harp in ***Touchstone Magazine***, of the book ***The Essential Russell Kirk***.[124]

1. There is *"a transcendent moral order."*

    There is universal moral law that is transcendent to man and human society. This law applies to all men in all places and at every moment of history. Ethical principles and the capacity for virtue are inherent in the Creator's design. The individual and the society must honor these laws and principles if there is to be freedom, order and human flourishing. Rejection of these laws can have consequences that are fatal to the individual and catastrophic to society. Christian conservatives and Natural Law conservatives heartily agree with Kirk about the transcendent moral order.[125]

    If there is a transcendent moral order, then it is reasonable to think that God can reveal his order to man by sending his anointed one, the Christ, from heaven to teach us, and by giving revelations to his apostles and prophets. If there is a transcendent moral order, the historicism of Hegel and Marx is unreasonable. Universal truth is fixed and contradicts the assertion of a changing truth.

---

[119] (Kirk, The Russell Kirk Center for Cultural Renewal - Ten Conservative Principles 2007-2011)
[120] (Russello 2008)
[121] (Kirk, The Conservative Mind: From Burke to Eliot 1953, 1960, 1972, 1985 - 2001 Printing)
[122] (Nash 2007)
[123] (Harp 2007)
[124] (Kirk and Panichas, The Essential Russell Kirk: Selected Essays 2007)
[125] (Jenkins 2011)

2. A society is a *"community of souls"* stretching back to the primordial past.

Our forefathers still live through us in our inherited wisdom and through our inherited culture. They live through us and we live in them in mysterious spiritual ways. When we are cut off from our forebearers, we become orphans and strangers in the world and lose our capacity for authentic community. Abandoned on the shores of a vast alien world, we suffer alienation, anomie and acedia.

The old Western idea of honor originally meant the honor of family. Purely individualist honor is a decadent modern version of honor. The idea of the family included many generations of the living and the dead. The honor of the family was celebrated by a coat of arms with a family motto. The family honor was at stake in the life of one carrying the family name. Children were taught how to behave so as not to dishonor the family. Every Southern boy in the nineteenth century was exhorted by his mother to become a Southern gentleman – and was exhorted by his father to become a man of honor.

The Western Christian origin of the idea of family honor was a spiritual grace passing down through the family line. Before the light of the gospel came to Europe, the worship of ancestors centering on the hearth prevailed in the Roman world. A tribal warrior cult that preserved the memory of heroes prevailed in the pagan north.

3. Deference should be given to the wisdom of our ancestors.

C.S. Lewis

C.S. Lewis spoke of the *"tyranny of the present"* by which modernists give preference to the contemporary ideas over older ideas. Lewis believed that stopping our ears to the voices of the past is a sure road to folly. The deep folly manifested in our contemporary popular culture is in part the result of a turning away from the Western past and stopping our ears to the voices of our parents and our ancestors.

Edmund Burke spoke of the social fabric woven by the wisdom of past ages that provides a lush culture for the nourishment of human nature. Once the social fabric is broken by liberal social engineering projects, it is difficult to restore.

4. A measured prudence should guide political change.

Hastily designed social programs often are unsuccessful and breed unexpected social problems. For example, Section 8 housing often brings drug dealers and teen gangs to the suburbs. The social problems of slum neighborhoods are reproduced in middle class neighborhoods. Welfare programs that reward idleness and penalize marriage have done much to destroy the black working class family.

The destruction of traditional society and culture is most striking in Communist countries, but it is also quite notable in the socialist countries in Europe. Socialists specialize is social engineering experiments – the very antithesis of Kirk's measured prudence in political change.

Modernists are addicted to the cult of change. Many politicians assume the voters will prefer the candidate most likely to bring *"change"* – even if that candidate is vague about what the change will be. A bias for *"change"* works against rationality in the design of legislation. Measured prudence is required for rationality to triumph over haste and political pressure.

5. Accept class differences.

Class conflict is destructive. Ideas about *"social justice"* based upon leveling fantasies of utopian thinkers are pernicious. From Karl Marx to John Edwards, the left has been poisoning political discourse with class conflict and social justice ideas.

An unequal distribution of talent, ability, wisdom and fortune is natural to man. A difference in economic fortunes among men is not evil. It is natural. The Puritans called it *"God's economy"* and his providential ordering of the world. Social traditionalists regarded social classes as the natural order of things.

Literary traditionalists have taught that social classes are essential to a high culture and a brilliant civilization. This is difficult to dispute when we consider that: a) the Renaissance was a cultural transformation of the aristocracy; and b) the leveling tendencies of modernism was accompanied by a sharp decline in the quality of culture, as Alexis de Tocqueville predicted.

Richard Weaver

6. Cherish private property.

Intellectual historian Richard Weaver (1910-1963) said that private property provides a refuge for the individual from the utilitarian state and from the materialist forces of commerce. I would add, property is a sanctuary for the family in an anti-family world. God's blessings are upon the homes of godly families. The home is a refuge against crime. Property owners demand law and order because the criminal is the enemy of the rights of the property owner.

According to Weaver, property encourages personal responsibility and providence in the long term maintenance and improvement of property. The sheer toil, planning and expense required to administer and maintain property develops a sense of personal responsibility.

Interestingly, Weaver believed that property encourages rationality. A return to reason is necessary before citizens are able to hearken to a man of principle who is running for political office. A man of principle who leads a rational people is indispensable for freedom, order and the viability of a republic.

Property encourages a sense of the neighborhood and of the community. A piece of property is a fixed point with links to the past and the future. It provides a stable refuge from Hegel's nightmare world of continuous flux. As one is blessed on his property, he enjoys a heritage from the past, and is made aware that he will pass on his property as a legacy to future generations.

Property invites the expression of personal individuality and creativity as one embellishes one's house and cultivates one's yard. In the privacy of one's property, one exercises his volition, carries out his plans, experiments with his ideas, and learns what it means to be free. That freedom is hedged about within the wholesome limits of prudent property management. Finally, property provides a place for the display and storage of memories, which I learned as I sorted my parent's attic.

7. The need for order is the primary social need.

Liberals and libertarians do not understand the pressing need for order, but most conservatives have always understood it in the marrow of their bones. The worst of all worlds is anarchy. The second worst condition is the

tyranny of protection rackets. Strong men and their gangs take control of the streets, rule through intimidation, and loot the people through protection money, extortion and the exploitation of vice.

The foremost purpose of government is to bring order, suppress crime, and to protect the citizens from foreign aggressors. Only then is civilization possible. Oratorical lines like *"government is the problem"* and *"government is a necessary evil"* are purely libertarian. Conservatives have traditionally believed that the state is good because it is ordained of God – yet also believe that the legitimate role of government in human affairs is limited.

8. Human nature is flawed and is not perfectible.

The best of men face an inner battle between good and evil. Therefore, man is a contradiction. One reason for reading the literary classics is to learn about the complex and contradictory nature of man.

Liberal social engineering programs are based on the utopian notion that government can perfect human nature. This idea is based on Rousseau's theory that man is naturally good and that he can be perfected by external influences. The young Ronald Reagan abandoned liberalism when he noticed that government social programs make men worse and inevitably backfire with disruptive unintended consequences. Man is damaged when he is manipulated according to false ideas about human nature.

ONE WORLD CULT

Chapter 8 will explore the concept of one-world pantheism, which is an essentially modernist and utopian idea that liberal dreamers use to gain political cover in a Christian culture.

Chapter 7 considered how Hegel propagated the cult of modernism by building faith in the inevitability of progress based upon impersonal forces of history. *"Progress"* must eventually lead to *"utopia"* in which the great *"oneness"* of pantheism will be fully manifested worldwide. The magical thinking of German Idealism, the cult of pantheism, the New Age Movement, and the United Nations Agenda 21 action plan[126] are the fabrication behind this befuddled myth.

Defined by The Global Oneness Commitment,[127] **one worlders** are *"those who advocate the abolition of nations, working to hand over power to a single-world government similar in structure to the present United Nations; off-shoots of the United World Federalists founded in the 1930s."* Progressive political parties developed in the United States around the turn of the 20th century, to assist the ideology advocating power and structure changes necessary for this governmental action. Some one worlders deny they are pantheists – Deists, Freemasons, Unitarian-universalists and Christian liberals believe in God but are ideologically modernist and utopian. The Masons use the motto *"The brotherhood of man under the fatherhood of God."* Under this winsome slogan, the functional pantheism of one-world dreams can get political cover in a Christian culture – Nelson Rockefeller, a one worlder, often quoted the Masonic motto. Paradoxically, many Masons abhor one worlders.

MAGICAL THINKING

The presumption that wishful thinking is a defining characteristic of liberals is incomplete – unfortunately, their views are not merely a case of childish faith in what they desire to believe. Progressively liberal individuals are bewitched when they open their hearts and minds to the seduction of **pantheism** (belief in a Cosmos of complete unity with sacred Nature amid a vision of progress leading to one-world utopia) and **neopaganism** (the idolatrous worship of nature). The dangerous combination imprisons their hearts and blinds their minds.

Social liberals have fallen under a sort of evil enchantment, resulting in spiritual bondage – they indulge in magical thinking because of spiritual beguilement. Modern progressives hate conservatives who throw cold water on their delusions and call their principles nonsense – they are as deeply obsessed with enchanted dreams as Gollum[128] was with the magical ring he called *"my precious."* The fantasy of world-wide utopia *"oneness"* accounts for the obsession with transnational associations. – coalitions like the United Nations and European Union are considered building blocks towards a world federation that would lead to a centralized global government.

From the *Lord of the Rings* movie

Conservatives believe in American national sovereignty and are opposed to the *"one world"* dreams of modernists. According to the American founders' natural law theory, man was designed to live in nations, not empires or international commonwealths. According to Montesquieu, national republics are more likely to provide citizens with

---

[126] (Strzelczyk and Rothschild 2009) (United.Nations, Agenda 21 Core Publication 1992) (United.Nations, Resolution Adopted by the General Assembly 1997)
[127] (Global Oneness 2010)
[128] A fictional character introduced in J. R. R. Tolkien's fantasy novel **The Hobbit**. (Tolkien, The Hobbit 1937) (Jackson 2001-2003)

freedom, order and protection of rights than any monarchy, empire, transnational commonwealth or international association. Some current conservatives are concerned that globalists are fomenting a secret power grabbing conspiracy involving the international elite. Unfortunately, the danger is far greater than imagination – millions of liberal modernists have openly spoken of one world government objectives for the last two and a half centuries.

WE SHALL BE BROTHERS

"Daughter of Elysium... Thy magic powers re-unite what custom's sword has divided. Beggars become Princes' brothers where thy gentle wing abides. Be embraced, you millions! This kiss to the entire world!" Excerpts from **Ode to Joy**, *Friedrich von Schiller, 1785*

The false hope of world brotherhood began in the West during the 18th century Romantic Movement, most notably with Genevan political philosopher, Jean-Jacques Rousseau and German romantic poets such as Johann Wolfgang von Goethe and Friedrich von Schiller (1759-1805). Schiller, who was either a Freemason or was sympathetic to their ideals, wrote the poem *Ode to Joy*, which celebrates the brotherhood and unity of all mankind – Ludwig van Beethoven (1770-1827) later put it to triumphal music in the final movement of his Ninth Symphony that was completed in 1824. Subsequently, Hegel's Idealism, New England Transcendentalism, the New Age Movement and environmentalism have further circulated the dream.

Global aspirations are not limited to the elite, and there is no need for secrecy or conspiracies. Millions of Europeans have been deceived by one-world fantasies and the cult of multiculturalism, speaking about it openly. Classicist Louis Markos[129] met an Austrian man who rejected the idea of being *"Austrian"* and insisted on life as an *"earth-man."* Some Europeans are so adrift and disoriented that they have lost the will to propagate Western culture or have enough children to perpetuate their national identities.

BLATANT NAZI INTENTIONS AND INSISTENT LIBERAL DENIALS

Winston Churchill

Utopian modernist leaders who made no secret about their one-world aspirations were the primary cause of great cataclysms in the 20th century. Nazism was not a secret conspiracy – Adolf Hitler (1889-1945) spoke publically and wrote blatantly about all his intentions.[130] To the Western world's amazement, Germany accomplished almost every objective. Hitler's Western progressive contemporaries refused to believe that he actually meant what he said. Sir Winston Churchill (1874-1965) rejected the temptation to live in denial and warned the world to take him seriously. This stand annoyed the British government, so Churchill was consigned to political wilderness, where he remained until the German invasion of Poland on September 1, 1939.

The Western liberal denials about Hitler's ambitions are an example of magical thinking – present liberal insistence that Muslim jihadists pose no danger is a similar enchantment. Liberals of the 1950s and 1960s likewise demonized those who warned about Communism. The Communists were more deceitful than the brazen Nazis about their plans, yet nearly every horrible action was predicted by J. Edgar Hoover (1895-1972), Bureau of Investigation Director (FBI predecessor), in the 1920s. Hoover simply read the published Marxist-Leninists works and considered the words sincere. Progressive liberals refused to consider it, of course.

---

[129] (Louis Markos n.d.)
[130] (Hitler 1925)

FABIANS VERSUS MARXISTS

A century ago, liberal progressives openly called for socialism through gradual democratic measures instead of a revolutionary approach. This **Fabian socialism** technique was named after the British Fabian Society in honor of the Roman general Fabius Maximus, who advocated a strategy of harassment and attrition tactics rather than head-on battles against Hannibal. Their utopian goals were identical to the ultimate goals of Communism, however they proposed a milder, gradually developed democratic socialism as the means of *"progress,"* thinking that education and social engineering would gently refine human nature in preparation for one-world perfection. Fabians wanted to bring about world government through democratic socialism, the spread of democracy, nation-building and world federalism.

In contrast, Marxist-Leninists (the correct name for Soviet communists) wanted to bring about totalitarian socialism by grinding men down, then building new communist men out of the ashes – using deliberately harsh methods to improve human nature quickly. They employed conquest, proxy-wars, secret police, terror, genocide, subversive front groups, propaganda and instigation of revolution, to achieve their global goals. It was thought that once man achieved faultlessness, the state would spontaneously wither away and all people would enjoy utopian bliss in perfect freedom. The preposterous theory that a totalitarian socialist dictatorship would gently dissolve while the military commissars went fishing and the secret police happily flung wide the gulag doors is beyond laughable – both Marxist-Leninists and liberals are magical thinkers.

AMERICAN MODERNIST POLITICS

American Republican progressives of the Teddy Roosevelt (1858-1919) variety put faith in economic, scientific and technological progress, and selective governmental reforms and interventions applied on a pragmatic, piecemeal basis. They believed in *"progress,"* but were vague about where progress was heading. Although Teddy was ambivalent about the captains of industry, Republican progressives of his day generally valued large international corporate enterprise as the engine of economic progress and prosperity – some CEO's of international corporations were one worlders.

The Fabian vision captured the left wing of the Democratic Party in America, even attracting some moderate Democrats like Harry Truman (1884-1972) and Hubert Humphrey (1911-1978), who cherished one-world dreams. Republican leaders like Wendell Willkie (1892-1944), Herbert Hoover (1874-1964), Thomas Dewey (1902-1971), Nelson Rockefeller (1908-1979), Richard Nixon (1913-1994) and Henry Kissinger (1923-) were essentially modernists.

A NEW WORLD ORDER

> *"We stand today at a unique and extraordinary moment. The crisis in the Persian Gulf, as grave as it is, also offers a rare opportunity to move toward an historic period of cooperation. Out of these troubled times...* ***a new world order*** *can emerge: a new era – freer from the threat of terror, stronger in the pursuit of justice, and more secure in the quest for peace. An era in which the nations of the world, East and West, North and South, can prosper and live in harmony. A hundred generations have searched for this elusive path to peace, while a thousand wars raged across the span of human endeavor. Today that new world is struggling to be born, a world quite different from the one we've known. A world where the rule of law supplants the rule of the jungle. A world in which nations recognize the shared responsibility for freedom and justice. A world where the strong*

respect the rights of the weak. This is the vision that I shared with President Gorbachev in Helsinki. He and other leaders from Europe, the Gulf, and around the world understand that how we manage this crisis today could shape the future for generations to come." George H.W. Bush, 1990

Former Bush Presidents

On September 11, 1990, President George H.W. Bush (1924-) spoke before a joint session of Congress, concerning the Persian Gulf War[131] – stating that the war offered an opportunity for *"a new world order"* to emerge. On February 27, 1991, he halted the American military when it had almost encircled the elite Iraqi forces, because he questioned his own authority to finish the job under the United Nations allies association, enabling the Republican Guard to flee home to Saddam Hussein.[132] The President's immersion in internationalism blunted his sense of national sovereignty, and weakened his confidence in his Constitutional authority as Commander-in-Chief.

President George W. Bush (1946-) had a somewhat stronger sense of national sovereignty in matters of war than his father, which earned him the hostility of internationalist Europeans and liberal Democrats. However, his sense of United States authority was not strong enough to enforce standing law concerning illegal immigration, or secure the border with Mexico.

The educated progeny of modernist businessmen became ambitious and talented in scientific and technical pursuits, and developed science fiction cult fantasies about human beings traveling in space to confront other humanoids on distant planets. Many futuristic authors wrote about a future earth ruled by one world government. The *Star Wars*[133] movies and *Star Trek*[134] television series portrayed planetary confederations that had supplanted earthly governments as galaxy power bases. According to these story lines, the *"one-world"* dreams of today will ultimately seem quaint, when *"one galaxy"* ideology will become the next enlightened fad, and the *"force"* will be with us – to be exact, spiritual pantheism will reign.

GRANDE DAME OF CONSERVATISM

As explained in Chapter 7, all modernism programs are alien to Western conservative values and Christianity. This includes the Republican version of modernism that Phyllis Schlafly (1924-) repudiated in her famous book, *A Choice, Not An Echo,*[135] which sold 6,000,000 copies. The work detailed how the liberal *"Rockefeller Republican"* wing had manipulated the Party's choice of nominees in several elections to recommend candidates like Wendell Willkie and Dwight Eisenhower, and called on conservatives to rally against the liberal agenda and offer a true conservative for the presidential nomination. Schlafly's implicit rejection of Republican modernism was the indispensable foundation for the conservatism of the culture war.

Interestingly, this Grande Dame of conservatism co-sponsored the September 17, 2007 Republican candidate *"values voters"* debate. Rudy Giuliani (1944-), Mitt Romney (1947-) and John McCain (1936-), who have tried to blend conservatism and modernism, were conspicuously absent from the debate. Alan Keyes (1950-), who rejects the dilution of conservatism with modernism, was prominently present.

---

[131] (Bush, Public Papers - 1990 - September 1990)
[132] (Bush, Public Papers - 1991 - February 1991)
[133] (Lucas 1977)
[134] (Roddenberry 1966)
[135] (Schlafly 1964)

Conflict between three mutually exclusive world views will take place during the first half of the 21st century, namely: 1) Modernism and Postmodernism versus; 2) Conservatism and Christianity versus; 3) Radical Islam. Each of these three antagonists must repudiate the other two. Only one philosophy can remain standing in the end – tolerance is not an option. Conservatism and Christianity are increasingly intolerant towards modernism and postmodernism – as the evil implications of those doctrines become clearer, a radical repudiation will be unavoidable. Meanwhile, the jihadist Muslims hate everyone and seem determined to generate hatred in all non-Muslims.

Citizens today are better prepared to fight for Christianity and conservatism than society was in 1920-1945, when modernists had taken over mainstream Protestant denominations, and orthodox doctrine disappeared from the pulpit in a majority of churches. The conservative political movement was on the ropes as progressives took over the Republican Party and Fabian style socialists took over the Democratic Party. There are also better odds of defeating Darwinism, the creation myth for modernism, today than in 1945.

CREATION MYTH FOR MODERNISM

Charles Darwin

Every world view must include a creation myth or story of origins in order to have intellectual, cultural and historical traction. Charles Darwin (1809-1882) supplied the creation myth for biological sciences, while Albert Einstein (1879-1955) completed one for physics and astronomy. Darwin lived during the same generation as Karl Marx – both men were science buffs who posited that progressive development can emerge from material elements. The cult of science as the engine of progress reached its apex when the Crystal Palace was erected in Hyde Park, London, England, to house the **Great Exhibition of 1851**, when more than 14,000 exhibitors from around the globe assembled to demonstrate the latest Industrial Revolution technology.

In 1851, Darwin and Marx both lived in England. Marx was the London correspondent for the New York Herald Tribune. Darwin's works entitled *Geological Observations on Coral Reefs, Volcanic Islands, and on South America* and *Fossil Circhipeda of Great Britain, Section Lepadidae, Monograph of the Circhipeda* would earn him the Royal Society's[136] Royal Medal[137] in 1853, and solidify his reputation as a biologist.

MARX AND DARWIN

Hegel slipped the mystical idea of continuously changing and improving mankind into Western imagination – this mysticism is incompatible with science, which deals with the empirical study of material things. Marx appeared on the scene with a solution to this problem – he offered a system of progress towards utopia through strictly material means. His theory of economic determinism was compatible with both materialism and science. Furthermore, his premise was

---

[136] The Royal Society is a learned society for science, possibly the oldest in existence. Founded in 1660, it was granted a Royal Charter by King Charles II and was initially an extension of the "Invisible College," with the founders intending it to be a place of research and discussion. The Society today acts as a scientific advisor to the British government, receiving a parliamentary grant-in-aid. The Society also acts as the UK's Academy of Sciences, funding research fellowships and scientific start-up companies. (Royal Society n.d.)

[137] The Royal Medal, also known as The Queen's Medal, is a silver-gilt medal awarded each year by the Royal Society, two for "the most important contributions to the advancement of natural knowledge" and one for "distinguished contributions in the applied sciences" made within the Commonwealth of Nations. The award was created by George IV and first awarded in 1826. (Royal Medal n.d.)

congruent with historicism, progress and utopia, and filled a gaping hole in modernism by reconciling science with the utopian cult of progress.

Once progressives recognized that Marxist presumption was essential to their program, they refused to entertain questions concerning the model's illogical aspects (i.e., harsh materialism welded to magical *"progress"* thinking and mystical utopia.) The formula, [*material thesis + material antithesis = mystical synthesis*], is obviously preposterous, but enchanted beliefs enabled an outrageously glossed over version of the Marx method to succeed. Human agendas often trump the search for truth because most men are rascals and few are angels – the rascals of modernism swallowed Marxist nonsense because it served their agenda.

Marx and Darwin needed each other to gain widespread popularity. Scientifically minded people had to envision biological advancement emerging from mere matter before they could accept the notion of economic determinism resulting in human progress. Economically oriented people had to see progress rising from economic class warfare before they believed biologic evolutionary progress. Evolution was institutionally established as the creation myth of modernism and became indispensable to modernist plans, which is precisely why public exposure of the scientific anomalies and fallacies meets with fierce political opposition from the left. Liberals fear that if the evolutionary story of origins were exposed as a myth, modernism would be threatened — they are correct.

EVOLUTION MYTH

Thomas Kuhn

One weakness of modern science was described by American physicist and philosopher Thomas Kuhn (1922-1996) in *The Structure of Scientific Revolutions*.[138] He noted that **prevailing paradigms** (the preferred scientific model) often become official doctrine for the science establishment. Most subsequent research is then devoted to supporting the standard and reconciling **anomalies** (facts that contradict the model) with the established system.

The education establishment indoctrinates students in the prevailing paradigm, propagates the creation myth, and goes to great trouble to conceal that it is a manufactured fairy tale by teaching evolution stories. The *Just So Stories for Little Children*,[139] by British author Rudyard Kipling (1865-1936), are highly fantasized origin stories with fantastic imaginary accounts of how various natural phenomena came about – such as *How the Leopard Got His Spots*. These fictional narratives explain facts using legend and folk tale themes to explain how a particular animal was modified from an original to its current form by the acts of man, or some magical being.

Contrary to popular belief, evolution science did not win on scientific merit. The agenda of modernism to have a story of origins trumped the search for truth, and myths became the prevailing paradigm. The evolution model cannot stand without magisterial authority from the science establishment and educational indoctrination.

> ### *Fred Critique*
>
> *The education establishment indoctrinates students in the prevailing paradigm, propagates the creation myth, and goes to great trouble to conceal that it is a manufactured fairy tale by teaching evolution stories.*

---

[138] (Kuhn 1962)
[139] (Kipling 1902)

VULNERABLE EVOLUTION THEORY

Evolutionary theory is open to challenge on the following grounds:

1. The mechanism for evolving from one species to another through random genetic mutations does not work. Evolutionists themselves cannot agree on the method or support various theories with hard facts.

2. The fossil record shows that species stasis is the norm and large gaps always exist between species. A new school of evolutionists, inspired by Stephen J. Gould (1941-2002), accepts this fact. The alleged missing links between species are invariably invalidated by evidence, although the withdrawal process is slow. Yet the education establishment continued teaching discredited missing links for generations after cutting-edge scientists rejected them.

3. Cambrian rock has fossils of 70+ phyla of animals – no ancestors for any of these animals appear in Precambrian rock. No new phyla of animals have appeared after the Cambrian era, and over half of original phyla are now extinct.[140]

4. The incredible complexity of species is harmonized through integrated and sophisticated designs. Collections of genetic accidents cannot spontaneously produce a design – a creature that is a jerry-built monstrosity of accumulated accidents cannot survive the harsh wilderness and compete with sophisticated species that enjoy integrated designs.

5. Teachers of evolution routinely display variations within species (microevolution) as examples of evolution to other species (macroevolution). Since the discovery of DNA in 1953, evolutionists have known that such claims are fraudulent. Variation within a species requires no new information in the DNA code – evolution to new species requires an immense amount of new information.

6. Science authorities respond to criticism by persecuting dissenters, who are often denied university tenure and publication of papers criticizing the evolution model in peer review journals. These nonconformists are then rebuked as illegitimate scientists because of the lack of published papers. The establishment has rigged the game to make sure the favored theory wins. It is an agenda of power that has nothing to do with the pursuit of truth.

THE GREAT RATIONAL MODERNIST

Albert Einstein

Albert Einstein (1879-1955) was born into a Jewish family, but became a pantheist after reading the work of Dutch philosopher Baruch Spinoza (1632-1677). Spinoza was excommunicated from his Jewish congregation for heretical beliefs about the Hebrew Bible's validity, the nature of divinity, and pantheism – his books were later added to the Catholic Church's *Index of Forbidden Books*.[141]

Pantheism is the myth that "god" is everything, everything is "god," and everything is "one" – it embraces the notion that the sacred universe (nature) and God are identical in all-encompassing, cosmic unity. Pantheists do not believe in a personal creator god who shares human form or attributes. Hegel's pantheism was the basis for his historicism, progressivism

---

[140] (Cambrian Fossils 2002-2011)
[141] The Index of Forbidden Books was a listing of publications prohibited by the Catholic Church, first printed by order of Pope Paul IV in 1559, that aimed to protect faith and morals by banning immoral and theologically incorrect books. The final (20th) edition was published in 1948, and was officially discontinued in 1966 by Pope Paul VI.

and utopianism – mystical, impersonal forces of history would compel the world of man to progress. In contrast, Spinoza and Einstein held to a rational pantheism that believed all things are connected to each other in a systematic way. In other words, the cosmos is like a mathematical systems model, or a machine – a closed system of interlocking parts that is all-inclusive and self-supporting.

Christians, Jews and Muslims believe a transcendent God created the world – Creator and creation are radically different. An interlocking system is not necessary to hold the cosmos together because God sustains His open system creation.

Einstein assumed his theory of relativity must be true because it was simple, elegant, aesthetically satisfying and easily grasped with simple principles. His model's beauty is the purely rational design of a harmonious cosmos, which is more complete and convincing than any previous concept. Unfortunately, Einstein painted a picture that is inconsistent with the real world – his universe is fundamentally different from God's creation.

EMBARRASSING DISCONTINUITIES

Einstein spent the second half of his career searching for a *"unified field theory."* Quantum mechanics, which governs the behavior of atoms and molecules, is incompatible with general relativity. So Einstein sought a model that would unite the greater world physics of matter and energy with the microcosmic world of atoms. He failed, and no one has yet succeeded. The **String theory** of multiple dimensions and multiple worlds is the latest and most bizarre attempt of theoretical physics to produce a unified field theory. Without one, Einstein's cosmos collapses – all things must tightly interconnect or his vision of creation is proven false. However, if God sustains an open, loosely woven system, discontinuities are not a problem.

The goal of physics is to devise comprehensive rules that organize and explain all perceptible phenomena, but the real world has proven to be stubbornly irregular. The physics of atoms is discontinuous with the physics of falling apples. Einstein's model has no practical use for explaining falling fruit – scientists still rely on Isaac Newton's (1642-1727)

Johannes Kepler

structure of matter. The best Massachusetts Institute of Technology (MIT) physicists argue that Einstein is reconciled with Newton concerning the force of gravity, but they cannot logically clarify why apples fall straight down. Relativity mathematics cannot be readily used to chart the velocity of a falling apple, if at all.

Likewise, the physics of a falling apple is discontinuous with the physics of an orbiting satellite. The concept of using Einstein's theory to calculate orbits and guide space ships through the solar system is scientific propaganda. MIT scientists actually use an updated version of Johannes Kepler's (1571-1630) laws of planetary motion[142] to compute orbits around planets, while giving Einstein credit.

The expectation that Einstein's general relativity is useful for computing the spiral movement of galaxies, since his idea of a warped space-time continuum seems logically appropriate for the curving motion of a fluid vortex, does not work. There are only two possibilities for this failure: 1) Einstein's gravity is too weak to account for galaxy behavior; or 2)

---

[142] In astronomy, Kepler's laws give a description of planet motion around the Sun. The laws are: 1) The orbit of every planet is an ellipse with the Sun at one of the two foci; 2) A line joining a planet and the Sun sweeps out equal areas during equal intervals of time; 3) The square of the orbital period of a planet is directly proportional to the cube of the semi-major axis of its orbit. Kepler's laws are strictly only valid for a lone (not affected by the gravity of other planets) zero-mass object orbiting the Sun; a physical impossibility, but they provide a useful starting point for calculating planet orbits. (Kepler's laws of planetary motion 1609)

there is not enough cosmic matter. The science establishment ruled out the possibility that Einstein might be wrong. Instead, they use two plug figures to make the math work – **dark matter** is an imaginary substance that has no grounds for existence other than to make Einstein's theory work, and **black holes** are imaginary vortexes of immense gravitational pull. Einstein even used his own plug figure, the **cosmological constant**, which modified his original theory to achieve a stationary universe. He abandoned the concept after American astronomer Edwin Hubble (1889-1953) discovered that the degree of *"Doppler redshift"* observed in light spectra from other galaxies increases in proportion to its distance from Earth, which helped establish that the universe is expanding.

The 1998 discovery of cosmic acceleration has renewed interest in a cosmological constant, but scientists are cheating by using plug figures. These rascals have an agenda to support the prevailing paradigm, which is necessary to maintain the modernist program. Einstein must succeed, even if a tailor-made, imaginary universe is required. The physics of orbiting satellites and galaxies is discontinuous – the mathematical explanation for galaxies and the infant data from galaxy clusters may also be discontinuous, early reports indicate surprise.

A DISCONTINUOUS UNIVERSE

What is wrong with having a cosmos that is 1) discontinuous between molecules and apples, 2) discontinuous between apples and orbiting satellites, and 3) discontinuous between planets and galaxies? If the cosmos must sustain itself though tightly interlocking connections in a closed system, the existence of three internal discontinuities must inevitably cause it to fly apart. Scientists prefer the interlocking system because it is understandable through mathematics, and most of Einstein's work was blackboard math. They refuse to concede to erratic unpredictability and reject Einstein because he is essential to progressive dogma. Nothing is wrong with a discontinuous universe if God is the creator and sustainer of a loosely woven cosmos.

THE BIG BANG MYTH

The Big Bang theory is based on Einstein's assumption that everything in existence is tightly interwoven. If the cosmos was once confined to a single dense spot that exploded, the idea of interrelation is plausible. Astronomers noticed a Doppler redshift in distant galaxy light that implied movement away from center. If proven true, the cosmos is expanding, perhaps as a result of an initial explosion. This highly speculative idea offers a story of origins in accordance with the modernist world view.

Many controversies and difficulties plague the Big Bang theory, and it has been reformulated many times. The following critique was independently developed by Fred Hutchison, and has been limited to three points.[143]

1. Einstein assumed a stationary universe but his mathematics did not work, so he invented a plug figure to make the math succeed and produce a stable and symmetrical cosmos. He called his plug figure the *"cosmological constant,"* which he abandoned when he learned that the cosmos is not stable. Some big bang theorists have continued to play with cosmological constants in pursuit of symmetry, because Einstein said the cosmos must be symmetrical. Unfortunately, the pursuit of symmetry through plug figures has eluded science. This undermines the foundation Einstein laid for a big bang theory.

[143] (F. Hutchison, Brief History of Conservatism 2009)

2. Big Bang theory cannot account for the three discontinuities mentioned above. If they can be explained away with plug figures, the premise can survive for a while. However, if the attempt to gloss over the asymmetrical discontinuities fails, then the theory must collapse.

3. Einstein's theory is a mathematical model of a closed system. Such models are unstable and fragile because a slight change in variables can produce a radical difference in output, and the slightest glitch can produce a system collapse. Anyone who has worked with computers understands this observable fact.

Einstein's cosmos exists on a knife edge. If things were slightly different in one direction, the cosmos would collapse; in the opposite direction, the universe would explode. Therefore, Big Bang theorists have been riding the bucking bronco of an unstable and fragile creation. They adjust the formula a little and are thrown off the horse, which is why the theory has never stabilized after forty years.

A FRAGILE COSMOS

*"There does not exist today a general scientific consensus about the importance of greenhouse warming from rising levels of carbon dioxide. In fact, many climate specialists now agree that actual observations from weather satellites show no global warming whatsoever... Energy is essential for all economic growth, and fossil fuels provide today's principal global energy source. In a world in which poverty is the greatest social pollutant, any restriction on energy use that inhibits economic growth should be viewed with caution. For this reason, we consider 'carbon taxes' and other drastic control policies ... to be ill-advised, premature, wrought with economic danger, and likely to be counterproductive... We believe the Kyoto Protocol – to curtail carbon dioxide emissions from only part of the world community – is dangerously simplistic, quite ineffective, and economically destructive to jobs and standards-of-living. We consider the drastic emission control policies deriving from the Kyoto conference – lacking credible support from the underlying science – to be ill-advised and premature." **Leipzig Declaration, 2005**

Some Christians have accepted the idea of an unstable and fragile cosmos, marveling at how precise God's creation is in light of the detail that any slight variation would dissolve everything. Unfortunately, it only seems volatile when viewed through Einstein's frail and unbalanced mathematical systems models. The cosmos is actually incredibly secure – let computer models crash as they will, the solid creation remains.

GLOBAL WARMING FALACY

Because the science establishment believes the universe is unsound, they assume disasters will occur when man tinkers with the environment. The latest episode of disaster paranoia is the global climate theory that makes fluctuating warming and cooling predictions based on mathematical computer programs. Since the models are erratic, scientists think earth's climate is wobbly and prone to disaster – any fiddling will cause calamitous reactions.

Computer programs with multiple variables are an invitation to cheating. Programmers have no alternative but to tweak models to make them behave. Every adjustment has the implicit bias of making the model perform as desired. If global warming is expected, the fine-tuning continues until the model coughs up worldwide sweltering.

The amount of global climate change varies radically from model to model, which is probable with heavily tweaked plans. Global *"green"* conferences touting huge government, corporate, media and community sponsors are the latest fad to promote one-world thought, with themes of pulling together to save the globe. International forums (many are influenced by The United Nations) cherry pick agendas to ensure reporting only on curriculum that illustrates the desired view. The push for environmentally friendly design, technology and business to converge into global green initiatives has become a sacred conviction – often times labeling good products *"sinful"* in order to boost special interest favorites claiming new and *"sustainable"* products.[144] Then the moderator takes the microphone, states that the official committee is in unanimous agreement with the tweaked findings, declares the case closed, and asserts that no further discussion is needed.[145] We are then admonished to get busy rescuing the world. In the end, they will warn us that the only workable solution is world federation.

THE CULTURE WAR

Four self-destructive properties of modernism and postmodernism have brought forth our present culture war, as explored here in a somewhat rhetorical fashion. The implications of these ideas and movements will be discussed further starting in Chapter 10.

1. **Denial of American National Sovereignty.** If the forces of progress are moving us towards world government, then American national sovereignty stands in the way of progress. For this reason, when America goes to war on the authority of the Constitution and the assumption of national sovereignty, liberals call it an *"arrogant"* and *"illegal war."* They believe the only legal war is one fought under the aegis of an international body or alliance. Unfortunately, such bodies are unlikely to put a premium on American safety.

   Liberals approve of open borders because a flood of illegal aliens will promote multiculturalism and progress towards the great *"oneness"* of a one-world government. If America were to enforce its borders, it would be acting like a sovereign state – and liberals do not want America to be a real nation. They want it to be a province under the auspices of world government.

   Modernists incorrectly blame World War I and II on nationalism. World War I was caused by competition between European empires that did not respect nation-states. As explained earlier in this chapter, World War II in Europe was initiated by conflict between two modernist, one-world ideologies that did not respect nation-states. World War II in the Pacific was instigated by the Japanese Empire's belligerency. The Western patriots who opposed and defeated Hitler and Japanese Prime Minister Hideki Tōjō (1884-1948) were nationalists.

2. **Denial of the Existence of Evil.** If we are creatures of a pantheistic world evolving towards one-world utopia, there can be no such thing as evil because *"everything is god"* and *"god is everything."* Everyone must be included and interconnected in such a world. People assumed to be evil are merely slower in progressing towards utopia, or are stuck in the past. However, conservatives who seek to exclude those presumed to be evil are not tolerated. Wars against governments that conservatives consider evil must be forbidden. Therefore, the current President of Iran, Mahmoud Ahmadinejad (1956-) – who wants an atomic bomb, seeks to destroy Israel, denies the holocaust, and is sponsoring terrorists – should not be perceived as evil and should be invited to speak at Columbia

---

[144] Governments around the globe have created legislation to phase out incandescent light bulbs, aiming to encourage the use and technological development of more energy-efficient alternatives, such as compact fluorescent and LED lamps, which are more expensive, more dangerous and less effective.

[145] **The Leipzig Declaration on Global Climate Change** is a Science & Environmental Policy Project (SEPP) statement seeking to refute the claim of scientific consensus on the global warming issue. The declaration opposes the global warming hypothesis and the Kyoto Protocol. (Leipzig Declaration 2005)

Mahmoud Ahmadinejad

University. Divisive conservatives who think that Columbia is promoting evil by inviting Ahmadinejad should not be allowed to speak.

Richard Weaver (1910-1963), an American scholar primarily known as a shaper of mid-20th century conservatism, wrote that *"those who have a false view of the world cannot properly understand current events."* Liberals have a distorted concept of Ahmadinejad's visit because they have a twisted view of the world. Though not crazy, they cling to a foolish world view. Just as scientists would rather create an imaginary universe than give up on Einstein, liberals are more willing to sputter nutty things about current events than surrender their insane mental orientation of global society.

3. **Denial of a Universal Moral Law.** If we are participating in a march of progress toward utopia, the moral law established in biblical days has no bearing on the present *"enlightened"* generation. As future peoples become more progressive, they will cast off retrograde ethics and develop better moral codes. Regrettably, when universal moral law lapses, mankind immediately descends to behavior that is right in their own eyes and the wicked run amok. When this happens, the populace self-destructs.

4. **Denial of Western Spiritual and Culture Heritage.** Modernists want to break free from Western heritage and practice multiculturalism in order to usher in the glorious one-world culture of the future. Alas, to renounce Western high culture is to rebel against civilization itself. When cut off from the rich intellectual, cultural and spiritual treasuries of the past, humans cease to be civilized and revert to barbarism. The primitivism of current music and art indicates that society has fallen from brilliant culture into degradation while under the influence of modernism.

SAVING CIVILIZATION

In the name of civilization itself, we must rid ourselves of the delusions of modernism, so that we can defend culture from the barbarians. The external barbarians who hate our society are the Muslim jihadists. The internal barbarians are multiculturalists who systematically deconstruct our traditions in the name of progress. Ridding ourselves of the fantasy utopia will free us to rebuild culture. Many tools for rebuilding are found in the five historical streams of conservatism: Christian conservatism, Traditionalist conservatism, Natural law conservatism, Neoconservatism and Libertarianism.

Modernism is an enchantment of dark spiritual forces; therefore we face a spiritual battle. Only the power of God can defeat such a formidable enemy. We participate in God's cosmic battle through prayer and faith. Let us fall to our knees and pray our way to mighty victories, and rise up to be about our Father's business.

MODERNISM'S WAR AGAINST THE PAST

The first call to intellectually dismiss the past was made by 17th century philosophers who conceived of an odd proto-modernism in the midst of an essentially conservative Baroque civilization. Modernists of the 19th century were increasingly hostile to the West's cultural heritage. This trend culminated in the shocking radicalism of John Dewey, the most influential voice in the education establishment during the 20th century. Chapter 9 will explore how great cultural disillusionment after World War I lent credibility to many anti-western modernist fads.

Edith Wharton

Pulitzer Prize winner and American writer, Edith Wharton (1862-1937), told a story about high society in Old New York during the 1870s in *The Age of Innocence*,[146] in which she borrowed from historical wisdom to understand and critique the follies of her own generation. Victorian conservatism of that era was the result of the spiritual revival during the Civil War, and the reaction to the upsurge of modernism and the unconventional lifestyle revolt against aristocratic social and political norms (a.k.a. bohemian romanticism) earlier in the century.

As explained in Chapter 4, the call to intellectually dismiss the past was first made by 17th century philosophers Francis Bacon and Rene Descartes, who conceived of an odd proto-modernism in the midst of the essentially conservative Baroque civilization. The misguided 18th century French Enlightenment philosophers were hostile to the Catholic High Middle Ages, and falsely labeled the blossoming civilization a continuation of the Dark Ages. Although this outrageous **canard**[147] has been thoroughly debunked by historians, the myth continues to be propagated by modernist narrators on the History channel.[148]

Hostility toward Western cultural heritage increased during the 19th century. In contrast to the way Wharton considered past wisdom, arch-modernists Sigmund Freud (1856-1939), William James (1842-1910) and John Dewey (1859-1952) argued that the cultural past should be dismissed and replaced with a whole new enlightenment of modernity. This trend culminated in the shocking radicalism of John Dewey, the most influential voice in the education establishment during the 20th century.

CULTURAL DISILLUSIONMENT

The great cultural disillusionment after World War I lent credibility to many anti-western progressive fads. Freud, James and Dewey were among the writers who wanted to dismiss cultural and intellectual heritage. From the start, modernists have had no interest in sharing the stage with proponents of traditional wisdom – they wanted to program the future as the new masters. This was just as true of Francis Bacon as it was of John Dewey.

THE CONSERVATIVE REACTION

It is encouraging to note that the foolishness of modernism is the breeding ground for traditional conservatism. Modernist deceptions concerning human nature have provoked many conservative reactions. Men such as Edmund Burke, G.K. Chesterton, Richard Weaver, J.R.R. Tolkien, C.S. Lewis and Russell Kirk became traditionalists in response to modernism and the positive influence of Christianity. However, not all reactionary conservatives were Christians.

Edith Wharton, who was at best a nominal Christian, became a traditionalist conservative after attempting to live her youth according to modernist notions of personal *"liberation,"* which she found unlivable. In *French Ways and*

---

[146] (Wharton, The Age of Innocence 1920)
[147] An unfounded or false, deliberately misleading story.
[148] (A&E Television Networks, LLC. 1996-2011)

Their Meaning she wrote, *"There is nothing like a revolution for making people conservative."*[149] Wharton was not interested in political theory, but in the complex interplay of men and women in society. She was a trenchant observer of the attitudes, ideals, illusions, denials and frustrations of individual people as they groped their way through the labyrinth of life – critical of the *"childish and self-deceiving"* ways that modernists try to *"refuse to themselves pain."* She debunked the modernist delusion that human nature can be remade to serve our purposes – one of her fictional characters believed that denying evil prevents it from coming into being, and threw herself into all the foolish self-help fads and faux spiritual cults of the 1920s. Humorously, Wharton was a mischievous closet traditionalist. She amused her reader by laughing at traditional society, while setting the stage for defending the best elements of tradition and exposing the folly of modernism.

FROM REBEL TO REACTIONARY

Edith Wharton was born into the respectable Jones family of old money. The family was so prominent in New York society that social climbers spoke of *"keeping up with the Joneses,"* an expression that survived the fall of the dynasty into obscurity. As a style setter, young Edith attempted to become the best dressed young woman in New York, as her mother had been. After surveying the artistic grandeur, brilliant conversation and bohemian ways of Paris, the famous Jones girl stopped trying to keep up with the Joneses. She rebelled against the traditional convention-bound New York high society and ridiculed the social system in print.

As a writer, Wharton tried to follow the example of Charles Dickens (1812-1870) and William Thackeray (1811-1863) in her satires and caricatures of society. She gradually began to see through the follies of modernism and discovered that the social mores and traditions of old New York embodied heaps of wisdom about human nature, and advanced from rebel to reactionary.

THE HUMAN TRAGEDY

Wharton embraced the two classical masks of comedy and tragedy – her novels are full of wit, levity and sarcastic teasing, but end conveying a tragic view of life. She observed modernists flinging themselves into disaster, while traditionalists lived decent and dignified lives of quiet tragedy. The traditionalist stoically endured personal tragedy and the confining limitations of society because he enjoyed the consolations of virtue, family and society, and the agreeable amenities of a civilized and cultured life. The old regime French had this pleasant solace in mind when they spoke of *"the sweetness of life."*

Wharton did not formally subscribe to the Christian doctrine of original sin and the fall of man. However, she had an instinctive understanding that there is no escape from the self-defeating tangles of human perversity and the iron decrees of nature. Therefore, she recognized the futility of modernist hopes of escaping depravity traps and natural tragedies.

NO ESCAPE TO A WORLD OF DREAMS

Newland Archer, the dreamy and inarticulate protagonist of Wharton's 1921 Pulitzer Prize-winning book ***The Age of Innocence***, fell in love with the exotic and articulate Madame Ellen Olenska, who was born into a prominent New

---

[149] (Wharton, French Ways and Their Meaning 1919)

York family, but lived for years at the summit of the rich and elegant Paris society. Wharton does not give Olenska many lines to speak in the book, but puts the most memorable words into her mouth. Newland, as a personification of culture at its best, embodied a goodness and innocence of which Olenska was more aware than he. He unwittingly convinced her that they could never be together. She said, *"...you had felt the world outside tugging at one with all its golden hands – and yet you hated the things it asks of one; you hated happiness bought by cruelty and indifference. That was what I'd never known before – and it's better than anything I've known... and don't let us undo what you have done! I can't go back now to that other way of thinking. I can't love you unless I give you up."*

At another time, she continued her explanation to Newland, *"...it was you who made me understand that under the dullness [of conventional society] there are things so fine and sensitive and delicate that even those [things] I most cared for in my other life look cheap by comparison... but it seems as if I'd never before understood with how much that is hard and shabby and base the most exquisite pleasures may be paid for."* In other words, to allow the sordid things of bohemian society to trample upon the fine things of conventional culture is too heavy a price to pay, even for the seemingly exquisite pleasures of romantic dalliance and aesthetic refinement.

As a new convert to the old ways, Madame Olenska had a deeper understanding and stronger commitment to the good things she had learned from Newland than he did himself. He was shaken from his dutiful and upright resolve by his overwhelming love and dreamy longing to run away with her.

> *"And you'll sit beside me, and we'll look not at visions but reality,"* she said.

> *"I don't know what you mean by realities,"* he responded. *"The only reality I know is this."*

> *Olenska startled him out of his dreamy trance by asking, "It is your idea, then, that I should live with you as your mistress – since I can't be your wife?"*

> *As a man of delicate manners, he was shocked by the crude word "mistress." "I want – I want somehow to get away with you into a world where words like that – categories like that – won't exist. Where we are simply two people who love each other, who are the whole of life to each other; and nothing else shall matter."*

> *She drew a deep sigh that ended with a laugh. "Oh my dear – where is that country? Have you ever been there? ... I know so many who have tried to find it; and believe me, they all got out at the wrong stations... and it wasn't at all different from the world they left, only rather smaller and dingier and more promiscuous."* [150]

AMERICA'S TRAGIC LOSS

As a writer who lived in Paris, Wharton observed the tragic lives of those who had fled New York for Paris in order to be *"modern."* She concluded that they would have been better off to stay in New York – many of them were emotionally dislocated and alienated from one another. Ernest Hemingway (1899-1961) referred to the American expatriates in Paris during the twenties as *"une génération perdue"* or *"a lost generation."* [151]

---

[150] (Wharton, The Age of Innocence 1920)
[151] (Hemingway, The Sun Also Rises 1926)

Life within old social boundaries was comfortable and safe, but frustrating, as Wharton well knew. The inability to find satisfaction in such a system emanates from the deep disorders of human nature – a change of regime will not eliminate these disorders. The quest to find *"free love"* and freedom from restraint in Paris often led to the seduction and debauching of naive Americans, leaving them jaded at best, and depraved and suicidal at worst. In contract, Wharton discovered that the customs and traditions that embodied deep wisdom about human nature were foundational to society. She grieved that a lost generation of post-WWI moderns were dismantling the old social system, and that something good about America was being lost forever.[152]

BUILDING A BRAVE NEW WORLD

The writings of Sigmund Freud, William James and John Dewey helped dismantle traditional society – all offered a substitute for the cultural heritage and wisdom of the past. Freud's substitute was the human subconscious; James' was the quick payoff of practical action; Dewey's was pragmatic techniques for adapting to a contemporary society in flux. Each man was trying to build a brave new world on the ashes of the old, in his own way.

A newspaper cartoon of Chairman of the Communist Party of China Mao Tse-tung's (1893-1976) **1968 Cultural Revolution**[153] depicted Chinese youth reading Mao's *The Little Red Book*[154] while turning their backs on a great mountain of books labeled *"3,000 years of tradition."* When thinking of Freud, James and Dewey, the old cartoon comes to mind. Like Mao, the three cultural usurpers would replace an immense treasury of wisdom with peculiar speculations from their cramped minds.

Aldous Huxley

Fred Critique

Cultural usurpers would replace an immense treasury of wisdom with peculiar speculations from their cramped minds.

Aldous Huxley (1894-1963) wrote **Brave New World**, a book about a utopian world where war and poverty had been abolished.[155] The people were stimulated and tranquilized through promiscuous sex and drugs. One particular drug, called soma,[156] imparted escape from pain and bad memories and offered pleasant hallucinations. Complacent escape from responsibility became the norm, while the government abolished the family, culture, art, literature, science, religion and philosophy. In short, civilization, culture, virtue, faith, friendship, love, and all that is noble about man was replaced with indulgence of contented human cattle by the pandering and controlling government.

A number of college students in the late 1960s were asked if they would take a drug that would make them gloriously happy at the cost of turning them into a vegetable. Many of them were ambivalent, not wanting to be a vegetable, but also not wanting to miss the happiness drug. They wanted instant happiness without consequences. The long series of modernist thinkers such as Hegel, Darwin, Marx, Freud, James and Dewey culminated in the gathering of human cattle at the 1969 Woodstock Festival in Bethel, New York. Many Woodstock zombies were stoned on drugs, brought to sensual

Fred Critique

The long series of modernist thinkers culminated in the gathering of human cattle at Woodstock.

---

[152] Inspired by a book review of the biography, **Edith Wharton**, by Hermione Lee. (Miller 2007)
[153] The Great Proletarian Cultural Revolution was a socio-political movement in the People's Republic of China from 1966-1976. Mao Tse-tung's goal was to enforce socialism by removing capitalist, traditional and cultural elements from Chinese society.
[154] (Tse-tung 1964)
[155] (Huxley, Brave New World 1932)
[156] (Huxley, Soma in Aldous Huxley's Brave New World 1932)

oblivion through a perpetual sex orgy, and pounded into insensibility through drums and electric guitars amplified to the threshold of pain. The sedated automatons made inarticulate grunts that war, poverty, family and religion should be abolished, and that all people should be united through promiscuous sexual embrace and drugged euphoria.[157] [158]

Huxley's **Brave New World** was prophetic about the direction modernism was heading – he saw it coming but probably did not expect the debauchery to be so ugly and degrading, or the political slogans to be so mindless. George Orwell's (1903-1950) book **Animal Farm**[159] warned us about slogans. Madame Oleska's words, *"smaller, dingier, and more promiscuous"* were on the right track.

A MADMAN'S MYTH ABOUT HUMAN NATURE

> *"Finally, brethren, whatever is true, whatever is noble, whatever is right, whatever is pure, whatever is lovely, whatever is admirable – if anything is excellent or praiseworthy – think about such things."*
> *Philippians 4:8 (NIV)*

Prior to Sigmund Freud, Western society generally acquired an understanding of human nature through relationships, experience, family, society, the Bible, church and the literary classics. Freud wracked his fevered brow, brought forth dark speculations, and built a new model of man that radically contradicted all older concepts – psychoanalysis. Science has been unable to validate the effectiveness of traditional (Freudian-style) psychoanalysis, which has largely passed out of use among psychologists.[160] It is now known that Freud had no solid scientific evidence for some of his more controversial theories, but speculated upon his clinical observations to establish them.[161] His personal mental pathologies suggest that he was a driven man – not driven to follow evidence, but by his own neurotic agendas. He was subject to depression, phobias, exaggerated fears of dying, and psychosomatic illnesses. Cocaine was his drug of choice, which he rationalized as a therapeutic anti-depressant.[162]

Fred Critique

Freud wracked his brow to bring forth dark speculations, and built a new model of man that radically contradicted all older concepts.

Freud did a great deal of psychoanalysis on himself – which a self-absorbed, drug-addled psychologist was bound to do. During his obsessive journeys into his inner darkness, he discovered perversions that he used as the basis for his theory of infantile desires for incest as the source of neurosis. He also theorized that religious joy was a delusional relapse to an infantile state, during which one freshly experiences the remembered joy of a mother's arms. Incredibly, such drivel was popular for several generations.

Modernists have foolishly entrusted themselves to guidance from a drug-addicted madman in their quest to discover who they are. Unfortunately, Freud's baleful influence lingers on in literature, films and philosophy – and in Marxist and feminist

Fred Critique

Modernists foolishly entrust themselves to a drug-addicted madman in their quest to discover who they are.

---

[157] Author's secondhand opinion, as he was not in attendance. (F. Hutchison, Brief History of Conservatism 2009)
[158] According to an actual attendee, while some used drugs and engaged in sex, most listened to music or looked for food and water – it was not a giant orgy of sex and drugs. It also poured rain several times, soaking the unprepared festival goers who had to sit in the sun to dry off, and making the farm field muddy and slippery. (Tomassini 2011)
[159] (Orwell 1945)
[160] (Tyler 2009)
[161] (Webster 1995)
[162] (Markel 2011)

theory. His self-medication and preoccupation with the most primitive impulses of his psyche are often reenacted in modern culture. Freud created a mythology of human nature that the modernist program adopted – Freudian science may be dead, but the Freudian cult is alive and well.

FREUD AND MODERNISM

Sigmund Freud

How does Freud fit in with the agenda of modernism? To start with, he was an atheist and materialist like Darwin and Marx – he considered man a dynamic biological system. As a biological determinist, he believed that perceptions of free will are delusions, and asserted that the conscious mind plays a minimal role in actual behavior. Humans are thereby reduced to the status of mere robots running on primitive impulse fuel. Freud's primeval man accords well with Darwin's classification of man as an animal descended from apes. One cannot negate God without negating man as well.

If man has no freedom of choice and is not guided by the conscious mind, he is free from moral accountability. Freud treated *"guilt-feelings"* as a psychological disorder that can be treated with therapy. He rejected as a religious myth that an objective moral guilt can exist. Beginning with Freud, the psychological profession has battled mightily to remove moral stigma from crime, and rationalize criminality and sexual immorality. Their encouragement of liberation from Freud's idea of sexual *"repression"* gradually led the profession to the formal acceptance of homosexuality and sexual perversion.

Modernists have consistently followed Jean Jacques Rousseau (founder of liberal modernism and a co-founder of the Romantic Movement) in denying the existence of innate evil in man, and in arguing against individual moral responsibility. Modernism and the Freudian model are popular because they fit the progressive agenda, and because most people are rascals and wish to escape ethical accountability. A being that rejects honorable liability is unfit for freedom, and must be supervised by an authoritarian socialist government. This happens to be one of the objectives of the malicious program – encourage moral depravity and then call upon big government to clean up the mess. If this is not evil, nothing is.

Fred Critique

Modernism and the Freudian model are popular because they fit the progressive agenda, and because most people are rascals and wish to escape ethical accountability. A being that rejects honorable liability is unfit for freedom, and must be supervised by an authoritarian socialist government. This happens to be one of the objectives of the malicious program – encourage moral depravity and then call upon big government to clean up the mess. If this is not evil, nothing is.

FRESH RATIONALIZATIONS

Wharton spoke of the modern desire to break free from the restraints of traditional society. Freud offered fresh rationalizations for breaking free from restraint, theorizing that the subconscious mind represses primeval desires and urges – the result of this repression is neurosis. The objective of Freudian psychoanalysis was to bring repressed desires up to the surface from the ocean depths of the unconscious, where the consciousness mind could observe it for purposes of therapy. Notice that after minimizing the role of the conscious mind, Freud attributes therapeutic powers to the alert and observing intellect. Freudianism is self-contradictory.

Freud did not advise his patients to surrender to the primitive impulse, but just to liberate it from repression and observe it for therapeutic effect. Whether the mere exposure and observation of repressed desire has value for therapy is a matter of controversy. An acquainted psychologist suggested that playing with the buried complexes of identity is unwholesome because it stirs up those dark entities and gives them power. Tampering with secret obsession can cause more neurosis – just as Freud became more neurotic after his own self-analysis.

FREUD AND THE SOCIAL SCIENCES

Margaret Mead

Tragically, as Freudian thought moved into the social sciences, emphasis shifted from therapeutic observation to acting out the impulse. The Freudian voyeur became a libertine experimenter. Social scientists began to recommend that after one was freed from repression, the repressed impulse should be actualized. Freud opened Pandora's Box, and enlightened experts encouraged the demons to fly out of their cages – Freud rationalized the monstrosities, and the social sciences introduced them to society.

Anthropologist Margaret Mead (1901-1978) brought sexual Freudianism into the social sciences. She wrote about the *"sexual liberation"* of Polynesian girls in **Coming of Age in Samoa**.[163] Mead favorably contrasted the sexual promiscuity of Samoan adolescents to the *"sexual repression"* of American girls. However, it is now known that the Polynesian girls soon caught on to Mead's agenda and invented lurid sexual stories to titillate her morbid preoccupation with sex – and then laughed behind her back.[164]

FREUD AND THE ARTS

As Freud's pernicious influence spread throughout Western culture, his effect upon the visual arts was particularly striking and shocking. Performance art, the acting out of one's primeval impulses, is merely the exhibitionism of the narcissist who is pretending to be an artist. A second Freudian influence is art as therapy, which is most obvious in the abstract impressionist.

Jackson Pollock

Jackson Pollock (1912-1956), the inventor of abstract impressionism, tossed together atrocious pictures that appear to be paint randomly splashed upon canvas. The effect might not be so hideous if purely random methods were used, but Pollock obeyed primeval urges as he splashed, dripped and smeared the paint. The depressing, haunted and demented quality is no accident – it is the depraved work of a Freudian madman.

Pollack, who was a frequent psychiatric patient, used his paint drippings for self-therapy, much as he had used Rorschach inkblot tests. Just as he had seen his demons in the ink blots, he conjured up fiends as he splashed with paint. His psychoanalysis freed him of inhibitions that had kept the monsters of his haunted forest in the woods. Pollock brought the ogres out of the forest to haunt his *"art."* The manic *"authenticity"* of his arm movements as he followed his demented impulses was more important to him than what the mess looked like on canvas.

The hideous ugliness Pollock created bespeaks of an insane man in hell. This is what the brave new world must be in the end – the utopia turns into a hellish haunted house.

> ### *Fred Critique*
>
> *The hideous ugliness Pollock created bespeaks of an insane man in hell. This is what the brave new world must be in the end – the utopia turns into a hellish haunted house.*

---

[163] (Mead 1928)
[164] (Freeman 1999)

Pollack turned to alcohol to escape his tormented madness. When that did not work, he killed himself by crashing his automobile, taking a young party girl with him. If C.S. Lewis had included Pollock in his book **The Great Divorce**,[165] he would have said that Pollock was in hell before he died and continued in hell after he died. Jackson Pollock was evil, not just through the perversion of art, but in his personal abuse of everyone who tried to help him. His murderous hatred of life was expressed in his suicide and the vehicular murder of Edith Metzger. His paintings are a record of his descent into hell.

THE SUBVERSIVE NATURE OF MODERN ART

Modern art often involves a radical renunciation of the Western aesthetic tradition. Traditional art exalts beauty; seeks order, harmony and proportion; and is committed to form and reason. Modern art often wallows in ugliness and rejects beauty; revels in chaos; shatters form and seeks disordered experiences that undermine reason. Saint Augustine (354-430) defined evil as *"that which undermines and subverts the good."* By this definition, modern art can be evil.[166] Since the modernist agenda lays aside Western cultural tradition, resulting in the loss of much goodness, it can be argued that the progressive program is, in large part, an evil agenda.

WILLIAM JAMES AND PRAGMATISM

American psychologist and philosopher William James (1842-1910) wrote **Pragmatism**,[167] a popular book that applied the empiricism of Bacon, Locke and Hume to religious and literary ideas – testing validity by whether or not the beliefs worked in practice. His standard for judgment was the existence of a short-term, practical pay-off measured by a pleasing outcome when the idea was acted upon. If the action had merit, James referred to it as having *"cash value."* In other words, truth is equal to the realistic cash value.

Niccolò Machiavelli (1469-1527), a famous master of Greek and Roman philosophy and political pragmatism, would have been embarrassed by expediency that stooped to sordid calculations that negated all thinking beyond the most elemental level. Cash value practicality as the judge of an idea's worth is both vile and unworkable in practice. A program based upon valid truth might disappoint due to uncontrollable circumstances – failure might occur from a timing problem or incorrect methods of application. On the other hand, a bad idea might enjoy temporary success – many powerful fads are based on foolishness. Such discernment would be impossible for a disciple of James.

Many Americans practice cash value simplicity in their workaday lives, often bringing it to church in an attempt to serve God. Even congregations that embrace orthodox doctrine have been known to utter the catch phrase, *"Do not learn any more until you are practically applying what you have already learned."* This is not logical Christian inspiration – it is a false, secular, modernist proposal. Pragmatism is not only antithetical to Christianity, it simply does not work.[168]

> *Fred Critique*
>
> *Many Americans practice cash value simplicity in their workaday lives, often bringing it to church in an attempt to serve God.*

To judge the validity of religious ideas by immediate applicability or outcome when put into practice is impossible. Some deep spiritual concepts cannot be boiled down to simple cookbook directions for instant action, requiring years

---

[165] (Lewis, The Great Divorce 1945)
[166] To include all modern art as evil or a product of base desires, is not accurate. For example, Salvador Dalí (1904-1989), a surrealist not a modernist, painted many beautiful religious works – perhaps demonstrating a real battle in his soul. Not all modern work can be categorized with Jackson Pollock.
[167] (James 1907)
[168] (F. Hutchison, Brief History of Conservatism 2009)

of reflection to sink deep into the heart and mind – eventually changing lifelong perspectives that slowly bubble up into attitudes and actions. An adult might suddenly understand the application of something learned as a child. Some truths drive crowds away with information people should heed, as opposed telling them what they want to hear. According to James, such ideas are not valid because they have no cash value.

Looking for an instant application will, at best, render the shallowest possible concept comprehension, and at worst will totally miss the point. Followers of Christ's teachings often tend to be unpopular in exclusive cliques, which can be construed pragmatically as a negative outcome. Effective methods for attracting crowds are now popular in many American evangelical churches – unfortunately, the cool, crowd-pleasing Christ is an imaginary person, the fantasy of shallow pragmatic minds. The crucified Christ is offensive to individualistic, self-sufficient Americans who are complacent in their inordinately high self-esteem, and addicted to instant gratification.

William James

William James' version was particularly vicious, since his measure of the outcome's cash value was determined by subjective feelings. If it feels good, do it. Elemental pragmatism amounts to a narcissistic self-indulgence that is deceiving and corrupting. Feeling good about an action's outcome is a very unreliable basis for judging an idea's validity – a greedy man may feel bad about results that fail to make him richer; a cruel man might experience positive emotion over a conclusion that hurts someone; someone could suffer unpleasantness relating to assenting effects if they are in a bad mood, or if they had hoped for a different end product. It is impossible to apply this program without becoming self-seeking and calculating. Such people are destined for the misery of a shallow and grasping life.

PRAGMATISM AND INTELLECTUAL SHALLOWNESS

Pragmatism yields intellectually and morally shallow people who are impatient with ideas devoid of readily conceived applications. As a rule, shallow ideas offer the easiest applications. Pragmatists are innocent of deep intellectual reflection, and therefore doomed to follow imprudent fads and cults. They are vulnerable to conspiracy theories based on one simple concept pertaining to injustice or wrongdoing in the world.[169]

> *Fred Critique*
>
> *Pragmatism yields intellectually and morally shallow people who are impatient with ideas devoid of readily conceived applications.*

Practicing simplicity indirectly cuts individuals off from their cultural, literary and intellectual past. Literary classics are immortal because they sink into the human heart and impart deep wisdom about life and human nature. James' approach to literature negates this effect – if folks read literature while searching for snippets that are of immediate practical use, they will come away with little of lasting value. The harvest of wisdom is arrived at through sympathetic immersion in the lives of the story's characters, reflection about their life accounts, and stimulation from the dramas. Universities are full of scholars who have read the classics, yet appear to be illiterate because the interpretation methods students are taught ensure they learn nothing of value.

PRAGMATISM AND LEARNING

The connection of pragmatism with learning introduces us to John Dewey, whose prominent educational theories were heavily influenced by William James. Both James and Dewey were deceived about the way humans learn. Most

---

[169] (F. Hutchison, Brief History of Conservatism 2009)

children can memorize lists of rules for practical action, but learning by rote does not guarantee retention. Education is a slow process of exposure, meditation, digestion and assimilation – the deepest lessons may take years to absorb. More time is often required to incorporate discernment for the right settings, contexts and opportunities to apply truth. The awareness of human motivations, attitudes and reactions to life events is often necessary before truth can be properly applied. It is questionable that pragmatists have any hope of understanding human nobility and depravity, or applying truth concepts, when they know nothing about mankind's hopes, dreams, fears and follies.

A BIAS AGAINST LEARNING

Pragmatism is anti-metaphysical – William James valued only ideas with a quick payoff. The meaning of life, the nature of being, the inquiry into what man can know and how he knows it, and the true nature of reality are issues with a very slow payoff. The historical hostility of pragmatists to metaphysics reveals their anti-intellectual bias – metaphysics probes the ocean depths, pragmatists paddle on the surface.

> *Fred Critique*
>
> *The mind that is unfamiliar with metaphysics can never fully develop its cognitive powers, and will be unable to learn deep truths.*

The mind that is unfamiliar with metaphysics can never fully develop its cognitive powers, and will be unable to learn deep truths. Since pragmatism is intellectually superficial, the pragmatist must remain second-rate in academic prowess. Pragmatic students tend to become annoyed when assigned to read great classical literature because they are impatient for action. The rationally lazy do not want to dig for wisdom, and despise profound truths that have no instant applications. They want easily accessible, cookbook rules to guide their actions.

DEWEY'S THEORITIC HAND HOLDS

> *"Woe to you experts in the law, because you have taken away the key to knowledge. You yourselves have not entered, and you have hindered those who were entering." Luke 11:52 (NIV)*

John Dewey is famous for **instrumentalism**,[170] which is an imaginative word for convenient handles to depend on for theoretic support. For example, if Dewey wanted students to work in groups, he would teach them practical techniques for doing so. He developed these methods through experimentation and empirical processes with built-in scientific patina, which gave him academic respectability. Students developed a recipe book of instrumental techniques, but were actually trained to simply look in a menu for canned procedures as a substitute for thinking.

> *Fred Critique*
>
> *As schools adopt regurgitation teaching routines that lower the intellectual content, students become so simplified in culture, education and thought that bright kids are turned into slow learners.*

Employees who come up through the ranks of CPA firms that insist on canned approaches are often ignorant of basic auditing concepts that should have been learned during their first year in the profession. This learning approach makes developmental growth stages impossible. Fred Hutchison, a former auditor whose work involved both teaching and quality review, found that individuals who used a cookbook system never matured professionally. They could not clarify the rationale for completing assigned tasks; could not tailor audits based on the special problems and unique structures of auditees; lacked the intellectual power to correctly interpret test results; and could not explain the reasoning behind their own conclusions. In the professional world, these

---

[170] Instrumentalism is the idea that scientific theory is a useful instrument to understand the world – a concept or theory should be assessed by how successfully it explains and predicts phenomena, as opposed to how correctly it describes impartial reality.

folks are hard to re-teach.[171]

Dewey's instrumental methods involve many techniques, but it is impossible to learn this way. Christ's rebuke to lawyers in Luke 11:52 – that they had *"taken away the key to knowledge"* – is reminiscent of Dewey. By substituting canned procedures for serious analysis, he removed the key necessary for deep learning, comprehension and advanced intellectual maturity. Just as years of rote auditing create habitual beginners in the conceptual understanding of fiscal review and inspection, Dewey's mechanical methods produce college professors who are literary criticism novices, leading to academic paralysis. As schools adopt regurgitation teaching routines that lower the intellectual content, students become so simplified in culture, education and thought that bright kids are turned into slow learners.

THE MAD SKIPPER OF THE EDUCATIONAL SHIP

John Dewey

John Dewey believed human culture is in continuous flux. As a strict pragmatist, he believed the only relevant learning equips students with short-term payoff techniques that manage the existing world at the moment. Dewey emphasized that tricks which worked a generation ago are now irrelevant, because society and people have changed. Georg Hegel, the father of historicism, would have been shocked at how extremely far Dewey carried the theory – his radical philosophy involves rejection of historical lessons and contempt for the past. For example, Dewey dismissed traditional ideas about good and evil, reasoning that mankind had been transformed and time-honored views were inappropriate – normative societal ethics in present existence are the only standards students require. *("But Mom, all the other kids are doing it!")*

This very popular idea in America happens to be absurd and destructive. It is preposterous to accept that human nature is constantly unstable; it is madness to assume that human customs of thinking, feeling and acting change as quickly as unpredictable street fads. John Dewey was a unique madman who sat at the tiller of the educational sinking ship. In spite of generations of failure in applying his methods, the educational establishment still holds him in high esteem – apparently debilitated intellectually by Dewey's guidance, leaders lack the mental capacity to learn from his mistakes. The present multiculturalism in education involves a suppression of Western cultural heritage. This subversion would not have been possible without John Dewey.

FLOWERS BREAKING THROUGH THE CONCRETE

As modernism destroys Western culture, one might despair amidst the dismal gloom. Edith Wharton reacted to the madness of modernism by learning deep truths about traditional society – when a culture becomes inhuman, human nature rebels against it. The contemporary conservative movement came into existence in reaction to the inhumanity of modernism and the shocking moral depths to which the decadent culture has fallen. In a brave new world paved over with concrete, flowers are growing through the cracks.

The remaining chapters will deal mainly with the postmodern era. The ancient roots of Western civilization are being destroyed by contemporary culture. In order to fully understand these foundations that are under multicultural threat, Chapter 10 is obliged to consider Ancient Greece and the High Middle Ages.

---

[171] (F. Hutchison, Brief History of Conservatism 2009)

Ruins of ancient Greek theater

The 20th century culture war began in the 1920s, and accelerated during the late sixties counter-cultural revolution and the seventies sexual revolution. The remaining journey through history will deal mainly with the **Postmodern Era**.[172] The ancient roots of Western civilization are being destroyed by contemporary culture. In order to fully understand these foundations that are under multicultural threat, Chapter 10 will take a brief visit back to Ancient Greece and the High Middle Ages.

REASONING FROM UNIVERSALS TO PARTICULARS

As you recall from Chapter 1 (see page 7), there were important building blocks of today's conservatism in the ideas of Saint Anselm, Peter Abelard and a host of others. Thanks to Saint Anselm, the father of the scholastic movement, the Western mind was opened to new dimensions of rationality. He taught his disciples to reason by starting with universals received by faith – *"Credo ut intelligam"* (*"I believe so that I may understand."*)[173] He formulated presuppositions based on the universal truths, then worked down to particulars in a logical and systematic fashion. This method of deductive reasoning is uniquely resistant to logic fallacies when correctly performed, and opens minds to objective rational thought. As one steps outside himself to reason in an impartial manner, he can recognize subjective bias in his own thoughts and discipline himself against such biases. These heightened powers of wisdom profoundly enhanced philosophy, literature, music, art, architecture, and the military and political arts.

THE RISE OF SCIENCE

It is no accident that the systematic, intellectual discipline of science originated in Western Europe, although many earlier civilizations produced talented scientific amateurs. The West was first to generate a critical mass of men with heightened powers of rationality, who systematically collaborated in scientific communities encouraging research and discovery (i.e., the Royal Society in London and the Encyclopedia in Paris.)

Many who have analyzed the rise of science notice the common belief that nature conforms to law – that the Creator incorporated His design of natural laws into creation. This faith in natural law and laws of nature comes naturally to those who trust that universals exist and subsist within particulars. God's gift of reason permitted human thoughts to discover the laws of nature. Aquinas is famous for optimism concerning the high level of correspondence between reason and nature. Western man was not afflicted with doubt about this connection until being exposed to Hume's skepticism and Kant's equivocations in the late 18th century.[174]

> *Fred Critique*
>
> *Faith in natural law and laws of nature comes naturally to those who trust that universals exist and subsist within particulars.*

---

[172] Postmodern Era describes the economic and cultural condition of society after the end of modernity (1980s or early 1990s) and includes the conscious adoption of postmodern philosophies in art, literature and society.
[173] (Sidney N. Deane 1962)
[174] See Chapter 4

The universal/particular dilemma is closely related to **the one and the many** (see Chapter 1, page 13), which is the second founding principle of Western civilization.[175] God has one being, but three persons – this archetype is the contributing notion behind the rise of republics. Considered a de facto motto of the American Republic, *"E Pluribus Unum,"* meaning *—Out of Many, One,"* was adopted by an Act of Congress in 1782.[176]

Americans recognize the nation as a mysterious union of many individuals, since people are ontological beings (i.e., personhood is undeniably real.) In like manner, the one nation really exists – it is not just a conglomeration or collective, as some Libertarians suppose.[177] E Pluribus Unum is conceptually similar to the biblical doctrine of the church as one body with many members.

Conceptualists like Abélard assume American Republic *"oneness"* is just an idea – Nominalists similar to Roscelin, Occam and postmodern skeptics think the *"one"* is just an arbitrary name. It takes a Trinitarian Realist to believe in the nation's authentic existence as a unity that emerged from the populace. Those who consider the emergent oneness of the nation to be just an idea, have trouble understanding the unabashed patriotism of those who realize that E Pluribus Unum is much more. The emotional and spiritual love for the elusive entity called America could hardly exist apart from a Trinitarian public. The lump in the throat while pronouncing the words *"the American Republic"* is inconceivable to postmodern multiculturalists. That which we would die for is nonsense to them.

E PLURIBUS UNUM VERSUS LIBERTARIANISM AND SOCIALISM

E Pluribus Unum conveys that membership and participation in a political body can honor healthy individualism – we can be both team players and individualists without contradiction. This is precisely what some Libertarians cannot understand, insisting that the collective must, of necessity, be a threat to the individual. Trinitarian wisdom suggests that Socialists have gone off track in one direction, and hyper-individualistic Libertarians have derailed the opposite way. God designed the world so that the community would enhance individuals, and the individual would contribute to community.

E PLURIBUS UNUM VERSUS NEOPLATONISM

E Pluribus Unum reverses the paradigm of **Neoplatonism** (a syncretism of platonism and pantheism), which presumes that the many flow from the one, emanating as inferior individual manifestations. According to that false paradigm, individuals are lesser precipitated lumps from the emissions of the great platonic One. Interestingly, scientists posit that

---

[175] The third founding concept is the incarnation of Christ – God becoming man and bridging the gap between infinite God and finite man.

[176] The United States Congress passed an act (H.J. Resolution 396) in 1956, adopting *—In God We Trust"* as the official motto.

[177] This is not an official Libertarian position or platform plank. The genesis of the thought lies in the Libertarian insistence on individual liberty as the foundation of social living. In other words, the purists in libertarianism would claim that the rights of the individual supersede any claim that any government would have on them. This view can be called *"orderly anarchy."* While it may be the philosophical basis for liberty-oriented society, it does not represent practical reality. It is estimated that fewer than 10% of Libertarians hold this view. (Earl 2011)

stars are spontaneous chunks from the Big Bang. Einstein's scientific theories were based upon concepts similar to the pantheistic elements of Neoplatonism.

In contrast to Neoplatonism, E Pluribus Unum suggests that the one emanates from many individual people, i.e., the American Republic emerges from the people – first the person, then the union. The result is a healthy balance between individualism and collective solidarity. A bottoms-up approach is not politically unstable for a Trinitarian people. The ordering principle descends from God and is imparted to people. There can be one nation as long as the God of the one and the many is Master. A collection of mere individualists will fly apart through centrifugal forces.

THE TRINITY VERSUS TRIBALISM

It is no accident that the Lord's special blessing has rested upon the American Republic, since it is a form of government in accord with His nature. Such a formulation is almost impossible for a Muslim state, because Islam

denies the Trinity. Oneness under Allah compels the individual to submit and conform – authoritarian rulers must extinguish political individuality. The democracy experiment in Iraq made no headway until the parliament found an unsteady equilibrium as a confederation of tribes. Individual submersion in the tribe makes Jeffersonian democracy very difficult.

The Teutonic tribes that overran the Roman Empire were Aryan Christian heretics who rejected the Trinity. As long as they remained Aryans they could not understand civilization, and retained their tribalism. Once Trinitarian Christianity was introduced among the barbarians, tribes gave way to organic feudalism, empires, nations and cities. Many Medieval settlements became little Republics containing elements of democracy.

Fred Critique

If society dissolves into the tribalism of identity politics, the Republic shall surely perish. Principled citizens are obliged to fight with all their strength...

The Trinity makes the extinction of tribes and birth of Republics achievable. In contrast, postmodern multiculturalism encourages a tribalism that is antithetical to a Republic. If society dissolves into the tribalism of identity politics, the Republic shall surely perish. Principled citizens in politics are obliged to fight with all their strength against the cancer of notions like *"I am entitled because I am black, Hispanic, gay, working class, a woman, etc."*

HUMAN FLOURISHING

Ty Cobb

The concept of the one and the many is necessary for full human flourishing. A culture flowers to the extent that both individuals and the community are prosperous. The model meets two primary needs of every person: 1) the desire to be special and unique; and 2) the desire to be an accepted and cherished member of a community. Every baseball player wants to be a superstar and a team player. A star who is shunned by the team, like Ty Cobb,[178] is never happy – neither is an unnoticed team player.

In daily life, folks may not want to be celebrities, but they desire to feel special and unique in

---

[178] Ty Cobb was famous for being a vicious racist, even supposedly avoiding Babe Ruth because of his allegedly black facial characteristics.

114

some way, and want friends to recognize and value them. Individual people might not aspire to be reduced to the tightly interlocking system of a baseball team, but everyone wants to feel accepted as a member of a family, business team, fraternity, church or community. Everybody has the secret need to be part of something greater than ourselves. These conflicted yearnings are hard to meet apart from Trinitarian social consensus. Life in the American Republic prior to the Triune God's banishment from the public square and the rise of group-think, political correctness and tribal identity politics was conducive to both celebrating the individual and honoring the group.

TRADITIONAL MULTICULTURALISM

Prior to the 20th century, the West practiced a good form of multiculturalism made possible by Trinitarian Realist assumptions – the one and the many can apply to multiple cultures. All the national cultures of Europe were reasonably compatible under the aegis of an overarching Western culture, because they shared the same founding principles. Christian scholars were educated in classics from all the nations of Europe.

However, traditional European multiculturalism cannot be extended worldwide because the base assumptions of Trinitarian, Realist and Logocentric European culture are unique and incompatible with most non-Western societies. This does not mean that international cultural exchanges cannot be fruitful, but that traditional diversity and ethnic variety cannot be practiced on a global scale. The 19th century European empires discovered the incongruity of pagan and Christian cultures. However, when colonies converted to Christianity and accepted the Trinity, as Latin America did, they were included in the cultural and intellectual dialog of Europe's multicultural world.

DESTRUCTIVE MULTICULTURALISM

Postmodern multiculturalists irrationally insist that there are no necessary barriers to an international cultural community. Scholars of comparative religions would have us believe that differences in world religions are superficial, and that they are compatible at the core. This is nonsense, of course. These fuzzy-thinking intellectuals blur the differences with sweeping cloudy metaphors, and typically greet logical criticisms with charges of bigotry. The older, Western multiculturalism enshrined reason – the postmodern variety is based upon a revolt against logic. Reasoning faculties must be checked at the door to think that Christianity, Islam, Hinduism, Buddhism and Animism are essentially the same.

Traditional Western culture has been correctly recognized as a barrier to the dream of an international community of cultures. Trinitarian rationality, Realism and Logocentricity stand against the internationalist agenda. As a result, many multicultural proponents either exclude the West from their carnival, or demonize Western culture. Hatred of the West is one of the passions shared by America's left-wing radicals.

> *Fred Critique*
>
> *Traditional Western culture has been correctly recognized as a barrier to the dream of an international community of cultures.*

Postmodern professors hired to teach Western classics train students to deconstruct the text to find coded messages concerning the ruling class power agendas – as if Shakespeare was part of an elite conspiracy. In this way, academia tries to neutralize the effect of classic Logocentric words. Feminist lecturers warn students about the *"patriarchy"* of dead, white European males – as though **Romeo and Juliet** is patriarchal propaganda, and the tale of star-crossed young lovers is Shakespeare's clever gambit to seduce and deceive the reader.

William Shakespeare

TRINITARIAN CREATIVITY

The Trinitarian universals/particulars concept is an excellent guide to good and bad creativity. Since universals dwell in particulars, great works of art and literature use particular circumstances to convey universal truth and beauty. Artists do not create universals like God does, they discover them – original creativity occurs in the organization and communication. Each artist is a uniquely talented individual, and cannot avoid infusing personal eccentricity into their work. There was only one Shakespeare, one Rembrandt and one Tolstoy.

Great literary classics are saturated with strange idiosyncrasies, yet the universals of truth and beauty shine through. Aristotle and Aquinas insisted that particulars are not just vessels for carrying universals, but have independent idiosyncratic features called **accidents**.[179] The property of an accident has no necessary connection to the essence of the thing being described.[180] An author's idiosyncrasies are accidental features that do not impair the ability to be a messenger of universals, unless egocentric self-absorption allows the peculiarities to interfere.

DUMBING DOWN

The dumbing down of literature involves saturating readers in rambling particulars and averting universals. As particulars were divorced from universals, meaning was drained and they became *"dumb"* – not in the sense of being stupid, but of being mute. As the Logocentric voice of words was muted and gagged by postmodern writers, the shelves of Christian bookstores were gutted of meaty substance to make way for fluff and fad books, and a great jumble of knick-knacks, flashy junk and tasteless kitsch.[181] These stores are struggling to stay in business, and have become a metaphor for the dumbing down of Christian writers.

BAD CREATIVITY

Beginning with the 18th century Romantic Movement, the false notion that artists are creators took root, and artistic genius began to be equated with the divine power of creation. This was tremendously stimulating to Western culture for a time. The view was already taken seriously when Viennese opera composer Christoph von Gluck (1714-1787), Austrian symphony composer Joseph Haydn (1732-1809), and the enduringly popular Austrian composer Wolfgang Amadeus Mozart (1756-1791) were inventing classical music. Their great compositions include some of the most beautiful pieces of music ever written – Mozart added sensuality to music with counterpoints that made the music come alive. Yet the movement contained the seeds of its own destruction. All the

---

[179] According to Aristotle, there are nine kinds of accidents: quantity, quality, relation, habits, time, location, situation (or position), action and passion (*"being acted on"*). For example, a chair can be made of wood, metal or plastic, but this is accidental to being a chair – it is still a chair regardless of the material.

[180] Thomas Aquinas used Aristotelian concepts to explain the theology of the Eucharist, particularly the transubstantiation. According to this tradition, the accidents of the bread and wine do not change, but their substances change to the Body and Blood of Christ.

[181] Kitsch is a form of art considered to be inferior, tasteless copies or worthless imitations, and is associated with the deliberate use of cultural icons and cheap mass-production.

works of man, even the most noble, inspired and refined, are tainted by original sin.

The quality of composition declined in the late 19th century as innovation became valued over the intrinsic merit of the piece. The cult of originality led to the 20th century idea of music as self-expression, of which jazz is the most complete exemplar. After 1920, symphonic music critics began to praise ugly compositions that disintegrated into chaos, if the piece was original and expressive of the composer. Counter-cultural dissonance was taken as a sign of originality, and the trend of non-conformity led to new conformism. New compositions based on 19th century models are now regarded as *"inauthentic"* for postmodern culture.

An old, eccentric architect of Fred Hutchison's acquaintance once condemned the design of a beautiful new church because *"it is not of this era,"* causing Fred to recoil at this statement of resounding stupidity and decadence.[182] This mindless new fashion elbows aside intrinsic merit as it stubbornly insists that art is only valid as an expression of contemporary culture. The craze for novelty and freedom has morphed into a prison of cultural determinism. Originality for the sake of originality is not sustainable, and the fad has collapsed into a cult of conformance to a chaotic culture – the worst of all possible worlds for the arts.

CONCLUSION

Western culture can be restored by radically renouncing the cults of modernism and postmodernism, but to do this will require learning to accept persecution. Rejecting the notion that all religions are essentially the same, or that **Romeo and Juliet** was a conspiracy of the patriarchal power elite will attract demented, post-modern scholars intent on persecution. If the grizzled old architect was told that the new church is beautiful, and that denouncing it on the grounds of modern validity was a mindless alternative, a tremendous battle would ensue. This decadent culture is perishing, but its denizens will go out fighting because they are loyal to their tormenting demons.

Once the false and wicked culture has been rejected, the foundations of truth that were laid in the 12th and 13th centuries must be rebuilt. It will be necessary to focus on grounded Realism that vindicates both universals and particulars. It will be essential to honor the one and the many. It will be vital to listen to Logocentric words once more. It will be crucial to admire artistic creation solely on the intrinsic values of beauty, harmony, meaning and humanity.

> *"Your people will rebuild the ancient ruins and will raise up the age-old foundations; you will be called Repairer of Broken Walls, Restorer of Streets with Dwellings." Isaiah 58:12 (NIV)*

---

[182] (F. Hutchison, Brief History of Conservatism 2009)

Figure 3. Chapter 11-Epilogue Timeline (1830-2010 AD)

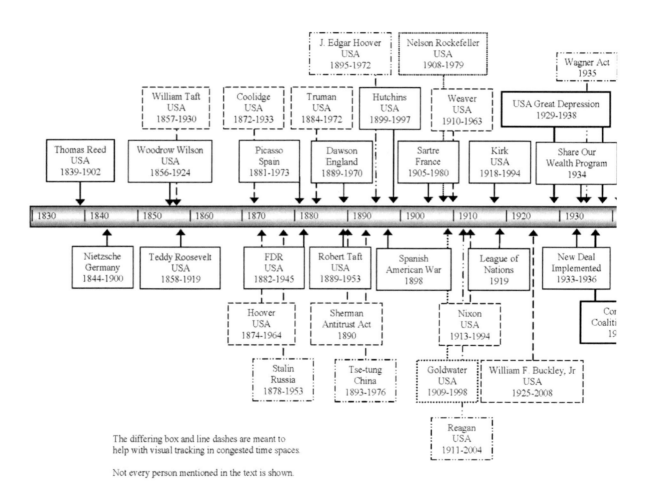

The differing box and line dashes are meant to
help with visual tracking in congested time spaces.

Not every person mentioned in the text is shown.

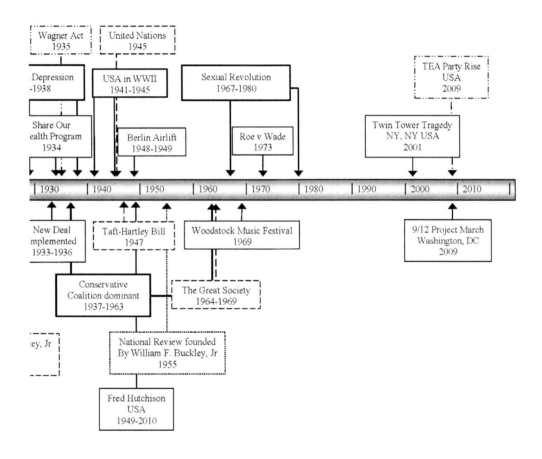

The 1940's conservative intellectual movement coincided with the arrival of atheistic **Nihilism**[183] and **Existentialism**[184] to American shores. While French existentialist philosopher and political activist Jean-Paul Sartre (1905-1980) was sitting in a Paris coffee shop writing ***Being and Nothingness***[185] and ignoring Nazi occupation, four great thinkers were laying foundations for a Western renewal of Traditionalist Conservatism (refer to Chapter 1). As Existentialists claimed that man is empty and alone in an absurd world, the conservative pioneers stressed that Western man has a rich cultural and spiritual heritage to draw upon for renewal.[186] This chapter covers the five kinds of conservatism spawned by that inevitable restoration, listed in historical sequence.

THE FIVE POSTWAR STAGES OF THE CONSERVATIVE MOVEMENT

Liberalism/modernism/progressivism is historically recent, and since it presents false views about human nature, is doomed to eventual failure. In contrast, conservatism is ancient precisely because it is inherent to human nature – strains of Western Traditionalism go back to 800 BC. Five developmental stages of 20th century conservative restoration began with the ideas of intellectual writers.

1. **Traditionalism.** The intellectual foundations of Traditionalist Conservatism were laid by Christopher Dawson, Robert Hutchins, Richard Weaver and Russell Kirk over several decades, but the movement boasted a significant band of adherents by the late 1940s. This chapter considers three main varieties of Traditionalism.

2. **Libertarianism.** American Libertarianism originated with the American founder's Classical Liberalism, which was a synthesis of classical economics and Natural Law theory, and provided some of our cherished free Republic conceptions. Modern Libertarianism has many variations, retaining some classic traits and drifting away from others. Three major branches that emerged in the 1940s are reviewed in this chapter.

3. **Christian Conservatism.** The synthesis of Christianity and Traditionalist conservatism was developed by Christopher Dawson and Richard Weaver. In 1980, the rationale provided Evangelicals and conservative Catholics the motivation to enter politics and vote for Ronald Reagan, driven by the desire to correct the nation's moral decadence.

4. **Neoconservatism.** The complicated and fascinating genesis of Neoconservatism will be summarized in Chapter 14, including the roles played by Robert Hutchins, Mortimer Adler, Leo Strauss, Irving Kristal and Norman Podhoretz. William F. Buckley, Jr. also participated by offering his microphone and print space to friendly Neocon

---

[183] Nihilism is an extreme form of skepticism that denies all existence, claiming that all values are baseless and nothing can be known or communicated.
[184] Existentialism emphasizes the unique and isolated experience of individuals in a hostile or indifferent universe. The philosophy regards human existence as unexplainable, and stresses freedom of choice and responsibility for the consequences of actions.
[185] (Sartre 1943)
[186] (Various 1961)

intellectuals. Neoconservative contributions to the restoration of American literary culture and President George W. Bush's foreign policy will be briefly enumerated.

5. **Natural Law.** The American founders were guided by Natural Law,[187] which has 21st century political philosophy value. Natural Law provides a rational framework and action guide, in a constitutional law context, that can restore the Republic according to founding principles. Natural Law standards can draw extreme Libertarians back from their radical drifts – the doctrine summons them like a lighthouse in the stormy seas of hyper-individualism, towards the safe haven of Classical Liberalism and the home port of the conservative movement.

FOUR GIANTS

Four great men restored Traditionalism and got the 20th century conservative movement rolling. While Sartre sat in a sidewalk café, watching Nazi storm troopers march by and scribbling nihilistic counsels of despair, these men were laying groundwork for the restoration of Western civilization. We are grateful dwarfs who are privileged to sit upon the shoulders of these giants.

CHRISTOPHER DAWSON

Christopher Dawson

Christopher Dawson (1889-1970) was an English **Anglo-Catholic**[188] scholar with a philosophic bent who converted to Roman Catholicism. He was an Oxford contemporary of C.S. Lewis, also an Anglo-Catholic who briefly considered converting, but decided against it. Both Dawson and Lewis were Medievalists and Renaissance men. Dawson's focus was medieval history, theology and culture – he was essentially an **Anglo-Saxon**[189] intellectual. Lewis, a lyrical **Celt**[190] from Northern Ireland, concentrated on literature and was deeply immersed in the humane letters.

Oswald Spengler (1880-1936), a German historian and philosopher, is best known for writing ***The Decline of the West (Der Untergang des Abendlandes)***,[191] which is a cyclical theory of the rise and decline of civilizations. British historian Arnold Toynbee (1889-1975) wrote a twelve-volume analysis of the rise and fall of civilizations, *A Study of History*,[192] a synthesis of global history based on the rhythms of rise, flowering and decline. Dawson originally set out to write a similar theory of history, and his studies provided an intellectual foundation for his writings. However, his life work focused mainly on Western history and Christianity's role in the formation, inspiration and preservation of culture.

Dawson was as consistently a Christian Conservative as he was a Traditionalist Conservative. Traditionalist thinkers are drawn to cultural history, and the Western record is permeated with Christian influences, which is why the two are

---

[187] (Barton, Natural Law Articles 2011)

[188] Anglo-Catholic describes people, beliefs and practices within Anglicanism that affirm Catholic heritage and identity, rather than Protestant – it represents either a form of Catholicism without papal control, or a form of Protestantism with more elaborate liturgy and ritual, or a fusion of the two traditions.

[189] Anglo-Saxon designates the Germanic tribes who invaded the south and east of Great Britain beginning in about 550 AD, establishing the English nation – they remained in power until the Norman Conquest in 1066.

[190] The Celts were a diverse group of tribal societies in Iron Age and Roman-era Europe.

[191] (Spengler 1927)

[192] (Toynbee 1934-1961)

compatible. Dawson's essay, ***The Study of Christian Culture***,[193] explains the six historical ages of the Church – Chapter 15 of this book borrows the *"four ages of Christian traditionalism"* concept from this document. This loaned perspective is like being a dwarf sitting upon the broad shoulders of a giant – viewing distant vistas from the vantage point of great height.

RELIGION AND CULTURE

> *"It is the religious force which supplies the cohesive force which unifies a society and a culture...a society which has lost its religion becomes sooner or later a society which has lost its culture."*
> Christopher Dawson

Spiritual aspirations emanating from religious faith revive the heart, expand the imagination, and awaken and inspire the verbal, lyrical and intellectual faculties. People who are thus vivified are often overflowing with ideals, thoughts and sentiments that find expression through cultural channels. In this manner, the prevailing religious faith of a society gives birth to culture, which then inspires and sustains it. European high culture prior to 1750 is a tribute to the powerful spiritual aspirations stimulated by Christian passion.

Western civilization's decline is related to the deterioration of Christianity after 1750. Cultural decline accelerated in the 20th century, when the interpretation of *"separation of church and state"* began to hermitically seal off Christian faith.[194] Some present Evangelical mega churches, reputed for being seeker-sensitive entertainment centers, seem to be more influenced by contemporary culture than the other way around. This kind of church captivity happens when shallow and watery spirituality proves incapable of motivating the soaring aspirations that can change society.

> ***Fred Critique***
>
> *Church captivity happens when shallow and watery spirituality proves incapable of motivating the soaring aspirations that can change society.*

THE ARCHENEMY OF MODERNISM

Dawson called for the recovery of a medieval world view (or neo-scholasticism), wherein individual rationality, freedom and moral effort are of central importance and are well suited for present intellectual needs. The specter of a *"collective mind"* swallowing up modern individuals horrified him, and he occasionally sounded like a Libertarian inveighing against identity politics. The nihilistic (existentialist) and **positivistic**[195] spirit of the age were abhorrent to Dawson – he angrily vented that *"positivism equals negativism,"* since Positivists skeptically reject everything except observation and material proof.

Dawson also rejected the cult of *"progress,"* protesting that Modernists had discarded the golden Western heritage to revive cultural barbarism in the name of progress. When Pablo Picasso (1881-1973) stopped painting stylized Harlequins and clowns after observing a tribal African mask, his art quickly disintegrated into ugly fragments – our barbarous culture highly values his abominations.

---

[193] (Dawson 1959)
[194] (Barton, Wallbuilders: The Separation of Church and State 2001)
[195] Positivistic philosophy states that sense perceptions are the only admissible basis of human knowledge and accurate thought, rejecting metaphysics as meaningless.

All five kinds of conservatism play an essential role in the fight against modernism and postmodernism. However, it was the great Christian Traditionalist, Christopher Dawson, who sounded the alarm about our common enemy. His discernment signaled the culture war in a historically, spiritually and intellectually satisfying way.

ROBERT HUTCHINS

Robert Hutchins

Robert Maynard Hutchins (1899-1997) was president (1929-1945) and chancellor (1945-1951) of the University of Chicago, and the editor of **Great Books of the Western World**[196] and **Gateway to the Great Books**.[197] The son and grandson of Presbyterian ministers, Hutchins became a secular **perennialist**,[198] holding that all people everywhere should be taught the things of everlasting value. His conversion from legal realism (all law is made by human beings and is therefore subject to human foibles, frailties and imperfections) to metaphysical philosophy (ideas that are universal, immutable and everlasting) occurred while studying Neo-Scholastic philosophy, Aristotle and Saint Thomas Aquinas.

After Hume and Kant in the late 18th century, metaphysicians wandered in the wilderness of skepticism and withering critique for a century. The exile of Western metaphysics resulted in an increasing divorce from reason, reality and morality, and a loss of transcendent aspirations. A Victorian Era, Neo-Scholastic, **Thomist**[199] revival restored metaphysics for a season. Hutchins lived in the academic afterglow of this renewal as a college student – his awakening to abstract rationality was the basis for great contributions he subsequently made to Western culture.

Hutchins circulated the concept of *"great ideas,"* a set of timeless concepts that has been enthusiastically discussed by Western thinkers in every generation from Homer to Hemingway. These notions have an everlasting quality because men in every generation and every place are interested in them, hence the perennialist philosophy. Every great Western thinker and writer wrestles with and is inspired by the great ideas of previous philosophers – each generation of leading theorists behaves as though they are sitting around a table discussing and debating the great ideas with the immortal thinkers of the past. Hutchins called this *"the great conversation,"* an indispensable design for Traditionalist Conservative and Neoconservative thinkers. Hutchins identified 130 great Western thinkers and writers, and his colleague, Mortimer Adler (1902-2001), identified 102 great ideas. Adler's **Syntopicon**[200] summarizes what these great thinkers said about each of the great ideas.

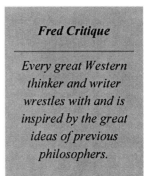

Fred Critique

Every great Western thinker and writer wrestles with and is inspired by the great ideas of previous philosophers.

Hutchins proved that great ideas are exciting to modern college students – slumbering learners are capable of awakening from the intellectual anesthesia of Modernism to become earnest **bibliophiles**[201] as they eagerly gather to discuss great ideas. The great ideas fill their minds with a large inventory of expansive ideas that provoke rational discussion and reflection. Musing on them can gradually turn a bright young barbarian into a rational and civilized man.

---

[196] (Hutchins, Great Books of the Western World 1952)

[197] (Hutchins and Adler, Gateway to the Great Books 1963)

[198] Perennial philosophy stresses the notion of the universal recurrence of philosophical insight independent of epoch or culture, including universal truths on the nature of reality, humanity or consciousness.

[199] Thomism philosophy is based on the legacy of the work and thought of St. Thomas Aquinas.

[200] (M. Adler 1952)

[201] Bibliophiles are book lovers.

Hutchins was an archetypal traditionalist because he gathered together the best Western values from the Classical, Medieval, Early Modern and Modern eras. He was also a conservative, since he wanted to preserve the intellectual culture in which the great ideas are regularly discussed. When Hutchins came on the scene, the great conversation was flagging for the first time in 2,800 years – a cleavage had opened between the best contemporary writers and the great conversation. Modernists had succeeded in cutting Western writers off from their intellectual and literary heritage. Hutchins became a hero of Western culture when he restarted the great conversation.

A CONSERVATISM CENTERED ON IDEAS

Robert Hutchins ensured that the developing conservative movement would be about ideas. Conservative debaters often have a superior grasp of ideas than their liberal opponents, partially because of exposure to Hutchins' *Great Books* program and discussion groups, which creates a debate culture that sharpens their wits. In contrast, debating about ideas is blocked in liberal circles by group-think, multiculturalism, codes of political correctness and identity politics. Conservative jurist Robert Bork (1927-) went to the University of Chicago in order to become an intellectual. Alan Keyes (1950-), conservative American activist and author, studied political philosophy under the Jewish thinker Allan Bloom (1930-1992), who was deeply influenced by the Great Books program. Both Bork and Keyes have exceptional debating skills.

The Jewish intellectual Mortimer Adler, who enumerated, cataloged and summarized Hutchins' great ideas, seems to have been an inspiration to Allan Bloom, Adler's colleague at the University of Chicago (UC). German Jewish immigrant Leo Strauss (1899-1973) was also a professor at UC, and spoke highly of Hutchins' *Great Books* program. Adler, Bloom and Strauss were the first Neoconservatives – all three were disillusioned by the intellectual and aesthetic decay of the humanities in modernist academia. Allan Bloom's critique of academia's neglect and subversion of the classics in his book *The Closing of the American Mind*[202] appears to have been inspired by Hutchins' critiques of academia and formal examinations about the nature of education. Irving Kristol (1920-2009), leader of the second generation of neoconservatives, transformed the literary program for Jewish intellectuals into a broad-based political movement.

RICHARD WEAVER

Richard Weaver

Richard Weaver (1910-1963) was a Platonist who championed transcendent truth and shunned Nominalism. As a son of the South, Weaver promoted agrarian ideals and traditional community values – he loved the Anglican/Episcopal spirit of the Old South that honored tradition and nature.

Weaver taught English at UC, the alma mater of Hutchins, Adler and Bloom. Although he was intellectually stimulated at Chicago, his formation as a conservative intellectual seems to have occurred at an elite Southern preparatory school, at the University of Kentucky, and at Vanderbilt University in Tennessee. In his famous book *Ideas Have Consequences*,[203]

---

[202] (Bloom 1987)
[203] (Weaver 1948)

Weaver wrote that private property is the last metaphysical right of the individual – an indispensable idea to Traditionalist, Libertarian and Natural Law conservatives. His theory of communitarian individualism, that emphasizes the balance between individual responsibility to the community and the social importance of the family unit, is cherished by many conservatives.

Weaver considered America's lamentable cultural degradation a result of the sad reality that citizens no longer believed in transcendent values, and lacked the moral ambition to discover higher truth – the inevitable fate of metaphysic ignorance. Allan Bloom reiterated Weaver's idea in his critique of elite students who had no interest in searching for higher truth.

> **Fred Critique**
>
> *Cultural degradation is a result of citizens no longer believing in transcendent values, and lacking the moral ambition to discover higher truth – metaphysic ignorance.*

THE CHRISTIAN GENTLEMAN

Weaver valued the old idea of landed aristocracy – when a tract of land was linked to a respected family name for several generations, honor, dignity, responsibility and stability was often the result. Traditional Western gentry produced a code of chivalry and perpetuated the Christian gentleman image – a vision dating back to Castiglione's Renaissance book *The Courtier*, and to the intellectual foundations laid by Petrarch's Renaissance schools for Christian gentleman.[204]

Weaver rejected egalitarianism[205] and approved social hierarchy that placed the gentry at the summit, claiming that the pursuit of excellence produces a cultural elite, while Egalitarianism produces mediocrity. The Old South planter class embodied the ideals of honorable Southern gentlemen, whose sons were carefully trained and brilliantly educated to become society's next generation of elite leaders. They all read *The Courtier* and attended elite schools for Christian gentleman – Presidents Washington (1732-1799), Jefferson (1743-1826) and Madison (1751-1836) were sterling products of the agrarian gentry culture.

PALEOCONSERVATISM

Weaver's intellectual followers split into Paleoconservative and Agrarian branches – both are heirs of the Old South blood and soil romantics, except Paleocons emphasize blood and Agrarians emphasize soil. Paleocons and Agrarians both advocate states' rights, as did the Old South; therefore, they join hands with Natural Law conservatives on issues of federalism.

Rush Limbaugh

Sometimes called *"classical conservatives,"* Paleocons are anticommunists and champion America-first ideas stressing tradition, civil society and federalism. They seek to find identity in family roots, religious tradition, community, regional traits and practices, patriotism and European culture – customs of sanctified memory. When Paleocons research their cultural roots, they often look back to Anglo-Saxon and Scots-Irish Americana. Some are unabashed nativists, favoring the interests of established inhabitants over those of immigrants.

Paleocons differ from Neocons on immigration, international trade, affirmative action, foreign wars, international associations and the welfare state. The anti-authoritarian tendencies of populist Paleocons run against Weaver's hierarchicalism, and represent scraps

---

[204] See Chapter 2
[205] Social equality or classlessness

borrowed from Buckley and Goldwater's synthesis of traditionalism and libertarianism. However, in the age of Rush Limbaugh, when Paleocon radio talk-show hosts despise the liberal elite, populist paleoconservatism has more political traction than Weaver's elitist hierarchy.

Paleocons with an *"America first"* mindset sometimes reject the military culture and imperial expansionism of the Old South, but family military traditions remain strong in many regions. Hunting and gun ownership are an integral part of this culture, since pursuing game and soldiering were favored vocations of Southern gentry. John Kerry (1943-) may have lost the 2004 presidential election because of his gun-control policy. Democrats who are avid hunters turned against him, depriving him of the electoral votes from Iowa, New Mexico and Ohio, and almost costing him Pennsylvania and Michigan.

The first Paleocon with national political traction was Senator Robert Taft of Ohio (1889-1953), who failed in his quest to win the Republican Party presidential nomination in 1940, 1948 and 1952. His Conservative Coalition included conservative Republicans in the North and conservative Democrats in the South. Rush Limbaugh and Pat Buchanan are the two most politically influential Paleocons of the present generation.

AGRARIANS

> *"Why, land's the only thing in the world worth working for, worth fighting for, worth dying for, because it's the only thing that lasts... It'll come to you, this love of the land. There's no getting away from it if you're Irish."* Gerald O'Hara, **Gone with the Wind**, 1936[206]

Agrarians are more likely to have Southern roots, sympathies and nostalgic memories of rural life than Paleocons – and are more likely to be hunters. As the name implies, Agrarians are interested in Weaver's virtues of staying close to the land. Agrarian men aspire to be gentlemen of honor, chivalry, courtesy and hospitality. The landed gentry model of families living on the same property for generations has faded, due to the decline of family farms and the restless wanderlust of young country folks. However, the paradigm of agrarian writers and poets who stay close to the soil has flourished and spread from the South to the Midwest plains.

In the summer of 2007, a lady poet friend of Fred Hutchison told him that she sank her feet into the rich soil of her small Iowa farm to gain poetic inspiration and insight. Like Scarlett O'Hara in **Gone with the Wind**, she seemed to draw her strength from the land,[207] bringing to mind the above words of Gerald O'Hara to Scarlett. Notice how the gentleman's agrarian love of the land is mingled with love of family Celtic blood lines. On the O'Hara plantation, nativist ideals of blood mingled freely with romantic dreams about folk culture rising from the soil.

---

[206] (Mitchell 1936)
[207] (F. Hutchison, Brief History of Conservatism 2009)

RUSSELL KIRK

Russell Kirk

"In its immediate influence upon culture, perhaps the most important aspect of the genius of Christianity is its account of human personality: the doctrine of the immortal soul, the belief in the unique character of every human person, the concept of human dignity, the sanction for rights and duties, the obligation to exercise Christian charity, the insistence upon private responsibility." Russell Kirk, 1960[208]

Russell Kirk (1918-1994) was an American political theorist, historian, social and literary critic. His formation as a Conservative was not through Christianity like Dawson, or through metaphysics like Hutchins, or through blood and soil traditions and ideals like Weaver. Kirk's development came through literature and histories of scholarly value, and literary stories about leaders. He gleaned his ideas from great works of fiction and the ideas, words and actions of great statesmen.

Although Kirk became a well-known writer much later than Weaver, he developed a tremendous following as a writer for Buckley's magazine, ***National Review***. Buckley, an agile Irish storyteller and literary buff, preferred lyrical writers like Kirk and C.S. Lewis over heavy intellectual/philosophic types like Toynbee, Dawson and Hutchins. Indeed, Kirk's histories sometimes read like epic tales – in a different age, he may have been a poet like Homer or a legendary Scottish bard like Ossian. Kirk's Scottish roots grafted ideals from the Celtic world, when bards were typically aligned with clan chiefs who valued blood and soil traditions, to modern folk culture.

Edmund Burke

Kirk's version of Traditionalist Conservatism overlaps Weaver's – he had a formative influence upon some Paleocons. Both Kirk and Weaver were inspired by Edmund Burke to preserve the *"social fabric"* that embodies the accumulated wisdom of many generations. Kirk had a facility for colorful historical narratives in which he described the development of the social fabric. He was particularly talented at explaining how English common law developed over the centuries through the legal decisions of local judges. He pointed to Sir William Blackstone's (1723-1780) ***Commentaries on the Laws of England***[209] as the repository of this treasury of legal wisdom – the four volume work is divided into the rights of persons, the rights of things, of private wrongs and of public wrongs. The American founders had a profound understanding of the rights and duties of Englishman because they read Blackstone. Constitutional scholars of the *"original intent"* school of thought sometimes search Blackstone to gain understanding of what the founders meant by particular words, phrases and passages of the Constitution.

KIRK'S FIVE OVERARCHING PRINCIPLES

Kirk's overarching conservative principles are:

1. A transcendent order exists that one can observe in tradition, revelation and Natural Law.

2. The variety and mystery of human experience should be respected.

3. Society requires social classes that demarcate natural distinctions.

4. Freedom requires private property.

5. Political innovation should be prudent and compatible with existing traditions and customs.

---

[208] (Kirk, The Common Heritage of America and Europe 1960)
[209] (Blackstone 1765-1769)

The three main branches of traditionalist conservatism are: 1) Dawson's religious and historically based cultural conservatism and anti-modernism; 2) Hutchins' metaphysical and literary conservatism of great ideas; and 3) Weaver-Kirk Burkean conservatism. The Weaver-Kirk Burkean conservatism (named after Edmund Burke) can also be called *"social fabric"* conservatism – Weaver and Kirk wanted to preserve the social fabric from the depredations of Modernism. The three branches of Weaver-Kirk Burkeans are Paleocons, Agrarians and the intellectual heirs of Kirk.

STAY TUNED

Chapter 12 will deal mainly with the emergence of traditionalist conservatives in American politics from 1912-1952, starting with the presidential election of Woodrow Wilson, who was the first in a series of progressive presidents.

This chapter deals mainly with the emergence of traditionalist conservatives in American politics from 1912-1952, starting with the presidential election of Woodrow Wilson, who was the first in a series of progressive presidents. Many traditionalists began entering politics to oppose the progressives. In 1952, Senator Robert Taft of Ohio, often called *"Mr. Conservative,"* was at the peak of his political influence as the bane of progressives.

THE PROGRESSIVE MOVEMENT BEGINS (1890)

"One of the greatest delusions in the world is the hope that the evils in this world are to be cured by legislation" Thomas Bracket Reed, 1886

Woodrow Wilson

Although it is difficult to find a definitive starting date for the progressive movement, the **Sherman Antitrust Act of 1890**,[210] the most famous early bill, provides as good a date as any. A group of reform-oriented journalists called *"muckrakers"* were loosely associated with the progressive movement. They wrote mainly for popular magazines and were extremely critical of business monopolies. Progressives and muckrakers sought a wide variety of social reforms. The anti-business element of progressivism caused a reaction from pro-business conservatives, providing a convenient guide for tracing the movement's rise.

The first powerful conservative in government to openly oppose the progressive movement was Thomas Bracket Reed (1839-1902) from Maine, who served as Republican Speaker of the House (1889-1891 and 1895-1899). Known for his sharp wit, Reed's quotable remarks contrast conservative views with progressive doctrine.

CONSERVATIVE RESTORATION VERSUS REACTION

Herbert Hoover and Franklin Roosevelt

The progressive movement gained steam under the progressive presidencies of Theodore Roosevelt (served 1901-1909), Woodrow Wilson (served 1913-1921), Herbert Hoover (served 1929-1933) and Franklin Roosevelt (served 1933-1945). Conservative response steadily increased until the apogee of Senator Robert Taft's powerful opposition to the **New Deal**,[211] a series of economic programs in response to the Great Depression that were passed by Congress during Franklin Roosevelt's first term. Implemented between 1933 and 1936, the plans included the **National Industrial Recovery Act**,[212] the **National Labor Relations Act**,[213] and the **Social Security Act**,[214] and focused on the *"3 Rs"*: Relief

---

[210] The Sherman Antitrust Act requires the U.S. federal government to investigate and pursue trusts, companies and organizations. It was the first Federal statute to limit cartels and monopolies, and still forms the basis for most antitrust litigation today. Politicians were unwilling to refer to the law until Theodore Roosevelt's presidency (1901-1909). (Sherman 1890)

[211] The New Deal represented a significant shift in U.S. political and domestic policy, including increased federal government economic regulation. It also marked the beginning of complex social programs and growing labor union power. The effects remain a source of controversy and debate among economists and historians.

[212] (Roosevelt 1933)

for the unemployed and poor; Recovery of the economy to normal levels; and Reform of the financial system to prevent a repeat depression.

Progressives believed the reforms benefitted the common good, labeling conservative opposition as *"reactionary,"* a term coined by Marxists as the standard expression for conservative opposition.[215] Conservatives sought to reinstate true constitutional government as established by the founders – they were *"restorationists"* seeking to refurbish the old republic, and were not mere opponents of change as progressives alleged.

NATURAL LAW VERSUS LIBERTARIANS AND PROGRESSIVES

Contrary to modern libertarians like American businessman Gary Johnson (1953-), former Governor of New Mexico and 2012 candidate for the Libertarian Party nomination for President, early 20th century conservatives did not view increased government spending or new government programs as necessarily bad. They rejected the libertarian conception of struggle between the citizens and government in a zero sum game, in which individual freedom diminishes in direct proportion to the increase in government activity. Conservatives applauded vigorous and effective government action when it stayed within the scope that natural law assigns to government, and within the boundaries imposed by the Constitution. However, when progressives launched federal programs that transgressed natural and wholesome boundaries of government, and trespassed upon natural prerogatives of individuals, families, churches, businesses, communities and states, conservatives opposed them as a matter of principle. They were not blindly anti-government, but insisted that government play by the rules and function within proper boundaries.

> **Fred Critique**
>
> *Conservatives applauded vigorous and effective government action when it stayed within the scope that natural law assigns to government, and within the boundaries imposed by the Constitution.*

This progressive willingness to violate constitutional boundaries, thereby breaking the rules of government, has tempted current liberals to do likewise. The most obvious examples are liberal judges who tweak the Constitution to interpret it as they please, and cases of voter fraud. A specific case began when political candidate Lyndon Johnson (1908-1973) violated rules to win a close election, rationalizing that cheating is permitted for progressive causes. When he ran for Vice President on the 1960 Kennedy/Johnson ticket, he also sought a third term in the U.S. Senate. After changing Texas law to allow him to seek two offices, he won both and later resigned the senate seat. In 1988, presidential candidate Michael Dukakis' VP running mate, Senator Lloyd Bentsen from Texas, took advantage of *"Lyndon's law"* and retained his Senate seat despite Dukakis' loss to George H.W. Bush. Senator Joe Lieberman of Connecticut used the same strategy in 2000 after Al Gore lost to George W. Bush. In 2008, Joseph Biden of Delaware was elected Vice President and was re-elected Senator, as Johnson had done in 1960.

FIVE PROGRESSIVE HERESIES PLUS ONE

There are a number of fundamental theological doctrines essential to Christianity – false teachings that undermine these principles are heresies. Progressives and populists have introduced six political heresies that are destructive to republics. Five are attributable to progressives and are listed below. The populists take credit for the sixth heresy, which is described later.

---

[213] (S. R. Wagner 1935)
[214] (Wagner and Lewis 1935)
[215] (marxists.org 2008)

Thomas Brackett Reed

Rational minds know change can be good or bad – it is equally irrational to be either blindly for or against change. However, life experience teaches that most new ideas are worthless, while only a few are valuable. Thomas Reed said, *"Most new things are not good and die an early death; but those that push themselves forward, and by slow degree force themselves on the attention of mankind, are the unconscious productions of human wisdom and must have honest consideration and must not be made the subject of unreasoning prejudice."* Reed's reference to a slow-working unconscious wisdom indicates that he was a traditionalist conservative similar to Edwin Burke.

Wise conservatives are not opposed to new ideas, but call for a slow sifting process. Those who pan for gold may find a few precious grains among thousands of worthless sand particles – gold is like the few good ideas, and sand is similar to the many worthless ones. Most management and church fads that passed through during recent decades are now forgotten, but a few survived in modified form because of proven value. Human susceptibility to temporary trend craze is mitigated by the common sense to discard most fashions after they run their course.

Businesses and churches can easily drop bogus manias, but governments cannot – once fads become government programs, they are often granted everlasting life and the folly becomes entrenched. When a legislature rejects Reed's caution, government becomes a repository for the unlimited accumulation of human recklessness. That is why tax experts must possess encyclopedic knowledge, and reforming the labyrinthine tax code is like cleaning the Augean stables.[216]

> *Fred Critique*
>
> *Mobs hear rhetorical vows and cheer wildly, while having no clue what they applaud. Magical thinking lends itself to easily inflamed passions while rational faculties close down.*

This heresy is based on nonsense and is very popular – current political candidates routinely promise *"change"* without bothering to explain what it means or where it leads. Mobs hear rhetorical vows and cheer wildly, while having no clue what they applaud. Magical thinking lends itself to easily inflamed passions while rational faculties close down. Shakespeare put these words in Mark Antony's mouth after he incited a Roman mob to hysteria and riot – *"Why friends, you go to do you know not what."*[217] In like manner, Barack Obama's (1961-) crowds get into a tremendous uproar over... they know not what.

It is no accident that so many progressive/populists were skillful **demagogues**.[218] Some conservatives called them *"rabble-rousers"* because they provoked the masses and transformed them into mindless, hysterical mobs. Huey Long (1893-1935), the charismatic and immensely popular Governor of Louisiana (1928-1932), was noted for his radical populist policies – he created the **Share Our Wealth Program**[219] with the motto *"Every Man a King,"* proposing wealth redistribution measures to curb poverty and homelessness during the Great Depression.

---

[216] In Greek mythology, Augeas was best known for his stables, which housed the greatest number of immortal livestock in the country and had never been cleaned – until the great hero Heracles succeeded by rerouting the rivers Alpheus and Peneus to wash out the filth.

[217] (Shakespeare, The Tragedy of Julius Caesar: Act III, Scene ii 1599)

[218] Demagogy is a political strategy for gaining power by appealing to the prejudices, emotions, fears, vanities and expectations of the public – typically via passionate rhetoric and propaganda, and often using nationalist, populist or religious themes.

[219] (Long 1934)

PROGRESSIVE HERESY 2 – THERE ARE NO NATURAL BOUNDARIES FOR THE SCOPE OF GOVERNMENT.

According to this heresy, the appropriate scope for government changes with the times. *"Modern times"* require a wider reach for governmental powers than the 19th century American Republic *"simpler times."* The odd suggestion that former days were simpler and therefore needed less government betrays a deep ignorance of history. The civilized, cultured, literate and articulate people of previous eras lived in socially complex communities. Their high culture and sophisticated society contrasts auspiciously with the primitivism of modern neo-barbarians.

When people believe government has no natural limits, it steadily expands until dominating every aspect of life. All the liberties we hold dear will gradually be crushed in the slowly closing vice of tyranny. Progressives took the brakes off a truck careening

down a steep hill with this assertion. By default, they left it entirely to conservatives to stop the runaway vehicle before it runs over people – this liberal elusion reveals deep irresponsibility imprinted on their hearts. Wisdom dictates that loaning money to people living in a magical fantasy world is reckless, because they behave irresponsibly. Likewise, progressives are untrustworthy since their universe is imagined – expect broken promises.

Rational people know that government and private life are two different entities – only children confuse issues of public and private, often becoming an embarrassment to parents. The slightest hint that the public sector has no natural boundaries is childish. The careless intrusion of government into private spheres betrays an awkward lack of responsibility. Conservatives view progressive antics as juvenile, i.e., when liberals turn private funeral memorials into political speech opportunities, the stunt is regarded as sophomoric and disrespectful.

PROGRESSIVE HERESY 3 – GOVERNMENT IS AN ORGANIC LIVING ENTITY.

This heresy claims that government grows, develops and matures in an *"evolutionary"* fashion. Similarly, the United States Constitution is given *"living document"* status, which means it grows through judiciary interpretation to accommodate the developing government. After all, *"change is good"* and we should not block *"the path of change"* or *"turn back the clock."* Rational adults disregard magical paths of change and mystical clocks of history – only children believe such nonsense. Yet this childish drivel is widely believed.

Like many progressive myths, the claim of organic government is an assertion that must be taken on faith, or left alone. The only way to believe this fantasy is to never see the administration from inside. Prussian statesman Otto Von Bismark (1815-1898) said, *"Laws are like sausages. It is better to not see them being made."* Idealism concerning sausages and governments is preserved by maintaining perfect ignorance.

After years of working with many state agencies, Fred Hutchison was reminded of a Rube Goldberg contraption.[220] He saw nothing organic in auditing, however he did observe *"biology"* that motivated a manager to promote an inept young woman. Unfortunately, government management is plagued with this kind of natural science.[221]

---

[220] A Rube Goldberg device is a deliberately over-engineered machine that performs very simple tasks in a very complex fashion, usually including a chain reaction. The expression is named after American cartoonist and inventor Rube Goldberg (1883-1970).
[221] (F. Hutchison, Brief History of Conservatism 2009)

PROGRESSIVE HERESY 4 – GOVERNMENT IS INNATELY GOOD AND IS THE AGENT THAT FORCES OF HISTORY HAVE CHOSEN TO USHER IN A BETTER WORLD.

Jean Jacques Rousseau

If the magical forces are impersonal, how can they choose and/or care about human welfare? Progressives posit that government is a distillation and expression of the people – what Rousseau vaguely called *"the general will."* Government is imagined as the *"friend of the people"* because *"government is the people."* Notice the mystical fuzziness and naiveté of such conceptions.[222] Liberals then claim that capitalists, plutocrats and aristocrats are *"enemies of the people"* because their private interests block the social engineering *"path of progress."* They declare that business is not *"the people"* but government is, in spite of the fact that trade and commerce offer a much freer scope for individual human thought and action.

Thomas Brackett Reed (1839-1902), Speaker of the U.S. House of Representatives from 1889-1891 and 1895-1899, said, *"One of the greatest delusions in the world is that all the evils in the world are to be cured by legislation."* This fantasy flows from the assumption that government is innately good, wise and trustworthy. The fact that Reed's warning came during the 1890s is a reminder of how old this heresy is – something stubborn in human nature perpetuates a popular myth's endurance. Recall that most theology heresies are more than 1,500 years old. This fallen race has always bred more rascals and fools than those who are rational, responsible and astute.

> ### *Fred Critique*
>
> *This fallen race has always bred more rascals and fools than those who are rational, responsible and astute.*

PROGRESSIVE HERESY 5 – HUMAN RIGHTS ARE GRANTED BY THE GOVERNMENT, NOT BY GOD OR NATURAL LAW, THEREFORE THEY CHANGE OVER TIME.

Conservatives view this idea as absurd and pernicious, never dreaming how quickly mischief accumulates. The idea that rights are created by government enabled judges and legislators to concoct a *"right to privacy"* in which anything goes behind closed doors. They invented the right to an education; to not be poor; to medical care; to gay marriage; to gay adoption of children; to black equal representation in colleges and jobs; to non-exclusion of women, blacks and gays from private clubs; and for officially protected *"victim"* groups to never hear a personally demeaning utterance. Progressive governments routinely devise such rights as part of the brave new world program. Many newly-minted rights diminish freedom, order, or both.

The Unites States Constitution **Bill of Rights** amendments[223] enhance freedom without compromising order. The American founders taught that human rights come from God or natural law, and are therefore limited in number, universal, fixed and unalienable. On rare occasions a government can discover rights, but can never create rights – it is

---

[222] It is almost as blurry as an Obama speech. (F. Hutchison, Brief History of Conservatism 2009)

[223] 1st – Establishment Clause, Free Exercise Clause; freedom of speech, of the press, and of assembly; right to petition

2nd – Militia (United States), Sovereign state, Right to keep and bear arms

3rd – Protection from quartering of troops

4th – Protection from unreasonable search and seizure

5th – Due process, double jeopardy, self-incrimination, eminent domain

6th – Trial by jury and rights of the accused; Confrontation Clause, speedy trial, public trial, right to counsel

7th – Civil trial by jury

8th – Prohibition of excessive bail and cruel and unusual punishment

9th – Protection of rights not specifically enumerated in the Constitution

10th – Powers of States and people

not a god to mold and manufacture human nature and bestow contrived rights. Leading officials are not a force of nature that brings forth living beings to be nurtured and provided for, like a mother caring for her children. When the bowels of most large state agencies are examined, it is like treading the labyrinths of a dark, troubled underworld. No father god is found to give name or nature; no warm nursing mother is located to suckle. The suggestion that this wasteland is where personal nature is molded and rights are conjured up would be frightening if it were not ridiculous.

Why must government play God? Can government just be the government? Leaders must be mature grown-ups to understand the boundaries of government and resist representing a magical entity meant to dazzle and bewitch citizens. They must honor the true God before they can stop looking for false gods. They must experience the real God before they can be real humans. All these problems have numinous roots – progressivism is a symptom of spiritual sickness.

> **Fred Critique**
> _____
> *Progressivism is a symptom of spiritual sickness.*

PROGRESSIVES AND POPULISTS

Robert La Follette

There was considerable overlap between the progressive and populist movements in the 19th and early 20th century. Robert La Follette (1855-1925) ran for president in 1924 as the Progressive Party candidate, was more progressive than populist, and is a key figure in Wisconsin's long history of political liberalism. Huey Long was more a populist than a progressive. Al Gore (1948-) is descended from a line of leading Tennessee political populists.

The populist motto, *"Power to the People,"* implied the notion *"down with the elite."* Populists were social levelers who favored the little guy – they hated hierarchy, emphasized equality, were anti-regime and wanted to overthrow the establishment. They emphasized popular democracy and viewed government as *"the voice of the people."* When Fred Hutchison's outspoken grandmother heard populists tout, *"The voice of the people is the voice of God,"* she would respond with, *"The masses are asses."*[224] Paradoxically, the elite Gore political machine was populist in agenda. In contrast, progressives liked elites if they were progressive, or were congenial to the movement – they did not mind hierarchy if they were at the top of the pyramid, or could influence those at the top.

> **Fred Critique**
> _____
> *The masses are asses.*

Progressives and populists agreed on their dislike of big business and conservative, middle class institutions. They both valued labor unions, family farmers, and unlimited, untamed democracy as they cried, *"Let the people speak."* They did not concur with the founding father principles that democracy unleashed runs wild, but when tamed and harnessed by the Constitution and the rule of law it ensures freedom.

THE SIXTH HERESY – DEMOCRACY IS THE HOLY GRAIL

Populists added a sixth heresy to the movement: Democracy is the Holy Grail. They believed that **democracy**[225] is inherently good, that anything limiting or filtering it is bad, and that it is the hope of the world – if delivered to all

---

[224] (F. Hutchison, Brief History of Conservatism 2009)
[225] Democracy is a form of government where all people have an equal say in decisions that affect their lives, ideally including direct participation in the proposal, development and passage of legislation into law. It can also involve social, economic and cultural conditions that enable the free and equal practice of political self-determination.

mankind, every world ill would simply fade away. This global messianic democracy was particularly prominent in Woodrow Wilson's international policies and the G.W. Bush administration.

The American founders had read Locke, Bolingbroke and Montesquieu, and thereby understood that democracy can be either good or bad. Unchained democratic systems run rampant and easily yield to social upheaval, popular demagogues, mob rule, and men on horseback rescuing the mob from itself. Men like Caesar, Napoleon and Hitler quickly rise to power on the fragments of regimes shattered by popular passions.

If a **republic**[226] is devoted to personal freedom and liberty, the elected legislature must provide for a carefully restrained representative democracy. When legislators are tamed, instructed in law and stoic rationality, and civilized with genteel self-restraint, there is hope for a governing body – human nature demands structural restraints. When elected representatives are balanced with an aristocratic senate, an executive, a judiciary, and state and local bodies, the legislature can be a true defender of freedom. Such a system is essentially a republic, and only secondarily a democracy.

Since the 6th and 7th Presidents, John Quincy Adams (1767-1848) and Andrew Jackson (1767-1845), the United States has had two major parties; one believing America is a democracy and the other considering it a republic. The populists who embraced the sixth heresy a century ago had predecessors dating back to Andrew Jackson. Thomas Jefferson entertained populist views, but indulged them more in theory than in practice.

Hutchison's forthright grandmother always stamped her letters with *"This is a Republic, not a Democracy. Let us keep it that way."* The word "repu*blic*" has always stirred deep feelings within liberty minded citizens, while *"democracy"* lacks the same emotional punch. God fearing patriots can imagine themselves dying for The Republic, but cannot conceive of dying for democracy.[227]

THE COOLIDGE QUASI-CONSERVATIVE PRELUDE

Calvin Coolidge

Calvin Coolidge (1872-1933) is a perfect example of an honest and self-restrained gentleman who was of great service to the Republic. Contrary to popular belief, Coolidge was not a philosophical conservative – he was a de facto conservative by default. He was torn between the Republican Party's progressive faction, led by Teddy Roosevelt (who wrested control of the progressives from La Follette), and the moderately conservative wing, led by William Howard Taft (1857-1930). While serving as Governor of Massachusetts (1919-1921), Coolidge's program included a few dashes of progressive legislation.

---

[226] A republic is a form of government in which a significant portion of the people retains supreme control over the government, and where offices of state are not granted through heritage.
[227] (F. Hutchison, Brief History of Conservatism 2009)

As the 30th President (1923-1929), Coolidge employed his keen legal mind, and took the Constitution and its federal separation of powers seriously, concluding that the presidential role was limited. His policies may have superficially resembled a **laissez faire**[228] economic conservative, but were determined by pure and simple federalism, not political or economic theory. Although a business booster, Coolidge dissociated business cheerleading from his executive policy.

Coolidge was a scrupulously honest lawyer – he abided by his oath to uphold the Constitution and refused to claim executive powers not clearly granted to the president. His refusal to act on various occasions was not passive or lazy; he resisted breaking the supreme law of the land. He often declined speaking unless he had something specific to say, and did not take executive action unless it was legal and had a legitimate objective. Coolidge set the standard for future constitutional conservatives who would defend federalism, fight the executive branch expansion beyond constitutional boundaries, and oppose judicial interpretation of the Constitution according to ideological bias and social engineering fancies.

TRADITIONALISTS BECOME POLITICAL

As noted in Chapter 11 (page 127), the three varieties of Traditionalists include Burkean (or social fabric) conservatives, which also grew three branches: 1) Paleoconservatives, 2) Agrarians, and 3) Russell Kirk followers. The paleocons first gained political power through the Republican Party, and were called *"classical conservatives."* Unlike Coolidge, paleocon political philosophy was based on transcendent moral order world view and belief, as previously outlined. Their substantial political ideas contrasted favorably with the insubstantial principles of liberal progressives, which were based on vague notions of progress and cloudy dreams of utopia. The 33rd President, Harry Truman (1884-1972), believed in the inevitability of progress leading to future utopia, touting vague and incoherent ideas – his views of *"progress"* were almost as indistinct as Barack Obama's rhetoric of *"hope and change."*

PALEOCON REACTION TO THE NEW DEAL (1932-1952)

No one reacted to the New Deal with greater hostility than paleocons – when President Franklin Roosevelt (1882-1945) died, some threw parties to celebrate. To the end of her life, Hutchison's paleocon grandmother could not hear the name Franklin Delano Roosevelt (FDR) without expressing disgust.[229] Although we must not tolerate the FDR hatred of that generation, we should realize they considered his march the vanguard of forces determined to undermine constitutional government and tear apart the cherished American way of life, and they were not mistaken.

> ### *Fred Critique*
>
> *FDR's march was the vanguard of forces determined to undermine constitutional government and tear apart the American way of life.*

Paleocons objected to high taxes, deficit spending, creeping socialism, the inefficiency and waste of New Deal programs, the regulation of business, farm subsidies, programs favoring labor unions, nationalized health insurance, the "packing" of the Supreme Court by FDR, John Dewey's progressive education program, aggressive involvement in foreign affairs, the League of Nations, excessive immigration, and the influence of the U.S. Conference of Catholic Bishops upon New Deal social policies. The most intense period of political reaction was 1932-1952. Paleocons gained significant traction during the 1938 congressional elections – after four years, the New Deal had failed to cure

---

[228] Laissez-faire describes an environment where transactions between private parties are free from state intervention, including restrictive regulations, taxes, tariffs and enforced monopolies. The French phrase literally means "let do," and broadly implies "let it be," or "leave it alone."

[229] (F. Hutchison, Brief History of Conservatism 2009)

the Great Depression and FDR Democrats were falling in public esteem. It was World War II that finally restored the country and revived fortunes.

ROBERT TAFT AKA "MR. CONSERVATIVE"

Robert Taft

Robert Taft of Ohio (1889-1953) was elected to the Senate in 1938 and organized the **Conservative Coalition of Congress**,[230] an alliance of Republican conservatives and conservative Southern Democrats. The coalition's mission was to oppose New Deal agendas and abolish or curtail existing New Deal programs. Taft's most famous legislation was the **Taft-Hartley Bill of 1947**[231] that corrected the untoward federal favoritism towards labor unions inherent in the **Wagner Act of 1935**.[232]

Although Taft supported social security and federal housing programs, as a general rule he advocated free markets and limited government. His libertarian tendencies were a precursor to William F. Buckley, Jr.'s synthesis of Traditionalism and Libertarianism, as described in Chapter 13. Taft was a strong presidential candidate in 1940, but liberal Republicans objected to his non-interventionist foreign policy and opposition to New Deal programs. In those days, the Party still had many liberal heirs of Teddy Roosevelt's progressives. The Republicans nominated dark horse nominee Wendell Wilkie (1892-1944), the second of four weak campaigns for the presidency (Landon, Wilkie, Dewey and Dewey).

Taft did not run for president in 1944 – his opposition to America's entry into World War II made his election impossible because of the war's general popularity and the remarkable surge of American patriotism during those years. Taft tried again in 1948, but was bested by Thomas Dewey (1902-1971), who was also making his second run. Then the memorable 1952 brouhaha in Chicago arrived.

TAFT'S COLD WAR DILEMMA

Harry Truman

In order to understand the Chicago brouhaha,[233] we must first understand Senator Taft's Cold War dilemma. Paleoconservatives always had an isolationist streak. President William McKinley and Senator Thomas Brackett Reed were almost alone in their opposition to the popular Spanish American War (1898). Senator Henry Cabot Lodge opposed American membership in the League of Nations (1919) on the grounds that it would impair American national sovereignty. Senator Taft opposed American entry into World War II – the America First Movement of the 1940s was a non-interventionist paleocon affair. Pat Buchanan (1938-) and Robert Novak (1931-2009) opposed sending American troops to Iraq (2003) because their paleocon instincts told them America would not benefit.

Communism was uniquely abhorrent to Paleocon conservatism. Whereas liberal reformers were slowly unraveling the social fabric one strand at a time, Communists wanted to throw the whole structure into the furnace. Joseph Stalin

---

[230] The Coalition was dominant in Congress from 1937-1963, remained a political force until the mid 1980s, and eventually died out in the 1990s. (Jensen 2009)

[231] The Labor-Management Relations Act, or Taft-Hartley Act, is a United States federal law that monitors the activities and power of labor unions, and is still in effect.

[232] The National Labor Relations Act, or Wagner Act, is a United States federal law that limits employer reaction to workers in the private sector who create labor unions, engage in collective bargaining, and participate in strikes and other concerted activity to support their demands.

[233] A brouhaha is a state of social agitation when a minor incident gets out of control, and is typically marked by controversy and fuss that can afterwards seem to have been pointless or irrational.

137

(1878-1953) and Mao Tse-tung (1893-1976) conducted mass exterminations of the middle class and murdered a large portion of the intelligentsia and professional class. Taft hated communism with a passion, and at the same time was a moderate isolationist during the war years – his paleocon urge to fight communism was checked by his paleocon aversion to international entanglements. In contrast, President Truman ordered the Berlin Airlift,[234] shored up anticommunist nations through the Marshall Plan,[235] manipulated the United Nations to frustrate the Soviets, and fought a proxy war in Korea to check communist expansionism. Progressives like Wilson, the two Roosevelts, and Truman were enthusiastic internationalists. The conservative opposition was not.

PALEOCONS TORN BETWEEN ISOLATIONISM AND ANTICOMMUNISM

Fred Hutchison's paleocon grandmother and her daughter went to the 1952 Republican convention as delegates. The daughter was loyal to Taft. The grandmother was a politically active isolationist during World War II, while her son was flying P-51 Mustangs in North Africa, Sicily and Italy, but defected from Taft to Douglas MacArthur (1880-1964) when the same son was flying Mustangs in Korea.[236] These two conservative Republican women perfectly manifested the inner conflict of paleocons – to remain true to the isolationist *"America First"* principles, or hate communism so much that they voted for General MacArthur, whose motto was *"There is no substitute for victory."* Triumph over the evil foe was imperative. American author William Manchester (1922-2004) wrote that MacArthur was like Julius Caesar in that, *"He was as great as a man can be without being good, and as wise as a man can be without being humble."*[237] This truly great but deeply flawed man dazzled Fred's grandmother.

> *Fred Critique*
>
> *The inner conflict of paleocons – to remain true to isolationist "America First" principles, or hate communist infiltration.*

In 1952, Truman's popularity was at a low ebb because he was perceived as soft on communism – too weak to insist on victory in Korea and too soft to root out communist infiltration of the State Department. Irony of ironies, that year Senator Taft's influence in the Party was at its zenith; this was his golden moment to ascend to the White House at last. Unfortunately, his anti-New Deal paleocon dominance occurred when American anti-communism was white hot. What should a good Republican's priority be? The ideal moment had come for Republicans to nominate generals like MacArthur and Dwight "Ike" Eisenhower (1890-1969), and anti-communist crusader Richard Nixon (1913-1994). This conflict of loyalties brought about a tremendous collision – the shockwaves are still with us.

THE BROUHAHA IN CHICAGO

Taft went to the 1952 Republican convention in Chicago as the leading presidential candidate. Republicans wanted to line up a winning candidate before the voting began, and manic haggling for delegates commenced in rooms filled with cigar smoke, whiskey, filthy spittoons and sweaty deal-makers. Fred's grandmother, who had marched in the

---

[234] The Berlin Blockade (June 1948-May 1949) was the first major international crises of the Cold War that resulted in casualties. During the multinational occupation of post-World War II Germany, the Soviet Union blocked the Western Allies' rail and road access to sectors of Berlin under Allied control, aiming to force the western powers to allow the Soviet zone to supply food and fuel, thereby giving the Soviets control of the entire city. In response, the Western Allies organized the Berlin Airlift to carry supplies to the people in West Berlin, providing up to 4,700 tons of daily necessities.

[235] The Marshall Plan (European Recovery Program, ERP) was the large-scale American program to aid Europe with monetary support to help rebuild economies after World War II, in order to combat the spread of Soviet communism.

[236] (F. Hutchison, Brief History of Conservatism 2009)

[237] (Manchester 1978)

Women's Christian Temperance Movement,[238] was utterly disgusted and sickened – her motto was, *"Lips that touch liquor shall never touch mine."* In contrast, her big, hearty, back-slapping, belly-laughing daughter drank whiskey and was as rough and tough as the men in the smoke-filled rooms – a jolly but formidable woman, Hutchison made it his business to stay on her jolly side and avoid her formidable side.[239]

The delegate wheeling and dealing astonished those watching the debate on television, as the fight over credentials got ugly. Ike's handlers were superb propagandists and deal-makers, and his bandwagon traversed the streets with fog-horns blaring, *"Thou shalt not steal,"* accompanied by actors dressed like bandits pretending to steal delegates. The real agitation in the qualification battle was the dirty tricks played by Ike's moderates, and Eisenhower beat Taft 595 to 500 on the first ballot. If Taft had only been a little more overtly anti-communist, a bit better at oration, and more of an impromptu deal maker in the smoke-filled rooms, the Republican nomination and the presidency would surely have been his. His courtly, magisterial oversight of the Senate unfitted him for the Chicago knife fight.

ELEPHANTS STAMPEDE THE COW PALACE

Elephants have long memories. Conservative delegates to the 1964 GOP convention had bitter memories of stolen delegates and lying propaganda during the 1952 convention. A tough young woman named Phyllis Schlafly (1924-)

Nelson Rockefeller

aroused and enraged the elephant herd with her book, *A Choice, Not an Echo*.[240] She lambasted the New York establishment party leaders for foisting a series of weak *"me too"* candidates, for cheating Taft of his rightful nomination, and for attempting to shove the moderate Nelson Rockefeller (1908-1979) down their throats. *"For once let us real Republicans have a choice, instead of tamely submitting to the decrees of the party leaders of the New York establishment,"* she exclaimed. The raging elephants stampeded the Cow Palace in San Francisco, where the 1964 convention was held. They denounced Rockefeller moderates, defied national GOP leaders, and pushed through Barry Goldwater's (1909-1998) nomination for president. Do not torment angry elephants!

NEXT TIME

Chapter 13 will allude to Buckley's role in drawing conservative Catholics into politics, and the Libertarian rebellion drama. By the time Goldwater ran for president, his political philosophy had become an example of fusionism, a blend of traditionalism, libertarianism and anti-communism. This new mix opened the door to his presidential nomination and the Reagan presidency.

---

[238] The Woman's Christian Temperance Union (WCTU) is the world's oldest non-sectarian women's association. Organized in Cleveland, Ohio in 1874, the group spearheaded the prohibition crusade.

[239] (F. Hutchison, Brief History of Conservatism 2009)

[240] (Schlafly 1964)

Robert Taft

Chapter 12 ended with Barry Goldwater's (1909-1998) GOP nomination for president in 1964. Senator Robert Taft, the preeminent conservative figure from 1938-1952, paved the way for young Goldwater's rise, who was an enthusiastic foot soldier for Taft's conservative coalition. By the time of his presidential campaign, he was materially different in political philosophy from the late paleoconservative Robert Taft – Goldwater had embraced a blend of traditionalism, libertarianism and anti-communism known as **fusionism.**[241]

FUSIONISM, PROMISING BUT PROBLEMATIC

Barry Goldwater

Goldwater's free-wheeling, colorfully eccentric and outspoken manners were ridiculed by Democrats during the 1964 presidential campaign – his eccentricity was indicative of the intense individualism of a deeply libertarian man. As Senator Goldwater aged, he became increasingly open-minded and unconventional, expressing blunt annoyance with his party's opposition to abortion, the gay agenda and the individual use of drugs. This decline in moral reasoning often accompanies emerging hyper-individualism as libertarians drift away from fusionist moorings, and is common among unanchored conservatives today. Goldwater's slide was unusual because it occurred during fusionism's heyday – an early warning sign of troubles to come.

Fusionism was generally good for the conservative movement for several decades, as some important ideas were extracted from libertarian writers. The tension between traditionalist moral codes and implicit libertinism seemed to hold the process of decadence in check. This was particularly true prior to the sexual revolution (1967-1980). Libertarians who faithfully read *National Review (NR)*,[242] the fountainhead and flagship of fusionism, were regularly exposed to moral reasoning that kept some of them from running amok. Fred Hutchison remembered making jovial comments about *"libertarians running rampant"* when his group could not determine the whereabouts of some of their unfettered fellows at a conference.[243]

The political awakening of Evangelical moral conservatism occurred during the later part of fusionism's zenith, leading to Ronald Reagan's (1911-2004) electoral landslides (1980 and 1984) and another influence that slowed moral decay. Libertarians were enthusiastic supporters of Reagan and remained a loyal and indispensable part of the Republican team – for a season, their enthusiasm for the crusade against big government trumped individualist rationalizations for the sexual revolution.

> *Fred Critique*
> _____
> *The tension between traditionalist moral codes and implicit libertinism seemed to hold the process of decadence in check.*

---

[241] Fusionism is an American political strategy for combining traditional conservatives with some libertarian and social conservatives. The movement was promoted and named by *National Review* editor Frank Meyer.

[242] National Review is a biweekly magazine founded by William F. Buckley, Jr. in 1955 and based in New York City, self described as *"America's most widely read and influential magazine and web site for conservative news, commentary, and opinion."*

[243] (F. Hutchison, Brief History of Conservatism 2009)

THE HEYDAY OF FUSIONISM (1960-1988)

William F. Buckley, Jr. (1925-2008) had a long personal association with Goldwater, encouraging the budding fusionism. Brent Bozell (1955-), Buckley's brother-in-law, was ghostwriter for Goldwater's book, *The Conscience of a Conservative*.[244] This famous and influential publication is a convenient marker for the beginning of fusionism's peak. Ronald Reagan was a fusionist; therefore his last year in office (1988) is a good indicator for the end.

William F. Buckley

Buckley was in the prime of his influence on American political philosophy. Prior to 1960, he was the colorful upstart and **enfant terrible**[245] who dared challenge the liberal establishment. From 1960-1988, he and his memorable team were the leaders of American conservative political philosophy; after 1988, Reagan and Buckley became the elder statesmen. Reagan's retirement in 1989 and Buckley's departure as editor of NR in 1990 left a huge leadership void in the movement. Although still involved with NR and active in conservative causes, Buckley's absence from the tiller created an irreplaceable vacuum. Buckley's powerful and winsome presence had encouraged leading conservative American thinkers to affiliate with NR and thoughtfully discuss different opinions.

PIONEER DEBATER AGAINST STATISM

Buckley used libertarian arguments against the creeping socialism and statism advocated by liberals, reaching a mass audience with his TV debate show, **Firing Line**.[246] Through this pioneering enterprise, he taught conservatives how to debate and defeat liberal arguments, an example followed for several decades. Rational reasoning trumped collective ideology, as conservatives generally had the best rationale for free enterprise and personal freedom, which is part of the reason liberalism lost appeal after 1970.

BABY BOOMER FUSIONISTS AND FRED HUTCHISON

Fred Hutchison

Conservative baby boomers formed the greatest mass of fusionists. Their political instruction occurred on college campuses when Buckley, Goldwater and Schlafly were heroes, as they read NR and books written by traditionalists and libertarians. It is impossible to understand the conservative movement in the second half of the 20th century apart from fusionism.

Fred Hutchison was already a traditionist when he entered Miami University in Oxford, Ohio – his early conservative awakening was inspired by the Goldwater campaign. He joined the fusionist led Conser-vative Club, where he found himself in perpetual debate with an intellectual libertarian who shared a common resistance to fusionism. Hutchison was a traditionalist Christian with no admixture of libertarianism, his fellow was a libertarian atheist with no traces of traditionalism – at two poles of the philosophical spectrum, their defiance of fusionist tides were the exception in the club. Hutchison's praise for fusionism in no way implies that he was ever a fusionist, although he did appreciate the movement's remarkable historical achievements.

> ### *Fred Critique*
> ---
> *Hutchison's praise for fusionism does not imply that he was a fusionist, although he did appreciate their achievements.*

---

[244] (Goldwater 1960)

[245] An unconventional badly-behaved person who causes embarrassment or shock to others.

[246] Firing Line (1966-1999), founded and hosted by William Buckley, was the longest-running public affairs show in television history with a single host. The program featured many prominent intellectuals and public figures, and won an Emmy Award in 1969.

FUSIONISM AND THE GREATEST GENERATION

President Richard Nixon, a lifelong main street Republican, lapsed into **Keynesian economics**[247] and price controls; this move is remembered by fusionist conservatives as an unexpected and painful setback in the middle of a great advancement in ideas. Nixon, a naval officer in World War II, was a leading anti-communist crusader in the late 1940s and early 1950s. He belonged to a generation of Republicans who had a hard time understanding libertarianism and fusionism.

William F. Buckley, Jr., the pioneer of fusionism who was twelve years younger than Nixon, had none of that generation's insularity, and none of the self-absorption, moral declension or cultural decadence of baby boomers. For all his published protests concerning Yale's liberalism, his alma mater, he lived during a marvelous time for education and unique opportunity in the world. Buckley was raised amidst a community of international elites in a day when high culture still meant something to members of the American patrician class. His father was a professor of romance languages, a lawyer and a Texas oil industry tycoon.

William F. Buckley, Sr. (1881-1958) was part of T.S. Eliot's (1888-1965) generation. Ernest Hemingway (1899-1961) called this the *"lost generation,"*[248] but in one important respect it was actually the last to not be lost – this was the last time Americans were assured of getting a fine classical education untainted by John Dewey's ultramodern and anti-traditional depredations. The children of Eliot's generation were nourished by the environment of a brilliant culture.

Ronald Reagan

Ronald Reagan, fourteen years older than Nixon, was an enthusiastic fusionist. A New Deal Democrat in his youth, Reagan became a Hollywood Republican around age forty, and continued his philosophical formation until he was fifty. His famous televised speech for Goldwater in 1964 had the excitement, passion and conviction of a recent convert. Interestingly, several great pioneers of conservatism switched from liberalism in their mature years – this hall of fame includes Locke, Montesquieu, Burke, Goethe, Churchill and Reagan.

As a young man, Buckley was encouraged by his father to read books by libertarian author Albert Jay Nock (1870-1945), so the ideas were essential to his conservative formation. Reagan was not introduced to libertarian ideas until his forties, and never listed as far to the libertarian side as Buckley. The two disagreed about giving the Panama Canal away; Reagan opposed it while Buckley was in favor. While Buckley advocated legalizing drugs, Reagan strongly opposed it and launched a war on drugs.

BUCKLEY AND THE MULTIPLE STREAMS OF CONSERVATISM

Buckley's practice of blending several conservative streams is highly relevant to the main thesis of this book – namely, that reconciliation and philosophical interaction between conservatism's five historical forms can restore an intellectually vigorous, culturally fruitful, morally coherent and politically potent society. Apparently, Buckley had insight along these lines more than fifty years ago, when he used libertarian and traditionalist writers to encourage and promote fusionism. Often arguing along libertarian lines on **Firing Line**, he managed to incorporate anticommunism into the conservative movement, while rejecting paranoid conspiracies.

---

[247] Keynesian economics is based on the ideas of 20th century English economist John Maynard Keynes, and argues that private sector decisions may lead to inefficient macroeconomic outcomes, therefore advocates active policy responses by the public sector, including monetary policy actions by central banks and fiscal policy actions by governments to stabilize output over the business cycle. The global financial crisis in 2007 caused world leaders to use Keynesian economics through government stimulus programs in an attempt to assist the economy.

[248] (Hemingway, The Sun Also Rises 1926)

Buckley encouraged his brother-in-law, Brent Bozell, to found **Triumph**,[249] a pioneer magazine for Catholic theological, intellectual and political conservatives. **Triumph** was the precursor of Richard John Neuhaus' (1936-2009) **First Things**[250] journal, and the inspiration for founding the Catholic liberal arts Christendom College in Front Royal, Virginia, in 1977. The restoration of classical orthodox Catholicism and traditional intellectual, moral and literary culture was desperately needed following the embarrassing meltdown after Vatican II – statistics show a significant decrease in membership, vocations and conversions, plus substantial monetary asset loss. The general public's view of priests has since eroded from Bing Crosby's portrayal of a slightly whimsical but loveable cleric, to distrust of priests and disdain for the bishops who failed to weed out child molesters. Serious Catholics still wince at the memory of hideous clown masses, when frolicking priests dressed as clowns celebrated mass while jamming to rock music. No one winced more than Buckley and Bozell.

THE PASSING GLORY OF A CLASSICAL EDUCATION

"The purpose of education is to help us to know a good man when we see him." Tracy Lee Simmons

Tracy Lee Simmons

According to legend, nine goddesses devoted to Apollo sang, danced and played musical instruments atop Mount Parnassus – Greek poets would climb the mountain hoping to dance with and be inspired by the muses. Buckley encouraged Tracy Lee Simmons, an Associate Editor of NR, to write **Climbing Parnassus: A New Apologia for Latin and Greek**.[251] In this work, Simmons made the case that students ought to learn Latin and Greek so they could read Western classics in these languages. Classical education develops the mind, helps impart wisdom and virtue, inculcates a taste for quality, stimulates the pursuit of truth and excellence, and transmits the traditional culture of the West.

Fred Hutchison was a friend to the last Latin teacher in the Columbus Public Schools, who taught interested friends to be writers in her spare time. Her unfailing good judgment in matters of critiquing, editing and the formulation of words was a testimony to her classical education. When she retired from teaching, the school system abolished the Latin and classics programs. The foolish education establishment replaced these gems with wretched courses that included multicultural quilt making – this is a symptom of public education's meltdown, just like clown masses indicated degrading Catholicism.[252]

[249] Triumph was a monthly American magazine published from 1966-1975 and based in Spain, which analyzed religious, philosophical and cultural issues from a traditional Catholic perspective.

[250] First Things is an ecumenical journal founded in 1990 that is focused on creating a "religiously informed public philosophy for the ordering of society," and is considered to be widely influential for exploring broad aspects of religion and society.

[251] (Simmons 2002)

[252] (F. Hutchison, Brief History of Conservatism 2009)

THE COMPLETE MAN

In the Renaissance sense, Buckley was the complete man. As the product of a classical education, he mastered Latin, spoke several European languages fluently, and was the maestro of English vocabulary. Imagine him bandying with Samuel Johnson and holding his own with the great craftsman of words. Visualize the clever and lighthearted man in a contest of wit with Voltaire, the grand master of intellectual parlor games.

Buckley played Baroque music on the harpsichord with a technique worthy of a chamber music soloist. He opened his television show with music from Bach's 1721 *Brandenburg Concerto*. The joy, charm, complexity and playfulness of the Brandenburg is a perfect expression of Buckley's temperament. Even though the show had a pedantic and polemic quality, it had a big audience because of its joyous and playful mood.

As a man who exhibited the *"full human flourishing"* we often write about but seldom see exemplified, Buckley had an extraordinary zest for life. He had a gift for friendship, even with liberal opponents – he was fascinated with the variety, irony, mystery and surprise of human nature. When he met random acquaintances, he would beam with pleasure and wonder at encountering a remarkable and unique specimen of humanity. In like manner, he took pleasure in each of the historic streams of conservatism.

THE PIED PIPER

Many questions exist concerning Buckley's motivation. His long profession of opposing the ruling establishment seemed to wane in the shadow of success that gave him a respected position in reigning society. His attack on the John Birch Society was rewarded with liberal respect and acknowledgment that he was conservatism's representative. Some long time acquaintances actually questioned whether he really was a conservative.[253]

CLASSICAL LIBERALISM

In order to learn from this stormy voyage through the seas of fusionism, we must be properly introduced to libertarianism and understand its glories and horrors. Libertarianism originated with the classical liberalism of the late 18th century, a political philosophy that deeply influenced the American founders – these roots are the greatest of its glories. The original definition of **liberal** is *"that which is fitting for a free man."* Hence, the phrases *"liberal education"* and *"liberal arts,"* and classical liberalism. Renaissance ideals of the complete man were the context for what is suitable for a free man.

Classical liberalism came into existence through the combination of classical economics and natural law philosophy – the 18th century's version of fusionism! It was the merger of freedom of the complete man and economic liberty. The love of freedom during America's founding era influenced the development of classical liberalism. These ideas led to founding the Liberal Party in Great Britain in the early 19th century. To understand libertarianism demands an appreciation for individualists' passion for freedom, and knowledge of classical economics.

> *Fred Critique*
>
> *The love of freedom during America's founding era influenced the development of classical liberalism.*

---

[253] (McManus 2002) Chapter 18 explores this more fully.

CLASSICAL ECONOMICS

The free market economic theories of Scottish pioneer of political economy, Adam Smith (1723-1790), and English political economist David Ricardo (1772-1823) explain how competitive market forces can lead to a dynamic economy and the production of better goods at lower costs in abundant quantities that are efficiently distributed to

convenient markets. The goods are priced high enough to make a profit, but low enough to be sold in the face of competition from similar or alternative products. Products that compete mainly in terms of price are standard commodities or part of the thrift market. Products that compete mainly in terms of quality, uniqueness, service, specialty tailoring, craftsmanship, reputation, prestige, new technology, scarcity or limited availability through ordinary markets are franchises, market niches and luxury markets.

For example, extremely expensive art glass by prestigious artists is displayed in an anonymous warehouse in Cleveland's "Little Italy." After a gourmet Italian meal, Fred Hutchison stumbled through the door of the warehouse by accident – which is the only way to know about this art collection apart from word of mouth. The buyers of these curious objects are museums, international art brokers, and multimillionaires of many countries who all know about the warehouse through conversation. Every glass piece is unique. The collection has an aesthetic range from gorgeous, to incredible, to revolting, to weird. Some of the glass pieces are the size of a refrigerator. Moving the larger and more fragile pieces requires expensive specialty movers. The name of the artist is the most important determiner of price. The turnover of inventory is very slow and the mark-up can be extremely high. The market value of a piece might change radically as it sits in inventory, due to the haggling and speculating of international art collectors – it might increase tenfold from the acquisition price or fall to one tenth the original price. This is the very archetype of a niche market for luxury collector goods.[254]

In contrast, corn in a silo in Iowa is the ultimate commodity for which price, supply and demand trump all other considerations in the market. Thrift market retail goods are sold in large quantities in big box stores or strip malls. The inventory turnover of these goods is very rapid and the mark-up is a very small percentage. Some grocery items commonly have a one percent mark up.

DOWN WITH SOCIALISM

A socialist regulated economy is radically incompetent in these activities. When regulators mandate low prices, the invariable result is a scarcity of goods. Some goods that are urgently desired by people can only be obtained through bribes or the black market. Corruption kept the Soviet economy in motion – without fraud, fatal stagnation would have settled in. When soviet regulators decreed an abundance of products, the stores filled with surplus goods that no one wanted.

When products are protected from competition, quality falls drastically. The quality of goods in stores of the Soviet Union often fell below what was acceptable in rummage sales and flea markets of slum neighborhoods in Western cities. In contrast to the declining socialist economies, free enterprise tends towards a bustling marketplace, a resilient economy, innovation, human dynamism and increasing productivity.

---

[254] (F. Hutchison, Brief History of Conservatism 2009)

THE BUSTLING WEST

Interestingly, the bustling market town seems to be a Western innovation. The frenetic activity of the medieval city or trade fair market place was almost unique in the world of that day. Most markets in large cities of other civilizations did not bustle, they concentrated on luxury trade goods for the aristocracy and subsistence staples for the poor. Rome of the Republic was too poor to have a bustling market – Rome of the rich Empire was a central bazaar for imported luxury goods, trinkets for tourists and bread for the rabble. In contrast, medieval towns had a manic and busy bourgeois class and large numbers of eager, bustling artisans. Luxury goods for the aristocracy, specialty items for the church, and staple goods for the servile classes were secondary specialties.

The hum of animation can still be heard on certain streets in New York and Chicago, a fading clue of the merry mayhem in thronged medieval streets. During the Renaissance, the commercial energy of cities increased in intensity. The cities of renaissance Italy and the trading towns of northern Germany invented modern capitalism. After the industrial revolution came to England, Adam Smith wrote ***The Wealth of Nations***,[255] in which he explicated his seminal theories of classical economics.

> ***Fred Critique***
>
> *The cities of renaissance Italy and the trading towns of northern Germany invented modern capitalism.*

THE FREE MARKET AND PERSONAL FREEDOM

To the delight of those who love freedom, free markets can, to some degree, set consumers free from direct government supervision. The realization of a connection between free markets and personal freedom was an epiphany to natural law theorists who loved freedom and preferred republics to monarchies. These philosophers provided a metaphysical basis for private property and access to free markets as human rights based upon the laws of nature. Aristotle, St. Thomas Aquinas, John Locke, Viscount Bolingbroke and Baron Montesquieu laid the Natural Law foundations of classical liberalism that inspired the American founders. The classical education and well-stocked personal libraries of the founders gave them access to these writers.

> ***Fred Critique***
>
> *Modern libertarians have wonderfully preserved the love of freedom and a devotion to classical economics.*

Modern libertarians have wonderfully preserved the love of freedom and a devotion to classical economics. Unfortunately, libertarians have preserved only remnants of natural law philosophy. As a result, contemporary libertarianism has become metaphysically anemic.

NATURAL RIGHTS LIBERTARIANS

Modern libertarians who come closest to classical liberalism are the *"natural rights"* adherents who hold that *"life, liberty and property"* should be protected as ends in themselves. The phrase was coined by John Locke and enshrined in the ***English Bill of Rights***[256] and the ***Fifth Amendment to the American Constitution***,[257] to wit: *"No person*

---

[255] (A. Smith 1776)
[256] The English Bill of Rights was passed by Parliament on December 16, 1689.

shall be... deprived of life, liberty, or property, without due process of law..." Accordingly, natural law theory, life, liberty and property are indeed natural rights based on the imperatives of human nature. Those *"certain unalienable rights"* endowed by the Creator are proclaimed by the **Declaration of Independence**[258] and enumerated in the **Bill of Rights**, which consists of a set of early amendments to the Constitution. These rights are unalienable precisely because they are based on natural law. Human nature never changes, and therefore natural law never changes. As a result, human rights derived from natural law never change. The old rights are unalienable, and judges cannot logically create new rights at will.

> *Fred Critique*
>
> *Human rights derived from natural law never change.*

THE CHIEF ENDS OF NATURAL LAW

Plato and Aristotle

Natural rights libertarians believe these rights end in themselves, but that cannot be if the principles of natural law philosophers are true. Beginning with Aristotle, all natural law philosophers have said something like: *"The chief end of man is the full flourishing of his nature according to the design of that nature."* Thus, the discovery of that nature, perhaps through classical education, and the disciplined and developmental application of man's design can lead to human flourishing. As Plato and Aristotle explained, the practice of virtue is imperative to the formation of a complete man. Natural rights provide the opportunity to pursue virtue, but do not ensure that men will seek virtue.

> *Fred Critique*
>
> *Natural rights provide the opportunity to pursue virtue, but do not ensure that men will seek virtue.*

VOCATION OF RENAISSANCE MEN

The complete Christian gentlemen of the Italian Renaissance were recognized as the natural political leaders of those republics. Leonard Bruni, Sir Thomas More and Thomas Jefferson are excellent exemplars of this model. They exhibited their flourishing lives to an awestruck public through amazingly versatile talents as they steered the affairs of state.

Life, liberty and property are natural rights, but are also means to higher ends. The natural law theorist asks, *"After securing freedom, property and leisure, what then shall a man do to fulfill his nature and design? Collect expensive art glass, build a business, or rule a republic?"* The Renaissance answer was that the best employment of complete Christian gentlemen was leadership in politics, literature and education for the cultural and political renovation of society. Cosimo de Medici ran an international business, ruled a republic, dabbled in papal politics, established a premier school and a library, collected art and classical documents, and sponsored literary scholars and artists – two of his apprentice artists were Michelangelo and Botticelli.

> *Fred Critique*
>
> *The best employment of complete Christian gentlemen is leadership in politics, literature and education for the cultural and political renovation of society.*

---

[257] The Constitution was adopted on September 17, 1787, by the Constitutional Convention in Philadelphia, Pennsylvania, and ratified by conventions in each U.S. state in the name of *"The People."* It has been amended twenty-seven times; the first ten amendments are known as the Bill of Rights.

[258] The Declaration of Independence is a statement adopted by the Continental Congress on July 4, 1776, announcing that the thirteen American colonies at war with Great Britain regarded themselves as independent, and no longer part of the British Empire.

ABSOLUTE FREEDOM

What should free men do? Some libertarians are so zealous about freedom and privacy that they are offended such questions are even asked. They feel that freedom requires a hermitically sealed personal solitude during which the individual is alone and at counsel with himself concerning his mode of living and freedom of choice. Questions about what he ought to be or do are reckoned as an intrusion and trespass into the holy of holies of his sacred personal solitude. Libertarianism is a very poor substitute for religion.

Unfortunately, if questions about what men ought to do with their freedom are not admissible, freedom will be drained of its meaning. Plato said, *"The unexamined life is not worth living."* Existentialists like Jean-Paul Sartre (1905-1980) and Albert Camus (1913-1960) discovered that when they insisted on an absolute existential freedom, life became absurd – absolute freedom is a one-way ticket to madness.

John Milton (1608-1674), the great poet who wrote **Paradise Lost**,[259] said, *"Liberty hath a double edge, fit only to be handled by just and virtuous men; to the bad and dissolute, it becomes a mischief unwieldy in their hands."* Tracy Lee Simmons wrote concerning classically educated people, *"Books and life both teach them that a freedom without discipline may not only be useless, but a hindrance to grasping something true beyond the veil of illusion."* Undisciplined freedom leads to illusions instead of truth.

RIGHTS AND DUTIES

According to natural law theory, all rights are balanced by obligations and duties. Therefore, citizens are obliged to inquire what implicit duties free people have to family, neighbors, community and country. The marvel of freedom is that it opens the eyes of conscience to see true duties and obligations. Nothing merits the name of virtue apart from meeting these true duties and obligations.

The very idea that individuals have rights but not duties is metaphysically impossible – such a world cannot logically exist. There cannot be a creature that requires rights based on the imperatives of his nature, but is free from duties that are required by his nature. Renaissance men often discussed what it meant to be human, agreeing that it is inhuman to deny natural duties and obligations, and a sign of humanity to fulfill them.

"Noblesse oblige" is a French phrase literally meaning that nobles have duties – suggesting that they had responsibilities to lead, manage and so on; not to simply spend time in idle pursuits. By virtue of their power, wealth, education and free time, aristocrats have obligations to society. But this principle applies in some measure to every person. All humans are endowed with a measure of reason, free will, talent and other human faculties, therefore they all have duties. When the idle rich or the idle poor reject their duties, vices multiply and they become wretched creatures living an inhuman half-life.[260]

---

[259] (Milton 1667)
[260] (F. Hutchison, Brief History of Conservatism 2009)

Some libertarians argue that their obligations consist solely of those duties they have agreed to by their own choice. They are correct in the contractual and legal sense, but not in the metaphysical sense. Man does not live by contractual obligations alone. Human affiliations and obligations cannot be reduced to the perfunctory formality of mere contracts. One must fulfill overt contracts while not ignoring implicit obligations. Every wife of a workaholic businessman understands this.[261]

INDIVIDUALIST LIBERTARIANS

Individualist libertarians, offshoots that regard the individual person as an end in himself, believe that humans are absolute owners of their lives and property, and should be free to do anything they please, provided they do not infringe upon others who are trying to enjoy their freedom and property. This is a conception of liberty as absolute freedom from boundaries and limitations, with the sole exception that one may not hurt others or deprive them of their rights and freedom. Although this has become a popular idea, it represents the triumph of wishful thinking over rationality. Human nature has a design. All designs must function within limits and according to rules. All of human life must be conducted within boundaries. To refuse to recognize limits and boundaries is to deny we have a nature. If we have no nature, we can claim no rights.

> ### Fred Critique
>
> *To refuse to recognize limits and boundaries is to deny we have a nature. If we have no nature, we can claim no rights.*

INDIVIDUALIST LIBERTARIANISM IS SELF-REFUTING

From *Lord of the Flies* movie

The presupposition that we have a nature designed by God provides us with the only grounds we have for claiming natural rights, which are based on the design of our nature. The denial of personal limitations is a denial that we have a nature, which undercuts our claim to rights. Therefore, individualist libertarianism is self-refuting, and a short route to nihilism and chaos.[262] In Sir William Golding's (1911-1993) book ***Lord of the Flies***,[263] the boys on the deserted island began with freedom without boundaries, the lawless freedom led to chaos, and chaos led to tyranny and the absolute denial of rights. The impossible belief in absolute rights and freedom from boundaries represents the magical thinking of spiritual cultists, half-mad existentialists, illogical hyper-individualist libertarians, and boys running wild.

> ### Fred Critique
>
> *The impossible belief in absolute rights and freedom from boundaries represents the magical thinking of spiritual cultists, half-mad existentialists, illogical hyper-individualist libertarians, and boys running wild.*

Thomas Jefferson was a classical liberal, but occasionally slipped into an individualist libertarian frame of mind. He wrote, *"Rightful liberty is an unobstructed action according to our will within the limits drawn around us by the equal rights of others."*[264] Unfortunately, individualist libertarianism is becoming the default position of many Americans, as they can be heard everywhere saying, *"I can do anything I want provided I do not hurt anyone else."* Conservatives, liberals and moderates casually repeat the same illogical mantra.

---

[261] (F. Hutchison, Brief History of Conservatism 2009)
[262] Libertarians running rampant at the conference are a hint at this chaos. (F. Hutchison, Brief History of Conservatism 2009)
[263] (Golding 1954)
[264] Fred Hutchison never cared for Jefferson. (F. Hutchison, Brief History of Conservatism 2009)

THE LIBERTARIAN UBERMENSCH

Russian-American novelist, philosopher, playwright and screenwriter Ayn Rand (1905-1982), known for her two best-selling novels *The Fountainhead*[265] and *Atlas Shrugged*[266] and for developing a philosophical system she called **Objectivism**,[267] made important contributions to the corpus of individualist libertarian ideas, but ran far afield. A

Ayn Rand

student of Aristotle, Rand determined that human rights are grounded in man's rational faculties; therefore individualist libertarians are not utterly devoid of metaphysics. However, her principle of the virtue of selfishness is a metaphysical impossibility. No coherent design for human nature can make self the chief end of self. Full human flourishing must include reaching out to something that is transcendent to self. The Renaissance man might start a school or rule a republic. The Christian reaches up to God and out to his neighbor.

Rand's novels feature the romantic worship of the superior man of ability who is an end in himself and despises lesser beings that need others. Her self-enclosed heroes sound like Nietzsche's *"ubermensch"* (superman) who has the *"will to power,"* and contempt for lesser beings and those who are compassionate for lesser beings. Buckley drummed Ayn Rand out of the conservative movement. Complete men do not like hollow men. Ubermenschen are empty of humanity.

> *Fred Critique*
> ___
> *Full human flourishing must include reaching out to something that is transcendent to self.*

LIBERTARIAN REDUCTIONISM

Fred Hutchison's original objection to individualist libertarianism when he first encountered it in college was that it posits a reductionist view of man – when metaphysics gets anemic, the view of human nature contracts.[268] If the mind and will of the individual is the only thing that exists, humans are very poor creatures indeed. We must then lead a narrow and barren existence that is the opposite of the humanity and versatility of Renaissance men.

HATRED OF GOVERNMENT

> *"The disturbing symptoms which I have in mind are a growing disregard of the first principles of justice and jurisprudence, even among judges and lawyers; and the tendency toward concentration of power in Federal and state executive branches and bureaucracies." Russell Kirk, 1960[269]*

Individualist libertarians insist upon a very limited role for government and regard it a necessary evil. They believe government should protect property and contract, and defend citizens from crime, foreign invasion and infringement of rights. Beyond that, it can establish a currency and perhaps build roads (they cannot agree about the roads.)

---

[265] (Rand, The Fountainhead 1943)
[266] (Rand, Atlas Shrugged 1957)
[267] Objectivism holds that reality exists independent of consciousness, that human beings have direct contact with reality through sense perception, that one can attain objective knowledge from perception through the process of concept formation and inductive logic, that the proper moral purpose of one's life is the pursuit of one's own happiness or rational self-interest, that the only social system consistent with this morality is full respect for individual rights embodied in laissez faire capitalism, and that the role of art in human life is to transform man's widest metaphysical ideas, by selective reproduction of reality, into a physical form – a work of art – that one can comprehend and to which he can respond emotionally.
[268] (F. Hutchison, Brief History of Conservatism 2009)
[269] (Kirk, The Common Heritage of America and Europe 1960)

An intelligent political philosophy cannot regard the government as a necessary evil – after all it is natural law, not pragmatic necessity, which assigns a role to government. If it has a legitimate role to play in society, completes that task well, and does not go beyond the boundaries as defined by natural law, then government should be praised. Malice towards government is the source of the grudging epithet *"necessary evil,"* and is based upon disappointment and fear. One may be disappointed when government overruns its natural boundaries and mishandles those tasks not assigned to it by Providence. One may rightly fear that a growing government authority and jurisdiction might take away rights and freedoms. We must be vigilant good citizens to prevent this, but do it without calling government a *"necessary evil."*

> **Fred Critique**
>
> *An intelligent political philosophy cannot regard the government as a necessary evil.*

CONSEQUENTIALIST LIBERTARIANS

Consequentialist libertarians are inspired by philosopher-economists Milton Friedman (1912-2006), Ludwig Von Mises (1881-1973), Friedrich Hayek (1899-1992), and British Utilitarians John Stuart Mill (1806-1873) and Jeremy Bentham (1748-1832). The consequentialists justify human freedom and free enterprise by its good fruits, concentrating on the economic prosperity of free markets and the economic stagnation and dislocations caused by socialism. From the point of view of individual people, consequentialists dwell on the tyranny and horrors of living under socialist rule. In contrast, free markets enable the individual to be happily free of such tyranny.

> **Fred Critique**
>
> *Consequentialists justify human freedom and free enterprise by concentrating on economic prosperity.*

When Fred Hutchison was in college, he recalled briefly arguing for free markets on the grounds of economic prosperity. A natural rights libertarian asked him, *"Are you a pragmatist?"* From this reproof, he understood for the first time the difference between consequentialists and natural rights libertarians.[270] Consequentialists are practical and realistic – *"Freedom makes us richer."* Natural rights libertarians stand on principle, *"I would choose freedom even if it makes us poorer."*

HISTORICAL CONCLUSIONS

The remarkable achievements of the fusionists put the conservative movement in a much stronger position than it was in 1960. At the Iowa straw poll in August 2007, most of the Republican candidates were in competition to see who was the most traditional. Conservatives are now the majority of Republicans. This could not have happened without the fusionist movement. However, everything created by man has within it the seeds of its own destruction. The fusion of traditionalists and libertarians has fallen apart, and many individuals have gone through a decline in moral reasoning. Rights without responsibilities and freedom without boundaries is the ideology of narcissists. Republican narcissists have embarrassed the party with corruption and lack of spending restraints.

> **Fred Critique**
>
> *Republican narcissists have embarrassed the party with corruption and lack of spending restraints.*

---

[270] (F. Hutchison, Brief History of Conservatism 2009)

FINAL REJOINDER

When libertarians broke free from natural law, they implicitly rejected transcendent moral order and universal moral law. Those who reject universal moral law are de facto atheists, for a denial of universal law and truth implies a denial of the God who is the source of absolute rule and fact. Libertarianism can become new version of an old heresy called **antinomianism**, which means *"against law"* or *"usurper of law."* Those who are against law become lawless rebels and nihilists. Usurpers of law become little gods making their own arbitrary laws according to their own whims.

When someone rejects the possibility of a transcendent moral authority, they implicitly reject authority and hierarchy. Everyone who rejects the invisible authority and hierarchy will chafe under visible authorities and hierarchies, and will go through life as a rebel. At best, he will pragmatically pander to authority while secretly despising it.

The existence of social order requires authority, hierarchy and tradition. Those who reject authority invariably wind up rejecting hierarchy, tradition and social order. Without hierarchy, the pursuit of excellence vanishes. The pursuit of excellence requires the ascent up a staircase of increasing perfection. The pursuit of truth involves a similar ascent. Without tradition, Western cultural heritage vanishes. Without a social order, only atomistic individualism remains. Such a world yields to chaos and barbarism. Chaos yields to tyranny. That is the reasoning behind traditionalists who avoid becoming a libertarian or fusionist.

> *Fred Critique*
> _____
>
> *The existence of social order requires authority, hierarchy and tradition.*

NEXT TIME

Chapter 14 will examine the early days of the culture war, which include a frenzied prelude and the development of a hideous counter-culture, running from the Woodstock Music Festival to Roe versus Wade.

This chapter will examine Fred Hutchison's understanding of the early culture war, including the chaotic prelude (1967-1968) and the development of a counter-culture proceeding from the Woodstock Music Festival (1969) to Roe versus Wade (1973).

UNJUSTIFIED REBELLION

The sixties rebellion was not a natural reaction to the bad things of the fifties, as often supposed – it was an evil reaction to wholesomeness. There has never been a rebellion with so little to rebel about. Since the affluent and pampered baby boomers had little to complain about, the unrest had little justification and was therefore wicked and shameful. Those who attempt to rationalize the sixties often depict the fifties as a dreadful time – looking through this prism minimizes and excuses wickedness. Evil hides behind false pretext, including absurd sham rationalizations.

IN PRAISE OF THE FIFTIES

The values of God, country, community and family still reigned in the fifties. An astounding 69 percent of Americans claimed local church membership in 1960, which may exceed the numbers for any nation at any time in Western history. The pews of churches were filled as never before or since.

Most mainstream Protestant denominations, which comprised about half of American church membership, still taught the universal moral law and traditional values – these same denominations claim only five percent today, and most never mention moral law. Negative cultural indicators such as existentialism, beatniks, greasers, bikers, early rock and roll and **cinema noir**[271] reflected fifties subcultures far removed from Main Street America. The massive box office hit films were not **Rebel Without a Cause** (1955) or **A Street Car Named Desire** (1947), but films of triumphal righteousness like **Quo Vadis** (1951), **The Robe** (1953), **Demetrius and the Gladiators** (1954), **The Ten Commandments** (1956) and **Ben Hur** (1959).

AMERICA UNITED

In the fifties, America's long racial nightmare seemed to be over – **Jim Crow laws**[272] ended in the North during the forties, if not in the South. President Truman integrated the military during the Korean War, and the integration of schools had a promising beginning. Civil rights leaders during the sixties recognized the progress, but complained that advancement was too slow. Conservatives argued that moderate and steady improvement in racial equity, in accord

---

[271] Cinematic noir is stylish Hollywood crime dramas, particularly those that emphasize cynical attitudes and sexual motivations.
[272] Jim Crow laws were state and local laws enacted from 1876-1965 (instituted by "progressive" Democrats in the 1920s) that mandated public facility racial segregation, with a supposedly "separate but equal" status for black Americans. In reality, treatment and accommodations were usually inferior to those provided for whites, systematizing economic, educational and social disadvantages.

with social order stability, harmony and freedom, is more lasting and blessed than sudden revolutionary change. The lingering Southern bitterness over the Civil War and reconstruction seemed to be a fading memory. We were united by memories of winning a patriotic war (WWII) and by a common cause against communism. America was whole once more – the founders' dream seemed to reach fulfillment.

SWEET TIME TO BE A CHILD

Economic prosperity had returned (only for whites) after the long Great Depression nightmare and the privations of war rationing. Many Americans now owned government program homes with modern appliances, grassy yards, white picket fences, kids and a dog. Men generally had steady jobs, most marriages were for life, and adultery was rare. Feminism had yet to introduce disdain toward men or unhealthy competition between men and women. Mothers were at home with pre-school children in real neighborhoods that cared about community. Only a sourpuss can deny that the American fifties were an agreeable time and place to live for an unprecedented number of people, and a sweet time to be a child.

FIE ON GOODNESS

"Fie on goodness, fie / It's been depressing all the way and getting glummer every day / Ah, but to burn a little town or slay a dozen men, Anything to laugh again… / There's not a folly to deplore, Confession Sunday is a bore / Oh, fie on goodness, fie"

In the original stage version of **Camelot**[273] (1960), knights sang the bawdy song *Fie on Goodness*. They were bored with the sweetness and harmony of Camelot and were eager to return to the fun of bloodshed and debauchery. The song was cut when the show went on tour because it was considered too racy for American audiences outside New York, but was retained when the play went to London. Like the rowdy warriors, sixties rebels were bored with prosperity, social harmony and cultural sweetness of the fifties, and wanted to break the monotony with rioting and debauchery. Just as the knights were unjustified for rising against Camelot's goodness, the sixties revolution against wholesome American culture was insupportable and deplorable. The prosperous, soft living and pampering of children spoiled and corrupted the baby boomer generation that subsequently rampaged – the sweet fifties led to the sour sixties.

Puritan lawyer John Winthrop (1587-1649) was a leading figure in founding the Massachusetts Bay Colony (1628), and served as governor for twelve years. Winthrop warned that God's grace brings righteousness, righteousness leads to prosperity, and prosperity corrupts so that men turn away from God and become wicked.

---

[273] Camelot is a musical by Alan Jay Lerner (book and lyrics) and Frederick Loewe (music) based on King Arthur.

GOING TO SAN FRANCISCO...

A culture war prelude occurred on college campuses and in San Francisco during 1967-1968. Recall from the song *San Francisco*,[274] *"If you're going to San Francisco, be sure to wear some flowers in your hair."* The tune chronicled *"the summer of love"* – that is, the 1967 summer of sex, when *"flower children"* gathered and established San Francisco as the holy land of depravity. The town remains the American Sodom to this day.

Fred Critique

San Francisco remains the American Sodom today.

"Summer of Love" in San Francisco

Elements of this strange overture included radicalizing the antiwar and civil rights movements, and the emergence of a weird psychedelic drug counter-culture. An equally bizarre spiritual subculture for the narcissist, the New Age Movement, includes neopaganism and the occult. During this time of deluded souls, confused minds, disordered passions and extreme ideologies, fringe elements of the anti-war and civil rights movements sometimes used vitriolic rhetoric to foment violent public insurrections. However, in spite of florid speech and riotous zeal on the streets, most activists craved participation in an improved America of their dreams. Only where Marxist ideology poisoned their minds was something akin to hatred of America discernable. Non-Marxist liberals did not despise America yet, because the postmodern program of deconstructing Western cultural heritage was not in full gear in the United States – in contrast, the cultural loathing of Europeans dates back to 1920.

BARBARIANS RENOUNCE CIVILIZATION

The debauchery at the **Woodstock Music & Art Fair**[275] was a brazen renunciation of Western culture and values. Our resilient society can weather storms from overblown antiwar or civil rights activists, but popular renunciation of civilization and all things decent, humane, excellent, beautiful and true cause society to sink like a floundering ship caught in a typhoon. We can survive passage through many social upheavals, but a voyage into barbarism may not offer return passage – when Rome was inundated by barbarians, the return of enduring culture was delayed by six hundred years of savagery. Woodstock revelry began an invasion of cultural and moral subversion.

Fred Critique

Woodstock revelry began an invasion of cultural and moral subversion.

A PERVERSE PREFERENCE FOR BARBARISM

Many individuals voiced a dislike of civilization, preferring barbarism. Art historian Kenneth Clark (1903-1983) wrote a splendid BBC television documentary and book, *Civilisation: A Personal View by Kenneth Clark*,[276] in which he said, *"People sometimes tell me that they prefer barbarism to civilization. I doubt they have given it a long enough trial... They are bored with civilization; but all the evidence suggests that the boredom of barbarism is infinitely greater. Quite apart from the discomforts and privations, there was no escape from it. Very restricted company, no books, no light after dark, no hope. On one side the sea battering away, on the other infinite stretches of bog and forest. A most melancholy existence, and the Anglo-Saxon poets had no illusions about it."*

---

[274] "San Francisco (Be Sure to Wear Flowers in Your Hair)" was written by John Phillips of The Mamas & the Papas, and sung by Scott McKenzie in 1967, to promote the Monterey Pop Festival.
[275] Woodstock Music & Art Fair was a music festival, held outside at Max Yasgur's 600-acre dairy farm in the Catskills near the town of Bethel, New York, from August 15 to August 18, 1969. During the rainy weekend, 32 acts performed for 500,000 fans.
[276] (Clark, Civilisation: A Personal View by Kenneth Clark 1969)

MIDDLE EARTH AND ANCIENT GIANTS

To illustrate the barbarian disillusionment, Clark quoted a translated passage from *The Wanderer*, a 10th century Old English poem of unknown origins. Here is a snippet from the poem with a few lines substituted from other translations shown in bold.

> *"A wise man will grasp how ghastly it shall be / When all this world's wealth standeth waste / Even as now, **throughout this middle-earth**, / Walls stand wind beaten, / Heavy hoar frost; ruined-habitations / The wine halls crumble; / their wielders lie bereft of bliss /... **And so he destroyed this city / He, the creator of men / That human laughter is not heard about it** / And idle stand these **ancient works of giants**."*

The wandering warrior returned to his old mead hall and found it in ruins and all his tribesmen slain. He lamented the ruined state of *"middle earth."* J.R.R. Tolkien borrowed this term and quoted several lines from *The Wanderer* in tales about hobbits, elves and dwarves in Middle Earth. Nomadic Anglo-Saxons conquered the civilized Celts living under Roman rule in Britain – the Celts were illumined by Christianity and enjoyed the brilliant Latin culture of antiquity. Brutes lamented over destroyed beer pubs, while early Christian Brits grieved the devastation of magnificent Roman structures. The poet called these elegant ruins *"ancient works of giants"* in contrast to puny barbarian projects.

THE BOREDOM OF BARBARISM

Kenneth Clark

Clark said, *"The boredom of barbarism is infinitely greater."* Those who cannot endure intellectual boredom are thrilled by civilization and horrified by barbarism. *"And so he destroyed this city; He, the creator of men, that human laughter is not heard about it."* If man were forced to live among boring barbarians, laughter would be rare.

Three intellectually stimulating streams of conservatism stand out as stalwart defenders of civilization and determined opponents of brutality: **1) Traditionalist conservatives** defend the social fabric of civilized society; **2) Neo-conservatives** uphold Western literary and intellectual classics, and **3) Christian conservatives** are vehemently opposed to paganism and the occult. Barbarism is invariably pagan, as demonstrated during the Dark Ages and at Woodstock. In contrast, from the fall of Rome until around 1800, Christianity was the most civilizing Western force. In today's culture war, we see doctrinally orthodox Christianity aligned with civilization against neopaganism and neobarbarism. If our civilization is to be saved, Christianity must defeat paganism in the 21st century as in the 10th and 11th centuries.

> *Fred Critique*
> ___
> *Three intellectually stimulating streams of conservatism stand out as stalwart defenders of civilization and determined opponents of brutality.*

WOODSTOCK – A DECLARATION OF CULTURAL WAR

Woodstock was the beginning of the culture war on two fronts. It marked the start of a protracted battle between liberals and conservatives about watershed moral and political questions. It was also the moment when Modernism began to transform into Postmodernism in America, and the deconstruction of Western cultural tradition became a priority of liberals. Despite postgraduate college degrees, these subverted elites turned into enemies of culture – a suicidal mission since without civilization, there are no academics.

Woodstock proclaimed to the world that anything subversive was now welcome in America, drawing a postmodern counterculture from Europe. As Chapter 1 of this book states, *"Conservative principles and values have consistently produced beneficial effects upon culture. In contrast, liberalism has often been destructive to Western culture, propagating false views about the nature of man, society, government and the cosmos – and only produces a mixed blessing."* During the modernism era, liberalism sometimes created a mixed cultural effect; postmodern liberalism has been almost entirely destructive.

SEX, DRUGS, AND ROCK AND ROLL

Woodstock was billed as *"An Aquarian Exposition: 3 Days of Peace & Music"* – but the theme appeared to be *"sex, drugs, and rock and roll"* with the motto of *"if it feels good, do it."* Antiwar protests, Marxism, the green movement, holistic mysticism, neopaganism and the occult were secondary themes, like sideshow freaks at Barnum's circus. Psychedelic drugs and promiscuity were rampant – many young fools attended just to get stoned or have sex. After being addled by the haze, they wandered through the carnival of subversive rubes and sampled the horrors according to whim and delusion.

Woodstock popularized *"acid"* or psychedelic rock music that featured long, rambling, screaming solos on the electric guitar designed to accompany drug use, and was a forerunner of heavy metal. Hard rock with harsh anti-social or raw sexual lyrics was also featured. It is no surprise that the most morally and visually squalid event in American history was accompanied by the ugliest music ever heard by human ears. A return to barbarism includes a preference for primitive music – Woodstock's version included the screams of the damned.[277]

Fred Critique

A return to barbarism includes a preference for primitive music – Woodstock's version included the screams of the damned.

MUSIC OF DEATH

Janis Joplin

Janis Joplin (1943-1970) and Jimmy Hendrix (1942-1970) screamed into the microphones at Woodstock as though they were being tortured. Joplin was addicted to heroin and Hendrix was widely known for using lysergic acid diethylamide (LSD). Within little more than a year after Woodstock, both these lost souls were dead. Their screams of agony to the crowds were subsequently made in the nether regions, with no listening audience to hear the wails and gnashing teeth. The doomed musicians came to the end of the rope while singing the music of death – a forerunner to the culture of death featuring abortion on demand.

Fred Critique

Screams of agony to the crowds were subsequently made in the nether regions, with no listening audience to hear the wails and gnashing teeth.

During the Woodstock era, rock musician performances on television displayed violent convulsions and hideous contortions; as though they were possessed by demons. Perhaps the foul imps who inspired the songs had no sense of musical taste or concept of beauty, and degraded the preferences of a lost generation. Some current musicians mimic the shudder of the damned, but come across as hokey and laughable, like low budget horror movies.[278]

---

[277] (F. Hutchison, Brief History of Conservatism 2009)

A MIDDLE CLASS REVOLUTION

For over a century, the West has had a small bohemian counterculture that sometimes uses drugs and has orgies – Woodstock surpassed this by gathering between 400,000-500,000 people. The majority were college students from affluent middle class families. The movie **Woodstock**[279] glorified the festival and celebrated the subculture. The

Jimmy Hendrix

documentary was cheap to make, was very popular with college students, and made money. Millions of baby boomers were seduced by the movie to join the rebellion. The hoard of rebels dwarfed the number of Greenwich Village beatniks in the 1950s and the Paris bohemians in the 1920s. Many rock concerts since have become little Woodstocks, flaunting characteristic elements of vulgarity, rebellion and moral decadence.

History teaches that lower class and labor revolutions usually fail, but middle class insurrections normally succeed. This new upheaval was the young against the old middle class; a battle of generations. The group that had once supplied the moral fiber of America was now leading an entire generation towards paganism and moral debauchery.

> **Fred Critique**
>
> *The group that had once supplied the moral fiber of America was now leading an entire generation towards paganism and moral debauchery.*

HIPPIES RIOT WHILE REASON TAKES A STAND[280]

By the time Fred Hutchison entered college, he had already realized that most people are generally deceived and most are rascals. This realization was confirmed by his misfortune of attending college when campuses were inundated with hippies who listened to acid rock. When he denounced acid rock to a collection of about twenty students, word spread through the dorm and made him a figure of controversy, celebrity and ridicule. His presence in a room full of hippies sometimes inspired mock celebrations of truth, justice and the American way. Hutchison became the designated Captain America of the campus to be celebrated and laughed at – a role he rather enjoyed playing with the hippies, who also savored the silly games.

> **Fred Critique**
>
> *Most people are generally deceived and are rascals.*

Hutchison once gave an impromptu lecture in the dorm living room to a group of perhaps fifty scruffy hippies about the evils of drugs and promiscuous sex. The spontaneous event drew a good crowd because of his colorful reputation. The mob sat in a semi-circle around his overstuffed chair as though he were a guru – it was a farce, of course. He decided to play out the charade because it gave him a chance to inveigh against sexual immorality, drugs

and riotous living. The merry hippies responded to his scolding as if it was entertainment, laughing with gusto. Fred genuinely enjoyed their high spirits – it was fun to be the center of attention in such a cheerful company of nitwits. His attempts to reason with them compared to trying to get serious with the three stooges. He thought they were morally insane for regarding sexual and chemical continence as a joke, and said as much to them. Even as he was drawn into their mood of hilarity, he felt like slapping those naughty knaves.

---

[278] (F. Hutchison, Brief History of Conservatism 2009)

[279] (Baez, Havens and Cocker 1970)

[280] This section chronicles the author's experience. (F. Hutchison, Brief History of Conservatism 2009)

CONSERVATIVES WERE AWOL

The other campus conservatives were AWOL while all this was going on. Libertarians had no objection to sex and drug abuse by hippies; fusionists felt inhibited about questioning the moral values of others; budding neoconservatives were reading the classics; serious scholars, who comprised a significant portion of the student body, were in the library studying. Evangelicals were preoccupied with evangelism and Bible studies, and were mostly missing from action when it came to politics and issues-oriented public forums – they had not yet joined the culture war.

Hutchison agreed with the evangelicals on most major points of doctrine, and admired their penetrating Bible studies. However, he could not understand their timid withdrawal from the world and strange indifference to politics. They seemed to come alive for organized evangelism, but faded into the wallpaper when things got political. The campus conservative club did recruit a few Southern Baptists – Southerners were more gregarious and amenable to active politics than the timid, well organized, Northern evangelicals.

> ### Fred Critique
> *Evangelicals were timidly withdrawn from the world and strangely indifferent to politics.*

EARS FILLED WITH WAX

Hutchison was sitting in the dorm recreation center one evening when a strange madness enveloped the place like a steamy fog – it was the paranoid enthusiasm of a mob. Many students rushed by him towards the campus riots. Some of them charged forward with heads lowered, hoping to get past before he issued a challenge. He hailed some of them, calling them to turn back, but they rushed by all the faster. They were like the crew of Odysseus who placed wax in their ears lest they should hear the siren songs.

A few fellows paused and talked with Hutchison for a moment – he warned them that what they were about to do was immoral, illegal, antisocial and unpatriotic. Some were pleased by the personal attention and amused that he should try to draw them back from the course, but after a brief exchange of words they plunged into the dark maelstrom. Others were annoyed by his nagging and interference with their personal affairs, waving him off and stalking sullenly into the night. Then there were the spoiled brats who were shocked by his rebuke – apparently, no one had ever said *"No"* to them before.

DUST IN THE WIND

"I close my eyes / Only for a moment and the moment's gone / All my dreams / Pass before my eyes a curiosity / Dust in the wind / All they are is dust in the wind / Same old song / Just a drop of water in an endless sea / All we do / Crumbles to the ground though we refuse to see / Dust in the wind / All we are is dust in the wind / Now don't hang on / Nothing lasts forever but the Earth and Sky / It slips away / And all your money won't another minute buy / Dust in the wind / All we are is dust in the wind / Dust in the wind / Everything is dust in the wind" **Dust in the Wind**, *Kansas, 1978.*

Another kind of fellow who drifted towards the riots seemed dazed and confused, like debris and wreckage floating on frothy and turbulent waves. Hutchison's voice seemed far away to them, as does a voice from dry land calling to those who are bobbing in the surf. The memory of these drifting ones reminded Hutchison of

Dust in the Wind,[281] a popular song released after the Woodstock frenzy had died down. The song captured a vein of dazed resignation to endless flux and a haunted acceptance of fate with the phrase, *"All we are is dust in the wind."*

CONSCIENCE CRIES OUT

Hutchison called out to the young men rushing to the riots, but not one turned back. The solidarity of revolt against morality and conscience among the white, middle-class men was reminiscent of the camaraderie at Woodstock. Years later, Hutchison came to realize that his was the voice of conscience in that dorm for a season. The designated public conscience is a lonely task when most people have hardened hearts and closed ears against ethics. Proverbs 1 describes wisdom crying out in public places – fools, scorners and simpletons refuse the rebuke of wisdom and rush to terrifying calamity and destruction, exactly explaining the riotous campus night.

> *Fred Critique*
>
> *The designated public conscience is a lonely task when most people have hardened hearts and closed ears against ethics.*

As darkness fell, Hutchison was alone in the empty dorm recreation center for over an hour wondering, *"Conservatives, where are you?"* They were either hiding under beds or had sneaked off to see the hideous riots out of voyeuristic fascination. Hutchison sat there wondering if he was the last sane man on earth. In terms of the moral health of our culture, this was an unusually sinister time.

THE SCAPEGOAT

Hutchison was still sitting in the overstuffed chair when the students stumbled back from the riot. Some were laughing, but some were depressed and ashamed. One of them was weeping from the effects of tear gas and the terror of being chased by police dogs. He railed at Hutchison, blaming him for the malevolent whirlwind he had escaped, sobbing, *"Your National Guard troops did this to me."* Apparently, the minds of mob rebels are so darkened that they cannot distinguish between different parties and groups who oppose them. In paranoid confusion, the rioter was convinced that Hutchison and the troopers were in cahoots. Mobs must have their scapegoats. Hutchison suspected that this particular young man was stung either by the scolding of the hippies, or the warnings to rushing protesters – the wound still hurt upon returning from the riot because of the inability to silence the voice of conscience. No man is angrier than the one fighting his own conscience.

> *Fred Critique*
>
> *The minds of mob rebels are so darkened that they cannot distinguish between different parties and groups who oppose them.*

The weeping accusations were Hutchison's first experience of being the object of paranoid conspiracy thinking by someone who really meant it; the student was not jesting or playing with metaphors and insults. Hutchison was subsequently accused by the school paper of being the tool of the college administration. In later years, he was accused of being a tool of oil companies in a letter to the editor of a major newspaper, because he disagreed with fad theories of global warming. He was also accused of being a Neocon and therefore a tool of the president's cabal, a Nazi, and a racist. Notice the similarity between contemporary liberal paranoia and the campus mob suspicion seeking a scapegoat.

---

[281] (Kansas 1978)

KING CANUTE DEFIES THE TIDE

King Canute

Was Hutchison foolish to make a lonely stand? Was he like King Canute, who sat on the sea shore commanding the tide not to come in? During times of public madness, if even one person publically says *"No"* it makes a difference. The consciences of troublemakers retain memory after participating in lunatic mobs – they remember it differently if anyone stood in opposition. If no one gave resistance or signs of disapproval, a collective event of irrationality and malice is remembered in a self-justifying way. A few agitators may actually repent of wickedness – they should be given the opportunity to change sides, to join wisdom, so they are not alone in renunciation of the mob.

Hutchison was not shunned because of his unpopular stand – he had more friends in his campus Captain America days than at any other time in life. No one should ever calculate the consequences of opposing the crowd. We must do what we know is right, and leave the outcomes to God.

> *Fred Critique*
>
> *No one should ever calculate the consequences of opposing the crowd.*

HIGH COST OF SITTING OUT THE CULTURAL APOCALYPSE

America sat out the first three years of World War I and the first two years of World War II, for reasons most Americans accept. Less justifiably, many conservatives sat out the first four years of the culture war (1969-1973). As a result, they came to the battle too late to prevent the sexual revolution, which could have been blocked. Whenever large numbers of citizens have risen up against sexual indecency, they won – IF they stood at the barricades BEFORE the libertines gained entrenched positions.

Many moons have passed since Woodstock. American sexual mores might not be as wayward now if conservatives had been involved earlier, although they have made some modest gains after decades of fighting the culture war. Nonetheless, sexual moral codes are vastly worse than before Woodstock and Roe v. Wade – damage to the American family has been incalculable. This is the high cost of sitting out the early phases of cultural apocalypse and moral pandemic.

> *Fred Critique*
>
> *There is a high cost for sitting out the early phases of cultural apocalypse and moral pandemic.*

CURE FOR SLUMBERING CONSERVATIVES

Winston Churchill

Young liberals were wide awake while their conservative counterparts were sound asleep, leading to speculation that a flaw is built into the nature of conservatives that makes them slow to respond to danger. This phenomenon was demonstrated in Winston Churchill's collection of speeches ***While England Slept***[282] and John F. Kennedy's book ***Why England Slept***.[283] Churchill's lectures from 1932-1938 were a vain attempt to awaken a slumbering England to the perils of Nazism and fascism. Kennedy was inspired by Churchill to publish his thesis, written during his senior year at Harvard University, in which he examined Britain's lack of military preparation to face the threat of Nazi Germany. Perhaps slumbering traditionalists have always been conservative, in contrast to men who

---

[282] (Churchill 1938)
[283] (Kennedy 1940 (published in 1961))

161

convert late in life, like Reagan and Churchill, who often notice emerging perils first. They remember their crazy years as young liberals and understand how dangerous the jungle can get.

An elixir to awaken snoozing conservatives is needed. Churchill read enormous quantities of history during his idle time with the British Army in India, which may have been the source of his remarkable foresight about the Nazis. Fred Hutchison's independent reading of history as a boy was more extensive than many of his campus colleagues, which may account for why he was awake during the cataclysms while they slumbered, his zeal for the pursuit of truth kept him alert – he also acquired an early hatred of evil, stupidity, mediocrity, mendacity, duplicity, group think, cliques, fads and propaganda at his mother's knee. Some propositions every young conservative should consider: 1) consume heavy servings of history as part of a reading diet – most will relish this dish because it is their nature to love history; 2) teach that metaphysical truth really exists, has meaning and is worth pursuing; 3) gain a healthy skepticism about the folly and stupidity of this world by reading the works of G.K. Chesterton.[284]

> ***Fred Critique***
> ---
> *An elixir to awaken snoozing conservatives is needed.*

WHAT CONSERVATIVES CARED ABOUT[285]

There were four major concerns young conservatives cared about during the early culture war that aroused them to action: 1) the Young Republicans takeover by moderates; 2) creeping socialism; 3) campus leftists; and 4) Communism. The moderate takeover reminded Hutchison and his friends of the *"me too"* Republican presidential candidates, since they all had read Schlafly's ***A Choice, not an Echo*** and fancied they could do for the Ohio Young Republicans what she did for Goldwater in 1964. Protests and credentials battles at the state convention were a humiliating failure. They distributed literature condemning high taxes, government regulation and social engineering with a net effect of a very small handful of students changing their minds. Debating issues with liberal professors in and out of class did not change anyone's mind. However, two initiatives regarding campus leftists and communists had a major impact.

CAMPUS COMMIES

Karl Marx

The big Conservative Club versus the Student Mobilization Committee (SMC) debate was well promoted and attracted a crowd of more than three hundred people. Fred Hutchison was one of two debaters for the conservative team. The SMC, a communist front group, also had two debaters. The topic was the Vietnam War.

The priority of campus commies was to teach students to hate America. As J. Edgar Hoover (1895-1972) had explained in his famous book about Communism, ***Masters of Deceit***,[286] few Americans are likely to believe the preposterous theories of Karl Marx unless they are first induced to hate their own country. This is precisely what the SMC was doing on campus, and were therefore regarded as the vanguard of evil forces.

> ***Fred Critique***
> ---
> *The priority of campus commies was to teach students to hate America.*

Hutchison's best line in the debate went something like this: *"If we precipitously withdraw from Vietnam, the press will be ejected, a curtain of silence will go down, and the 'night of the long knives' will begin."* (This was a quotation that he read to the

---

[284] (F. Hutchison, Brief History of Conservatism 2009)
[285] This section chronicles the author's experience. (F. Hutchison, Brief History of Conservatism 2009)
[286] (Hoover 1958)

students, but he could not recover the source.) He pointed out that every violent communist government takeover was always followed by a blood purge – a standard policy and practice for followers of the Marxist-Leninist doctrine.

NIGHT OF THE LONG KNIVES

Skulls of Cambodian victims

What Hutchison said concerning the night of the long knives was vindicated by subsequent history. President Nixon negotiated a peace settlement for Vietnam that was similar to the Korean War agreement – South Vietnam was saved. In a fit of madness, Democrats in Congress cut off all war funding, which forced an instant withdrawal of American troops and termination of aid. They turned a tactical victory into defeat, and South Vietnam was lost. The communists subsequently murdered about 1,000,000 civilians in South Vietnam and an estimated 6,000,000 in Cambodia.

TRIUMPH OVER MALEFACTORS

It is always amazing how oblivious liberals are to communist theory and practice. During Hutchison's debate with the SMC, he noticed startled faces in the crowd when he told them that blood purges always follow communist takeovers.

His team won the debate because their facts and logic were more appealing than the hysterical rant of student commies – one of their debaters was a hot-head who actually threatened to beat up a heckler in the crowd. After being told that communists murder their opponents, the undergraduates observed how a student communist threatened to beat up an opponent. This victory was sweet because the true malefactors were publically exposed as fanatics, tyrants and bullies. Hutchison's picture appeared on the front page of the college newspaper, waving his arms in a rhetorical flourish while refuting and rebuking the commies. This publicity paved the way for his next exploit.

> **Fred Critique**
>
> *It is always amazing how oblivious liberals are to communist theory and practice.*

THE STUDENT NEWSPAPER

Hutchison wrote a critique of the student newspaper, which was actually published! He accused the student staff of being a self-perpetuating clique that had turned the paper into a left-wing scandal sheet. He argued that it was unjust that an irresponsible paper, unwanted by many students, be supported by mandatory student fees. After enjoying and abusing a privileged arrangement like this, he thought the editor was self-serving and unjust to clamor for complete freedom from college administration supervision. The student editor responded in print with a rambling denunciation of Hutchison.

He had hit a nerve. The newspaper clique was an archetype of the powerful and privileged liberal establishment, in all its self-righteous hypocrisy, self-serving arguments, special pleading fallacies and manipulative games. Hutchison explicitly exposed the racket, and implicitly uncovered the self-interested game of the school's liberal administration. Even though the editor accused him of being a tool of the administration, Hutchison was actually a thorn in its side.

> **Fred Critique**
>
> *The newspaper clique was an archetype of the powerful and privileged liberal establishment, in all its self-righteous hypocrisy, self-serving arguments, special pleading fallacies and manipulative games.*

PAWN IN A CHESS GAME

Hutchison wondered why the liberal powers permitted him to publish the school newspaper critique and publically debate campus communists. In those days of campus disorder, perhaps the administration needed a visible Captain America to prove to alarmed alumni that they were not part of the insurrection. In the end, he was a chess pawn in a game played by powerful men.

"We are none other than a moving row / Of Magic Shadow Shapes that come and go / Round the Sun-illumed Lantern held / In midnight by the Master of the Show. / But helpless Pieces of the Game He plays / Upon his Chequer-board of Nights and Days; / Hither and thither moves and checks and slays / And one by one back into the Closet lays." **LXVIII & LXIX, The Rubaiyat of Omar Kayyam**[287]

RISING TO THE CALL

Abortion was legalized in 1973. The last year of Reagan's presidency (1988) marks the culture war peak when the Christian right rose to challenge the powerful secular left. Chapter 15 will consider the profound implications of this confrontation, and will explore the link between the spiritual health of Christianity and the vitality of civilization.

---

[287] (Kayyam 1120 AD)

Abortion was legalized in 1973. The last year of Reagan's presidency (1988) marks the culture war peak. This chapter considers the profound implications of the Christian right rising to confront the powerful secular left, and will explore the link between the spiritual health of Christianity and the vitality of civilization – it seeks to prove Christopher Dawson's thesis, refute secularists, and argue for Christianity's robust role in every area of American life, relying heavily on historical facts.

RELIGIOUS ASPIRATIONS AND THE RISE OF CIVILIZATIONS

Christopher Dawson

Historian Christopher Dawson devoted much of his life's work to studying and writing about the interaction of Christianity and civilization over the course of history. He claimed that every rising civilization had religion at its core, and was driven forward by religious zeal and spiritual aspirations. Dawson believed every civilization that loses touch with its religious roots must eventually fall, no matter how rich and powerful – he was alluding to a *"higher religion"* like Christianity, which is conducive to civilization, not to pagan religions that give rise to primitive tribalism.[288]

If Europe had not converted from paganism to Christianity, mankind would probably still exist as barbarian tribes. Civilization may fail if modern man fails to maintain religious heredity, leaving posterity to primordial lives. Similar collapse, dispersion and degradation has happened many times in history, i.e., the descendants of Mayan and Inca civilizations now live in jungle clans. If Dawson's thesis is correct, the secularist argument that religious concerns have no place in political debates or social/cultural dialog is false. Declining civilizations must heed the voices calling for a return to spiritual roots, in hopes of avoiding ruin.

> ### *Fred Critique*
> *Declining civilizations must heed the voices calling for a return to spiritual roots, in hopes of avoiding ruin.*

RISING ABOVE THE FLAT LANDS

New civilizations rise when an entire society unites in pursuing transcendent spiritual aspirations and ideals. In contrast to the powerful sense of transcendence in rising civilizations, the evaporation of meaning precedes the decline. A symptom of that loss is demonstrated when society enters what C.S. Lewis called *"flat land,"*[289] where higher callings and upward aspirations have vanished.

In contrast to contemporary spiritual flat land, people of new civilizations are permeated with a sense of the transcendent. Collective focus on God leads to the formation of strong, unifying ideals that can break the *"cake of custom"*[290] and liberate people from the bondage of primitive religion. This domination is not easy to break, which is why so few new civilizations are formed. The content of pagan religion wells up from the inner darkness of tribal shamans when

---

[288] (Dawson 1959)
[289] (Lewis, Bluspels and Flalansferes: A Semantic Nightmare 1939)
[290] Walter Bagehot (1826-1877) wrote Physics and Politics (1872), in which he coined the expression, "the cake of custom," to describe the tension between social institutions and innovations.

they go into trances – low shamanism holds followers in slavery to tribal taboos with terrifying threats surrounding violations. Individuals melt into the tribe and personhood is lost in the din of ugly, demented rites.

Higher religion is beautiful. Prior to 1880, European culture prized beauty more than any other culture, before or since. Beauty was cherished because of Europe's high religion, namely Christianity, which regards the triune God and his creation as beautiful.

HIGHER RELIGION AND UNIFYING IDEALS

In contrast to dark and ugly images welling up within paganism, a higher religion descends to people by revelation and is written down in sacred books by prophets and apostles. Divine disclosure sheds a glorious light of truth and beauty upon individuals, inspiring high aspirations. Human reason is awakened by truth, and conscience is aroused by universal moral law.

As citizens reach above and beyond themselves to a transcendent and glorious God, an extraordinary unity of purpose is realized. This powerful harmony can break them free from pagan fears and elemental selfishness, thereby liberating them to work with others of like mind for a higher cause. People in rising civilizations understand that selfishness is bondage, and devotion to solidarity with others is a special freedom. Rapidly growing cultures sometimes display remarkable levels of agreement, allowing ordinary people to cheerfully accept astonishingly heavy sacrifices to glorify God (refer to Chapter 1, Laying Foundations).

> **Fred Critique**
>
> *As citizens reach above and beyond themselves to a transcendent and glorious God, an extraordinary unity of purpose is realized.*

PERSONHOOD IN RISING CIVILIZATIONS

Henri Bergson

Contrasting personhood in rising civilizations with those in declining cultures, Philosopher Henri Bergson (1859-1941) wrote in *The Two Sources of Morality and Religion*[291] that there are two kinds of souls and two types of society: open and closed. Open souls and societies are receptive to *"the experience of transcendence."* Christians associate the transcendent realm with God, his supernatural works and the heavenly realm, which are beyond human understanding. Transcendence is essentially different from finite human thoughts and works.

Left to their own device, humans tend to close in on themselves and get smaller. Spiritual transcendence opens man to something greater, enabling spiritual enjoyment and psychological growth. Individuals become larger than life, outshining the closed and shrinking who need crutches for support, yet still become entangled in unhealthy co-dependency. Those who are *"larger than life"* have a heroic capacity to break free of dependencies and entanglements.

Bergson wrote that the experience of transcendence empowers man to sever *"natural cycles and processes,"* i.e., breaking the *"cake of custom."* Mankind must separate from primitive society customs before they can team up to build new civilizations. Bergson concluded that correct openness must rely on *"the Christian understanding of the person and universal brotherhood."*[292]

---

[291] (Bergson 1932)
[292] (Staal December 2008)

THE MODERN FLIGHT FROM GOD

Max Picard

Bergson's description of shattered individuals correlates with the shattered family of modernity that brings forth shattered individuals. When families are destroyed, civilization falls. Max Picard (1888-1965), a writer of mystic sensibility, described the *"closed soul"* of modernity in ***The Flight from God***,[293] although he did not use that term – when a critical mass of citizens have closed souls, the culture declines.

"Picard saw the modern, secular West as a self-perpetrating system of spiritual amnesia, frantically busy yet accomplishing nothing, full of communication yet bereft of conversation, loud and bright yet at the same time mute and senseless. Love, friendship, and loyalty exist only as fragments in the world of Flight from God: evanescent, snippets of experience that come and go. That is why in modern times, words have become merely signs, disconnected from the persons that utter them."[294]

Fractured, fragmented and scattered beings that live in a declining civilization bring to mind a haunting phase from the final line of T.S. Elliot's poem ***The Waste Land***, *"These fragments have I shored up against my ruin."[295]*

SHORING UP THE FRAGMENTS

"Everyone who does evil hates the light, and will not come into the light for fear that their deeds will be exposed. But whoever lives by the truth comes into the light, so that it may be seen plainly that what they have done has been done in the sight of God." John 3:20-21 (NIV)

Open souls enjoy wholeness along with humility, while closed souls are fractured, scattered and narcissistic – modest completeness versus egoistical devastation. Open individuals are humble for two reasons: 1) they are aware of their smallness and imperfection in relation to the greatness and perfection of God; and 2) wholeness enables them to clearly see themselves – realism about oneself breeds humility.

> ### Fred Critique
> *Open souls enjoy wholeness along with humility, while closed souls are fractured, scattered and narcissistic – modest completeness versus egoistical devastation.*

The closed soul of modernity is narcissistic for complex reasons. When people cannot gain a sense of self by sifting through fragments, they try in vain to shore up the fragments. Shattered individuals summon primeval delusions of pride to devise a schematic of self. The budding narcissist assembles these fragments, then worships this great idol and becomes self-absorbed. Since self-idolatry is delusional, they practice magical self thinking. The mosaic of fragments is futile because it is easily shattered by reality. People must live closed lives protected by layers of defenses to postpone the inevitable shattering – these layers are the narcissist's cocoon.

The narcissist fancies himself to be the godlike center of the universe. These shattered creatures are supremely selfish and therefore essentially evil, but with the help of magical thinking, they cherish their own false goodness. Divine light revealing the true goodness of God exposes the illusion. Therefore, reminders of the transcendent God Almighty are

---

[293] (Picard 1934 (1951))
[294] (Staal December 2008)
[295] (Eliot 1922)

painful, because they reveal the lie of their godlike pretensions and shattered reality. Divine transcendence is a death blow to human narcissism.

God is the epitome of wholeness and harmony. He is the opposite of a fragmented personality. God's presence strips off the self-deceiving veil of wholeness and exposes the hideous reality of a fractured life. It is no wonder that the shattered people of modernity are fleeing God – the modern *"self-esteem"* movement is a futile exercise of shoring up fragments, and is symptomatic of a declining culture.

> *Fred Critique*
> ___
> *The modern "self-esteem" movement is a futile exercise.*

REMOVING GOD FROM THE PUBLIC SQUARE

*"The lady doth protest too much, methinks." **Hamlet**, Act 3, Scene 2, William Shakespeare*

If people with closed souls are fleeing from God, the last thing they want is a reminder about Him. They become offended by any prompt, often disguising it as anger – but in many cases it is based upon fear, because God has become a bogeyman. Hollywood cleverly manipulates these primal fears by depicting gospel preachers as demented and frightening beings, and pandering to morbid and voyeuristic fascination with the object of the wounded paranoia – the God they are fleeing. The recent run of books by atheists that rage against God caters to the same injured suspicion.

An English woman found Fred Hutchison's internet essays that openly mentioned God *"alarming."* She insisted that his essays be removed from the shared computer of her rental community room.[296] Her protests and demands were unreasonable, of course, but a closed, fractured person who is fleeing from God is not a reasonable being. She could not just ignore the essays and allow others to enjoy them. Her voyeuristic bogeyman fascination enticed her to peek at the essays, and thus became alarmed and indignant.

Those who want to remove all trace of God from the public square are unreasonable in exactly this way. If they really did not believe in God, it would be easy for them to ignore it when he is mentioned publically, just as they ignore it when children speak of witches and goblins. But they secretly fear that God does exist, because they are afraid of him and stung by the mere mention of him. Angry narcissists make unconvincing atheists. They lie when they claim that they only care about the separation of church and state and the *"inclusion"* of all citizens. No one gets paranoid and hysterical about that. Paranoia and hysteria are reserved for the bogeymen and scapegoats of a shattered mind.

There is no constitutional right for neurotics to be free from the thing that sets off their paranoia. Unfortunately, many weak leaders are so afraid that someone, somewhere, might be offended, that they take the reassuring public mention of God away from everyone – no matter how unreasonable the placating, or how small the number offended. In order to indulge a tiny number of hypersensitive people, God is being expelled from the public square. The next step in this paranoid agenda is to squelch freedom of speech for fear that something might be said that offends the quick-

> *Fred Critique*
> ___
> *In order to indulge a tiny number of hypersensitive people, God is being expelled from the public square... When God is driven out of the public square, freedom soon follows.*

---

[296] (F. Hutchison, Brief History of Conservatism 2009)

tempered – then common references to God's standards are labeled *"hate crimes."* For example, pastors in Sweden can be arrested for preaching from biblical texts on homosexuality. When God is driven out of the public square, freedom soon follows.

THE BATTLE BEFORE US

Freedom first came to Europe through the urban republics erected to the glory of God. Freedom is now fading in Western culture as God is systematically cast out. We have no choice but to fight the battle to turn our culture around – not just for the sake of souls, but to save Western civilization itself. Those who choose to stand up and fight will be rewarded with persecution and hatred by the perishing world system. Unfortunately, the contemporary church is going through a prolonged lukewarm spell and is not prepared for battle. The deceitfulness of riches and watered-down *"seeker sensitive"* messages at various churches has rendered many Christians soft and self-indulgent. Many Evangelicals quit the culture war because they fear persecution, loathe personal sacrifice, and are no longer zealous about truth. All too many crave the approval of this wicked world, instead of God's approval.

> ### Fred Critique
> *We have no choice but to fight the battle to turn our culture around – to save Western civilization itself. Those who choose to stand up and fight will be rewarded with persecution and hatred.*

REMEMBER THE FORMER GLORIES

> *"You say, 'I am rich; I have acquired wealth and do not need a thing.' But you do not realize that you are wretched, pitiful, poor, blind and naked. I counsel you to buy from me gold refined in the fire, so you can become rich; and white clothes to wear, so you can cover your shameful nakedness; and salve to put on your eyes, so you can see." Revelations 3:17-18 (NIV)*

Remembering the former glories of what God can do through his people will give us courage and inspiration to face the battle. The dangers and sacrifices of building the kingdom of God on earth in 1050 were a hundred-fold greater than the cost to us of defying the secular left in America today. Yet peasants rushed to the daunting tasks with

> ### Fred Critique
> *Remembering the former glories of what God can do through his people will give us courage and inspiration to face the battle.*

rejoicing and becoming heroes. These athletes of Christ did not drag around the self-centered baggage that encumbers Christians in many contemporary churches. They died to themselves and to the world as they identified with Christ in His death. Therefore, they were not burdened with the dead weight of inordinate pride and selfishness.

The 11th century Christians were intoxicated with the glory of God and united in zeal. In sad contrast, the sense of transcendence has faded from seeker sensitive entertainment centers (i.e., evangelical mega-churches) that pander to spoiled Christians. God will receive our worship, but will not stoop to star in a stage show where the music director says, *"Give a round of applause to God."*

Considering the boldness and fury of the wicked, and the timidity of the soft contemporary Christian, turning society around before it shipwrecks seems impossible. However, creating a brand new civilization out of the Dark Age was infinitely more difficult. God is still the same. The difference lies in the hearts of men – the power of the cross is just as accessible to us as it was to them. The transcendent glory of God is just as ready to make our hearts sing as it was then. Alas, pampered Christians of today are strangely complacent and self-satisfied.[297]

COMING UP NEXT

Chapter 16 will explore the logical correlations between Christian doctrinal orthodoxy and conservative political philosophy. Orthodoxy in this sense means the great truths of historical creeds and confessions of the church. Chapter 1 proposed that the five streams of conservatism have always had a positive influence on Western culture. This is particularly true of Christian conservatism – when doctrine is orthodox and truths of the faith are propagated boldly and without compromise.

---

[297] (F. Hutchison, Brief History of Conservatism 2009)

Chapter 15 discussed the strong correlation between Christian spirituality and the vitality of Western culture. However, spirituality by itself is not enough. Issues of truth and doctrinal orthodoxy are equally important. A spiritually charged people who faithfully declare God's Truth can turn the tides of history, so we now turn to questions of doctrine. This chapter explores some of the logical correlations between Christian doctrinal orthodoxy and conservative political philosophy. Orthodoxy in this sense means the great truths of historical creeds and confessions of the church. Chapter 1 proposed that the five streams of conservatism have always had a positive influence on Western culture. This is particularly true of Christian conservatism – when doctrine is orthodox and truths of the faith are broadcast boldly and without compromise.

CHRISTIAN TRUTH CLAIMS TRANSFORM CULTURE

Christianity's truth claims preoccupied monastic and university scholars from the 11th-13th centuries. They pursued the truth with extraordinary enthusiasm, zeal and intellectual vigor. Watering down the truth to pander to the crowd, as is often the practice today, would have been unthinkable to these early ambassadors. Interestingly, some learned scholarly debates in the 12th century were attended by large crowds of ordinary people who shared the zest for truth. Common people had never been so enthusiastic about the battle for truth – students burned with intellectual excitement and displayed earnest striving after Truth.

Aristotle

The only comparisons for this passion are the students who sat in the olive groves of Plato's Academy, or those who walked in the gymnasium colonnade of Aristotle's Lyceum. European scholastic enthusiasm was ultimately shared by thousands more students than ever attended either Plato's school or Aristotle's colonnade. As marvelous as the Greek philosophic teachings were, it was small-scale compared to the Medieval European universities, and ill-timed in history for maximum cultural effect – Plato and Aristotle appeared after the golden age of Athens was over and culture had set in its ways.

In contrast, scholasticism appeared shortly after 1100, when European civilization was brand new. It therefore had a seminal influence in molding culture when it was impressionable and pliable. The 12th century was particularly flexible and dynamic, and the developing society was rapidly changing. The greatest scholar was St. Thomas Aquinas (1225-1274), whose works are still included in Western literary canons. **Thomists**, scholars who specialize in Aquinas, still appear when intellectual ferment rises among people with renewed interest in metaphysics.

SCHOLASTICISM GIVES EUROPE THE EDGE IN RATIONALITY

From the beginning of the High Middle Ages, Europe had a uniquely rational culture. Scholasticism was formally developed in the early growth stages of civilization. Europe became the premier society of rationality and remained so until the early 20th century. Historical advantages were mainly benefits of reason and educated intellect – natural resources like navigable rivers and natural harbors were aggressively developed by intelligent men. The proliferation of wind mills, water mills, stone cutting machinery, and treadwheel cranes for lifting heavy loads betokens a society of restless minds seeking to solve practical problems. The Dark Age slumbering minds were awakened for such tasks through scholasticism and education in Cathedral schools and monasteries.

Scholasticism was a truth-seeking venture sponsored by the church; therefore, Christianity gave Europe the edge over other civilizations in rational powers – a triumph of doctrinal orthodoxy. During scholastic debates, orthodox views prevailed over dissident heterodox and heretical opinion. Thus, European culture was shaped and enlightened by the theology of doctrinal orthodoxy.

CONSERVATIVE VERSUS MODERNISM

> *"The present threat to our civilization comes as much from indifference, apathy, and selfishness as it does from the totalist powers; and pessimism for pessimism's sake is as bad as optimism for optimism's sake." Russell Kirk, 1960[298]*

Just as conservative theology (orthodox doctrine) is compatible with conservative political philosophy, liberal theology is compatible with political liberalism and progressivism (modernism). Liberal theology can be characterized as modernism wrapped in a nominally Christian package. Modernism is the common enemy of conservative theology, political philosophy, reason and civilization – and has fallen to a shocking state of intellectual and moral decadence.

TIGHT THEOLOGY AND LOOSE POLITICAL PHILOSOPHY

The fact that there are logical connections between conservative theology and political philosophy does not imply a perfect fit – there are points of tension. It is a loose fit, not a tight fit, which is good enough for a political philosophy, but only logical precision is acceptable for orthodox theology. Whereas the great faith creeds required an exacting precision of language and concepts, political philosophy needs only to provide a general fit, like clothes purchased off the rack that do not need custom tailoring.

Fred Critique

Loose doctrine is an invitation to heretics. Tight political philosophies collapse into narrow ideologies that are not amenable to debate, alienating natural allies and making political compromise impossible.

Beware of doctrines that are woven too loosely and political philosophies that are woven too tightly. Loose doctrine is an invitation to heretics. Tight political philosophies collapse into narrow ideologies that are not amenable to debate, alienating natural allies and making political compromise impossible.

PERFECTIONISM AND POLITICAL DISASTER

The 2008 presidential campaign included a search for the perfect conservative candidate, and led to the destruction of all the candidates. Once the ground was littered with conservative bodies, John McCain (1936-), a moderate whose chances had long been written off, stepped forward and claimed the Republican nomination. He was beaten by a vague and inexperienced liberal Democrat named Barack Obama.

---

[298] (Kirk, The Common Heritage of America and Europe 1960)

Perfectionism is suicidal in politics. Many Americans were guilty of insisting upon the perfect conservative and fighting against the imperfect candidates who might have won. As sadder and wiser people, the mission now must be to unite the five historical streams of conservatism. This would be unfeasible if all five groups were perfectionists or defined their cluster of ideas as narrow ideologies – the schools can only work together if a loose fit is tolerated, allowing each to learn from the others. Each branch has specialized wisdom that is needed by the conservative movement as a whole.

MAN HAS A NATURE

"I believe in God, the Father almighty, creator of heaven and earth." ***The Apostles' Creed (390)***

This first line of the **Apostle's Creed**[299] confesses that God is the creator. If God created man, he also designed him. If man has a design, he also has an innate nature. An integrated design is not subject to material change, but is fixed over time. Thus, human nature is fixed throughout the centuries and is universally shared by all mankind. Doctrinally orthodox Christians and political conservatives almost universally insist that man has an innate nature, and that man has always been essentially the same. Therefore, they cherish the wisdom of the past.

In contrast, modernists almost universally deny that man has a universal nature, insisting that man is a construct of culture, environment, economics and biology. They believe that human nature is in flux and that mankind was essentially different in former centuries. They are therefore skeptical about past wisdom. There is a great gulf between modernism and theological conservatism, which explains how political conservatism lines up in opposition.

HUMAN NATURE AND LEGISLATION

If man has no nature but is a construct of society, as liberals think, legislators will tend to think they can fashion a better man through social engineering programs. In contrast, if man has a nature based upon a design that is fixed and unchanging, as conservatives believe, agendas designed to change human nature only inflict injuries or stifle his nature. Seventy years of Soviet Union social engineering failed to change human nature the slightest amount. The relentless attempts turned the entire society into a wretched and joyless prison filled with dysfunctional people.

In contrast to soviet tyrants, thoughtful conservative representatives will review proposed legislation to determine if it runs against the grain of human nature. Examining proposed new laws in an attempt to ascertain whether it is oppressive to human nature provides wholesome boundaries in which man can flourish. Political and theological conservatives usually unite to oppose social engineering programs – liberals and communists generally favor them. It is patently obvious why conservatives are invariably anticommunist and why many liberals have a secret

> ### *Fred Critique*
>
> *Examining proposed new laws to ascertain whether they are oppressive to human nature provides wholesome boundaries in which man can flourish.*

---

[299] The Apostles' Creed is an early statement of Christian belief that is widely used by many Western tradition Christian denominations for liturgical purposes, including the Catholic Church, Lutheranism, Anglicanism, Western Orthodoxy, Presbyterians, Methodists and Congregationalists.

sympathy for communism. This is why poorly informed conservatives have difficulty differentiating between liberalism and communism.

Although Christian and political conservatives generally agree about opposition to social engineering programs, Christian conservatives emphasize the principle that only divine grace changes the human heart. Traditionalists stress that governments rend the delicate social fabric. Libertarians are primarily concerned with how government programs interfere with individual initiative.

IN ADAM'S FALL WE SINNED ALL

Christian doctrinal orthodoxy requires acknowledging that although mankind is harmoniously designed with an innate nature that was originally good, he has been fatally corrupted by original sin – as if he has a well-designed constitution that has been contaminated. Man is **totally depraved**[300] in the sense that the contamination of wickedness has reached all his faculties and every part of his constitution. Man is not absolutely evil.

The most evil men, like Hitler, Stalin, Mao, Pol Pot and bin Laden, started with an innate propensity to sin, and willfully pursued evil thoughts and deeds through various stages of development. In the fullness of time, they brought forth highly developed evil. The human lifetime is too short and the developmental process too slow to produce absolute

evil. In like manner, a saint is overtaken by death long before he can realize the perfection of holiness.

This being understood, orthodox doctrine traditionally holds that there is no human faculty left pure and uncontaminated by original sin. The evangelist Charles Finney (1792-1875) is regarded by some doctrinally orthodox theologians as a **pelagian**[301] heretic, because he limited the scope of original sin. He asserted that the mind and will were not automatically contaminated with original sin, and that man is as sinful or righteous as he chooses. Finney preached the gospel with the assumption that men choose their way to faith. To the contrary, the doctrinally orthodox reformer Martin Luther (1483-1546) taught that man was originally good but became bad through Adam's fall because:

1. All of our faculties, including the mind and will, are contaminated by original sin;

2. We are in bondage to sin until God sets us free through His grace; and

3. Faith is a gift from God.

An example of alphabet rhymes that teach moral values in the **New England Primer**[302] is, *"In Adam's fall we sinned all."* Original sin was inherited by all Adam's progeny, meaning all mankind. The original design harmony was disrupted by deep-seated wickedness in the human heart. It is not possible to return to Eden and regain the original harmony and goodness of God's design by relying on human strength and effort, which is why we need a Savior.

---

[300] Total depravity is a theological doctrine from the Augustinian concept of original sin. It teaches that as a consequence of the Fall of Man, every person born is enslaved to sin and, apart from the grace of God, is utterly unable to choose to follow God or accept salvation.

[301] Pelagianism is a theological belief that original sin did not taint human nature and that mortal will is still capable of choosing good or evil without special Divine aid. Thus, Adam's sin set a bad example but did not have the consequences assigned to original sin, while Jesus set a good example that counteracted Adam and provided atonement for sins.

[302] The New England Primer was a student textbook used in English settlements in North America, and first printed in Boston in 1690 by Benjamin Harris, who had published a similar volume in London. It was used until the 19th century. Over five million copies were sold.

MAN IS A CONTRADICTION

Traditionalist conservatives believe man is a contradiction and is capable of evil. This is a mild, common-sense view about the dark side of human nature – what daily experience and history lessons consistently teach. There is a tension between this concept and the orthodox Christian position, but when it comes to politics and legislation most differences fade. Once again, observe the loose fit of conservative theology and conservative politics. These two groups are easily united in political ventures against liberals who have convinced themselves that man is inherently good.

BEWITCHING THE CONSERVATIVES

The ascendancy of liberalism unites conservatives as they perceive a common enemy. One reason conservatives were not united in the 2008 election cycle was that the eyes of many were blinded to the rise of leviathan out of the pit – that is, the increase of far left power. They were sightless, deceived and bewitched because they had slipped away from conservative principles. Christians who forget biblical truths can backslide and be deceived by the world and the devil. A political conservative who loses grip on principles and values can be deceived by liberals or compromised by deals with moderates. Some try to balance conservative principles with incompatible modernistic concepts – this practice debilitates and induces a slippery slide to the left.

> *Fred Critique*
>
> *A political conservative who loses grip on principles and values can be deceived by liberals or compromised by deals with moderates.*

WISHFUL THINKING

When liberals deny the palpable reality of human nature's dark side, they reject all the lessons of life and experience. Such denial suggests a powerful delusion or childlike naiveté. During his late teens, around the time he was thinking about becoming a conservative, Fred Hutchison remembers telling a liberal college instructor that his arguments were based on *"wishful thinking."* The stubborn notion that man is inherently good was behind much of his naiveté.[303] We live in a broken world and it does no good to wish otherwise, as immature children might do.

The willful denial of the evil lurking in human hearts has, in some cases, an element of malice. Such dismissal suggests a primal rebellion involving the indignant rejection of the broken world's harsh reality. The circular logic follows as something like, *"I refuse to believe that men are the rascals and knaves they appear to be. Therefore, I insist that they are otherwise."* The malice inherent in this contradiction is sometimes turned against conservatives who are pessimistic about human nature.

CAN FALLEN MAN BECOME VIRTUOUS?

Marcus Aurelius

Some theological conservatives believe that although man is depraved, he can cooperate in a development process leading towards virtue with the help of **common grace**,[304] an empowerment from God for believer and unbeliever alike. Through common grace, a noble pagan like Roman Emperor and Stoic philosopher Marcus Aurelius (121-180) reached a degree of understanding on truth questions – he knew the difference between good and evil, and virtue and vice. By all accounts, Aurelius made significant headway in his quest for

---

[303] (F. Hutchison, Brief History of Conservatism 2009)
[304] Common Grace refers to God's grace that is universal to all humankind. It is ‑common" because its benefits are experienced by the whole human race without distinction. It is "grace" because it is undeserved and sovereignly bestowed by God.

wisdom. However, common grace without the **special grace**[305] that comes with conversion to Christ is not enough – Marcus Aurelius wasted the substance of Rome with futile, tactically irrational wars against the northern barbarians. He persecuted Christians, and he designated his foolish, malicious and delusional son, Commodus, as heir to his throne. Socrates (469-399 BC) was wrong – the rule of philosopher kings is no panacea.

CONSERVATISM CAN BE PROBLEMATIC

There is a problematic dichotomy for creatures with a good design that have become evil through rebellion against their Designer and resistance to the design. According to Aristotle, virtue consists of thoughts and actions in agreement with man's design – vice is doing things that are against the nature and design of man. This is not an intellectually easy or intuitively obvious concept. A distinction must be carefully made between good design and deep corruption.

By failing to make this distinction carefully, fault lines have formed among conservative theologians and political philosophers along two kinds of errors: 1) downplaying human depravity by overemphasizing the design goodness; and 2) downplaying the design goodness and harmony due to preoccupation with human depravity. The first error leads to trusting in man too much and slipping towards the left, theologically and politically. The second error leads to rejecting Natural Law, which is indispensable to coherent systematic theology and rational conservative political philosophy.

> *Fred Critique*
> ___
> *A distinction must be carefully made between good design and deep corruption.*

The difficulties do not end there. Conservatives must carefully distinguish between the sinful nature and habitual propensities that have developed from a long series of choices. A mistake at this point can lead to all kinds of sloppy thinking. Theologian John Gregory Mantle (1853-1925) characterized this careless thinking by referring to self-righteous Christians as those who have built learned behavior on a corrupt root.[306] The opposite error is to downplay a sinner's wickedness by making excuses that the person is merely following bad habits. This inaccuracy leaves out a moral appraisal of the long series of wicked choices made to develop the behavior pattern. One can justly refer to someone as an *"evil man"* if he has spent a lifetime cultivating evil practices. Certain criminal psychologists have determined that hardened criminals often start cultivating evil imaginations in childhood, and perform many experiments in turning the thoughts into deeds. Through such experiments, they become proficient in increasing stages of evil.[307]

TUTELARY PARADOX

It is common to have a pessimistic view of human nature, and at the same time be optimistic that individuals can eventually fulfill the destiny inherent in their design, with the help of divine grace. However, the developmental process of maturing and getting ready for one's ultimate destiny can be very long and difficult. Many stray from the straight path that leads to this fulfillment. Some folks think that potential destiny and manifest depravity are an impossible contradiction. Yet both dimensions of human nature are a **tutelary**[308] paradox that can slowly lead to wisdom and personal growth. The paradox is a motivator to seek help from God and be delivered from the sins and vices that would bar the fulfillment of destiny.

---

[305] Special Grace is the Calvinistic understanding of God's grace by which he redeems, sanctifies and glorifies his people. It is bestowed only on those God elects for redemption to eternal life through faith in Jesus Christ.
[306] (Mantle 1974 (1896))
[307] (Samenow 1984)
[308] Tutelary – guardianship of a person or a thing.

THE PARTICULAR AND THE UNIVERSAL

Some libertarian conservatives and traditionalists emphasize the particular and unique qualities of individuals to such an extent that they doubt men have a core nature with universal qualities. This denial of universal human nature underlying individual particulars is why some libertarians reject universal moral law. The confusion of not seeing the forest of human nature for the trees of individual particulars can be cleared up by a refresher course in Aristotle or St. Thomas Aquinas – both taught how to differentiate *"essence"* and *"accidents."* Aristotle's universals subsist as the

St. Thomas Aquinas

"essence" of particular things; in other words, core human essence, or humanity, is universal. The *"accidents"* are those superficial, tangible details, particularities and eccentricities that make people unique individuals. Recognizing the unique personality but ignoring the underlying personhood is an error of logical distinctions; e.g., *"He is a rascal and a clown, therefore he is not a human being."* The error is insulting because it is reductionistic.

Precisely because Aristotle's and Aquinas' thought was so deeply woven into Western culture, the culture was able to avoid extremes in collectivism and individualism. The West lost this facility in direct proportion to the decline of metaphysics after 1800. Political liberals of today swing wildly between collectivism and lawless, atomistic individualism. It is no accident that metaphysics is anathema to them.

THE EXISTENTIAL MISTAKE

Another Libertarian mistake is the Existentialist type involving failure to differentiate between essence and existence. Existentialists are obsessed with finding an *"authentic"* mode of existence. It is an extreme version of the American quest for a self-defining and trendy life-style. Such preoccupation with modes of existence tends towards the neglect of *"essence,"* the inner humanity that is independent of existing. Aristotle and Aquinas can clear up the problem by clarifying the difference between essence and existence.

Man cannot be content to just exist and not be concerned about personal modes of existence, because he is a finite, contingent, insecure, proud being who must attach to the world by raising a banner. *"Look at me. I am right here, right now, and am expressing myself in a unique manner. Therefore, I exist!"* Those who are spiritually mature enough to completely dispense with *"raising the flag"* are very rare. However, an obsession with existential self-expression is a sign of abnormal insecurity and immaturity.

Unlike man, God's essence is the same as his existence, because he is complete and self-contained in the perfection of his being. If he raises the flag, it is purely an act of love and never an attempt to ground or vindicate his existence. Those who cannot differentiate between essence and existence do not understand man. Those who think God has modes of existence do not understand God. The West used to have a good balance between individual creativity and archetypal forms in art and literature – now the existential quest for radical individuality of expression has thrown the arts and literature into chaos.

A UNIVERSAL MORAL LAW

All designs have rules of operation. New kitchen appliances and yard tools come with written operation directions and malfunction instructions in case of emergency or dangerous use. Since man is a designed being, there are rules and laws concerning what is salutary to his nature, and what is destructive to him and his neighbors. These statutes, laws and precepts are the same for all people in all times – therefore universal moral law exists and has been unchanging and

universal ever since man's appearance on earth. The instruction booklet for man, provided by the designer, is called the Bible – the Old and New Testaments are in perfect agreement relating to core elements of the universal moral law summed up in the Ten Commandments. Old Testament ordinances specific to Israel and not universal in applicability were abolished in the New Testament – but not the principles of the Decalogue.[309]

Many modernists deny the existence of a universal moral law, and call such things individual *"value judgments"*. They assume that since they often invent their own moral cosmos, the conservative moral law is the same kind of personal invention. This presumption is revealed when they claim that the command against adultery is a personal assessment decision. Not so – universal moral law is the exact opposite of made-up values unique to the individual.

Positions on innumerable political issues hinge on whether people believe in universal moral laws, or dismiss them as individual value judgments. Consider an example of a free-floating value judgment: *"The fetus in my womb is part of my body. I can do anything I want with my body. Therefore, I have the right to kill the fetus. My free choice to do so makes it right."* The first sentence is contrary to scientific fact. The second sentence is opposed to natural law and biblical teaching. The third sentence conflicts with universal moral law. The fourth statement comes from the funny farm of **solipsism.**[310] This cluster of concepts ignores the spiritual reality that babes in the womb are people.

> ***Fred Critique***
> _____
> *Since man is a designed being, there are rules and laws concerning what is salutary to his nature, and what is destructive to him and his neighbors.*

The invention of tailor-made value stances gratifies personal comfort and unrestrained lusts. They promise freedom from consequences and personal responsibility. In contrast, authentic moral laws require self-denial, develop personal virtue, and promote the general good of the family, the neighborhood and the community.

SELF-CONTRADICTORY NATURE OF MODERNISM

In contrast to the fault-lines of conservatism, modernism has stark contradictions. Conservative fault lines can often be reconciled or reduced to a loose fit. However, it is dubious whether the contradictions of modernism can be reconciled or made to work together. Modernists say: 1) man does not have a nature; and 2) man is inherently good. These two propositions are contradictions – if man does not have a nature, he cannot be inherently good, inherently bad, or inherently anything. Modernism posits an impossible contradiction and is therefore a false, absurd world view. It is no accident that Sartre came to believe that life is absurd.

---

[309] The Ten Commandments, also known as the Decalogue, are a set of Biblical principles relating to ethics and worship and considered fundamental to Judaism and Christianity. They include: 1) You shall have no other gods before me, 2) You shall not misuse the name of the LORD your God, 3) Remember the Sabbath day by keeping it holy, 4) Honor your father and your mother, so that you may live long in the land the LORD your God is giving you, 5) You shall not murder, 6) You shall not commit adultery 7) You shall not steal, 8) You shall not give false testimony against your neighbor, 9) You shall not covet your neighbor's house, and 10) You shall not covet your neighbor's wife, or his male or female servant, his ox or donkey, or anything that belongs to your neighbor.

[310] Solipsism is the philosophy that only one's own mind is sure to exist, knowledge of anything outside one's own mind is unsure. The external world and other minds cannot be known, and might not exist outside the mind.

James Madison

James Madison (1751-1836), an American Founding Father and contributor to the Constitution, wrote, *"If men were angels, no government would be necessary."*[311] We would not need police or a justice system to punish evil doers. Liberals, who believe men are good unless they are mentally ill or emotionally damaged, sometimes propose that we substitute therapy for criminal punishment. Liberal judges have been known to let child molesters off on probation to get *"therapy."* These morally deranged judges are not impeached – they are defended by the liberal media and often re-elected.

Some liberals say, *"Society is the cause of criminality. Therefore, let us fix the root causes in society, instead of punishing criminals."* When there is a crime wave, conservatives talk of hiring more police and building more prisons, and liberals talk about therapy and social engineering projects. Christians who believe in the fall of man must be skeptical of therapy's ability to make an evil man good, or that social programs can cure the real cause of crime that lurks in dark human hearts.

In the novel ***The Lord of the Flies***, English school boys became island castaways and quickly reverted to savagery. When a seaman came to the rescue, a character named Ralph realized how far they had sunk into depravity – he wept for *"the end of innocence and for the darkness of the human heart."* It hurt to give up the pleasant illusion that man is naturally good.[312]

When Fred Hutchison was on the college debate team, an argument was made that welfare programs do not corrupt the beneficiaries because *"people have an innate desire to work."* This point was baldly asserted on the grounds that man is naturally good and therefore tends to prefer virtue to vice. Similar thinking prevailed when the New Deal and Great Society programs were designed. The result was a great mass of welfare families who remained on the government dole for generations. Idleness multiplied their vices and shattered their families – apparently, they did not sit at home studying Aristotelian virtues.

RIGHTS AND DUTIES

In political culture today, those who shout the loudest about rights are most likely to deny duties – dead beats, moochers and con men. While such moral decadence is expected from liberals, it is embarrassing when some libertarians carry individualism to extremes, demanding rights while denying duties. If man has a nature, he must have both rights and duties connected with that nature. Governments that respect human nature are obliged to protect the innate rights of individuals against the infringements of others. Since human nature is constant, these protections should be enduring principles of law. At the same time, no one should be offended by legitimate citizenship duties.

It is inconceivable that the creator would design man to soak up rights while denying duties. Those who demand every benefit but shun every duty are despicable, parasitic narcissists. It is unthinkable that man was designed solely to serve his own private ends, and that his innate dignity warrants special rights and privileges. It cannot be both ways. Either man has both rights and duties, or he has neither.

> *Fred Critique*
>
> *Either man has both rights and duties, or he has neither.*

---

[311] (Madison February 6, 1788)
[312] (Golding 1954)

SELF-GOVERNMENT

If humans have both rights and duties, full flourishing would require exercising those rights and meeting those duties. If people are capable of arousing themselves from self-seeking activities to carry out duties, the unavoidable implication is that they are capable of governing themselves. Moral and self-disciplined men who are thoroughly socialized as responsible members of the family and community are capable of governing themselves. The capacity to self govern makes it possible to have a Republic of free men with a limited role for government. The greater part of a Republic is self-governance – the lesser part is civil administration. It is no accident that when individual self-control is in decline, an increasing number of citizens call for enlarged government programs and regulation.

RESTORATION OF SELF-GOVERNMENT

It is not enough for conservatives to fight against the expansion of government. They must show the way towards restoring individual self-control by their own example and teaching – conservatives must be virtuous and teach classical values to the populace. America's pulpits must restore the long absent preaching of righteousness, holiness, personal responsibility and self denial. Perhaps an entire generation of indulging seeker-sensitive ministries must pass from the scene, so that a new wave of godly men, with hearts on fire for truth and zeal for righteousness and holiness, might rise up from the grassroots of America. The sharp edges of doctrinal orthodoxy, which have been blunted and rounded off for fear of offending someone, must be honed into a razor-sharp, two-edged sword. This has happened several times before in American history, which is why the country has had such a long run of self-government and personal freedom.

FREEDOM WITHIN BOUNDARIES

All designs are integrated with boundaries and limits. This truth is known to every engineer and architect. If man is a designed being, all of life must be conducted within limits. Virtually all doctrinal and theological conservatives understand this reality. However, liberals and modernists frequently talk about the absence of limits for an individual's possibilities. This popular idea passes for wisdom and enlightenment, but it is a notion so filled with fantasy and folly that even children know better. All ideas about life without limits are destructive to humans.

Many Americans are lured to their doom by the pied piper of no limits. They recklessly throw off boundaries, thinking it will set them free to do the impossible. This is madness – man is a created being, and therefore is finite and obliged to live within boundaries, like them or not. God has placed each of us on earth according to His *"appointed times,"* and has established the *"boundaries of our habitation" (Acts 17: 26)*. He placed us in a particular location at a specific time to do business for Him in a precise station in life. Our lives have starting and ending times, and the community, province or nation in which we live has boundaries. Every kind of work humans do is hedged with duties and boundaries. We flourish and find our freedom within these boundaries.

Everyone who knows they are not God but are mere creatures should understand this concept from within their bone marrow. Unfortunately, 20th century modernism promotes a powerful delusion that we are gods, and not men, and therefore have no limits. It was Friedrich Nietzsche (1844-1900) who opened this Pandora's Box to poison the souls of mankind.

CONCLUSION

Christian doctrinal conservatism allied with conservative political philosophy, is a good antidote to Nietzsche's nihilistic modernism. Christian conservatism is uniquely potent in fighting modernism, and is therefore indispensable as one of the five branches of conservatism. Without it, the other branches would be in constant danger of seduction by modernism and drifting to the left. Chapter 17 will explore the rise of neoconservatives in the 20th century, as modernism fell to a shocking state of intellectual and moral decadence – becoming the enemy of reason and civilization.

Augustus Caesar

Neoconservatism is the most misunderstood of the five conservative branches. Chapter 1 explained that tough minded and highly cultured Romans had a proto-neoconservative style – Emperor Augustus Caesar and his favorite writer, Virgil, are examples. More than two millennia later, neoconservatism made another historical appearance when President George W. Bush appointed a handful of highly visible and controversial neoconservatives (neocons) to positions of power and influence. Neocons became a convenient place to assign blame when foreign adventures went wrong, and conspiracy theories about them sprang up like weeds – government policies they developed sometimes divided conservatives. However, neocons are essential to the conservative movement – we should not throw them out, but embrace them as a permanent part of the conservative movement. Neocons should be accepted and accorded special honor for contributing great good for the country and civilization, and for suffering the liberal wrath as a result. Furthermore, we need to listen to them with special care.

> ### *Fred Critique*
>
> *We need to listen to neocons with special care.*

NEOCONSERVATIVE WISDOM

We should listen to the neocons for four reasons:

1. Neoconservatives have superior understanding of Western civilization's two deadly enemies: the three historical waves of modernism; and barbarism in both foreign and domestic guise.

2. Neoconservatives are committed to rejuvenating civilization and culture. They are devoted to classical literature, high culture, cultivating virtue, and the restoration of reason in an irrational age.

3. Neoconservatism provides an intellectual booster shot to the conservative movement.

4. Neocons matured after leaving their youthful liberalism – the conservative movement needs grown-ups.

LIBERALS GROW UP

President Bush

An old neocon joke is told that a conservative is a liberal who has been mugged. Many leading neoconservatives started as liberals and evolved into conservatives – hence the appellation meaning *"new conservative"* or *"new kind of conservative."* Neocons are grown up liberals who put childish magical thinking aside, packed like childhood toys in the attic. Chapter 5 observed that some founders of modern conservatism were liberals in their youth, becoming conservatives during mature mid-life years.

CROSSING THE RUBICON

As contemporary liberals evolve into neoconservatives, there is a **Rubicon**[313] crossing point in the journey where there is no turning back from becoming lifelong conservatives. The favorite motto of Leo Strauss (1899-1973), the great neoconservative political philosopher, was *"back to the Ancients."*[314] In other words, return to the political philosophy from a time before modernism began – implicitly renouncing modernism. Neocons pass a point of no return towards conservatism when they decisively renounce modernism, which can be exceedingly difficult and painful for them. Once they take the step, they are changed forever – scales fall from their eyes as they look back in horror at the crazy illusions, intellectual and moral decadence, false postures of self-righteousness, self-defeating passions and secret disgust of humankind they labored under as modernists. For this reason, neoconservatives are among the most astute critics of modernism and its political expression, liberalism.[315]

TURNING BACK FROM THE RUBICON

Budding neocons that turn back without crossing the Rubicon, and listen again to the siren songs of modernism, can be sucked back into liberalism. Some who turn back are like young adults who take a long look at the heavy responsibilities of adult maturity and balk – they become perpetual adolescents and are doomed to blighted lives. Some become squishy moderates, while still others find themselves awkwardly suspended between conservatism and liberalism, as was Robert Hutchins.

Robert Hutchins

Robert Maynard Hutchins, introduced in Chapter 11, laid an indispensable literary, intellectual and metaphysical foundation for neoconservatism, but never became a political conservative. He wasted the last 25 years of his life crusading for utopian liberal causes. However, Hutchins moved quite a distance from his youthful liberalism, to become the arch enemy of hyper-modernist John Dewey. Hutchins might have been remembered as the father of neoconservatism if he had crossed his Rubicon.

LEO STRAUSS FOUND A SOLUTION

One cannot renounce modernism unless he can clearly define its essential nature. That definition must be relevant to human action in general, and politics in particular – it is difficult to develop because of modernism's complexity through history. Leo Strauss found an effective way to do this through his background in political philosophy, history and the classics. He identified three waves of modernism: the first was in the 18th century; the second occurred in the 19th century, and the third appeared in the 20th century. Each wave can be reduced to its essential nature and explained so average people can understand, and renounce it.

---

[313] The idiom "Crossing the Rubicon" means to pass a point of no return, and refers to Julius Caesar's army's crossing of the Rubicon River in 49 BC, which was considered an act of insurrection.

[314] The "Ancients" were Socratic philosophers and their intellectual heirs who reacted to the irresolvable tension between reason and revelation, brought philosophy back to earth and the marketplace, and made it more political.

[315] Starting with Machiavelli, moderns reacted to the dominance of revelations in medieval society by promoting reason. They objected to Thomas Aquinas' merger of natural rights and natural theology.

The 18th century wave of modernism involved two rebellions: a philosophical rebellion against metaphysics; and a romantic revolt against civilization towards returning to nature. Both were camouflaged revolutions against reason. Neocons put great value on metaphysical rationality, high culture and civilization – these uprisings were hateful to them. Leo Strauss' exhortation to *"return to the Ancients"* essentially means seeking inspiration from the days when metaphysics was robust and Europe's high culture was blossoming.

18TH CENTURY REJECTION OF METAPHYSICS

Francis Bacon

Metaphysics deals with questions about principles, the meaning and purpose of life, and questions about realities underlying surface appearances. It deals with the nature of being and existence, and provides principles of rational understanding. The development of a mature, full-orbed rationality is not possible without metaphysics. Writers such as Machiavelli, Bacon, Descartes and Locke (per his **epistemology**[316]) gave early warnings that a rumbling against metaphysics had begun among intellectuals in the 16th and 17th centuries. (See Chapter 4 for details.) Francis Bacon had contributed the method and goal: practical empirical knowledge stripped of metaphysics for use in the quest for naked power and material gain. Niccolò Machiavelli made similar contributions to the unprincipled and ruthless program of modernism for power.

A radical renunciation of metaphysics came in the 18th century with the writings of Voltaire, Diderot, Hume and Kant. Voltaire provided satire and ridicule, Hume supplied the acid bath of skepticism, Diderot presented atheistic materialism, and Kant offered epistemological pessimism about what is knowable. Kant believed metaphysical realities exist, but concluded that they are beyond the human mind's reach – his critique was a death-blow to metaphysical rationality.

Modernism showed an ugly and sinister face to the world in these early beginnings. The rejection of metaphysics involved turning the mind away from lofty ideas and toward low pragmatic, materialistic, opportunistic considerations. This change narrowed the mind and soul of modern man – it made him more resourceful, but less rational and principled. The program of pragmatism prepared modern men to be more economically productive, but it also made them calculating, mercenary and ruthless.

ACID BATH OF SKEPTICISM

Leadership training programs for young conservatives should prepare them for the modernist acid bath of skepticism toward metaphysics. Every student who goes to college and tries to discuss metaphysics will run into this hostile skepticism. If he renounces it before university, the odds of falling into the acid bath and becoming a modernist skeptic are reduced. Students should be taught that the vicious attack is an irrational and arbitrary prejudice. They should be alerted that no enemy of metaphysics can offer logical reasons why they are against it. The bias is transferred like an infection in the swamps of modernist academia.

---

[316] Epistemology, meaning "knowledge, science", is philosophy concerned with the nature and scope of knowledge. It addresses the questions: What is knowledge? How is knowledge acquired? How do we know what we know?

BEAUTY, TRUTH AND THE GOOD

The rejection of metaphysics by modernists has led to denial that truth, beauty and the good have metaphysical reality. For example, college students will be told that there is no such thing as intrinsic beauty in the arts, poetry and music, because modernists feel that beauty is entirely a matter of personal taste. Scholars will be told that there is no such thing as metaphysical truth, and therefore the truths in theology, philosophy and literature are entirely matters of personal opinion. They will be told that there is no such thing as the metaphysical good, and therefore good and evil are private individual values.

Conservative students should be encouraged to renounce these fallacies of modernism and encouraged to diligently seek metaphysical beauty, truth and good. One such seeker on campus can turn many students away from self-destructive skepticism. The trick is to catch students soon enough, so that skeptical hostility toward truth, beauty and the good has not sunk too deeply into their hearts. The point of no return comes when they feel proud and superior in roles of self-appointed debunkers of all that is good – this is when subverted students join with forces of evil. In time, they become despoilers of all that is good. The modernist university is a launching pad for turning young men and women into monsters.

> ### *Fred Critique*
>
> *Conservative students should be encouraged to renounce these fallacies of modernism and encouraged to diligently seek metaphysical beauty, truth and good.*

MULTICULTURALISM

Students are encouraged to be aware of the celebration of mediocre works in art and literature solely on the grounds that they are produced by minorities, women, gays or people of non-western cultures – this predilection is not just a

politically correct fad. The West once had a grand civilization of metaphysics; primitive non-western cultures have no notion of metaphysics. Gays have rejected metaphysical moral standards and maintain that sexual practices are a matter of personal preference and taste. Feminists have equated metaphysical standards in history, literature and the arts with patriarchy and oppression – they reject great books written by *"dead, white, European males,"* claiming that only women can judge women's literature and history.

Black studies departments at universities have equated the application of metaphysical standards to black history and literature with racism. Assuming that there are no metaphysical realities outside black culture, we are told that only blacks can judge the literary value of black culture works. Start with the nonsense that there are no metaphysical standards, and you end up with the foolishness that only blacks can judge black art, music and literature. Suppose a white student attended a black history class and say to the professor, *"Cleopatra was not black as you are teaching, she was Greek – we know this because she was a descendant of Alexander the Great's Greek general, who acquired Egypt as part of his empire in 332 BC."* The professor would probably not ask for the student's source of historical facts, but he might question their racial sensitivity. If the student responded, *"It is not a matter of sensitivity, it is historical fact,"* the professor might fire back with the charge of racism.

A society in rebellion against metaphysics loses balance and common sense. Without a bulwark against irrationality, people can be bullied into believing nonsense. Thus, the recovery of metaphysics is necessary both for the protection of our sanity and the preservation of freedom. By this point, conservative students have realized the imperative of a radical renunciation of modernism.

REASONS, NOT CANNED STEPS – PRINCIPLES, NOT PAYOFFS

Students should be cautioned about modernists teaching them to ignore general principles, and learn by rote only those instrumental rules that have an immediate practical payoff. This was the approach of John Dewey and William James. Practical rules are not to be despised, of course, but to have actions divorced from reason, logic and meaning is irrational, inhuman, uncivilized and ultimately dysfunctional. The secret of long-term professional success is to refuse canned steps, and insist upon logical reasons for every step. In this way, judgment and skill steadily improve over time. Those who stick with bottled approaches quickly reach a limit in personal growth.

Conservative students should be told, *"Let modernists stagnate in their skepticism about general principles and their mindless, rote, cookbook approach to pragmatic actions. You should insist upon having a logical reason or principle for every step you take. You should always be able to explain what you are doing and why you are doing it, so you will grow into a leader with progressively growing wisdom, judgment and skill."*[817]

The life driven by principle and reason will tend to be less prone to the temptations and vices of mere pragmatists, who do whatever appears to work to get a practical payoff – even without knowing why it works. A principle-driven life leads toward virtue, while a payoff-driven orientation tends toward vice.

THE ROMANTIC RETURN TO NATURE

Who trusted God was love indeed / And love Creation's final law / Tho' Nature, red in tooth and claw / With ravine, shriek'd against his creed / Who loved, who suffer'd countless ills, / Who battled for the True, the Just, / Be blown about the desert dust, / Or seal'd within the iron hills?
In Memoriam, *Alfred, Lord Tennyson (1849)*

Jean Jacques Rousseau invented the Romantic Movement in the mid-18th century. Romanticism was the cultural wing of first-wave modernism, starting with literature and the arts in Germany. Rousseau's philosophy can be summarized this way: *Man in a state of nature was a noble savage. His nature was inherently good. The beginning of his corruption was when he first acquired property. He became further corrupted by civilization. Thus, all man's evils and vices are caused by society. Therefore, let us return to nature and release all those repressed urges that have been artificially bottled up by the strictures of society.*

The following points should be powerfully made to conservatives:

1. Blaming society for vices relieves individuals of responsibility for their actions, which is very bad for moral and spiritual condition. The separation of actions from consequences leads to irrational thought.

2. Belief that human evil comes entirely from society leads to seeking to fix society through legislation. All such attempts backfire with unintended consequences, precisely because society is not the cause of evil in human hearts. Social programs based on a misunderstanding of human nature always do more harm than good.

---

[817] (F. Hutchison, Brief History of Conservatism 2009)

3. Civilized society does more good than evil because it generally restrains men from antisocial and overtly destructive behavior. Civilization is more amenable to the development of virtue than living in the wilderness. Property ownership, civic involvement and family commitment also help in the development of personal responsibility and faithfulness.

4. Retreating to nature and allowing impulses to freely flow ensure that more evil will emerge than good – in time, reducing people to barbarian savagery. Barbarism blocks the development of human potential and often leads to violent depravity.

5. Nature should be respected, but never glorified or worshiped. In the words of Alfred Tennyson (1809-1892) as he coped with grief, nature is *"red in tooth and claw."* There is no such thing as a noble savage; this concept was unknown prior to the 18th century. Primitive tribal culture should not be emulated, in spite of Hollywood's infatuation with all things primitive.

6. The full flourishing of human nature comes when mankind's highest talents are fully developed and used for the development or renewal of advanced civilization.

7. The progressive education program fosters uninhibited expression of raw impulses that tend toward destructive narcissism and misanthropy.

Young conservatives should be told, *"Do not seek the path that will maximize your income. Seek what will maximize your wisdom, virtue, knowledge and powers of reason. Consider how a new job will develop your character and sense of personal responsibility."* Once conservatives have had time to comprehend and renounce the principles of first-wave modernism, they are ready to be introduced to the complex tangle of the second surge.

THE SECOND WAVE OF MODERNISM

The first wave of modernism consisted of skepticism and pragmatism – the second was a flood of mysticism and magical thinking. Some skeptics living in the 19th century debunked the infusion of mystics. Charles Dickens' (1812-1870) satirical novels contain a variety of skeptical examples in the form of hard-headed men trying to correct or harass dreamers. Dickens sided with the dreamers, because he was one of them.

In the realm of philosophy, thinking based in **utilitarianism**, [318] **consequentialism**, [319] **pragmatism** [320] and **instrumentalism**[321] made great headway during the 19th century through the writings of Jeremy Bentham, John Stuart Mill, William James, Elizabeth Anscombe (1919-2001), Henry Sidgwick (1838-1900) and John Dewey. Thus, more pragmatists and skeptics emerged, creating tension between tough-minded philosophers and dreamy new modernists. Karl Marx offered a synthesis between harsh materialism and wistful utopianism, which was the key to his success as a public intellectual.

The 18th century sweeping away of metaphysics enabled the rise of two seemingly opposite things: 1) extremely tough-minded pragmatism; and 2) exceptionally tender-minded mystical thinking. The world of modernism is loaded with both – the Victorian age, in particular, is filled with the dichotomy of tough and tender, as men were obliged to

---

[318] Utilitarianism teaches that the proper course of action is the one that maximizes the overall "good" of the greatest number of individuals.
[319] Consequentialism holds that the consequences of conduct are the ultimate basis for any judgment about the rightness of that conduct.
[320] Pragmatism distinguishes the meaning of ideas and propositions by observable practical consequences.
[321] Instrumentalism views scientific theory as a useful instrument in understanding the world – concepts or theories should be evaluated by how effectively they explain and predict phenomena, as opposed to how accurately they describe objective reality.

demonstrate rough masculinity and women were compelled towards gentle femininity. The mind swept clean of metaphysics is free to stare down at the hard ground of pragmatism, and to gaze up into the clouds and dream of heavenly castles. Manic-depressive pathology is the mental illness of modernism. Liberals are prone to unhealthy swings from living in cloud castles, to becoming overwhelmed by the gritty hardness of practical life – they sing with fairies and retreat to trolls under bridges. Rousseau sang with the fairies.

ROUSSEAU'S "GENERAL WILL"

Rousseau was the only original thinker for both the first and second waves of modernism. His political ideas influenced the French Revolution at the end of the 18th century. There was also a series of 19th century revolutions when Rousseau's quotations were read at barricades, such as his incendiary line, *"Man was born free, but is everywhere in chains."* Karl Marx could not resist stealing that line.

Jean Jacques Rousseau

Rousseau's theory of a social contract was intended to apply to republics in which people have sovereignty. However, his idea of *"the people"* was cloudy. Whoever the people are, they were supposed to rule through the *"general will,"* whatever that is, which Rousseau claimed is always right. Authentic reform and progress only comes through the general will, so as citizens trust it the magic of progress unfolds. If man is inherently good, as Rousseau taught his followers, the *"will of the people"* must be even better. A political-intellectual elite class sprang up to tell the public what the general will was. Members of the elite were perpetually hoping to be hired by rulers willing to be told what the general will was. Ministries of propaganda appeared to inform the people that the government was doing the general will.

When general dissatisfaction spreads through the land, charismatic candidates or leaders who vaguely promise *"hope"* and *"change"* might be trusted by many if people think they have the right instincts for divining the "general will. Remember, *"general will"* is alleged to be the sure way to *"progress."* Such an electorate abandons reason as it depends on the delicate tendrils of wishful thinking. Such was the bewitched American electorate of 2008.

Every 19th century political demagogue appealed to the general will – every revolutionary leader claimed that his revolution was the *"will of the people."* Most communist regimes publicize themselves as *"people's republics,"* even though they are as far from that as regimes can be. More political lies have been told in the name of that deception than any other pretext. One of the most pathetic moments in history was when President Franklin Roosevelt said to the sinister Joseph Stalin, the genocidal dictator of the Soviet Union, *"I know that we both govern according to will of our people."* When did the fiendish Stalin ever rule according to the will of the people?! That wooly-headed notion proceeded from a mind swept clean of metaphysics and filled to the brim with the cotton candy of 19th century wishful thinking and cloudy political mysticism.

The *"general will"* and *"the will of the people"* are undefined by modernists because the terms are indefinable. The phrases cast a cloud of confusion over political discourse. It is time to scuttle these vague expressions once and for all.

INEVITABILITY OF PROGRESS

Belief in the inevitability of progress has been an article of faith among modernists since the time of Georg Hegel – scarcely any American liberals doubted it in 1960. That faith was shaken by the time Hubert Humphrey (1911-1978) was the last presidential candidate (1968) to wholeheartedly embrace progress' certainty. His jovial voice on the stump seemed strangely outdated and tone deaf. The Democratic cadres lacked their customary pep and spunk – renditions of *Happy Days are Here Again* lacked conviction.

Soon afterward, Fred Hutchison predicted that faith in the inevitability of progress could never be restored and that liberalism was finished. He supposed that the temple of liberalism/progressivism could not survive the breaking of its key pillar. However, he failed to consider that modernist disillusionment after World War I was far more intense than the 1960s cynicism – both failed to kill off the incredibly resilient confidence.[322]

This belief is one of the most unsupportable ideas that ever entered the human mind, yet it is dear to the hearts of modernists. Unwillingness to give up the myth prevented Robert Hutchins from crossing his Rubicon to become the father of neoconservatives. Neocons must learn how to persuade moderns to give up the mystical faith in progress. Once they do this effectively, many more will cross the Rubicon and reach conservative maturity.

HEGEL AND THE FORCES OF HISTORY

Georg Hegel

Georg Hegel believed that impersonal *"forces of history"* are driving human history – therefore, progress is inevitable. Why would an impersonal force care about human progress? How can an impersonal force understand personal beings or help them progress? After all, progress has no meaning except to finite, personal and developmental beings like man. There is no meaning to an impersonal force. These notions are preposterous, but are sold by wrapping them in the fog of pantheism.

Pantheism holds that everything is *"god,"* therefore we are part of a great divinity and *"oneness."* Thus, the cosmos is god, nature is god, I am god and the coffee pot is god. No rational theology can be constructed from these hazy concepts because reasoning faculties shut down in the midst of this fog – one more way modernism is the enemy of reason. Hegel claimed that history is the story of the pantheistic cosmos assuming forms of greater and greater oneness in historical stages. At the end of history, the cosmos will roll itself up into perfect oneness – mankind will exist in perfect equality and oneness. The historical cycles leading ultimately toward utopia are *"progress."*

How can we be one with the pantheistic *"god"* if we are personal beings and the god is impersonal? Can the events of an historical age leave men less united and equal? Does the historical record show that this has happened many times? Hegel answered that antithetical forces collide and synthesize, moving a step closer to utopia.

Why would antagonistic forces synthesize instead of shattering? History is full of stories about regimes and institutions that collided, shattered and did not synthesize. Hegel claimed that impersonal pantheistic forces of history somehow cause things to synthesize instead of shattering – his followers just have to take his word, because there is no way to

---

[322] (F. Hutchison, Brief History of Conservatism 2009)

rationally support this. Modernists regard Hegel's *"thesis, antithesis and synthesis"* formula as prophetic. Neoconservatives should openly declare the formula to be preposterous – it was devised by Kant for developing metaphysical ideas, and he would have laughed to hear it used for stages of history.

KARL MARX

Karl Marx combined the magical ideas of Hegel with the hard-headed materialism of French philosopher Denis Diderot (1713-1784). His doctrine was a synthesis of modernism, which accounts for his popularity with modernistic intellectuals. He was an economic determinist, believing that: 1) social classes are economically determined; and 2) human nature is shaped by one's social class. Many modernist ideas are absurd at the surface, but this is not one of them. Marx's ideas have just enough truth in them to be plausible, if they are not examined too closely. As recently as the 1960s, these views passed among modernists without question. Even now, progressive liberals are trying to resurrect these oft-discredited notions, so let us pause and briefly debunk them.

A social class must have an economic foundation or it cannot exist. However, economics is not determinative of the ideals, mores or social codes of a class. Traditions, education, family ethos, concepts of honor, socialization, community participation, privileges and duties, and power structures have more to do with it. Marx's economic determinism in the context of class is a combination of three fatal errors: 1) vast overestimation of the role of economics in the human formation; 2) huge presumption error of the formative role of social classes; and 3) the mistake of determinism.

Jesus said, *"Man shall not live on bread alone, but on every word that comes from the mouth of God" (Matthew 4:4)*, meaning that man is more than a purely material creature. Humans have a complex personal nature that is partly spiritual, intellectual, emotional, social, imaginative and esthetic. Furthermore, the combination of these ingredients varies from person to person. A society that only recognizes material factors is reductionist and inhuman, therefore Marxism is inhuman.

Karl Marx

Contrary to the teachings of some liberal Christian ministries, the idea of *"social justice"* has Marxist origins, not Christian. The unequal distribution of wealth is presumed unjust because it must involve the upper classes preying upon lower classes, or so Marx claims. But it is not necessarily true – there are many honest ways to become rich without committing unjust deeds or oppressing the poor. The Bible does condemn the rich man who oppresses the poor through unjust dealings, but never insinuates that all rich men do this. However, Marx had the impudence to insist that all income inequality is de facto evidence of oppression of the poor via social classes. In his mind, any success occurs through unjust practices, or unfair class advantages. Concerning *"unfair advantages,"* although successful men of humble origin do not achieve through unmerited class rewards, Marx recognized no exceptions to his rule. He insisted that economically successful people are always tainted, either by overt injustice or by the collective wickedness and guilt of his class.

> ### Fred Critique
>
> *Contrary to the teachings of some liberal Christian ministries, the idea of "social justice" has Marxist origins, not Christian.*

Class advantages are considered unfair because of unequal distribution – fairness requires equal allocation only because modernism ideals declare so. Modernists presume that all people will be perfectly equivalent in the future utopia. This scenario cannot be a happy condition when humans have different talents, intellectual capacities, competencies and character qualities. Utopians insist that

190

mankind will be perfect, without explaining how uniform equality of mind, talent and competencies represent perfection.

The presumption of *"unfairness"* based on unequal distribution of advantages is irrational. English aristocrats had many advantages by birth, but the fact that the aristocracy was economically marginalized by the rise of industrial, financial and commercial interests that rarely included them made no impression on Marxists. Because he was a determinist, Marx clung tightly to the idea that class and economics account for everything. He rejected the innate nature concept, insisting that man is essentially an automaton programmed by impersonal forces. But questions immediately arise about how justice and fairness apply to automatons – and who can be morally aroused when automaton programming is unequally applied.

Marx thought progressive forces of history came from collisions of class and economics because of the exaggerated claims from the *"thesis, antithesis, and synthesis"* model. He borrowed the foolish nostrum from Hegel, who had utilized Kant. Marx applied it to class and economics, labeling it **dialectical materialism**.[323]

NEOCONSERVATIVES VERSUS MARXISM

Telling people they are automatons programmed by impersonal forces is a lie. As discussed in Chapter 7, declaring something that is false about human nature inflicts injury – no greater calamity befalls mankind than to believe they are soulless, mindless automatons. Neoconservatives should forcefully renounce all Marxist ideas for several reasons:

1. Marxist ideas are reductionist and inhuman;

2. They stir up popular discontentment in society that is abused by political demagogues;

3. They destroy creative, vibrant economy; and

4. They subvert the true ideas of justice and charity.

Liberal democrats cannot desist from using class warfare and social justice propaganda to win elections. America no longer has authentic social classes, only income strata and life style ranges. Any self-disciplined, reasonably intelligent and talented person may gradually climb upward through one or more income brackets in the course of a lifetime. But mindless class warfare propaganda goes on and on, casting a haze over political campaigns that make it hard to focus rationally upon real issues.

FREEDOM VERSUS SOCIALISM

There is more at stake than the prosperity free enterprise brings and the poverty socialism brings. Human freedom is at risk. An individual is not really free unless he has the liberty to buy and sell property, start a business, or offer his services to an employer or the public. Friedrich Hayek wrote the book ***The Road to Serfdom***,[324] in which he argued that citizens of socialist regimes are not free, but are not exactly slaves. They are bound to monotonous jobs, like serfs who were forbidden to venture out from the manor to the outside market place.

---

[323] Dialectical materialism means that every economic order grows to a state of maximum efficiency, while at the same time developing internal contradictions and weaknesses that contribute to its decay.
[324] (Hayek 1944)

SOCIAL JUSTICE, GUILT AND BITTERNESS

Social justice opinions have resulted in the prosperous giving alms to the poor out of guilt, and the needy receiving aid out of resentment. If an unequal distribution of wealth is unjust, the guilty rich will donate as atonement while the bitter poor will impatiently receive support believing it is owed to them. This is the exact opposite of Christ and the apostles' teaching to give in love and compassion, not from guilt, and to receive with gratitude, not resentment. Furthermore, it is absurd to ascribe guilt to one social class and entitlement to another. Unfortunately, Marx's false notions of social justice have undergone a revival in America.

> *"Many of the clergy tend markedly toward a sentimental and humanitarian application of religious doctrines to the reform of society, at the expense of the supernatural element in religion and the personal element in morality." Russell Kirk, 1960*[325]

NIETZSCHE UNLEASHES THE THIRD WAVE

Friedrich Nietzsche

Friedrich Nietzsche (1844-1900) disagreed with Rousseau, Hegel and Marx about the assertion that the historical process is caused by impersonal forces – theories that lead to a *"last man"* at the end, after history has played out. Nietzsche was personally disgusted with the feckless, equivocal, effeminate and wishful-thinkers of modernism he observed. Far from being ready for utopia, he thought modernists were good for nothing except making way for real men, who are prepared to demonstrate mastery.

In C.S. Lewis's ***The Screwtape Letters***, [326] the senior demon, Screwtape, was disgusted with the mushy quality of modernism's damned souls. He preferred *"crunchy"* traits and the great sinners of prior ages. Screwtape's reaction to modern man was similar to Nietzsche's, who thought modernism had a degrading effect on Western man. He was correct. In human terms, modernism brought about human regress, not progress. C.S. Lewis emphasized this in ***The Pilgrim's Regress***.[327]

> ### Fred Critique
>
> *Utopian social-engineering projects designed to perfect human nature actually leave them degraded and diminished.*

With visionary insight, Nietzsche saw through the crowning illusion of modernism's second wave – utopian social-engineering projects designed to perfect human nature actually leave them degraded and diminished. Nietzsche may have been the first man to understand that modernism is rotten to the core. He could easily have become the first neoconservative. Instead, he became the dark prince of hypermodernism, or Postmodernism. Instead of crossing his Rubicon to renounce modernism, he invented an exaggerated and sinister new model for strong, proud and ruthless men – not intended for wimps.

NIETZSCHE, THE DARK PRINCE OF MODERNISM

Nietzsche's deep insight about the delusion of second-wave modernism made him just the man to unleash the third-wave. Having rebuked the demons of second-wave modernism, he opened Pandora's Box and unleashed much worse demons upon the world. He was like an adolescent boy casting aside mildly scary Halloween masks with disgust, and enthusiastically reaching for the most hideous one in the store. *"Away with this mushy evil,"* he might have thought. *"I*

---

[325] (Kirk, The Common Heritage of America and Europe 1960)
[326] (Lewis, The Screwtape Letters 1942)
[327] (Lewis, The Pilgrim's Regress 1933)

will show them what a virile and manly evil looks like!" This fury may have begun as a revolt against his father, who was a Lutheran pastor.

Nietzsche was a ferocious rebel against modernism – paradoxically, he carried its worst elements to greater extremes than ever before. He was the first postmodern man. The 1960s youth rebellion was Nietzschean in nature, featuring zealous young radicals opposed to their parents' mild, wishy-washy modernism. This upheaval marked the beginning of Western democracy's disintegration.

Nietzsche also defied Christianity, as any arch-demon must. He wrote that Christianity was a religion for slaves, serfs and inferior people – the soft, over refined, liberal Christians he knew contributed to this perception. He believed that the meek submission commanded by Christ debilitates mankind, and denies a man's life-affirming vitality and will for power – that Christianity elevates weakness over strength, at the expense of dynamic energy. Having renounced soft modernism and delicate Christianity, Nietzsche set out to create a hard new world for the superior man.

THE SUPERIOR MAN AS CREATOR

Instead of impersonal forces driving history, superior men would become the agents of history in Nietsche's cosmos. He exhorted people to awaken from modernist slumbers, shake themselves and personally take responsibility for civilization and history. Although this philosophy sounds vaguely like neoconservative ideals, Nietzsche actually meant that superior men must become gods and recreate the world – which is anathema to all conservatives.

As gods, advanced mankind must recognize no higher gods or moral authority over them. Whereas the Christian God is bound by his own laws of righteousness, the new gods of Nietzsche's world are more like the Islamic Allah, who can break his own laws and change his mind about what those laws are. Nietzsche exhorted moderns to take responsibility for the formulation of their own values and rules – calling this the **transvaluation of values** in his book, ***The Antichrist***.[328] He asserted that Christianity inverts nature and is *"hostile to life,"* both as a religion and the predominant Western moral system.

THE STOPPER WAS OUT!

If everyone is a god creating his own personal moral cosmos, no social consensus is possible and society begins to disintegrate – there would henceforth be no restraints or boundaries holding self-assertive men in sane moderation. The stopper was out! Unrestrained madness was let loose on the world during the 20th century, since there was nothing blocking the pretense of proud man/gods. Narcissistic, hyper-modern men threw off all restraint as new *"superior man"* rejected the *"existence exists"* dictum of philosophical realism. German idealists had said, *"Things are out there when men acknowledge them."* The Nietzschean man/god now said, *"Things are out there if I will them to be out there, and whatever is out there is what I want to be out there."* Some call this solipsism – others call it madness.

PLAYING GOD DRIVES MEN INSANE

The presumption of personal deity leads to magical thinking, as in King Canute who believed he could command the tide. Nietsche's superior man is like the evil and demented Roman Emperor Caligula (12-41), whose god delusions drove him insane. Interestingly, Nietzsche had a mental breakdown in 1889, and was diagnosed with manic-depressive illness with periodic psychosis, followed by vascular dementia – the human mind is incapable of supporting the presumption of divinity without eventually cracking.

---

[328] (Nietzsche 1888)

Nietzsche's influence took two directions in Western culture: 1) toward American hyper-individualism, and 2) toward political messianism in Germany and Russia. Almost everywhere, political leaders adopted grandiose ambitions as they attempted to establish the cult of personality.

NIETZSCHE – THE FATHER OF NAZISM

Nazism evolved in three stages:

1. The Romantic Movement, part of the first wave of modernism, brought Nativism – the cult of blood and soil – to Germany. Mystical spirits were said to rise up from the soil to animate German folks who are close to the soil, turning them into an authentic people group with their own folk tales, heroes, myths, magic and culture. Some nativist cults believe in the inherent superiority of their own people or race. This was particularly true in Germany after nativists got a taste of Nietzsche's egomania. People at mass Nazi rallies seemed to go into a drunken euphoria when the *"master race"* was mentioned.

2.  During the second wave of modernism, Hegel's left-wing fought with right-wing Hegelians at the barricades. The right-wing sons believed the state leader, or *"der führer,"* was the vanguard of history. One task the leader must accomplish was to utterly crush Hegel's left-wing, which were the Communist vanguard rivals. Adolf Hitler rose to power because he fought the Communists, and he invaded Russia to stamp out Communism, which was his central objective for going to war.

3. Nietzsche, mastermind of third-wave modernism, taught the superior man to cultivate the will to power, to crush inferior men, and to indulge in unlimited political ambitions. The rising führer must use ideology as a weapon; seize power and rule on his terms; accept no limitations to his power; and develop the cult of personality, to be worshiped as a political messiah. The triumphant führer must subdue and rule the **obsequious**[329] natural slave peoples, thereby vindicating his mastery and superior vital powers.

The evil Nazi regime was incredibly successful, powerful, popular and united. German WWII achievements from 1939-1941 were almost unbelievable. Most Germans remained loyal to the führer until the bitter end – soldiers fought until they ran out of ammunition, and the Russians lost 300,000 men in taking Berlin. The incredible Nazi success was due to the fact that Nazism perfectly embodied all three waves of modernism – the German people were spectacularly unified, inspired and energized by the triple forces of modernism.

NIETZSCHE – THE GRANDFATHER OF COMMUNISM

Communism has a clear philosophical ancestry: 1) Rousseau, 2) Kant, 3) Hegel, 4) Marx, 5) Nietzsche, 6) Lenin, and 7) Stalin. Russian Bolshevik revolutionaries, Vladimir Lenin, Nikolai Bukharin (1888-1938), and Leon Trotsky (1879-1940) fused Marx and Nietzsche into a political philosophy – Lenin taught Marxists the radical ruthlessness he learned from Nietzsche. The Soviet Marxist-Leninist regime was called *"communism"* during the cold war. Soviet dictator Joseph Stalin was an absolute Leninist, or Nietzschean. He murdered far more of his own citizens than Hitler, sent far more people to concentration and work camps, and his secret police force was every bit as deadly as the Gestapo.[330]

Vladimir Lenin

---

[329] Exhibiting servile compliance; fawning.
[330] After the Soviet Union dissolved, archives containing official records determined that the various terror campaigns launched by the Soviet government under Stalin claimed between 15-20 million lives in the categories of: executed prisoners for either political or criminal offenses; deaths in Gulags and forced resettlements; deaths to POWs and German civilians; and victims of famine. Exact numbers may never be known.

THE CONTINUING CRISIS OF MODERNISM

Liberal democracy tends towards weakness when faced with the threat of third-wave regimes. The constant denial that Hitler and Stalin were threats by deceived liberal-modernists caused the West to balk until it was almost too late. During the cold war, American liberals were undecided about resisting Soviet Union expansion – they often opposed conservatives who wanted to fight communism. Although Nazism was defeated and the Soviet regime collapsed, a new third-wave horror has sprung up.

MUSLIM JIHADISM GOES THIRD WAVE

Vichy France, the puppet government under Nazi Germany, exported Nazi doctrine to the Muslim Middle East and North Africa, where the French still had colonies in Syria, Lebanon, Algeria, Tunisia and Morocco. Nazism fused well with certain jihadist verses Mohammed wrote while he was a war lord. The fruit of Nazi-jihadist synthesis was the Ba'ath Party, which produced Iraqi President Saddam Hussein (1937-2006). Frightening ruthlessness and blood thirstiness is a signature mark of the Nietzschean-Nazi touch.

While the Communists were making Middle East friends, they passed along the arts of subversion, insurgency and revolution to alienated Arab groups. Once again, Western powers are seen as soft, weak-willed modernists, dithering in the face of third-wave threats. Europe is particularly paralyzed by their denials of jihadist terrorists. The United States Congress is filled with members who are blind and deaf in their refusal to acknowledge the threat.

WELCOME THE NEOCONSERVATIVES

This chapter has sought to define the specific renunciations of modernism that budding neoconservatives must make to *"cross the Rubicon,"* and thereby complete the journey from liberalism to conservatism. The plan is applicable to first and second wave modernism – once a full renunciation is made at these two levels, the third wave automatically becomes repugnant. After crossing the first and second wave Rubicon, it is enough to educate conservatives about what third-wave people are saying to fill them with horror and indignation.

If the first two waves of modernism never occurred, no sane man would have listened to Nietzsche. Recall how pathetic and contemptible the *"last man"* of modernism was in Nietzsche's eyes – these ruined people were the very ones who listened to him. American patriots should heartily welcome neoconservatives into the conservative movement, seek to learn from them, and together combat the insanity of Nietzschean philosophy. Without them, who will lead the way through the minefields of modernism?

> *Fred Critique*
>
> _____
>
> *Patriots should welcome neocons, seek to learn from them, and together combat the insanity of Nietzschean philosophy.*

ON TO THE FINAL CHAPTER

Chapter 18 will conclude this book by considering the present crisis in conservatism, looking for remedies from this study of history. The old conservative fusionist movement has shattered. We must now seek new grounds for conservative unity, considering the fault lines and rifts between the five historic branches and the natural harmonies that have historically tended to unite them. The chapter will also discuss potential new combinations of conservatives for a fresh new political alliance, and the two new kinds of leaders that are needed.

We have traveled a long way through the history of conservatism and are nearing present day. This chapter will post mortem the disastrous election year of 2008 and consider the present crisis in conservatism, hoping to find some remedies from this study. The old conservative fusionist movement has shattered. We must now seek new grounds for conservative unity, considering the fault lines and rifts between the five historic branches and the natural harmonies that have historically tended to unite them. The chapter will also discuss potential new combinations of conservatives for a fresh new political alliance, and the two new kinds of leaders that are needed.

> ### *Fred Critique*
>
> *We must seek new grounds for conservative unity, considering the rifts between the five historic branches and the natural harmonies that have historically united them.*

POST MORTEMS

From a conservative's point of view, there were three disastrous presidential elections in the past century. The first was the 1932 election, resulting in Franklin Roosevelt's New Deal programs. The second was 1964, leading to Lyndon Johnson's Great Society plan. The third and most disastrous election was 2008, quickly followed by Barack Obama's *"great leap forward"*[331] toward socialism and national bankruptcy.

Obama's election mandate and the domination of Congress by liberal Democrats seemed to predict that the triumph of a morally and intellectually bankrupt postmodernism is near. Historically, the sudden advance of depraved evil is sometimes quickly followed by its own precipitous collapse. On the other hand, the ascent of evil can also open the door to new evils. Conservatives began to pray for the first and prepare for the second. Chapter 17 made it obvious that modernism, hyper-modernism and postmodernism embody everything that principled conservatives abhor. The good news is that ascendant modernism might provide a rallying point to unite the five camps of conservatism in a common battle – bringing the divided movement into a badly needed unification.

---

[331] The Great Leap Forward of the People's Republic of China was a 1958-1961 economic and social Communist Party campaign that attempted to utilize China's vast population to transform China from an agrarian economy into a modern communist state through a process of rapid industrialization and collectivization. Chairman Mao Tse-tung led the plan even after learning of impending famine from grain shortages. His plan was to dominate and revolutionize China, and then transfer the process to the rest of the globe. Tse-tung was a radical progressive who believed in a Marxist revolution. Despite boasting that he fought *"for the People,"* his Great Leap Forward, Cultural Revolution, and other progressive policies resulted in the deaths of 77 million people. His Marxist vision of revolution was pure destruction. He said, *"the country must be...destroyed and then reformed... This applies to the country, to the nation and to mankind... The destruction of the universe is the same... People like me long for its destruction, because when the old universe is destroyed, a new universe will be formed."* Many have compared Obama's policies to Tse-tung's.

Anita Dunn, a member of Barack Obama's administration who served as White House Communications Director from April through November 2009, gave a high school graduation speech during which she referenced Tse-tung and Mother Teresa as two of her *"favorite political philosophers."* Inference leads one to assume that she considers the Chinese death toll and reign of terror as acceptable. U.S. Marxist and Obama mentor, Bill Ayers, was also influenced by Tse-tung. According to Weatherman infiltrator, Larry Grathwohl, Ayers stated that after America has been overthrown by communists, 25 million resisters might have to be executed. Since Obama hired his staff, conjecture seems to indicate that he also admires dictators.

MORE CONSERVATIVE THAN THOU

"Mirror, mirror on the wall, who is the most conservative one of all?" Fred Hutchison, 2007

In 2007, it appeared that 2008 was going to be a good year for conservatives. The 2007 Iowa Straw Poll was a beauty contest for conservatives – amazingly, eleven conservative Republican candidates attended, while none of the moderates showed up! It would have been embarrassing for moderate candidates to appear as contestants in the battle for the *"most conservative."* During the speeches, each candidate tried to convince the crowd that he was more conservative all than the others. In essence, each one said, *"I am more conservative than thou."*

During the straw poll, Fred Hutchison thought he was in conservative paradise. As he strolled the event grounds, the carnival of happy conservative hoopla spread out before him as far as the eye could see. His feeling of being in heaven took another leap upwards shortly afterwards, when he became a Policy Advisor for Alan Keyes' (1950-) presidential campaign.[332] Keyes, who seemed to be the ultimate conservative, told reporters, *"I am the only complete conservative in the race."* He would have fit in perfectly at the *"more conservative than thou"* straw poll if he had already declared his candidacy.

CIVIL WAR AMONG CONSERVATIVES

As the 2008 presidential primaries approached, the tide turned and gradually began to look like conservative hell – it was the **annus horribilis**.[333] As conservatives fought hard against other conservatives, many painful divisions opened up in the movement. Conservative energy, zeal, finances and organizational skills were scattered and dissipated by being spread among too many Republican primary candidates. Dirty tricks were used to keep media-labeled *"minor"* candidates out of debates and off television. Competing factions formed within individual campaigns. It was a tragic civil war among conservatives – the good guys were fighting the good guys! Fine candidates were stabbed in the back. What fifty years of the conservative fusion movement had built was now in ruins and ashes.

John McCain

There is no escape from the depravity of man in this fallen world – it is not to be found even in the company of the best men. This perishing world is not paradise, and it will never be, not even for conservatives. We should know better. The conservatives killed each other off.

As the ground lay littered with conservative bodies, there was one man left standing – John McCain (1936-), a moderate who had been left for dead – that is to say, politically dead. Fred Hutchison dubbed McCain the man with nine lives.[334] One of the reasons McCain lost the general election was that his team was divided, while Obama's was united. The man with nine lives could not survive the fatal divisions within his own squad.

---

[332] (F. Hutchison, Brief History of Conservatism 2009)
[333] Annus horribilis is Latin for 'horrible year' – an oft humorous reference to John Dryden's 1666 poem ***Annus Mirabilis*** (The Year of Wonders).
[334] (F. Hutchison, Brief History of Conservatism 2009)

THE DENOUEMENT

The denouement of the annus horribilis finally arrived as the proud *"more conservative than thou"* syndrome led to the election of the most liberal president in American history. The moral of the story is that when conservatives are divided, moderates dominate the Republican Party, and Democrats win general elections. However, judging by the legions of enthusiastic conservatives at the Iowa Straw Poll, if conservatives united behind one candidate, they would be hard to beat by a Republican moderate in the primaries or by a Democrat in the general election.

CAUSES OF CONSERVATIVE DIVISION

There were four causes of conservative division in the 2008 election:

1. There was no natural national leader of American conservatives – Reagan and Buckley were dead, and second tier leaders were weak. Influential conservatives of the 1980s and 1990s had died or retired without being replaced with men of commensurate maturity, talent, competence or moral authority.

2. The mutually destructive divisions among conservatives were caused by a disturbing lack of grown-ups in the movement. A quotation from the Apostle Paul illuminates the problem:

The Apostle Paul

"I appeal to you brothers... that there might be no divisions among you... there are quarrels among you. What I mean is this, one of you says, 'I follow Paul,' another 'I follow Apollos,' another 'I follow Cephas,' still another, 'I follow Christ'... Brothers, I could not address you as spiritual, but as worldly – as infants in Christ. I gave you milk, not solid food, for you were not ready for it... You are still worldly. For since there is jealousy and quarreling among you, are you not worldly? Are you not acting like mere men?" Excerpts: 1 Corinthians 1-3 (KJV)

Emotionally immature and unprincipled people might be politically motivated to become great, instead of pursuing a desire to serve the country and blessing the commonwealth. The inordinately ambitious are easily lured into destructive factions. In the spirit of faction and selfish ambition, ruthless conservatives have been known to stab others in the back – Julius Caesar was not stabbed by enemies, but by his friends. Such betrayals begin with a clash of egos and swollen competitive goals, as 2008 demonstrated. More Christian ministries and conservative political organizations have been ruined by extravagant personal objectives and proud rivalries than from any other cause.

3. There appeared to be a falling away from conservative principles or a failure to teach them to the young conservative generation. There was also a general lapse of biblical principles among Christians, both the theological liberals and those who professed doctrinal conservatism. The catastrophic spread of the **emerging church**[335] has played a role in drawing Evangelicals away from sound doctrine. Hopefully, this book will play a role in calling conservatives and Christians back to the historical principles and truths that made our nation and civilization great.

---

[335] The so-called ―emerging church" does not seek truth in determining a belief structure – they determine what to believe through consensus, on a church-by-church basis. Truth seekers who dissent from the local church consensus are usually thrown out. This is why the emerging church has become infamous as propagators of heresy, as well as of extremely peculiar ideas and practices. During the era of spiritual tepidness, seeker-sensitive mega churches and emerging churches have started to go soft on the atonement doctrine. This slide towards apostasy is facilitated by revisionist historians who wage war upon Christ's atonement by cherry-picking facts from history and using illogical arguments in an attempt to sell myths that are opposite to the historical realities surrounding the doctrine. (F. Hutchison, Brief History of Conservatism 2009)

It has been reported that a surprising number of Evangelicals voted for Obama. Some sources claim that certain Evangelicals have rebelled against their former commitment to conservative politics. If this is true, it can be attributed to an increase of worldliness among Christians, and a corresponding decline in doctrinal orthodoxy. Chapter 16 demonstrated the general compatibility of doctrinal orthodoxy with political conservative philosophy. Doctrinal orthodoxy is radically incompatible with the modernism of Barack Obama – obviously, many have become so fuzzy on matters of doctrine that they cannot recognize this incompatibility.

Many drifting Evangelicals who withdrew support from conservative candidates were disingenuous in their rationalizations, and in many cases they backed liberals. They had been seduced by the spirit of the age, or the spirit of modernism. Are we to conclude that an apostate church of the near future will fawn over the false political messiahs of modernism? Or, has the time come for a reformation of Evangelicalism?

4.   Some natural fault lines among the five kinds of conservatives had opened up into schisms. These rifts can be healed as we take advantage of the natural harmonies that unite these branches. The goal of this book is to unite conservatives so they will listen, learn and work with each other – to rebuild the conservative movement.

RISE OF FUSIONISM

William F. Buckley

The rise and fall of conservative fusionism offers clues about the way forward. Traditionalists, libertarians and anti-communists were fused together in a strong, conservative alliance – they were willing to join hands to fight the Marxist menace. The enduring threat and William F. Buckley's *National Review* held the movement together for thirty years. Buckley invited intellectual Catholics who were well-versed in metaphysics and literary classicists to write columns for the magazine – they provided a badly needed booster shot. A Roman Catholic himself, Buckley began the slow process of weaning conservative Catholics and Evangelicals away from the Democratic Party – his efforts laid the foundation for the political defection of perhaps half of them during Ronald Reagan's presidential campaign.

A winning conservative coalition can be assembled once again, if the formula is changed. The first step is to stop thinking and talking in terms of *"more conservative than thou."* It makes no sense. The spirit of fusionism says, *"I need you precisely because you are a different kind of conservative, and you have special insights, knowledge and talents that I lack."* The dream is to unite the five historic streams of conservatism – paradoxically, selective exclusion comes before inclusion and unity.

> **Fred Critique**
>
> *The dream is to unite the five historic streams of conservatism – paradoxically, selective exclusion comes before inclusion and unity.*

SELECTIVE EXCLUSION

Unity requires a measure of exclusion. Buckley had the courage and wisdom to bar questionable characters from the fusionist movement: conspiracy theorists, cranks, fanatics, nativists, the Hegelian right, bombastic loose cannons, and uncivilized paleoconservatives (while embracing the civilized ones.) Robert Welch (1899-1985), founder of The John Birch Society (JBS), financially supported Buckley in the mid-1950s on more than one occasion, and recommended that others do the same so the rising conservative could start his magazine. A few years later, Buckley rejected Welch in his magazine and systematically attacked and belittled him and the Society – often boasting of his intention to

Robert Welch

destroy JBS. Current JBS members refer to Buckley as a *"Trotskyite,"*[636] an accusation that may have led to their exclusion.[337]

Buckley's fusion movement was spared the divisive extremists that bedevil the conservative movement now – no one today has the authority to bar the door against cranks. Buckley understood that in order to unite the streams of historical conservatism, it was necessary to selectively exclude some mutations. True unity requires a measure of exclusivity – heaven will be united at the cost of casting some into hell. Interestingly, Buckley recognized the value of an ideological subgroup when he included libertarians in the mixture; his pet project was to reclaim them for the conservative movement.

THE RECLAMATION OF LIBERTARIANS

Libertarianism started as classical liberalism, which had one foot in the conservative past by embracing natural law philosophy, metaphysical rationality and morality. The other foot stood in early modernism with the elements of classical economics and individualistic pragmatism, which came into being during the early modern era and were metaphysically anemic. Ben Franklin's **enlightened self interest**[338] is a perfect example of individualistic pragmatism – his philosophy was shrewd and effective, but shallow and void of metaphysics. Franklin is credited with providing the foundational roots for American values and character by mixing the Puritan values of thrift, hard work, education, community spirit, self-governing institutions, and opposition to both political and religious authoritarianism, with the scientific and tolerant values of the Enlightenment.

For a time, the rich metaphysics of natural law philosophy adequately compensated for the metaphysical deficit of classical economics and individualistic pragmatism. Laissez-faire capitalism[339] did not revert to the unscrupulous and despotic state of the robber barons in Europe who, from 800-1800 AD, collected tolls from passing cargo ships sailing on the Rhine River to bolster finances. While people remained moral, rational and socially responsible through the influence of natural law philosophy and Christianity, individualistic pragmatists did not become narcissists or disorderly barbarians. Natural law is not a substitute for divine grace in setting men free from the power of sin; however, common decency, social civility, public integrity and good citizenship are quite possible.

Classical liberalism gradually transmogrified, changing into libertarianism. Natural law was retained when individual rights were spoken of, but rejected when moral laws and personal duties were addressed. Robber barons reappeared in powerful 19th century American businessmen and industrialists who used questionable practices to become wealthy. By the 20th century, libertarianism became prone to metaphysical anemia, moral relativism and untamed atomistic individualism. The sexual revolution had a terrible effect on libertarians, many became morally decadent. Their desire to rationalize immorality sent some back into metaphysical famine and the dark forest of moral relativism. Evangelicals became uneasy when working with libertarians, suspecting them to be devoid of moral restraint.

---

[336] Trotskyism is the Marxist theory advocated by Leon Trotsky, an orthodox Marxist and Bolshevik-Leninist, which worked towards a vanguard working-class party. The theory pushed for an authentic dictatorship of the proletariat based on working-class self-emancipation and mass democracy, rather than the unaccountable bureaucracy after Lenin's death. The terms Trotskyite and Trotskyist are historically derogatory.

[337] (McManus 2002)

[338] Enlightened self-interest is an ethical philosophy holding that people who act to further the interests of others (or of the groups to which they belong), ultimately serve self-interest. Alexis de Tocqueville (1805-1859) discussed the concept in his work *Democracy in America* – he believed that Americans voluntarily join together in associations to further group interests, thereby serving their own interests. (Tocqueville 1835)

[339] Laissez-faire describes an economic environment where transactions between private parties are free from state intervention, including restrictive regulations, taxes, tariffs and enforced monopolies.

Metaphysical shallowness creates a vulnerability to off-kilter ideas – doctrinal slackness among Christians opens the door to heresy.

Buckley reclaimed libertarians by cleverly placing their articles next to columns by natural law philosophers in the *National Review*, thereby regularly exposing them to robust metaphysics. Under his tutelage, libertarians revived from metaphysical anemia, and were prepared for fusion with traditionalists and anticommunists to become a valuable part of the conservative movement. Critics of libertarianism's tendency toward spiritual deficiency and the corresponding moral and intellectual shallowness should remember that no one loves liberty more than libertarians – as the statist threat to freedom grows more ominous, their zeal grows more passionate. The other conservative branches are well advised to listen carefully when libertarians wax eloquent about love of liberty.

DISINTEGRATION OF FUSIONISM

Ronald Reagan

The Soviet Union collapse represented both the triumph and the death blow of fusionism. Anticommunism was the glue holding the effective conservative movement together – after the glue disappeared, it began to fall apart. The aging and fading of the two master fusionists, Ronald Reagan and William F. Buckley Jr., left the assembly leaderless and divided. Libertarians became increasingly annoyed with the staid traditionalists and the morally judgmental Christian conservatives, so they seceded from the fusion movement and became increasingly known for third party bids. On the bright side, libertarians taught traditionalists about classical economics and how to debunk the creeping socialists during the thirty year movement. Therefore, libertarians were not needed as badly in 1990 as they were in 1960. Some libertarians might return when they realize that conservatives still believe in classical economics, while moderates and liberals reject it.

THE CORE THAT FAILED

A lasting movement must be harmonious at the core – tension between traditionalists and libertarians existed during the heyday of fusionism. Buckley was right to include libertarians in the conservative movement, but was wrong to make them co-equal with traditionalists at the core; he should have integrated them along the periphery. Only when libertarians return to the classical liberalism of the founding fathers can they be trusted as core members of the conservative movement. For this to happen, a renaissance in natural law philosophy must occur first, which would hopefully cure the libertarian lack of boundaries disorder. Then, as grown-up classical liberals, they would have the self-discipline, temperance and gravitas of conservative maturity and be ready for leadership.

"The founders of the American Republic learned the first principles of human nature and society from the Bible, Cicero, Plutarch, and Shakespeare. But the present generation of school children is expected, instead, to "learn to live with all the world" – through a rash of scissors-and-paste "projects." " Russell Kirk, 1960[340]

This Republic was founded under the steady hand of classical liberals. Now that the ship of state is in danger of floundering on the rocks of modernism, the country needs men like the founding fathers once more. Libertarians are likely candidates if they mature into classical liberals, but through some combination of hatred for metaphysics and moral laws, many have cast off essential natural law principles and have failed to grow up. As a result, they fall short of the ability to meet the great needs of the United States of America. Time is short. Millions of libertarians need to embrace natural law and develop into classical liberals – they must become men like the founders to save the Republic. Until then, a new core must grow.

A NEW CORE

A combination of Christian and traditionalist conservatism could become the core of a new fusionism, since they command the largest number of conservative voters and are robust and resilient. The grassroots mainstream of American conservatism consists mostly of these groups. The other three kinds of conservatives are too dependent on leaders, intellectuals and writers to recruit and sustain large masses of ordinary people – often starting from scratch in winning recruits from each new generation. In contrast, Christian and traditionalist conservatism can carry on for generations among regular citizens without much leadership and or help from intellectuals – they are naturally passed on to successive generations, and have natural affinities. The bonding of traditionalist and Christian values generally enhance, deepen and vivify conservatism.

> *Fred Critique*
>
> *A combination of Christian and traditionalist conservatism could become the core of a new fusionism*

Christians look to Scripture and creeds, while traditionalists reflect on the moral and intellectual signposts of Western cultural heritage, many of which were the work of Christians. An extensive exploration of European history uncovers that the further back in time, the more Christian the culture was.

AN ANCIENT FUSION

The fusion of Christianity and classicism was the native formulation of European culture. Charlemagne's scholars (800) laid the foundation for this synthesis, which dominated society from 1050-1750. It was the most successful and fruitful fusion movement of all time. Traditionalist conservatism often includes literary traditionalism and classicism. A return to the Christian/classical fusion will feel like going home to people of European heritage. In a cultural sense, it brings them back to who they are in their heart of hearts. If the saying *"We are who we are because of who we were"* is true, society should reflect on the cultural history of our ancestors. As a civilization, we have wandered far from the heritage God gave our forefathers, and have forgotten who we are.

---

[340] (Kirk, The Common Heritage of America and Europe 1960)

GRASSROOTS CONSERVATISM

Grassroots conservatism consists mostly of Christians and traditionalists. One of the weaknesses of these American streams is the failure to produce enough home-grown men and women with the breadth of knowledge and depth of understanding to educate, train and equip others. That is precisely why they are indebted to the other three schools that each has a surplus of intellectuals. There are many deep thinkers on the periphery – namely among libertarians, neoconservatives and natural law philosophers. Some Evangelicals are anti-intellectual, which is a good way to lose the culture war.

The process of grassroots conservatives reaching out to others for an intellectual booster shot has already begun. For example, Evangelicals have started to learn natural law philosophy and metaphysics from Catholic intellectuals – new culture warriors are beginning to use these logical arguments against the abortion and gay agendas. Citizens are turning to *The Weekly Standard*,[341] the neocon flagship magazine, for facts and arguments to support the culture war. Libertarians who have written about the virtues of free enterprise and the vices of socialism for forty years now have a grassroots traditionalist audience.

> ### Fred Critique
>
> *There are many deep thinkers on the periphery – namely among libertarians, neoconservatives and natural law philosophers.*

NEW LEADERSHIP

A new form of leadership that utilizes the knowledge and talents of libertarians, neoconservatives and natural law philosophers is needed to serve the grassroots conservative core. Two new kinds of leaders are needed:

1. **New think-tank leaders** would recruit literary, research and philosophical talent from all five branches of conservatism. Their first objective would be to educate and equip grassroots leaders and build a national network. Local leaders would do the real work of educating and training foot soldiers and leading them in activist projects. Their second objective would be to launch extensive conversations between deep thinkers from each of the five streams, with the goal of teaching them to communicate with each other, learn from each other, work together, and unite and harmonize the conservative movement.

Every major cultural change in European history began with intense conversations by a small number of intelligent persons. Ideally, the intense conversations would be replicated among students at college campuses and in the grassroots neighborhoods. The new think tanks might facilitate grassroots activism by issuing guides, such as **"How to Run a Tea Party"** (TEA = *"Taxed Enough Already"* or *"Totally Engaged Americans."*) Since the conservative mainstream live in suburbia, exurbia, rural, Main Street, and small town America, most activism should well up from the grassroots. The divisions that vex top-down conservative leaders tend to be less serious in the grassroots. America has a strong tradition of local civic and volunteer organizations, and the rich experience from such organizations mitigates against divisiveness.

2. **Local grassroots leaders** would assume responsibility for educating local conservatives and training, organizing and equipping them for action. Education in conservative principles is especially needed at the grassroots level,

---

[341] (Edited by William Kristol and Fred Barnes n.d.)

203

since conservatives have an admirable bias for action and a pitiful bias against sitting down with a book. Therefore, top priority should first be given to educating these folks in sound conservative principles.

A massive re-education program in the European Christian/classical heritage is needed, which must start in the new think tanks and then be transmitted to grassroots leaders. These leaders must carry the task of educating Christian and traditionalist conservatives in Western heritage. It is not enough to hand them books – some of them do not read books. Teaching sessions followed by discussion groups are needed.

BEING VERSUS BECOMING

The metaphysical formula should consist of *"being"* first, and then *"doing."* Doing flows from being, not vice versa. The education and formation of conservatives comes before conservative activism. Discourage young conservatives from running for office when they do not understand even the basic principles of conservatism. It is time for Americans to scrap **The Great Gatsby** idea of becoming – that we become through doing. Gatsby supposed that he had become part of the patrician elite by the money he had made, the clothes he wore, the house he lived in, and the parties he threw, but all he had was a strut and a pose. No one was fooled by the pose except himself.[342]

Many allegedly conservative office holders offer the semblance of being conservative, but theirs is an empty pose sometimes referred to as being a RINO (republican in name only). In many cases, they have risen to the top through tireless campaigning and sloganeering without ever deeply pondering conservative principles in their minds and hearts. The conservative meltdown of 2008 becomes completely understandable when we consider some of the so called *"conservatives"* we elected to represent us. The grassroots conservative core was not educated in conservative principles well enough to differentiate between the pose and the living reality.

NEW GLUE

Although Christianity and traditionalism have strong natural affinities, there are also tensions between them. There is a sense in which the grace of God sets us free from bondage to tradition – traditionalism can also resist faith and grace. This is doubly true when traditionalism is combined with legalism. These important and difficult questions are outside the scope of this essay. Suffice it to say that a fusion of Christian and traditionalist conservatism will require new glue.

> *Fred Critique*
>
> *The new glue can be:*
> *1) united opposition to modernism; and*
> *2) natural law philosophy.*

The glue of the old fusion movement was anticommunism, strong leadership and good writers in Buckley's magazine. The new glue can be: 1) united opposition to modernism; and 2) natural law philosophy. The case for uniting conservatives against the three waves of modernism was made in Chapter 17. To this end, core members of the new fusion must learn to rely upon neoconservative experience for guidance concerning the nature and tactics of modernists. If a Christian-traditionalist leader of the new fusion emerges, he would be well advised to recruit a neocon intellectual as a senior consultant about modernism's influence.

NATURAL LAW AND TRADITION

Nothing alleviates the tension between Christian and traditionalist conservatism as well as natural law philosophy, because the principles are compatible with both. For example, God created and designed man, thus human nature prior

---

[342] (Fitzgerald 1925)

to the fall of Adam was determined by that design. Natural law philosophers can discover that design through reason. When sinful men violate the design, they violate their own true nature and sin against God. When men are virtuous according to natural law, they are true to themselves and honor God.

Traditional wisdom is filled with lessons about what is good and bad for mankind. To a remarkable degree, these instructions correspond with natural law principles. For example, English common law as compiled in Blackstone's commentaries was a masterpiece of traditional wisdom, and was greatly prized by Bolingbroke, Montesquieu and Madison, who were steeped in natural law theory.

The American founders discovered that traditionalist wisdom is generally in accord with natural law. Accumulated experience validates the truths of natural law. 18th century Englishmen did not take risky actions contrary to the lessons of experience, no matter how good the theory sounded. They did not start revolutions without solid ground to stand upon. As grandsons and great grandsons of Englishmen, the founding fathers were similar – they were unwilling to found a new nation based on untested theory. Therefore, they did not trust natural law theory until they had validated it with the wisdom of experience. The natural harmony between classical law and traditionalist wisdom made the American Republic possible.

THE GLUE OF NATURAL LAW

St. Thomas Aquinas

Just as natural law has innate affinities with traditionalism and Christian conservatism, it is a likely glue to hold these two together – the two-part core can be bonded with natural law. Neoconservatism began when the young Robert Maynard Hutchins studied the metaphysics of Thomism. Thomas Aquinas is the father of natural law as a comprehensive philosophy, so natural law philosophy is welcome in the metaphysics-rich atmosphere of neoconservatism. Natural law appeals to libertarians because it is the missing piece of their innate classical liberalism, and they have a secret hunger for natural law ideas – only through natural law can libertarians return to being the classical liberals they were meant to be. Therefore, neoconservatism and libertarianism can both be glued on to the new fusion with natural law.

EVANGELICALS AND CATHOLICS TOGETHER IN CULTURE WAR

Ecumenism refers to initiatives aimed at Christian unity and cooperation, and is used by Christian denominations and churches separated by doctrine, history and practice – the literal concept advocates a single, worldwide Christian Church. Fred Hutchison was not a supporter of the ecumenical movement, including the well publicized **Evangelicals and Catholics Together**[343] conclaves. He felt that ecumenism is actually modernism in a Christian wrapper, and that almost every step forward in ecumenism is a step backwards for truth.[344] However, a conservative political league of

---

[343] Evangelicals and Catholics Together is a 1994 ecumenical document signed by leading Evangelical and Roman Catholic scholars in the United States, and was part of a larger reestablishment of cordial relations that began in the 1980s with collaboration in para-church organizations such as Moral Majority during the Reagan administration. The statement is written as a testimony that spells out the need for Protestants and Catholics to deliver a common witness to the modern world, and draws heavily from the theology of the New Testament and the Trinitarian doctrine of the Nicene Creed. It does not mention any specific points of theology, but seeks to encourage spiritual unity.

[344] (F. Hutchison, Brief History of Conservatism 2009)

Evangelicals and conservative Catholics to fight the culture war is possible – again, glued together with natural law philosophy.

Some of the most effective proponents of the conservative position on culture war issues are natural law thinkers. Whether the topic is abortion, homosexuality, sexual fidelity, stem cells or euthanasia, natural law writers make the most effective arguments. Many of the best debaters are Catholics. These are issues that conservative Catholics and Evangelicals care deeply about. Evangelicals can supply the majority of culture war foot soldiers, while Catholics furnish the majority of world-class natural law philosophers.

If natural law philosophy is the magical glue that holds the new conservative fusion together, Evangelicals will be wise to enlist the distinguished graduates of Catholic universities who have taken advanced classes in natural law philosophy. It should relieve the minds of Evangelicals to know that this can be done while shunning the ecumenical conclaves. Catholics and Evangelicals in the American army fought well together against the Nazis and Japanese without an ecumenical second thought. They can also fight the culture war together without the distraction and time-wasting, dead-end road of ecumenism.

CONSERVATIVES AND LIBERALS IN DIALOG

Hutchison was trilingual – he could give a speech in traditionalist, Christian or natural law lingo. He learned by experience that if he spoke to liberals in traditionalist or Christian language, they would not tolerate it – but liberals would accept a speech clothed in natural law words and concepts. They may not have liked it, but they respected it.

In September of 2008, Hutchison gave a speech to a mixed crowd of conservatives and liberals titled *"How Free is Free Speech?"* on Islamic propaganda broadcast from a radio station and college campus in Burlington, Vermont. All the conservatives were sitting to the right of the isle; all the liberals were sitting to the left. The speech was filled with legal and constitutional precepts and telling facts. During the question and answer period, he switched to natural law language. Both conservatives and liberals were eager to participate. The liberals gamely tried to air their arguments in

Fred Hutchison, MBA
How Free is Free Speech?

a natural law context. Hutchison did not think the arguments were successful, but their smiles indicated that they thought they were holding their own. When he listened to the recorded session later, he did not think they had anything to smile about except that they came to the table and participated in a valid conversation.

When a liberal made an interesting point, Hutchison forbade the conservatives from chiming in too fast. He carefully recapped the argument, explained why it was an interesting point, and finally clarified how the idea was ultimately false. Although liberals often throw a fit when contradicted, these liberals were still smiling. He had bypassed their pinched ideologies and addressed their rational faculties.

When the liberals were really clever, Hutchison let the crowd in on the cleverness before he exposed the underlying fallacies. These particular liberals seemed to care more about being recognized for their cleverness than being right, so they compromised – Hutchison let them win at being clever, and they let him win at being right. No one directly contested the two major propositions of the speech, and a distinguished liberal professor praised him for being a *"strong speaker."* The magic of natural law can bypass ideological knots and go straight to the higher faculties of reason.[345]

---

[345] (F. Hutchison, Al Jazeera and Burlington Telecom - How Free is Free Speech? 2008) http://www.cctv.org/node/64007

REALIZATIONS

In Chapter 1, the point was made that conservatism is ancient and is to a large extent responsible for the cultural flourishing of the West. It was also stated that liberalism is modern and is to a large extent responsible for Western cultural decline. If this journey through history with the five kinds of conservatism spanning eighteen chapters was successful in its intent, the reader will now probably accept these two propositions.

The decay of Western culture is far advanced and a rebuilding of the shattered conservative movement is desperately needed – this chapter suggested a way to accomplish that end. Some readers might have realized for the first time which of the five branches is their type of conservatism; others may have noticed the variety they want to become. It is recommended that all readers make a study of their favorite kind of conservatism and read esteemed books written by noted authors in that stream. The glory of conservatism is that we can stand on the shoulders of the giants who went before us to discover that which is true, beautiful and good.

Those who are well established in their own school of conservatism might consider making a study of the other four. Such individuals might be effective at educating grassroots conservatives and reaching out to other kinds of conservatives, towards the goal of learning to communicate, learn and work with each other. Then we will be ready to get busy restoring the Republic to the glorious destiny that the great architect of the universe has chosen for us.

> ### Fred Critique
>
> *The glory of conservatism is that we can stand on the shoulders of the giants who went before us to discover that which is true, beautiful and good.*

REFLECTIONS ON THE MYSTERIES OF DIVINE PROVIDENCE

> *"If my people, who are called by my name, will humble themselves and pray and seek my face and turn from their wicked ways, then I will hear from heaven, and I will forgive their sin and will heal their land." 2 Chronicles 7:14 (NIV)*

Ultimately, the rise and fall of a great superpower like the United States of America is in the hands of God. But who knows whether God might call for one last revival of the Republic before the end of the age? If so, he will work through people to accomplish it. Although our sins and follies are great, there might be enough time to repent and turn things around before His mighty judgments fall on us.

The puritan fathers established the Massachusetts Bay Colony to be a Christian Republic. As such, it was to be a *"city set on a hill,"* and a light and example to the nations of the world. For all we know, this may yet be the destiny of the American Republic. As we near the end of the age when the lights go out and darkness descends upon the earth, perhaps it will be within God's purposes to preserve one place on earth where the light of the world and the light of truth are still shining. It is not impossible that the USA will be that place. However, the greatest spiritual revival this nation has ever seen must arrive before that can happen. In this day of general apostasy, when even Evangelicals seldom talk about sin, repentance or the cross of Christ, and talk even less of judgment and hell, the churches must be turned upside down and transformed into the oracles of God's truth and righteousness once more. A great wave of deep repentance by worldly Christians is long overdue.

STANDING ON THE SHOULDERS OF GIANTS

American conservatives can still be used by God to rebuild the Republic. In spite of the conservative meltdown of 2008, we have a great treasure house of past wisdom, splendid history, truth principles and values, and sterling examples to build with. We can win the great battle against deeply entrenched progressivism if, and only if, we are humble and wise enough to stand on the giant shoulders of those who have gone before us.

"Some men among us are doing whatever is in their power to preserve and reinvigorate our common heritage. This is not a work that can be accomplished through positive law or the creation of international commissions. Yet if a people forget the ashes of their fathers and the temples of their gods, the consequences soon will be felt in the laws and in international affairs. Without cultural community…, there is little point in political alliance. If we have no real civilization, no enduring cultural bonds, to unite us…, we may as well let the alleged [Communist] culture have its way with us." Russell Kirk, 1960[346]

Conservatives may soon have one of the greatest pleasures in life: the joy of rebuilding with like-minded companions! Fred Hutchison believed that transformation was approaching – he was convinced that an imminent renewal would become a special blessing that unites people and restores history.[347]

THE SUBURBS IN REVOLT

The 2009 election victories can be credited to moderate and independent suburban voters swinging away from liberals and Democrats to vote for conservatives and Republicans. This happened in electorally important red (Republican) and blue (Democrat) states – normally blue New Jersey and Pennsylvania both swung into the red, while Virginia and New Jersey chose Republican Governors. Disillusionment with the Obama regime and Congress was nonpartisan and non-geographic – whatever the region, party, or lack of affiliation, moderates and pragmatists were disappointed with the government. Disaffection was strongest in the sprawling suburbs that contain a large portion of the needed electoral votes to select presidents – residents of the middle class burbs woke up to become engaged voters and politically active citizens. Pollsters took special note of political hostility from suburban moderates, independents and women.

POLITICAL PHILOSOPHY SHIFTS TOWARDS CONSERVATISM

The 2009 polls verified the swing toward conservative opinion on key issues of political philosophy. An increase from 38% to 45% of middle class suburban voters complained of excessive government regulation. Criticism of government intervention into arenas best left to private business jumped from 40% to 48%. Those demanding less union power and influence rose from 32% to 42%. Shifts toward conservative views were also noted on issues such as abortion, immigration and global warming. Many blue-state, suburban independents grew a red streak, which accounted for the increase from 29% to 35% among those defining themselves as conservative.[348]

JOYOUS MARCH OF PATRIOTS

"America! America! God shed his grace on thee / And crown thy good with brotherhood from sea to shining sea!" **America the Beautiful**, *lyrics by Katharine Lee Bates, melody by Samuel A. Ward, 1895*

---

[346] (Kirk, The Common Heritage of America and Europe 1960)
[347] (F. Hutchison, Brief History of Conservatism 2009)
[348] Source of statistical data (Brooks 2009)

Personal friends of Fred Hutchison who lived in a suburban neighborhood were not particularly politically active. They attended a 2009 Tax Day Tea Party Rally in Columbus, Ohio, became members of a local patriot group, and subsequently joined both the 9/12 Project[349] and 8/28 Restoring Honor[350] marches in Washington, DC. The couple sat in Hutchison's living room and agreed that the 9/12 march from Independence Park to the United States Capital was one of the greatest mountain-top experiences of their lives. The uncanny confraternity of ordinary Americans was personal, social, patriotic and spiritual. This couple rubbed shoulders with rich and poor, bankers and hell's angels, architects, athletes, ditch diggers, farmers, mechanics, and carpet cleaners – marchers represented every race and color, and every state in the union. Distinctions fell away, and the kinship of being fellow Americans remained. Brotherly love and a bold pride of citizenship endured – it was real brotherhood from the heart that took no account of superficial differences.

The march had no trace of the cramped self-righteousness of liberal political correctness – it was redolent with the fresh air of the spirit of freedom, in contrast to the stench of liberal group-think. When real Americans get together and cast off the shroud that liberal elites have thrown over the culture, they rediscover the joy of community known to prior generations of Americans.

The lady now seems to be a rising player in local political circles. Her husband can scarcely contain his feelings when talking about political issues. These people are motivated! It is the motivation of true patriotism. Hutchison had seldom seen such commitment, love of nation, and love of community.[351] During the general election of 2010, such people massed together and pulled down the monuments to political arrogance, driving many enemies of freedom out of office.

2010 VICTORIES

The rising conservative tide continued, and many new conservatives were elected to the House of Representatives and Senate in 2010, while battleground states like Ohio, Florida and Wisconsin chose Republican Governors. Liberal Democrats and RINOs were thrown out of office by the rising Tea Party electorate. This outcome was likely a result of continued high unemployment rates, and a Congress that continued to defy public sentiment in its legislative agenda. The victories placed stopping power in conservative hands that slowed the damage inflicted by the Obama/Pelosi agenda and the culture war progressives. The coming day of rebuilding will bring restoration to constitutional government, robust civic life, and a moral culture that values truth. Conservatives will be obliged to roll up their sleeves and get busy.

---

[349] The 9-12 Project is a non-political movement started by American television and radio host Glenn Beck (1964-), who states the primary purpose is to educate others and *"to bring us all back to the place we were on September 12, 2001... we were not obsessed with red states, blue states or political parties. We were united as Americans, standing together to protect the values and principles of the greatest nation ever created."* 9-12 also represents the *"9 Principles"* and *"12 Values"* that Beck believes represent the principles and values shared by the Founding Fathers of the United States. Some in the Tea Party movement served as sponsors for the Taxpayer March to the Capital Building in Washington DC on September 12, 2009. The 9-12 Project activists do not identify with any major political party.

[350] The Restoring Honor rally was held on August 28, 2010 at the Lincoln Memorial in Washington, DC and was organized by Glenn Beck to *"restore honor in America"* and raise funds for the Special Operations Warrior Foundation. Beck's speeches emphasized that Americans of all religions should turn to their faith in God, and unite despite political or religious disagreements. Attendance was disputed by various sources, with estimates ranging from 87,000 to 500,000.

[351] (F. Hutchison, Brief History of Conservatism 2009)

SOLIDARITY IN REBUILDING

The central point in this epilogue is the great joy a community shares in the solidarity of rebuilding. Examples of this special joyfulness reside throughout history, current events and the Bible. Human nature flourishes in camaraderie, which contains a built in spiritual aspect.

REBUILDING THE BARN

Federal bank examiners in Ohio check mortgage files to make sure property backing a loan is insured – adhering to a law designed to prevent bank failure. Occasionally, examiners inspect loan files to rebuild a barn and find no insurance. Instead, they find a promissory note signed by the Amish Bishop stating that the Amish community will rebuild the

Amish building a barn

barn. Amish law forbids the purchase of insurance, so the Ohio Department of Banks decreed that a Bishop's promise be accepted as the legal equivalent. In other words, a Bishop's word is as good as gold. The Director of the Department of Banks does not trust the Bishop – he trusts the amazing consistency of the Amish community. He does not trust their virtue – they sincerely enjoy getting together to raise a barn, because something in human nature treasures working with good friends. The Amish culture is successful because the leaders make wise use of human nature, which is highly admirable.

CONFRATERNITY AND REBUILDING

The 9/12 Washington march had a joyous confraternity that was a prelude to the spirit of festive rebuilding. To demonstrate how a march can be compatible with this kind of spirit, consider the historical example of such a march that ended in perhaps the most joyous rebuilding of a beloved church in recorded history. As quoted from Kenneth Clark's, *Civilization*, as he gazed at the faces of statues on the West portal of Chartres Cathedral:

> "We know from the old chroniclers something about the men whose state of mind these faces reveal. In the year 1144, they say, when the towers seemed to be rising as if by magic, the faithful harnessed themselves to the carts which were bringing stone and dragged them from the quarry to the cathedral. The enthusiasm spread throughout France. Men and women came from far away carrying heavy burdens of provisions for the workers – wine, oil, corn. Amongst them were lords and ladies, pulling carts with the rest. There was perfect discipline, and a most profound silence, all hearts were united and each man forgave his enemies...
>
> "This feeling of dedication to a great civilizing ideal is even more overwhelming when we pass through the portal into the interior. This is not only one of the two most beautiful open spaces in the world (the other is St. Sophia in Constantinople), but it is one that has a peculiar effect upon the mind...
>
> "Perhaps it sounds sentimental, but I can't help feeling that this faith has given the interior of Chartres a unity and a spirit of devotion that exceeds even the other great churches of France such as Bourges and Le Mans... The whole harmonious space seems to have grown up out of the earth according to some natural law of harmony."[352]

---

[352] (Clark, A Guide to Civilisation: The Kenneth Clark Films on the Cultural Life of Western Man 1970)

REBUILDING THE TEMPLE

"All that day they offered great sacrifices and rejoiced, for God had made them rejoice with great joy; ...so that the joy of Jerusalem was heard even afar off." Nehemiah 12:43 (KJV)

Nehemiah rebuilding walls of Jerusalem

The book of Nehemiah relates the rebuilding of the temple in Jerusalem after the Jewish captivity in Babylon. This was even more of a community, home-made job than the building of Chartres. The French were able to hire professional architects, masons and craftsmen to assist with the job, and had elaborate mechanical devices for lifting stones. Nehemiah and the Jews were starting from scratch. The work required the utmost effort and great personal sacrifice of every person of the community.

After the temple was complete, the Israelites celebrated with two thanksgiving choirs. They did not rejoice only because human nature cheered for the rebuilding. They had a spiritual joy. *"God made them rejoice."* Hutchison suspected that some of the joy his friends experienced during the Washington march was a gift from God. When God decides to rebuild a nation, he unites people and pours out joy upon them.

INDIVIDUALITY IN UNITY

"When the day of Pentecost came, they were all together in one place. Suddenly a sound like the blowing of a violent wind came from heaven and filled the whole house where they were sitting. They saw what seemed to be tongues of fire that separated and came to rest on each of them. All of them were filled with the Holy Spirit and began to speak in other tongues as the Spirit enabled them." Acts 2:1-4 (NIV)

9/12 March in Washington, D.C.

When God decides to send his message of life throughout the world, He gathers like-minded people together and pours out a fiery unction upon them. A true anointing produces: 1) increased group unity; 2) stronger individuals, each with their own anointing (i.e., their own cloven tongue); and 3) new gifts and enablements that break out of the box of their own private world (in the book of Acts they spoke foreign languages.)

Liberal elites produce a faux unity by crushing individuals into group-think. In contrast, the Washington marchers remained very individualistic in spite of their unity. The lady who sat in Hutchison's living room seemed to have increased her political skills. These American patriots received all three things that prove a true anointing of God – unity, stronger individuals and new capabilities enabled by grace. We have reason to be encouraged! God Bless America!

A&E Television Networks, LLC. *History.com.* 1996-2011. http://www.history.com/shows (accessed 2011).

Adler, Mortimer. *A Syntopicon: An Index to The Great Ideas.* Chicago: Encyclopaedia Britannica Inc., 1952.

Adler, Mortimer J. *Great Books of the Western World.* Chicago: Encyclopædia Britannica Inc., 1952.

Alighieri, Dante. *Divine Comedy.* Ravenna, 1315.

Allmand, C. T. *Hundred Years' War.* World Book, Web. 2012. http://www.worldbookonline.com.ref.ualibrary.org/advanced/article?id=ar267260&st=hundred+years%92+war (accessed January 2012).

Amis, Martin. "Dead Men Russian: book review of House of Meetings." *Touchstone Magazine,* 2007.

Aquinas, Thomas. "The Summa Theologica of St. Thomas Aquinas." *New Advent Online Edition.* Vol. 2. Edited by Kevin Knight. Translated by Literally translated by Fathers of the English Dominican Province. Catholic Church, 2008. 454, 465.

Bach, Johann Sebastian. *Piano Society Free Classical Recordings - The Well-Tempered Clavier.* 1722-1742. http://pianosociety.com/cms/index.php?section=101 (accessed December 5, 2011).

Woodstock: The Director's Cut. Directed by Michael Wadleigh. Produced by Wadleigh-Maurice. Performed by Joan Baez, Richie Havens and Joe Cocker. Warner Bros. Pictures, 1970.

Barton, David. *Natural Law Articles.* WallBuilders, LLC. 2011. http://www.wallbuilders.com/searchResults.asp?cx=017913191964562303374%3Ap_grmfhrw8c&cof=FORID%3A11&q=natural+law&sa.x=0&sa.y=0&siteurl=www.wallbuilders.com%2FABTbioDB.asp (accessed 2011).

—. *Wallbuilders: The Separation of Church and State.* January 2001. http://www.wallbuilders.com/LIBissuesArticles.asp?id=123 (accessed 2011).

Bergson, Henri. *The Two Sources of Morality and Religion.* Garden City, NY: Doubleday, 1932.

Blackstone, William. *Commentaries on the Laws of England.* Oxford: Clarendon Press, 1765-1769.

Bloom, Allan. *The Closing of the American Mind.* New York: Simon & Schuster Inc, 1987.

Boccaccio, Giovanni. *The Decameron.* Italy, 1353.

Brooks, David. "Poll Watch." *The New York Times.* New York, November 9, 2009.

Buckley, Jr., William F. *God and Man at Yale.* Washington DC: Regnery Publishing, 1951.

Burke, Edmund. *A Philosophical Inquiry into the Sublime and the Beautiful.* New York : P.F. COLLIER & SON COMPANY, 1757.

—. *Reflections on the Revolutions in France.* London: J. Dodsley, 1790.

Bush, George H.W. *Public Papers - 1990 - September.* September 11, 1990. http://bushlibrary.tamu.edu/research/public_papers.php?id=2217&year=1990&month=9 (accessed June 13, 2011).

—. *Public Papers - 1991 - February.* February 27, 1991. http://bushlibrary.tamu.edu/research/public_papers.php?id=2746&year=1991&month=2 (accessed June 13, 2011).

Cairns, Scott, interview by MARS HILL AUDIO Journal. *How the Writing of Poetry Requires Attentiveness to the Life of Words* (March/April 2004).

Cambrian Fossils. 2002-2011. http://www.fossilmuseum.net/Paleobiology/CambrianFossils.htm (accessed June 29, 2011).

Carr, Karen. *Kidipede - Holy Roman Empire, High Middle Ages: Germany.* 2011. http://www.historyforkids.org/learn/medieval/history/highmiddle/hre.htm (accessed 2011).

Castiglione, Baldassare. *The Book of the Courtier.* Italy, 1528.

Chaucer, Geoffrey. *Canterbury Tales.* late 14th century.

Churchill, Winston. *While England Slept .* London: Putnam's, 1938.

Clark, Kenneth. *A Guide to Civilisation: The Kenneth Clark Films on the Cultural Life of Western Man.* New York: Time-Life, 1970.

Civilisation: A Personal View by Kenneth Clark. Directed by Michael Gill. Produced by British Broadcasting Corporation (BBC). Performed by Kenneth Clark. British Broadcasting Corporation (BBC) (1969) (UK) (TV) (BBC 2); Time Life Films (1970) (USA), 1969.

Convention, Delegates of the Philadelphia. *The Constitution of the United States.* Philadelphia, 1787.

Darwin, Charles. *Geological Observations on Coral Reefs, Volcanic Islands, and on South America.* London, New York and Melbourne: Ward, Lock, and Co., 1890.

Dawson, Christopher. *The Study of Christian Culture.* Westminster, Maryland: The Newman Press, 1959.

Donnelly, John Patrick. *Counter Reformation.* World Book, Web. 2012. http://www.worldbookonline.com.ref.ualibrary.org/advanced/article?id=ar137000&st=catholic+reformation (accessed January 2012).

Earl, Charles, interview by Julie Klusty. *Former Ohio State Congressman* (August 27, 2011).

Earle, E. Cairns. *Christianity Through the Centuries: A History of the Christian Church.* Third Edition, Revised and Expanded. Grand Rapids, MI: Zondervan, 1996.

Edited by William Kristol and Fred Barnes. "The Weekly Standard." Washington, DC: News Corporation.

Edwards, John. *The Washington Post.* July 28, 2004. http://www.washingtonpost.com/wp-dyn/articles/A22230-2004Jul28.html (accessed November 28, 2011).

Eliot, T.S. *The Waste Land.* 1922.

Fitzgerald, F. Scott. *The Great Gatsby.* New York: Charles Scribner's Sons, 1925.

Fletcher, Richard. *The Cross and the Crescent.* New York: Viking, 2003.

Freeman, Derek. *The fateful hoaxing of Margaret Mead: a historical analysis of her Samoan research.* Boulder, Colorado: Westview Press, 1999.

Gibbon, Edward. *The History of the Decline and Fall of the Roman Empire.* London: Strahan & Cadell, 1776-1788.

Civilisation: A Personal View by Kenneth Clark. Directed by Michael Gill. 1969.

Glaber, Rodulfus. *History in Five Books from 900 AD to 1044 AD.* Cluny, Saône-et-Loire, France: Cluny Abbey, 1027.

Global Oneness. 2010. http://www.experiencefestival.com/a/One_Worlders/id/191308 (accessed June 2011).

Golding, Sir William. *Lord of the Flies.* London: Faber and Faber Limited, 1954.

Goldwater, Barry. *The Conscience of a Conservative.* Shepherdsville, Kentucky: Victor Publishing Co., 1960.

Greenblatt, Stephen, et al., . *The Norton Anthology of English Literature, Volume 1.* 8th. New York City: W. W. Norton & Company, 2006.

Harp, Gillis. "Conservative Fundamentals, review of the book The Essential Russell Kirk edited by George Panichas." *Touchstone Magazine*, 2007.

Hayek, Friedrich. *The Road to Serfdom.* Routledge Press (UK): University of Chicago Press (US), 1944.

Hemingway, Ernest. *The Sun Also Rises.* New York: Charles Scribner's Sons, 1926.

—. *The Sun Also Rises.* New York City: Charles Scribner's Sons, 1926.

Hesiod. *Works and Days.* Milan: Demetrius Chalcondyles, 1st Printed Edition 1493.

Hitler, Adolf. *Mein Kampf (My Struggle or My Battle).* Germany: Eher Verlag, 1925.

Hoover, John Edgar. *Masters Of Deceit: The Story Of Communism In America And How To Fight It .* New York: Henry Holt & Company, 1958.

Huffman, Carl A. *Stoic philosophy.* World Book, Web. 2012. http://www.worldbookonline.com.ref.ualibrary.org/advanced/article?id=ar534240 (accessed January 2012).

Hutchins, Robert. *Great Books of the Western World.* Chicago: Encyclopædia Britannica Inc., 1952.

Hutchins, Robert, and Mortimer Adler. *Gateway to the Great Books.* Chicago: Encyclopædia Britannica Inc., 1963.

Hutchison, Fred. *Al Jazeera and Burlington Telecom - How Free is Free Speech?* September 17, 2008. http://www.cctv.org/node/64007 (accessed October 21, 2011).

Hutchison, Fred, interview by Julie Klusty. *Brief History of Conservatism* Columbus, Ohio, (2009).

—. *RenewAmerica - Fred Hutchison column.* 2009. http://www.renewamerica.com/columns/hutchison (accessed 2011).

Hutchison, Frederick J. *The Stages of Sanctification.* Bloomington, Indiana: Xlibris, 2000.

Huxley, Aldous. *Brave New World.* London: Chatto and Windus, 1932.

—. *Soma in Aldous Huxley's Brave New World.* 1932. http://www.huxley.net/soma/somaquote.html (accessed 2011).

The Lord of the Rings Film Trilogy. Directed by Peter Jackson. 2001-2003.

James, William. *Pragmatism: A New Name for Some Old Ways of Thinking.* New York: Longmans, Green, 1907.

Jenkins, David. *FrumForum - Russell Kirk Would Not Recognize These 'Conservatives'.* December 2, 2011. http://www.frumforum.com/russell-kirk-would-not-recognize-these-conservatives (accessed December 26, 2011).

Jensen, Richard. *Conservative Coalition.* September 12, 2009. http://www.conservapedia.com/Conservative_Coalition (accessed 2011).

Jesseph, Douglas M. *Metaphysics.* World Book, Web. 2012. http://www.worldbookonline.com.ref.ualibrary.org/advanced/article?id=ar358000&st=determinism (accessed January 2012).

Josephy, Jr., Alvin M. *500 Nations, An Illustrated History of North American Indians.* New York: Random House, 1994.

Kansas. *Dust in the Wind.* Cond. Woodland Sound. Comp. Kerry Livgren. 1978.

Kayyam, Omar. *The Rubaiyat of Omar Kayyam.* Persian, 1120 AD.

Kennedy, John F. *Why England Slept.* New York: Wilfred Funk Inc., 1940 (published in 1961).

Kepler's laws of planetary motion. 1609. http://en.wikipedia.org/wiki/Kepler%27s_laws_of_planetary_motion (accessed July 20, 2011).

Kipling, Joseph Rudyard. *Just So Stories for Little Children .* London: Macmillan & Co., 1902.

Kirk, Russell. *The Common Heritage of America and Europe.* Vers. Christianity Today, Vol. 4, pp 259–62. January 4, 1960. http://www.kirkcenter.org/index.php/detail/the-common-heritage-of-america-and-europe/ (accessed 2011).

—. *The Conservative Mind: From Burke to Eliot.* Washington DC: Regnery Publishing, Inc., 1953, 1960, 1972, 1985 - 2001 Printing.

—. *The Russell Kirk Center for Cultural Renewal - Ten Conservative Principles.* 2007-2011. http://www.kirkcenter.org/index.php/detail/ten-conservative-principles/ (accessed December 24, 2011).

Kirk, Russell, and George A Panichas. *The Essential Russell Kirk: Selected Essays.* Wilmington, DE: ISI Books, 2007.

Knight, Kevin. *Catholic Encyclopedia: New Advent - Henry IV.* 2009. http://www.newadvent.org/cathen/07225a.htm (accessed 2011).

Kuhn, Thomas. *The Structure of Scientific Revolutions.* Chicago: University of Chicago Press, 1962.

Kyle, Richard. *New Age movement.* World Book, Web. 2012. http://www.worldbookonline.com.ref.ualibrary.org/advanced/article?id=ar714261&st=new+age (accessed January 2012).

Leipzig Declaration. 2005. http://en.wikipedia.org/wiki/Leipzig_Declaration_on_Global_Climate_Change (accessed July 21, 2011).

Lerer, Seth. *Inventing English: A Portable History of the Language.* New York: Columbia University Press, 2007.

Lewis, C.S. *Bluspels and Flalansferes: A Semantic Nightmare.* 1969. Edited by Walter Hooper. London: Cambridge University Press, 1939.

—. *The Great Divorce.* London: Geoffrey Bles (UK), 1945.

—. *The Pilgrim's Regress.* London: J.M. Dent and Sons, 1933.

—. *The Screwtape Letters.* London: Geoffrey Bles, 1942.

Locke, John. *An Essay Concerning Human Understanding.* London: Tho. Baffet, 1690.

—. *Two Treatises of Government.* London: Awnsham Churchill, 1689.

Long, Huey. *Share Our Wealth .* February 23, 1934. http://hueylong.com/programs/share-our-wealth.php (accessed 2011).

Louis Markos. http://www.hbu.edu/hbu/Louis_Markos.asp (accessed June 2011).

Star Wars Series. Directed by George Lucas. 1977.

Luke. *The Acts of the Apostles.* 60-64 AD.

Madison, James. "The Federalist No. 51 - The Structure of the Government Must Furnish the Proper Checks and Balances Between the Different Departments." *Independent Journal*, February 6, 1788.

Manchester, William. *American Caesar: Douglas MacArthur, 1880-1964.* New York: Little, Brown and Company, 1978.

Mantle, John Gregory. *Beyond Humiliation: The Way of the Cross.* Washington, DC: Testimony Book Ministry, 1974 (1896).

Markel, Dr. Howard. *An Anatomy of Addiction: Sigmund Freud, William Halsted, and the Miracle Drug Cocaine.* Toronto: Pantheon Books, 2011.

marxists.org. *Glossary of Terms.* Edited by Andy Blunden. 2008. http://www.marxists.org/glossary/terms/r/e.htm (accessed 2011).

McCarthy, Harry. *The Bonnie Blue Flag.*

McManus, John. *William F. Buckley: Pied Piper for the Establishment.* Appleton, Wisconsin: John Birch Society, 2002.

Mead, Margaret. *Coming of Age in Samoa.* New York: William Morrow and Company, 1928.

Miller, Cheryl. "The Genius of Old New York." *Claremont Review of Books*, Fall 2007.

Milton, John. *Paradise Lost.* London: Samuel Simmons , 1667.

Mitchell, Margaret. *Gone with the Wind.* New York: Macmillan Publishers, 1936.

Montaigne, Michel de. *Essais .* 1580.

Montesquieu, Charles-Louis. *Persian Letters.* Amsterdam: Jacques Desbordes, 1721.

—. *Reflection on the Causes of the Grandeur and Declension of Romans.* Amsterdam, 1734.

—. *The Spirit of the Laws.* London: Thomas Nugent , 1750.

Nash, George. *The Heritage Foundation - The Life and Legacy of Russell Kirk.* June 22, 2007. http://www.heritage.org/research/lecture/the-life-and-legacy-of-russell-kirk (accessed December 26, 2011).

Neuroscience of Free Will. 2010. http://en.wikipedia.org/wiki/Neuroscience_of_free_will (accessed August 18, 2011).

Neuroscience of Free Will. http://en.wikipedia.org/wiki/Neuroscience_of_free_will (accessed August 18, 2011).

Nietzsche, Friedrich. *The Antichrist.* Germany, 1888.

Orwell, George. *Animal Farm.* London: Secker and Warburg , 1945.

Paine, Thomas. *The Rights of Man.* London: J.S. Jordon, 1791.

Picard, Max. *The Flight From God.* Washington, DC: Henry Regnery Company, 1934 (1951).

Protestant School Systems - Colonial and Nineteenth-Century Protestant Schooling, Early Twentieth-Century Protestant Schooling. 2011. http://education.stateuniversity.com/pages/2339/Protestant-School-Systems.html#ixzz1hho8bxvX (accessed December 26, 2011).

Rand, Ayn. *Atlas Shrugged.* New York: Random House, 1957.

—. *The Fountainhead.* Indianapolis, Indiana: Bobbs Merrill, 1943.

Star Trek Series. Directed by Gene Roddenberry. 1966.

Roosevelt, Franklin D. *National Industrial Recovery Act.* Seventy-third Congress of the United States of America. June 16, 1933. http://www.ourdocuments.gov/doc.php?doc=66 (accessed 2011).

Royal Medal. http://en.wikipedia.org/wiki/Royal_Medal (accessed June 15, 2011).

Royal Society. http://en.wikipedia.org/wiki/Royal_Society (accessed June 15, 2011).

Russello, Gerald J. *First Things - Russell Kirk & Postmodern Conservatism.* October 24, 2008. http://www.firstthings.com/onthesquare/2008/10/russell-kirk-postmodern-conser (accessed December 26, 2011).

Samenow, Dr. Stanton. *Inside the Criminal Mind.* New York: Crown Publishing, 1984.

Sartre, Jean-Paul. *Being and Nothingness: An Essay on Phenomenological Ontology.* Paris, 1943.

Schlafly, Phyllis McAlpin Stewart. *A Choice Not An Echo.* St. Louis: Pere Marquette Press, 1964.

Shakespeare, William. *Hamlet.* London, 1600.

—. *King Lear.* London, 1608.

—. *The Tragedy of Julius Caesar: Act III, Scene ii.* London, 1599.

Sherman, Senator John. *Sherman Anti-Trust Act (1890).* First Session Fifty-first Congress of the United States of America. July 2, 1890. http://www.ourdocuments.gov/doc.php?flash=true&doc=51 (accessed 2011).

Sidney N. Deane, editor. *Proslogion: St. Anselm's Basic Writings (English Translation).* Chicago: Open Court, 1962.

Simmons, Tracy Lee. *Climbing Parnassus: A New Apologia for Latin and Greek.* Wilmington, Delaware: Isi Books, 2002.

Singer, Marcus G. *Philosophy.* World Book, Web. 2012. http://www.worldbookonline.com.ref.ualibrary.org/advanced/article?id=ar427200&st=ontology+philosophy (accessed January 2012).

Smith, Adam. *An Inquiry into the Nature and Causes of the Wealth of Nations.* London: W. Strahan and T. Cadell, 1776.

Smith, Robert William. *Manichaeism.* World Book, Web. 2012. http://www.worldbookonline.com.ref.ualibrary.org/advanced/article?id=ar342040&st=manichaeism (accessed January 2012).

Spengler, Oswald. *The Decline of the West.* New York: Alfred A Knopf, 1927.

Staal, Rein. "The Forgotten Story of Postmodernity." *First Things*, December 2008.

Strauss, David Friedrich. *Das Leben Jesu .* Berlin: Pressedienst Adventgemeinde Berlin Spandau, 1835.

—. *On Christian Doctrine.* 1840.

—. *The Life of Jesus, Critically Examined - English Translation.* New York: Calvin Blanchard, 1860.

Strzelczyk, Scott, and Richard Rothschild. *American Thinker - UN Agenda 21, Coming to a Neighborhood near You.* October 28, 2009. http://www.americanthinker.com/2009/10/un_agenda_21_coming_to_a_neigh.html.

Thornton, Bruce. "Cultivated Taste - A Review of Two Books on the Georgics." *Claremont Review of Books*, Spring 2007.

Tocqueville, Alexis de. *Democracy in America .* London: Saunders and Otley , 1835.

Tolkien, J.R.R. *The Hobbit.* London: George Allen & Unwin, Ltd., 1937.

—. *The Lord of the Rings.* London: Geo. Allen & Unwin, 1954.

—. *The Silmarillion.* London: George Allen & Unwin , 1977.

Tomassini, Eve. (October 2011).

Toynbee, Arnold. *A Study of History.* Oxford: Oxford University Press, 1934-1961.

Trevena, Judy, and Jeff Miller. "Brain preparation before a voluntary action: Evidence against unconscious movement initiation." *Consciousness and Cognition, Volume 19, Issue 1*, 2010: 447-456.

Tse-tung, Mao. *The Little Red Book - Quotations of Chairman Mao Tse-tung.* Beijing: Government of the People's Republic of China, 1964.

Twain, Mark, and Charles Dudley Warner. *The Gilded Age: A Tale of Today.* American Publishing Company, 1873.

Tyler, David. *Science Literature - Clinical Psychology called to abandon unproven therapies .* October 20, 2009. http://www.arn.org/blogs/index.php/literature/2009/10/20/clinical_psychology_called_to_abandon_un (accessed 2011).

United.Nations. *Agenda 21 Core Publication.* June 14, 1992. http://www.un.org/esa/dsd/agenda21/.

—. *Resolution Adopted by the General Assembly.* June 28, 1997. http://www.un.org/documents/ga/res/spec/aress19-2.htm.

Various. *Determinism.* Wikimedia Foundation, Inc.,. 2012. http://en.wikipedia.org/wiki/Determinism (accessed January 2012).

—. *Masterpieces of World Philosophy in Summary Form.* Edited by Frank N. Magill. New York City: Harper & Row, Publishers Incorporated, 1961.

—. *Nativism (politics).* Wikimedia Foundation, Inc. 2012. http://en.wikipedia.org/wiki/Nativism_(politics) (accessed January 2012).

—. *Ontology.* Wikimedia Foundation, Inc. 2012. http://en.wikipedia.org/wiki/Ontology (accessed January 2012).

Voltaire. *Candide.* Paris: Cramer, Marc-Michel Rey, Jean Nourse, Lambert, and others, 1759.

Wagner, Senator Robert R. *National Labor Relations Act.* Seventy-fourth Congress of the United States of America. July 5, 1935. http://www.ourdocuments.gov/doc.php?doc=67 (accessed 2011).

Wagner, Senator Robert, and Representative David Lewis. *Social Security Act.* Seventy-fourth Congress of the United States of America. August 14, 1935. http://www.ourdocuments.gov/doc.php?doc=68 (accessed 2011).

Weaver, Richard M. *Ideas Have Consequences.* Chicago: University of Chicago Press, 1948.

Webster, Richard. *Why Freud Was Wrong: Sin, Science and Psychoanalysis.* New York City: Harper Collins / Basic Books, 1995.

Wenzel, David T. *One Morning at the Shire.* http://www.davidwenzel.com/home.html.

Wharton, Edith. *French Ways and Their Meaning.* London: MacMillan, 1919.

—. *The Age of Innocence.* New York: Grosset & Dunlap, 1920.

Wikipedia. *Crisis of the Late Middle Ages.* December 13, 2011. http://en.wikipedia.org/wiki/Crisis_of_the_Late_Middle_Ages (accessed December 26, 2011).

—. *High culture.* November 12, 2011. http://en.wikipedia.org/wiki/High_culture#cite_note-0 (accessed December 26, 2011).

—. *Manichaeism.* November 22, 2011. http://en.wikipedia.org/wiki/Manichaeism (accessed December 26, 2011).

—. *Stoicism.* December 17, 2011. http://en.wikipedia.org/wiki/Stoicism (accessed December 26, 2011).

CPSIA information can be obtained at www.ICGtesting.com
Printed in the USA
BVOW051545190212

283262BV00002B/1/P